R.I.P.

R.I.P.

THE

COMPLETE

BOOK

OF

DEATH

AND

DYING

CONSTANCE JONES

A Stonesong Press Book

HarperCollins*Publishers*

HarperCollins books may be purchased for educational, business, or sales promotional use. For information, please write to: Special Markets Department, HarperCollins Publishers, Inc., 10 East 53rd Street, New York, New York 10022.

FIRST EDITION

Designed by Joseph Rutt

A Stonesong Press Book

Library of Congress Cataloging-in-Publication Data

Jones, Constance, 1961–
    R.I.P. : the complete book of death and dying / Constance Jones.
—1st ed.
        p.   cm.
    "A Stonesong Press book"—T.p. verso.
    ISBN 0-06-270140-1
    1. Funeral rites and ceremonies—History.   2. Burial—History.
3. Death—Social aspects.   4. Death—Psychological aspects.
I. Title.
GT3150.J65   1997
393—dc20   96-30420

97 98 99 00 01 ❖/RRD 10 9 8 7 6 5 4 3 2 1

Contents

Editor

Constance Jones

Contributors

Carleen Brice
Marion Dreyfus
Diedre Elliott
Liza Featherstone
Linda Greer
Ken Packman
Jordan P. Richman, Ph.D.
Julia Banks Rubel
Karen Sbrockey
Susan Walton

Introduction

All interest in disease and death is only another expression of interest in life.
—THOMAS MANN

Nothing fascinates the living quite so much as death. One of the few experiences that all people share, it yet remains a mystery. Perhaps the most frightening, terrible fact of life, it is nonetheless powerfully seductive and undeniably romantic. Death has fueled the imagination since the first spark of intelligence ignited in the human brow. It has nourished religion, politics, art, science, economics and social custom, touching every aspect of everyday existence.

Failing (so far) to conquer death in this world, humankind has variously found ways to control the process of dying, to integrate death into life, to make use of it for assorted purposes and to reckon with its impact. But underlying all this effort is an implicit denial of death, in the form of an almost universal belief in immortality. Even if the body perishes, the idea goes, some component of the self lives on, whether in another world, in another incarnation, through one's work or in the memories of loved ones. In the persistent light of this conviction, life's inevitable conclusion is far from certain.

This volume examines the many pieces of the mortality puzzle, from dead baby jokes to organ donation. Topics include near-death experiences and serial killers, physician-assisted suicide and necromancy, mummies and life insurance. The wide range of information reflects the remarkable diversity of responses that people around the world and down through history have had to the single experience they all share. It makes for great reading, at times comical, at times horrifying, at times poignant, but always engrossing.

Divided into two sections, the material presented here is both entertaining and useful. Part One surveys the practices and attitudes surrounding death and dying. Cultural tradition, scientific study, demographic statistics, funerary customs, religious belief, creative expression and historical anecdotes each receive attention in a separate chapter, providing a snapshot of death's place in human society. In Part Two, practical information appears in a series of chapters on preparing for death, financial concerns, funeral arrangements and the mourning process. Interesting in its own right to the casual reader, Part Two is also a valuable resource for those who are personally coping with the issue.

Broken down into self-contained segments, the book lends itself both to browsing and to being read as a whole. Those who choose to browse and dabble will find numerous headings and sidebars to guide them to specific areas of interest, while those who choose to read straight through will find the sections arranged logically, with them in mind. An index provides directions to related text throughout the book, and an appendix offers a list of publications, organizations and other sources of further information.

The volume thus represents a sweeping overview of death and dying, useful to those seeking an introduction to the topic. By no means comprehensive—and admittedly subjective—it is nonetheless a rich compendium unlike any previously assembled. If nothing else, it won't bore anyone stiff.

Part One

I

The Traditions of Death

According to an African legend, at the beginning of time God delivered a clay jar to Toad and said, "Be careful with this because it contains death." Toad, pleased to have been chosen for such an important job, promised to guard the death jar well.

One day Toad was walking down the road when it met Frog.

"Oh, please let me carry the jar," Frog begged. "I know how to be careful."

Toad shook its head, but Frog whined and pleaded until Toad gave in.

Frog began to hop about and juggle the clay jar on first one foot and then the other.

"Stop!" Toad shouted, but it was too late. The jar slipped from Frog's grasp and fell to the ground. When it broke open, death flew out. Ever since then, all living creatures have had to deal with death.

Death has never been a stranger to humankind. The necessity for dealing with the dead is a universal experience. Stories such as the one about Frog and Toad helped accommodate the mystery of death in preliterate societies. Other stories portrayed two creatures who were ordered to carry important messages to humankind but, inevitably, the one who carried the message of death arrived first. Some mythical heroes, such as the Babylonian Gilgamesh, found the balm of immortality, but lost it to another creature. Death, then, became the fate of all living beings.

Attitudes Toward Death: Historical Overview

Neanderthal Attitudes

The first people, hunters and gatherers who followed seasonal migration routes, knew death intimately. Cold, hunger, illness and injury made death a familiar visitor. While it is impossible to fully understand ancient attitudes toward death, archeological evidence offers intriguing clues.

The early hominids seemed simply to have cast their dead aside. Bones have been found scattered among rubbish heaps in excavations older than 100,000 years. It appears that no special care or burial rites were given. Bodies were merely abandoned.

Neanderthal sites, however, indicate greater concern for the dead. Many of the objects retrieved mirror present-day burial practices. For instance, the excavation at Shanidar Cave in northern Iraq revealed remains surrounded by the pollen of several flowers, including thistles, cornflowers, grape hyacinths and hollyhocks. Scientists speculate that the flowers might have had medicinal significance. In other words, perhaps the Neanderthals were trying to "cure" death. Or, they simply might have wanted to decorate the final resting place of someone close to them.

In the western Himalayas, a Neanderthal child's grave is marked by a ring of wild goat horns, as if to invoke protection from both predators and evil spirits. A French burial reveals a teenage boy covered with red ocher powder and buried in a pit with his head resting on flint flakes. Many Paleolithic remains are found together with common, useful objects such as flints, weapons and food.

Neanderthal bodies sometimes are bound in a flexed position, arms folded, knees drawn up to the chest. In this way, the body resembles a child in the womb or a person curled in sleep. Some bodies are found facing east, as if they were positioned so that their spirits might awaken to some future dawn.

Of all the many clues concerning Neanderthal beliefs about death, discovery of the bear cult is one of the most intriguing. In 1917, Emil Bèchler, a German archeologist, discovered a systematic arrangement of cave bear bones at Drachenloch, high in the Swiss Alps. A similar find in Regourdu, France also contained bear bones, along with a Neanderthal buried with a cave bear's arm bone.

At Drachenloch, a rectangular stone "chest" contained carefully arranged bear bones and skulls. Other skulls rested in stone niches along the cave wall and one bear skull had a thigh bone thrust through its eye socket. Such evidence leads to speculation that Neanderthals set about creating ceremonial crypts for the powerful cave bear, a creature they revered.

Neanderthals may have been trying to evoke the restorative powers often ascribed to bears in preliterate societies. Because bears hibernate, falling into a deep winter sleep that outwardly resembles death, members of the bear cult might have been reflecting on rebirth and immortality. They may have held ceremonies and even "funerals" for both humans and bears. Burying cave bear remains next to Neanderthals might have been an attempt to transfer the power and mystery of hibernation. At any rate, it appears that over 30,000 years ago, Neanderthals made attempts to mitigate the finality of death.

Cro-Magnon Attitudes

Around 35,000 years ago, Homo sapiens known as Cro-Magnons began to appear in Europe. They had better tools than Neanderthals and, as a result, a more highly developed society. They also seemed to have had a rich ceremonial life that includes the first evidence of regular burial practices.

Again, it's impossible to know exactly what Cro-Magnons believed about death, but excavations suggest a complex set of concepts. Cro-Magnon remains found at Sungir, northeast of Moscow, reveal a man buried with tools carved from mammoth bones. The man wears several necklaces made from over three thousand ivory beads and a woman's cranium rests on top of his grave.

Next to the man and woman is the double grave of an adolescent boy and girl. They are buried head to head, along with the teeth of an Arctic fox, several rings, over ten thousand ivory beads and more than a dozen daggers, spears and spear throwers.

Discoveries such as the one at Sungir, along with other burials and cave art from this period, suggest that Cro-Magnons believed in group affiliation and recognized varied levels of social status. In addition, the children's grave indicates that status could be inherited. Many Cro-Magnon weapons and ornaments are beautifully carved with both realistic and symbolic images. Perhaps shamans or a priestly class of Cro-Magnons presided over the ritual use of such objects. Whatever the case, from this time forward, death was attended to with ever increasing care, ritual and symbolism.

Mesopotamian Attitudes

As the earliest civilizations emerged, prehistoric attitudes toward death solidified into formal beliefs. The Mesopotamians had a pessimistic view of death, but an optimistic view of life. They did not believe the soul lived on after death, so they thought one should rejoice, have fun and make the most of life. Though in many other ways their culture was similar to that of the ancient Egyptians, their attitudes toward death were strikingly different;

Egyptians fetishized death, while the Mesopotamians treated it simply—their architecturally unmemorable graves are covered over with earth, a sharp contrast with Egypt's Pyramids.

Egypt: The Kingdom Obsessed with Death

O my heart which I had from my mother! O my heart of my different ages! Do not stand up as a witness against me, do not be opposed to me in the tribunal, do not be hostile to me in the presence of the Keeper of the Balance. . . Go forth to the happy place whereto we speed; do not make my name stink to the Entourage who make men. Do not tell lies about me in the presence of the god. . . .
—Egyptian Book of the Dead

Ancient Egyptians believed that the fate of the soul was tied to the fate of the body after death. A person's *kaò* or vital life energy, needed to be reunited with its spiritual energy, the *baò*, inside the tomb. Because the baò resided in the body, physical preservation of the corpse was essential. Egyptians became consumed with ever more complex funereal arts and elevated preparation for death and concern for the afterlife to an obsession.

Properly performed, Egyptian mortuary rites guaranteed a happy existence in the next life. These rites and accompanying procedures are outlined in a series of texts, commonly known as the *Book of the Dead*, that represent the earliest sacred literature in the world. The texts were inscribed on tomb walls, painted inside coffins, copied onto "books" preserved in wooden containers and written on papyrus scrolls buried with mummies.

The texts are a collection of magical spells and incantations meant to assure the deceased's well-being in the afterlife. The elaborate rituals and procedures outlined in the *Book of the Dead* were so pervasive that Egyptians followed the process of mummification from about 3000 B.C.E. until many Egyptians converted to Islam 3,500 years later.

An important concept concerning death for ancient Egyptians was the idea of judgment. They believed that a divine tribunal would evaluate each person. In the afterlife, the mummy's heart would be weighed against the Feather of Truth and Righteousness. Good deeds kept the heart light and assured eternal life. A heavy heart indicated sin and was consumed by the crocodile-headed monster, Ammit.

Assuming that the dead person passed the divine test and was granted eternal life, items from one's former life would be needed in the next. That's why Egyptian tombs are so large and contain so many useful objects. Beautiful women took their cosmetics with them. Musicians took harps. Children took games and toys. Food, clothing, furniture, models of servants and slaves, family pets. . . Whatever was available in this life was buried along with the mummy.

The pyramids, the largest tombs in the world, became the final resting place of many mummies. The Great Pyramid of Khufu at Giza is made up of over 2,300,000 stone blocks and stands 480 feet high. Elaborate tombs like the Great Pyramid could take a half-million workers several decades to complete.

Greek and Roman Attitudes

Greeks borrowed part of their philosophy about death from the Egyptians. They too thought that the gods weighed a person's soul after death. Greeks buried people with bits of food, wine, clothing and various forms of entertainment for use in the afterlife.

The Greeks feared death terribly; their mythology describes shades, or souls, in Hades as sorrowful, their environment dark and gloomy. Literature and mythology alike reflect a fascination with immortality and horror at the anguish of death. Socrates, though an iconoclast in his time, did influence future Western philosophers' views on this subject; he believed death was not to be feared, nor grieved over extravagantly, but accepted calmly.

Improper burial procedures and failure to provide adequate offerings led to torment in the "joyless region" of the afterlife called Hades. Conscientious Greeks made sure that their dead were buried with a coin for Charon, the boatman who ferried souls across the river Styx, and honeycake for Cerberus, the three-headed dog who guarded Hades's gates.

The Greeks bathed their dead, anointed them with oil and dressed them, but did not create mummies. They buried their dead, until about 1000 B.C.E. when cremation became the preferred method. Cremation was first used as a practical solution to death on the battlefield. Urns filled with the deceased's ashes were much easier to return to grieving relatives, especially when deaths occurred in faraway places. Ash-filled urns also allowed for state funerals to be held weeks or months after a hero's death. While most commoners in Greece were buried, cremation became the preferred method of disposal for the bodies of the elite.

Cremation was closely associated with virtue and patriotism. *The Iliad* describes many elaborate cremations, including the Trojan King Priam's funeral for his hero son, Hector, and the enormous funeral pyre Achilles built to honor his friend, Patroclus.

Common Roman citizens, like common Greeks, were often buried, but the Roman elite chose cremation. Cremations became status symbols for the powerful. Wealthy families bought elaborate urns and rented space for them in special vaults called columbariums. They even bought jeweled lachrymatories, vessels to catch and store the tears of professional mourners. A whole mortuary industry (including the need for the first funeral directors) grew up around the practice of cremation and its ostentatious Roman accoutrements.

In the *Aeneid*, the poet Virgil chastises Romans for their tasteless, nonreligious cremations and gaudy funeral displays. He describes the proper method of building a simple funeral pyre, details the preferred use of cypress wood and advocates that only sincerely religious mourners attend the ceremonies.

The practice of cremation subsided around 100 C.E., but the reasons are not fully understood. Two theories are most probable. First, Christianity was on the rise and the early church frowned on cremation. Second, because there had been so many cremations for such a long time, wood had become scarce. Romans now needed this precious resource more for shipbuilding and forts along the empire's boundaries rather than for funeral pyres.

Celtic Attitudes

While the classical civilizations flourished around the Mediterranean, the people of northern Europe developed their own cultures and belief systems. The ancient Celts had little fear of death; this is probably why they were such reckless warriors. This attitude is related to their religious beliefs: they believed that there was little separation between the spiritual and earthly worlds, and the afterlife was much like this life, only better. During the Christian era, European attitudes toward death would become much more elaborate.

The Evolution of Modern Attitudes Toward Death

The Early Middle Ages: Death as Collective Destiny

Fresh from a victory in Spain, the rear guard of Charlemagne's army became trapped by Saracens in the narrow pass at Roncevaux in the Pyrenees. The French epic poem, *Chanson de Roland*, celebrates their bravery, mourns their eventual defeat and offers insight into medieval attitudes toward death and the dying.

Once he is mortally wounded, Roland, the daring hero of the battle, begins the series of acts expected of a man of his status during the age of chivalry. He recounts his life, recalling the things he has accomplished and the people he has loved. He celebrates his troops, exalts in the lands he has conquered, emphasizes his love and respect for Lord Charlemagne. Roland does not mention the woman betrothed to him, nor his parents because, above all, his last and most noble thoughts must be for France.

Death was certainly not unfamiliar to medieval people. It was accepted and taken for granted, as it had been for centuries. Excessive emotion over death—whether grief or fear—was considered inappropriate. Part of the reason for this was that for most people, life was so full of hardship that death seemed a release. And life expectancies were so low that adults viewed their own death as imminent, and practically expected babies and children to die. Communities were considered more important than individuals, so people did not mourn too greatly the loss of one person.

Painful and prolonged deaths were all too common and yet sudden deaths were rare. Even battle-injured soldiers usually had time to prepare themselves. They would remove their armor, lie down facing Jerusalem, cross their arms over their chests, settle earthly accounts and say their prayers. Perhaps a priest would be present to hear confession and give absolution. Finally, the medieval person—warrior or peasant—simply lapsed into silence and waited for death.

Unexpected death offered numerous complications to the medieval mind. For one thing, deaths were public events. In a world that depended on order and relied on the code of chivalry, to die alone meant that no one would hear your last prayers or receive your last instructions. The dying expected to be surrounded by family and friends. Death was seen not as an individual destiny but as a communal experience. All people died and all people participated in death's rituals. Sudden deaths broke this pattern of community involvement.

Because of the pervasiveness of Christian thought during the Middle Ages in Europe, death was seen by most people as a period of relief and repose where the dead waited, according to church promises, for resurrection. Burials were simple and, until the sixth century or so, most occurred outside of towns, a holdover perhaps from pagan times when the dead seemed able to return and haunt the living.

During the sixth and seventh centuries, monasticism and many cults dedicated to martyrs developed. Great numbers of pilgrims visited martyrs' grave sites and many wanted to be buried next to them, as an extra guarantee for the afterlife. Gradually chapels and then churches were built beside these grave sites. People began to be buried inside churchyards rather than in the countryside.

Charnel houses were another place of safekeeping for remains. These ossuaries were public places that stored bones, often of the poor or unknown or remains from old graves disinterred to make way for new burials on the same ground. Sometimes charnel houses arranged bones in geometric designs or, as in the famous Paris catacombs, made piles of femurs and skulls as much as eight feet high and ten yards deep.

Written on the walls of charnel houses might be phrases such as "Death is all around us." Indeed, it was. People gathered in charnel houses to do business, dance and gamble. A Breton song declared, "Let us come to the charnel house, Christians; let us see the skeletons of our brothers." Such burial practices reflect the belief that death was a collective destiny and not something greatly feared. After all, theirs was the promise of resurrection.

The Late Middle Ages and Renaissance: The Individual's Fear of Death

Item, my body I do bequeath
To our great mother, the earth. . .
Item, I with my grave to be
At Saint Avoye and nowhere else. . .
Item, four laborers shall carry
My body to the monastery. . .
And as for the lighting of my bier
I shall nothing say on it
Let my executor decide
And all dispose as he sees fit
The singing of a single Mass
of Requiem will suffice for me
But my heart would the more rejoice
If there might a descant be
And also I wish fervently
That all the singers who shall sing
Be given gold or currency
That their faces may be smiling.

—FRANÇOIS VILLON

Around the 12th century, medieval attitudes toward death began to change. More people had more access to the works of Greek and Roman philosophers. During the age of exploration, new continents and new cultures were discovered. Intellectual and geographic barriers fell and a new self-awareness arose. No longer were people certain of the Church's promise of communal resurrection. The concept of a divine balance sheet, tallied after each individual's death, developed. Anxiety, rather than repose, now accompanied thoughts of death.

This transformation in attitudes occurred in part because of the prevalence of disease, especially the plague. By the end of 1351, the first wave of the Black Death had wiped out over one-third of the population of Europe. Death seemed to be everywhere. The order of the age of chivalry had been upset. While much of church doctrine held fast, anxiety grew, especially surrounding the judgment of souls and salvation. As individualism strengthened, the family began to displace the community as a unit of social organization. Death took on dramatic, tragic overtones and, indeed, became a cultural preoccupation. The prospect of individual judgment after death grew even more frightening, as evidenced by images of heaven and hell in the art and literature of the time.

The act of dying took on greater significance. Angels and demons were believed to hover over the dying, battling for the soul. The moments before death were a time to justify one's time on earth and guarantee a place in the next world. The prayer, "Ave Maria," dates from this era and invokes the image of a good death.

Wills, penitences, patronages and endowments were often part of the deathbed scene. The revolutionary concept of free will brought with it moral responsibilities. Settling earthly accounts, giving personal testimonies and bequeathing property were seen as means to tip the eternal scales in favor of salvation.

During plague years, taboos and fears surrounded the dead. From this time forward, corpses were concealed. The faces of the dead, especially, were covered and burial shrouds and coffins cloaked dead bodies.

While the actual remains of the dead were more veiled, after-death images of them became more common. Plaques and tomb inscriptions proclaimed a person's life. Death masks and sculptures represented the body before and after death. Statues vividly detailed decomposition and warned of mortality and the need to be individually responsible for one's fate.

The Age of Industry: Science, Faith and Family

Up until the end of the Renaissance, each individual was consumed with anxiety over his or her own death. Death was frightening and seemed arbitrary; salvation elusive, rather than divinely guaranteed. Then, beginning around 1700, the focus shifted from one's own death to the death of others. Attachments between individual people—lovers, parents and children, husbands and wives, friends—became a more acknowledged part of life. Death was seen as a dissolution of passionate bonds, even more unbearable, but also erotic and romantic. More and more, people thought that families—believers and nonbelievers alike—had a chance to be reunited in heaven. Focus on the fate of others provided a way to cope with the frightening possibility of personal, eternal damnation.

But what happens when death comes to a person's only secure environment, the nuclear family? Ideas such as the beautiful death, the cult of memory and exaggerated mourning rituals resulted. Death came to be seen as the preface for a long-anticipated heavenly reunion with deceased family members. Rather than fear the hellfire and brimstone of their Puritan ancestors, Romantics of the 18th and early 19th centuries compared death to the unfolding of a butterfly from its chrysalis. Deathbed scenes, á la Romeo and Juliet, became events of grand drama and opportunities for final exchanges of beautiful intimacies.

In colonial America, death was treated as a familiar part of everyday life, just as it had once been in Europe, for similar reasons. Adults died young and the death of children was a regular occurrence. By the 1800s, though, American attitudes, especially those of the white middle class, were similar to those of Europeans.

In 19th-century Europe and North America, elaborate mourning ceremonies and memorials to the dead helped assuage loss. Ornate tombs, statues and monuments celebrated the dead. Because so many people spent time there, designers made cemeteries into huge parks, lush and inviting. Most deaths still occurred at home, and wakes, complete with coffins resting in the family parlor, were spirited, social affairs. Jewelry such as earrings, broaches and bracelets made from the hair of deceased loved ones was popular.

Victorians used special black-bordered mourning stationery. The bereaved usually stayed at home for a month after a funeral (except to attend church) and, for a year, attendance at celebrations of any sort was considered tasteless. The fashion industry responded to society's obsession with the deceased by designing somber mourning clothes. Accepted mourning colors were black for the first year and then purple and gray.

During this time, the modern view of death started to emerge. With improvements in medicine people lived longer and death was slower. Diseases lasted longer, thus becoming more frightening; this fear of disease made death itself repellent. The emerging notion of privacy, for individuals and families, gradually made mourning or even open discussion about death far less acceptable.

The Modern Age: Avoidance and Denial

Most deaths occur in hospitals now. Advances in drug therapies and other medications help suppress the agonies of disease and injury. Society and science view death as a biological transition and strive to make it painless. A hundred years ago, a thousand years ago, most deaths happened at home but, for most people today, death is invisible. Such is not yet the case in the developing world, where death still occupies the niche it has for eons—as an everyday fact of life. In contemporary Brazil among the very poor, the death even of children is such a frequent event that it is accepted without a great deal of grief.

Even with the act of death concealed by modern technology, anxiety remains high. Death may have been tamed by science and pain greatly alleviated, but many people fear the impersonal, clinical aspect of dying alone in a hospital. Because of population mobility and demographic shifts, faith in the community and support from the nuclear family may prove transitory. Religion comforts fewer and fewer people. Understanding life's or death's significance eludes many. With fewer rituals to depend on, lack of certainty about an afterlife and less solace available from loved ones, dying in the last part of the 20th century is indeed troublesome.

Funerals now are mostly short and discreet, handled by professionals rather than families. Cemeteries discourage elaborate grave markers and ornate statuary, recommending instead small, ground-level nameplates. Counselors often advise that children not attend funerals. Friends and family, unused to dealing with death, frequently remark, "I don't know what to say. I'm not sure what to do." Death in modern society seems almost shameful and is nearly taboo. Consequently, the bereaved and the dying alike can find themselves quite isolated.

The AIDS crisis has exposed American culture's unwillingness to acknowledge death. Its association with stigmatized groups and sexuality marries the historic connection between sex and death with the contemporary conviction that death is, as sex used to be, shameful. The extreme ostracism of AIDS victims and their survivors seems a grotesque extension of the treatment of the ordinary dying and their survivors—others do not want to know or hear about it. Ironically, the denial of AIDS only hastens its spread. Work to bring the disease into the open may help break down the wall of silence around human mortality.

The hospice movement defies the conventional denial of death. Hospice caregivers help demystify and deinstitutionalize death. Through death education, they encourage openness and frank discussion about life and death options and offer support for both the living and the dying.

Non-European Attitudes

The culmination of Western civilization's complex system of beliefs about death contrasts with beliefs held by the rest of the world's diverse peoples. A representative assortment of current attitudes includes the following.

Native American tribes vary a great deal in their cultural practices and beliefs, but there is some consistency in their views of death. They tend not to fear it, but to see it as part of the natural life cycle, a companion, not an enemy; it is also seen as something to be constantly aware of, because it might happen at any time.

By contrast, Australian Aborigines see death not as natural, but as an evil intrusion brought about by the magical powers of enemies. In traditional Ghana, too, there is no such thing as a natural death.

In Japan, for centuries Samurai knights had a code of honor known as *bushido*, which was influenced by Zen Buddhism, Confucianism and Shinto. Bushido meant resignation in the face of death and suffering and loyalty to one's commander—loyalty one would be willing to die for. Chinese attitudes are influenced by Buddhism, Taoism and most of all, Confucianism. Chinese tradition discourages anxiety about death. For Taoists, life and death are crucial partners: they make each other possible. Confucius taught that grief after a death was appropriate, but that it should not last too long, because all things end. He refused to speak directly about death, believing one could not yet know anything about it. The traditions combine into a general acceptance of death. The Chinese also have great respect for the dead, honoring them regularly with offerings and prayers; these practices contribute to a sense that death is an accepted part of daily life. Tibetans believe that more than anything in life, people learn from change. Since death is the greatest possible change, it is potentially the most liberating moment of human life, the time when it is easiest to attain peace and enlightenment. During life, therefore, one should instruct oneself in how to die, especially by reading the *Tibetan Book of the Dead*, the definitive source of Tibetan Buddhist teachings on the subject.

Funerals: History and Cultural Overview

Six feet of earth make all men of one size.
—OLD PROVERB

Funerals have always functioned as symbols to mark the passage from life to death. The Latin origins of the word "funeral" mean a torchlight procession, a way for the living to help the dead find their way to the next world. Funerals help the living overcome the stress that accompanies the death of others and help reunite the community after the loss of a member. In some cultures, funerals are necessary to provide safe passage into the afterlife and to protect the living from the power of dangerous, newly dead spirits. According to culture and historical era, this rite of passage can take many forms.

History of the American Funeral

Any history of American burial rites properly begins with the hundreds of Indian nations that lived in North and South America at the time of European contact. Each nation had its own funeral rites and burial practices. In Peru, excavations of Inca ruins revealed pyramids and mummies. The Aztecs and Mayans also built pyramids and, like the early Egyptians of the Old World and the Incas of the New World, worshipped the sun. Funeral rites in these cultures reinforced a person's obedience to the gods.

Forms of tribal burial in the Americas included:

- **INHUMATION:** placing the body in pits, graves, urns, mounds, caves and beneath the floors of dwellings. Embalming or mummification was sometimes performed.

- **SURFACE BURIAL:** placing the body in hollow logs or covering it with rock cairns or loose branches.

- **CREMATION:** burning the body and then collecting or scattering the ashes.

- **SEPULCHER BURIAL:** placing the body in a container that remained above ground such as a special lodge, canoe or carved wooden box.

- **AERIAL BURIAL:** placing the body in tree branches, baskets, lashed scaffolds or canoes.

- **AQUATIC BURIALS:** placing the body in rivers, lakes or oceans.

Just as methods of burial varied greatly among Indian nations, so did funeral rites. However, mourning songs were characteristic of most native funerals before the advent of European religions. These chants expressed sorrow, guided the dead to the afterlife and protected the living from otherworldly spirits.

When white people arrived in the Americas, they brought European burial customs with them. In colonial America, people often made plans for their own funerals. They realized that injury or illness could claim them at any time and so they stockpiled lumber for coffins or "cooling boards." Closets held special burial clothing (women sometimes saved their wedding gowns) and weavers loomed shrouds. Front parlors were kept tidy so that they could be used for wakes and funerals in case of sudden deaths. In Pennsylvania, German immigrants even built special rooms called *doedkammers* or dead rooms, with doors wide enough to permit pallbearers to enter and exit carrying a casket.

In the colonies and on the frontier, church bells tolled to announce deaths, yet it was considered poor taste to attend a funeral uninvited. The New Amsterdam Dutch hired *aanspreeckers*, men who dressed in black and wore crepe ribbons on their hats, to invite people to services. By the late 19th century, formal, black-bordered invitations announced funerals.

Family members (usually women) washed and dressed the body and wrapped it in a winding sheet. Often the family built the coffin. After a wake in the parlor, the family carried the coffin to the church for religious services and then to the graveyard.

Since funerals were occasions for gathering the community together, food played an important role. When Callie Dawes died in Boston in 1797, her funeral feast cost $844. The menu included beef, ham, poultry, fish, oysters, eggs, potatoes, peas, onions, cheese and fruit. Funeral foods for the Pennsylvania Dutch could be ham, stewed chicken, mashed potatoes, applesauce, red beets, doughnuts and sandwiches. In the South, mourners might be served rum punch, hot cider and cakes as well as entire meals.

Nathaniel Hawthorne described funerals as "the only class of scenes. . . in which our ancestors were wont to steep their tough old hearts in wine and strong drink and indulge in an outbreak of grisly jollity." Wakes might become drunken free-for-alls. An 1845 account recalls that "fathers have been known to stagger to the grave, husbands to fall down and sons to be drunken at the burial of all that is dear."

Not all funerals lacked decorum. Consider this description of a rural funeral from the 1800s:

> *Everyone as he entered, took off his hat with his left hand, smoothed down his hair with his right, walked up to the coffin, gazed down upon the corpse, made a crooked face, passed up to the table, took a glass of his favorite liquor, went forth upon the plat before the house and talked politics or the new road or compared crops or swapped heifers or horses, until it was time to lift.*

Individual sections of the country had funerals that reflected their culture. For example, New Orleans developed jazz funerals. Musicians led the cortege to the cemetery.

By the early 1800s, tradesmen provided some funeral services. Carpenters

Funeral Bill for Widow Ryseck Swart, Albany, New York, February 1700

Guilders	3	6 gallons of Madeira for women and men	84
dry boards for coffin	7	Sugar	5
¾ of a pound of nails	1	150 sugar cakes	15
Charge for making coffin	24	Tobacco and pipes	5
Cartage	10	Use of pall	10
Half a vat and anker of good beer	27	Wife of Jans Lockermans (to lay out body)	36
1 gallon of rum	21	(From: *Death in Early America*, by Margaret Coffin)	

might advertise themselves as coffin-makers. Church sextons not only rang steeple bells, but dug graves. Stable keepers provided carriages. Ornate hearses became popular in the late 19th century and came complete with glass windows, coach lamps, carved pillars and heavy, tasseled draperies. Matched teams of beautiful, well-trained horses drew the funeral coach.

The Civil War initiated a change in funeral customs. Because so many families wanted their dead soldiers returned home for burial, the practice of embalming came into wider use. Then, President Lincoln was assassinated. His funeral caravan lasted 14 days as the train traveled 1,700 miles from Washington, D.C. to Springfield, Illinois. Over seven million people saw Lincoln's embalmed body. His coffin was removed from the train and opened at every major stop along the way.

By the end of the 1900s, undertakers directed most aspects of the funeral. Embalming, now quite common, might be done in homes with portable embalming equipment or performed in separate rooms within funeral parlors. Undertakers sold or supplied all sorts of funeral materials: caskets, door badges, wreaths, memorial announcements, clothing, candles and cemetery plots.

Today national associations establish standards for the funeral directors' trade and government agencies license embalmers and morticians. Families seldom deal directly with the bodies of their deceased, leaving the orchestration of funerals to professionals.

Funeral Rituals in Various Religions

To every thing there is a season. . . A time to be born and a time to die.
—ECCLESIASTES 3:1

Throughout history, many cultures and religions have shared certain death rituals: laying out the body, watching over the dead (wakes), funeral services, burial ceremonies and mourning practices. According to religious beliefs, each event may be very simple or quite elaborate.

Judaism

"Yea, though I walk through the valley of the shadow of death, I will fear no evil, for Thou are with me; thy rod and thy staff they comfort me."
—PSALMS 23:4

Funeral customs vary within Jewish communities, but most dying Jews are comforted when they hear a special prayer called the *Shma:* "Hear O Israel the Lord your God, the Lord is One. You shall love the Lord your God with all your heart, with all your soul and with all your strength."

In traditional congregations the Chevrah Kaddisha, or burial society, cares for the remains. Members of this pious group cleanse and dress the body. Traditional Jews are buried as soon after death as possible in simple white shrouds to signify that all people are equal before God. A man's prayer shawl is placed over his shroud. Embalming is discouraged except when the practice is required by law. Coffins are simple and made from wood. Many less traditional Jews are cremated.

Funerals are usually held in Jewish funeral chapels, although they may take place in the synagogue. The rabbi reads from religious writings such as the Psalms and offers a eulogy for the deceased. The casket, though present, remains closed during the service.

As they carry the casket to the grave, it is traditional for pallbearers to stop seven times. This allows mourners time to reflect on the meaning of life. At the grave, the rabbi reads appropriate Psalms and offers prayers and people recite the Kaddish. Everyone tosses a handful of soil on the grave.

In strict religious communities, many rules govern the behavior of those in mourning, especially during *Shiva,* the first seven days after burial. Close relatives are not expected to carry on business or do everyday tasks during this time. Other family members and friends make their meals and comfort them while they grieve.

During Shiva, mirrors in the house are covered, so that mourners will reflect not on themselves but rather on the meaning of life and death. A candle is lit to signify the soul and burns for seven days. Mourners sit on stools or low chairs and wear cloth slippers and sandals instead of shoes. They may rend their clothing or wear symbolic ribbons as tokens of their grief.

The Kaddish is a prayer that praises God, affirms life and reinforces faith. It is recited daily during Shiva. In some congregations, Kaddish continues to be said for 30 days; in others it is said for 11 months less one day.

A year after the death, relatives and friends visit the grave site to dedicate the tombstone. Two Hebrew letters meaning "here lies a treasure" often appear at the top of the marker and other letters meaning "may his/her soul be bound in the bond of life" appear at the bottom. Each year thereafter on the anniversary of the death a memorial candle is lit in honor of the dead.

Islam

So glory to Him in whose hand is power over everything. Unto Him you shall be returned.

—The Koran

When Muslims feel close to death, they try to read the Koran, Islam's holy book, say prayers and profess their belief in the prophet Mohammed. They concentrate especially on repeating the phrase, "There is no god but Allah and

Mohammed is His messenger." Family members and friends also read the Koran, offer prayers and comfort the dying.

After death, the body is washed and wrapped in seamless white cloth. No cosmetics are used and burial preparations are very plain. If the person was a martyr, the ritual washing is not performed because blood is the emblem of martyrdom.

Mohammed said, "The sooner a good man is buried, the sooner he will reach heaven and be at peace," and so funerals and burials take place as soon after death as possible, usually within 24 hours.

Funerals may be held at home or in the mosque. Prayers are said by family, friends and, when present, the imam. Then someone asks the community whether or not the person who died had any debts. Worldly debts must be paid (usually by the family) or forgiven before burial. Questions are posed about the deceased person's conduct, similar to the questions asked of everyone on the Day of Judgment.

Coffins are not required because religious teachings say that people were created from clay and so they should return to clay. The dead are buried facing the direction of Mecca. A few simple prayers are said over the grave.

Christianity

In my Father's house are many mansions. . . I go to prepare a place for you.
—JOHN 14:2

Christian services emphasize the promise of life after death. Whether they are Roman Catholic, Eastern Orthodox or Protestant, Christian funerals mourn the loss of loved ones and celebrate anticipated spiritual rewards.

Catholic Practices   Anointing the Sick, a ritual formerly called Extreme Unction, is given to people who are very ill. The priest greets the person, offers a scriptural verse or litany, blesses the oil and says a prayer of Thanksgiving. Then the ill person's forehead and hands are anointed with oil and the priest says, "May the Lord who frees you from sin, save you and raise you up." Anointing the Sick concludes with prayers(including the Lord's Prayer), communion and a final blessing.

The last sacrament offered Catholics is the Holy Communion called the Viaticum. Via signifies that someone is on "the way" to heaven.

In the United States, most bodies are embalmed and prepared for burial by morticians. In the past and in some rural areas today, the Catholic family washed and prepared the body. The deceased are dressed in good clothes, typically suits for men and dresses for women and laid in caskets. Cremation, though permitted, is rare for Catholics.

The Order of the Christian Funeral includes three rituals:

- **THE VIGIL OR WAKE.** Family and friends gather to pray the Rosary and say other prayers. The vigil usually takes place at the funeral home on the evening before the funeral. Then the body is transported to the church.

- **THE MASS OF CHRISTIAN BURIAL (FORMERLY KNOWN AS THE REQUIEM MASS).** As Mass begins, the body is sprinkled with holy water to symbolize baptism. A homily called the Liturgy of the Word follows that recounts the person's life. Next comes communion, additional prayers and songs and the closing rite of commendation. During this closing, family members may speak and incense may be waved over the body.

- **THE RITE OF COMMITTAL.** During this last rite, the community follows the casket to the cemetery in a ritual procession. When practical, prayers and songs are sung or, in the case of an automobile cortege, attendees pray. At the cemetery, there are additional prayers and songs.

Catholic funeral masses are usually held in parish churches and Catholics are usually buried in Catholic cemeteries because they are consecrated ground.

Eastern Orthodox Practices   Many rites for the dead in Eastern Orthodox churches resemble those of Roman Catholic churches. If the dying person is conscious, he or she takes communion. Then the priest offers prayers and absolution and anoints the person with oil. In both churches, the chance for the dying to confess their sins and be offered forgiveness is important.

A vesper service or wake is held the evening before the funeral and prayers recited. Sometimes family members, deacons or priests stay with the body all night.

Eastern Orthodox funerals are also held in churches and conducted by priests. They include prayers, liturgical readings and eulogies.

Graveside services include short prayers and liturgical readings.

Protestant Practices   There is great variety among Protestant funerals. No special last rites are performed. However, ministers may be called to the bedside of the dying to pray and help the person come to terms with his or her life. As with Roman Catholic and Eastern Orthodox Christians, bodies are prepared by morticians, dressed in good clothes and laid in caskets for burial. Some Protestants are cremated following the funeral.

Prior to the funeral, the minister meets with the family to discuss the service. In particular, the minister seeks details of the person's life to include in the eulogy. The day or evening before the service the family gathers at the funeral home for a visitation, to view the deceased and to pray.

Protestant funerals are celebrations of life. Music and hymns, prayers, Bible readings, a eulogy and a brief sermon characterize most funerals. Family or friends also may offer tributes to the deceased. The casket is usually placed at the front of the church and may or may not be open during the service.

Attendees at some Protestant funerals show little emotion, preferring to express grief in private. Other funerals offer a means to openly express sorrow. Charismatic denominations and some African-American churches, for example, believe that the deceased has "crossed over" to a better world. While they are sad for the loss of loved ones, they rejoice in the dead person's release from earthly struggle. These funerals often are a mixture of intense crying and joyful praise.

Protestant graveside services usually are brief, consisting of a few prayers and maybe a song.

Hinduism

Worn-out garments are shed by the body;
Worn-out bodies are shed by the dweller within...
New bodies are donned by the dweller, like garments.
—THE BHAGAVAD GITA

Hindus believe in the cycle of life, death and rebirth. Repeated incarnations of the soul result from the moral law of cause and effect called *karma*. To break the eternal cycle of reincarnation, Hindus must free themselves from attachments to the material world, including attachments to the physical body. That's why Hindu funerals and cremations proceed quickly after death.

Prior to death and as a way to loosen earthly attachments, Hindus often meditate on disease or the aging processes occurring within their bodies. They may imagine the details of their own deaths and visualize their bodies being consumed on funeral pyres. Confronting mortality helps to conquer the illusion of individual human existence.

After death, the body traditionally is prepared for the funeral by the family and wrapped in a shroud. However, according to individual beliefs, morticians sometimes take on this responsibility. Funerals, whether they take place at home or at the mortuary, involve prayers and chants. Some families carry their dead to the cremation ground (or to the cremation chamber). This procession often is led by the eldest son, who also lights the fire.

In India, the pallet carrying the body is ceremoniously immersed in the Ganges River before it is taken to the *ghat* or landing along the river where the cremation occurs. Offerings of *ghee* (clarified butter), sandalwood and other fragrant woods and leaves may be added to the pyre. After cremation, the ashes are collected in an urn that is lowered into the Ganges.

Cremation signifies the soul's release and fire helps the deceased person to be born again. However, some Hindus believe that the period immediately following cremation is a difficult one for souls. The deceased may live on as ghosts and be dangerous to friends and relatives. As rites of passage, ritual offerings of food and drink may be presented to the dead from 12 days to up to one year following death.

Buddhism

Thus shall you think of all this fleeting world:
A star at dawn, a bubble in a stream;
A flash of lightning in a summer cloud.
A phantom, an illusion, a dream.

—BUDDHA, *The Diamond Sutra*

Buddhists celebrate death as a way to pass on to the next incarnation and move closer to *nirvana*. Specific funeral and burial practices vary from sect to sect, but how a person dies is extremely important to all Buddhists. They believe that the person's last thoughts, along with karma, determine what the next life will be like. Therefore, great care is given to the dying.

When a person is very ill, family and friends gather to say prayers and provide comfort. Priests offer guidance, telling the person what to expect at the moment of death, as well as after death. The goal is to allow the person to die without fear or regret in order to ensure a good future life.

After death, followers of the Tibetan tradition, for instance, wash the body, dress it and place it in a prayer position. Then the body is left undisturbed for three days so that the person's consciousness may separate from the body without shock.

Buddhist funerals are often more like celebrations. There is chanting, gongs and incense. Priests may speak directly to the dead and give instructions. The moments after death are considered unique opportunities for cosmic understanding.

After the funeral, most Buddhists are cremated. The funeral pyre may be sprinkled with consecrated oil and other offerings and wrapped with white scarves. Ashes either are scattered or placed in graves or urns. In countries such as Japan where Buddhist tradition mixes with ancestor worship, monks often make tablets for family altars in honor of the newly deceased.

Sometimes, funeral rites continue for several days and include ritual meals. A celebration meal also may be held three months later and on the anniversary of the death.

Wakes, Mourning, Remembering the Dead

In a bitter wind
a solitary monk bends
to words cut in stone

—BUSON, ZEN POET, 1715–83

Wakes

Before burial or cremation, people in many cultures keep watch over the dead in one way or another. Some sit with the dead only briefly; others stay for the entire time between death and burial. In ancient times someone had to stay with the body in order to keep away vermin and, depending on religious beliefs, to assure that the spirit of the dead remained safe and benevolent. Sometimes people were paid to watch over the body. In Scotland the longer a person's wake, the greater the charges. As a result, thrifty people buried their dead as soon as possible.

The Inca played complicated dice games as they sat with the dead. They believed that the dead could influence how the dice fell. At the game's conclusion, the person's belongings were divided up.

Celtic countries, especially Ireland and Scotland, had wakes that often developed into boisterous affairs. Even if they started off somberly, wakes soon became excuses for raucous parties. At a typical wake, the body was laid out in the home and family and friends gathered to pray. There might also be storytelling, songs and music.

As the night wore on and strong drink flowed, joke-telling, dancing, drunken brawling and rowdy behavior increased. Bread, cheese, pancakes and whiskey often were served at midnight. Mock battles might be staged, with one participant representing the dead person. Fighting sometimes grew violent. The deceased might be dealt a hand of cards or even removed from the casket so that someone who'd had too much to drink could sleep it off in comfort!

Many cultures partake of meals after funerals. In the Aragón region of Spain, a special bread is baked for the wake. In Ecuador, bread is made in the shape of people or mummies. The Amish in America bake "funeral pies" made with raisins. The first meal after a funeral among Jewish families is called *se'udat havra'ah,* the meal of condolence. Hard-boiled eggs and other round foods symbolizing life's continuity are served. Aztecs burned food for the deceased, often including a plump dog to help the dead cross the dangerous rivers of the afterlife. In Haiti, the funeral meal is called the *mange mort* and indeed some cultures practiced ritual cannibalism as a way, they believed, to spare the dead person's body the indignity of burial and decomposition.

Sin eaters are people who agree to take on the spiritual encumbrances of the dead by consuming ritual foods. India, England, Wales and Ireland are among the countries that employed sin eaters in the past. In Ireland, especially during the Great Famine, hungry people welcomed the opportunity to eat. Bread, beer and other foods were placed on the chest of the deceased. The bargain was that sin eaters mortgaged part of their eternal souls as they took on the weight of someone else's sins. Sin eaters often became societal outcasts.

Mourning

Just as the wake can take many forms, so do the period and methods of mourning. In some cultures and at some moments in history, mourning has followed elaborate precepts.

Victorian Mourning   Victorians were fascinated with death and had many elaborate mourning customs. In Cornwall, even bird cages and houseplants were draped in black. Parts of rural France went further—they tied crepe to pigsties and around cats.

Victorian attitudes persisted well into the next century. *Etiquette for Ladies*, published in 1925 in London, advised:

> "After the funeral the room should be thoroughly aired and before it is used again, the walls, ceiling and paintwork should be completely redecorated.
>
> Widows usually wear mourning for two years. Diamonds and pearls are frequently worn with very deep mourning. . . but gold is not usually worn until a year has passed.
>
> A widow is not expected to go into Society until at least three months have elapsed. Even then her visiting is confined to relatives and intimate friends. Gradually she reappears, though she should avoid dances and balls for at least a year.
>
> Children, daughters-in-law or sons-in-law, parents wear mourning for twelve months; ten months black, the last two months gray, white or mauve."

In both England and the United States, photographs of infants or other loved ones might be set in elaborate tufted frames and decorated with wax flowers and ribbons. As memorial tokens, watchfobs, bracelets, brooches, earrings and other jewelry was made from the hair of the dead. Black-bordered calling cards and stationery announced that a family member had died. The width of the border decreased after the first year of mourning.

Days of the Dead   Early Meso-American peoples did not fear death as much as they feared life's uncertainties. Many people believed that the dead helped the living connect with the gods and so they held festivals to invite the dead to return. Today, all over Mexico and throughout the southwestern United States, the Days of the Dead are celebrated October 31 to November 2.

In Michoacan, people build home altars to honor the dead. Bakers make anise bread called *pan de muerto* and children enjoy skull-shaped candies called *calaveras.* The community celebrates with dances that imitate old men and mock death.

At the cemetery, families tidy the graves and decorate them with marigolds, also known as *cempasuchilt.* The yellow and gold petals create paths that help the spirits find their way back to earth. At night, the cemetery glows with candles, as families gather to keep watch over the graves and commune with the dead.

Mexican-American Remembrances

Muriù como viviù. Tal vida, tal muerte.
(He died as he lived. Such a life, such a death.)
        —New Mexican saying

In traditional communities of northern New Mexico, wakes or *velorios,* last all night. The next day, after Catholic mass, friends carry the casket to the cemetery or *campo santo.* As they walk, church bells toll and mourners sing *alabados.* Sometimes, if the cemetery is far off, the pallbearers stop to rest and pray several times along the way. Each time the procession begins again, a family member places a small cross and a stone where the casket momentarily rested.

The cross is often inscribed with a short prayer for the deceased and a request that anyone who later happens along this way also pray for the dead. It is traditional to add another stone each time someone stops beside one of these crosses or *descansos.*

Throughout the Southwest, similar crosses mark the sites of accidental deaths. They are frequently found next to the scenes of highway accidents and along streams where people drowned. Erecting these crosses helps the living deal with the sudden and traumatic loss of loved ones.

Shrines to the dead as well as to saints are an important part of Mexican and Mexican-American tradition. *Nichos* are freestanding grave decorations. Large or small, these "niches" may be made of river stones, cement, brick or wood. They often contain statues of the deceased's favorite saints.

Some shrines are built not to honor saints but to honor sinners. El Tiradito in Tucson, Arizona, is a registered National Historic Landmark and "the only shrine in the United States dedicated to the soul of a sinner buried in unconsecrated ground." While the identity of the person to whom the shrine is dedicated is unknown, legend says that he or she died suddenly, possibly in an act of murderous passion. For generations, people have lit candles and prayed to El Tiradito, "The Little Castaway One," for help.

This shrine and many others like it across the Southwest, is dedicated to what folklorist Jim Griffith calls "victim intercessors," souls who suffered in life and so are able to understand the struggles of the poor. While they are not officially sanctioned by the Catholic church, shrines such as El Tiradito remain potent symbols of religious faith and ethnic identity.

Reliquaries and Death Masks

Among the many things people do in response to death is the manufacture of various symbolic accessories, such as the following:

Reliquaries

A reliquary is a container holding sacred objects that are venerated. In Gabon, polished, black, head-shaped boxes hold skulls and other ancestral remains. Solomon Islanders construct fish-shaped reliquaries for skulls.

Christian reliquaries hold the heads, hands or other body parts of saints. The container's shape may reflect the contents. The Eastern Orthodox Church, in particular, venerates relics as miraculous.

One of the most famous Christian reliquaries contains the arm and hand bones of St. Thomas Becket. A church in Rome preserved half the heart, one foot and a finger from San Camillo de Lellis.

Sometimes whole skeletons or mummified remains are displayed in ornate glass cases. The skeletons may be veiled in lace, wear armor or other clothing or be covered in brocade, pearls and velvet.

Death Masks

The ancient Romans made wax death masks and used them in plays. Actors wore the masks as they mimicked the gestures of the deceased. In medieval Europe, death masks often adorned the tombs of royalty.

To make a death mask, the face, ears and neck are first oiled and then plaster or wax is poured over. Once dry, the plaster or wax is removed and used as a mold to create a model of the deceased.

L'Inconnue de la Seine, the Unknown Girl of the Seine, is a famous death mask. Around the turn of the century, she was found in the Paris morgue and her likeness used by many artists. Death masks were made of Louis XIV, Marie Antoinette, Robespierre and Napoleon. Madame Tussaud, the famous founder of London's wax museum, began her career making death masks of those guillotined during the French Revolution.

European and American Stonemasons' Tombstone Symbols

Anchor: Hope

Butterfly: Resurrection

Clover Leaf: The Trinity

Crown: Reward in heaven

Ivy: Remembrance or friendship

Lamb: Purity

Lamp: Knowledge of God

Laurels: Fame

Lily: Purity

Palm: Victory

Shell: Pilgrimage

Rose: Sweetness or the Virgin Mary

Sword: Victory, Justice or Mercy

Violets: Humility

Wheat: Fruitfulness

Willow: Grief

Broken Column, Draped Urn, Upturned Torch, Skull, Scythe: Death

Photography, less messy and much quicker, replaced death masks as a way to preserve the image of the dead.

State and Military Funerals

If the funeral ranks among the most highly ritualized moments in a person's life, then the funerals of political rulers, military personnel and other major figures take death ritual to an even higher plane of ceremony.

State Funerals

When Queen Victoria died in 1901, her body was escorted from the Isle of Wight to England by eight torpedo-destroyers and several other ships. A team of cream-colored horses drew her bier across London. Many government buildings were draped in purple. Her state funeral was an immense affair and the flowers alone cost over £80,000. Australia's memorial wreath was made of rare orchids; the 7th Hussars military unit sent 60,000 Russian violets; the 9th Lancer's tribute was white azaleas, lilies of the valley, carnations and mignonettes; the King of Portugal sent a crown of lilies, orchids and violets.

When Abraham Lincoln was assassinated in 1865, the train carrying his body from Washington, D.C. to Springfield, Illinois was draped in black and wreathed with evergreen. Along the way so many people turned out that the train's engineer said, "History has no parallel to the outpouring of sorrow which followed the funeral cortege."

President John F. Kennedy's funeral reflected a similar outpouring of grief. His body lay in state in the Capitol Rotunda in a simple wooden casket. Heads of state, royalty and emissaries from 92 countries, including the Vatican, attended. Millions of people watched the televised event. Kennedy was buried in Arlington National Cemetery with full military honors. According to Mrs. Kennedy's wishes, the only flowers near the grave were a basket of blossoms from the White House garden. At the grave site, Cardinal Cushing gave the benediction after a 21-gun salute. A bugler sounded taps. Mrs. Kennedy was handed a folded American flag and then she lit the eternal flame.

It is not just kings, queens and presidents who receive governmental funerals:

- Huge lengths of black crepe draped the Arc de Triomphe for Victor Hugo's funeral in Paris in 1885.

- In 1852, the Duke of Wellington had what was described as "the most splendid funeral ever staged in Europe." There was a huge car (created in six foundries by one hundred men) made from cannon captured by Wellington's army, as well as the Duke's riderless horse, with boots reversed in the stirrups.

- When William "Buffalo Bill" Cody died in 1917, his body lay in state in the state capitol in Denver, Colorado, while 25,000 people filed past. For the funeral procession, a regimental band and infantry soldiers walked before the hearse, followed by Cody's riderless horse, McKinley.

Unknown Soldiers and Military Funerals

For thousands of years, burial on the battlefield was traditional. With hundreds or even thousands dead, no embalming facilities and scant transportation, it made sense to inter fallen soldiers where they fought and died. Burial at sea also has a long tradition. After a memorial service, the shrouded body is slid into the ocean.

During the Civil War embalming became more common for military dead and soldiers' bodies were shipped home for burial. Still, most World War I soldiers were buried in the huge European cemeteries dedicated to them. As a way to honor these servicemen, Congress voted to build a memorial amphitheater at Arlington National Cemetery to house a tomb of an unknown soldier.

Military funerals in general consist of an honor guard, military protocols, a salute and the playing of taps.

Deaths: Willing and Unwilling

The rituals of death include not only the customs surrounding the disposal of bodies and the migration of the soul to another plane, but also the

culturally sanctioned ways in which death is intentionally caused. Such practices—for example, execution, human sacrifice—may involve willing or
unwilling participants.

Sacrifices

Egyptians, Greeks, Romans, Phoenicians and Hebrews practiced the ritual sacrifice of their firstborn, other infants and older children. Infanticide of
babies born out of wedlock or as a result of rape or incest is common in many
cultures, as is the practice of killing handicapped babies. In some countries
(particularly China and India), female babies still are killed today, especially
when food is scarce or in order to make room for a male heir.

Sacrificing to create good crops or to prevent natural disasters has a long
history; so does sacrificing to appease the enemy. Around 1000 B.C.E., for
instance, Israel experienced a severe drought. King David deduced that the
cause was King Saul's massacre of the Gibeonites many years before. In order
to end the drought David directed that the Gibeonites execute several of Saul's
descendants. According to the Old Testament book of Samuel, the famine
ended when "the rains came and fell from heaven upon the bodies."

The Aztecs discovered their homeland in the valley of Mexico only after the
daughter of one of their chiefs had been killed by another tribe. At Teotihuacán,
huge pyramids celebrated the people's dedication to the sun. On ceremonial
platforms atop the pyramids, the Aztecs sacrificed thousands. Priests used flint
and obsidian knives to cut the living hearts from victims. Other victims were
thrown down wells, flayed alive or killed in other ritual ways.

The Toltecs too practiced human sacrifice. In one ritual, the leaders of
ceremonial ball teams were decapitated. Toltecs, Aztecs, Mayas, Incas. . . the
gods of the New World demanded blood.

Suttee

Not every sacrifice dies unwillingly. Many cultures allowed the wife of a
man to die when he did in order to ensure their afterlife reunion. Ancient
China, Thrace, Scythia, Egypt, Africa, Polynesia, Scandinavia and India all
practiced widow sacrifice. *Suttee* was banned by the British rulers of India in
1828, but before then it was quite common, however, because widows had
such low status in Indian society.

Executions

• In Rome, someone who sang rude songs could be executed.

• In ancient India, a person could be killed for stealing a royal elephant.

- Babylonians who sold bad beer received the death penalty.

- So did mediocre Assyrian barbers.

- In ancient Egypt, the punishment for merely injuring a cat was death.

Stonings were probably the first form of execution. Greeks and Hebrews generally limited stonings to people who committed crimes that affected the whole community. Courts determined who should be executed and the aim was "to purge the evil from the midst." Mobs might beat offenders to death with sticks, stones or their bare hands.

Romans practiced the spectacle of throwing criminals, Christians, slaves and foreign enemies to the lions or other wild beasts. They also set armed enemies against one another inside their coliseums and made them fight to the death. Another popular method of execution was crucifixion, which the Romans copied from the Phoenicians.

Noble Greeks and Romans sometimes were allowed to commit suicide. Socrates could choose the hour of his death and be surrounded by his students while he ingested hemlock.

Some cultures buried people alive. Rome's vestal virgins, if found guilty of immorality, were walled up in underground chambers. Unfaithful Inca wives of the sun god were buried alive. In the Middle Ages, monks, nuns and people of noble blood were sometimes allowed to avoid the scandal of a public execution and choose this method of death.

During the Middle Ages, trials were often held in the public marketplace. People believed that carrying out cruel and public death sentences served to deter crime. Executions often became gaudy entertainments and violent pageants. People were hanged at the gallows, disemboweled, drawn and quartered, mangled on huge wheels, boiled alive or pressed under weights until they stopped breathing.

Beheading is another historical execution method. The orator Cicero, sentenced by Rome for opposing the alliance between Mark Antony and Augustus, was beheaded. William the Conqueror introduced beheading to England. King Henry VIII beheaded some of his wives. Henry and Anne's daughter, Elizabeth I, executed her rival, Mary, Queen of Scots.

Another type of blade, the guillotine, promised "painless" death when it was introduced. Louis XVI, Marie Antoinette and thousands of French nobility and citizens died by the guillotine. When Marie Antoinette approached her execution, she stepped on her executioner's foot. Her final words were, "Monsieur, I beg your pardon. It was an accident."

Death by firing squad, the electric chair, gas chamber and lethal injection are more modern execution methods. Benjamin Franklin experimented with electrocution, discovering that it took six Leyden jars to kill a 10-pound turkey. In 1890, the first American electrocution, at Auburn Prison in New York state, took eight minutes and several jolts of electricity. The procedure was so gruesome that electrocution was almost abolished.

The gas chamber seemed technologically and morally superior to the electric chair. Attitudes toward the death penalty were beginning to change. The public now demanded that if there had to be executions, they should be more humane. In the gas chamber, some criminals died after only two minutes; but others took up to 11 minutes.

In 1976, in Huntsville, Texas, the first execution by lethal injection occurred. A saline solution, followed by a mixture of three chemicals, was injected through intravenous tubes. One chemical dulls the senses, one relaxes muscles to prevent breathing and one causes cardiac arrest. Today, lethal injection is the most common method of execution in the United States.

Harakiri and Kamikaze Pilots

In Japan and China, warriors practiced ritual suicide known as *harakiri* or *seppuku.* The act allowed soldiers to avoid execution by the enemy or to die honorably when they had fallen out of favor with the emperor. In the presence of official witnesses, the warrior drew a jeweled dagger across his abdomen, made an upward thrust and then was beheaded by a faithful friend. Harakiri persisted for generations. At the end of World War II, many Japanese soldiers, sailors and civilians chose to die rather than surrender.

Kamikaze pilots chose another form of suicide. During World War II, 3,913 pilots of "the divine wind" deliberately aimed their bomb-laden planes at enemy targets and died. Their moral code advised them: "Make it your joy to use every last bit of your physical and spiritual strength in what you do. Do not fear to die for the cause of everlasting justice. Do not stay alive in dishonor."

Dog Soldiers of the Western Plains

"It is a good day to fight! It is a good day to die!"
—Crazy Horse

Warriors held high status among Plains cultures. Although U.S. soldiers mistakenly labeled most Indian fighters "dog soldiers," the term applies best to the members of special warrior societies. In battle, dog soldiers attached a length of rope to one leg and tied the opposite end (about 10 feet long) to a

---

Dichos: Traditional Sayings from the Southwest and Mexico

"Achaque quiere la muerte." Death needs no excuses.

"Casamiento y palo mortaje del cielo baja." Marriage and death are both made in heaven.

"De la muerte y de la suerte no hay quien se escape." There's no one that can escape death or fate.

"Llegando al campo santo no hay calaveras plateadas." On reaching the grave, there are no gold-plated skulls (death makes equals of us all).

"No se puede cargar el muerto y cantar el alabado." You can't carry the corpse and sing the alabado (you can't do two things at the same time).

"Cuando se cae un santo, alguien de la familia va a morir." When a saint's statue falls, someone in the family is going to die.

"Si supiera el muerto que ando con la viuda, se volviera amorir en la sepultura." If the dead man knew that I was with his widow, he would die again in his grave (turn over in his grave).

"Cuando canta una gallina en el patio, un pariente se muere." When a chicken clucks on the patio, a relative is dying.

---

lance. After driving the lance into the ground, the dog soldier made his stand, determined to defend the narrow perimeter or die trying.

Dog soldiers were the epitome of their culture. They wanted to die well and their ferocious determination and bravery encouraged others.

II

The Science of Death and Dying

Stripped of sentiment and symbolism, dying and death are biological events. Nevertheless, their effects on the terminally ill and their survivors are profoundly social, emotional and psychological. The dying person experiences a sense of grief for the imminent end of his or her own life; family and friends mourn the loss of a loved one. But in scientific terms the event itself is simply the failure of a complex biological system. The mechanics of that failure produce a specific series of biological events that precede, coincide with and follow death, such as aging, clinical death and brain death. Where humanity has ascribed these events with layer upon layer of meaning, modern science has attempted to look beneath this mantle to understand mortality from a more objective—or at least different—point of view.

Evolution, Aging and Death

For those who elude an untimely death due to violence, accident or disease, death is the natural conclusion of growing old. In evolutionary terms, the aging process has no good explanation and does not enhance the survival of the species. Why, then, do living things age? The prevailing view is that aging is a secondary effect of a more important process: reproductive success.

In the 19th century, scientists began to wonder how aging fit into the newly proposed theory of evolution. At that time, the most common view was that aging was nature's way of clearing the population of worn-out members. This makes sense in some ways, because it makes more food and other resources available to members of reproductive age or younger. But if natural selection favors individuals who die when their reproductive years end, the theory doesn't explain why animals live beyond their productive years at all.

Another theory held that aging evolved as part of the ongoing process of development. Organisms are genetically programmed to develop to sexual maturity, when they can reproduce. According to this theory, age changes are just a continuation of that program. But like the worn-out members theory, this one doesn't explain why animals live beyond their reproductive years. The efficient answer, in evolutionary terms, would be for animals to die after they'd fulfilled their reproductive mission.

Enough and More: Biological Redundancy and Long Life

The answer to the aging puzzle that makes sense in evolutionary terms is that aging is a secondary effect of a more important process: survival of the species. Leonard Hayflick, a prominent researcher in the field of aging, explains that, according to this argument, natural selection favors animals that are more likely to live to sexual maturity and reproduce—those who are the fittest, in Darwin's words. To reach that age, animals must withstand nature's onslaughts, such as disease, predators, food shortages, freezing cold and other forces that kill off the weak. The survivors would be more robust than those who did not survive; they could hunt better, run faster (or otherwise outwit predators) and get food and shelter, very possibly at the expense of weaker members of the species. They would also be likely to have good, strong immune systems to survive disease and injury.

What characteristic do these survivors have in common? Biologically speaking, they share redundancy: not only are they strong enough to survive to sexual maturity, they are more than strong enough. With this excess capacity, the odds increase greatly that the animal will survive at least long enough to reproduce. Hayflick and others compare this excess to the backup system on a spaceship that gives the craft the capacity to travel beyond its destination, thus improving the odds that it will get at least as far as the target.

Redundancy means that some animals can survive insults that might finish weaker animals, because their vital systems have some backup. Thus, the animal with a heart whose pumping capacity exceeded the necessary minimum could survive even if part of that heart muscle were to be damaged and stop working. An animal so robust that it is more certain to survive to sexual maturity is also robust enough to survive longer after it has fulfilled its reproductive function. This "greater reserve capacity," as Hayflick terms it, is then passed on to the offspring. Longevity itself is not the point of evolution; the point is survival, but the same characteristics promote both ends.

Beyond basic survival traits, the capacity to live longer may also be related to an organism's ability to repair its DNA. In studies carried out in the 1980s in the laboratories of Roy Walford, a researcher best known for his work on low calorie intake and longevity, investigators bred mice for various life spans: short-lived, long-lived and in between. They then measured the animals' ability to repair DNA damage induced by ultraviolet light. They found that the short-lived mice had the lowest rates of repair, while the long-lived mice had the highest, with the midrange mice falling somewhere between the two extremes.

Even with the greatest reserve capacity and a high rate of DNA repair, no organism is immortal. At some point, a vital mechanism will fail and, either directly or indirectly, death will result.

Why We Age

You can ask for anything you like, except time.
—NAPOLEON

Although scientists have proposed and debunked many theories of why the human body changes with age, they still don't know what causes these changes. Today, however, the evidence clearly favors some theories and eliminates others. The strongest theories of aging explain it as a programmed event or as the product of random events; most theories incorporate elements of each. Likewise, many biogerontologists are coming to believe that aging can be explained by a combination of theories, not by one single theory.

Ancient Theories of Aging

Humans have speculated on the causes of aging for a long time, agreeing almost universally that aging is natural and inevitable. The earliest known hypotheses were based on the humoral theory, which held that four humors (body fluids) and their associated qualities rule the human body. Followers of Hippocrates, the ancient Greek physician, believed that old age occurred when the body was cold and moist, qualities attributed to phlegm.

Aristotle, writing in the 3rd century, varied slightly from the Hippocratic physicians; he saw old age as cold and dry. Galen, a physician in the 2nd century, viewed old age as the final stage of a process that began at conception. He believed the male's semen exerts a drying effect, which in turn leads to the formation of tissues and organs. Eventually, however, the drying ceases to be a good thing and instead begins to dry up the body's "innate moisture," which fuels it. Lacking this moisture, the body ages and dies.

Immortality is Elsewhere

Hopes for immortality have long been fueled by legends and stories of places where people lived forever or at least for a very long time. The Old Testament tells of the time before the great flood, when men lived almost a thousand years; Methuselah was supposed to have survived to 969. If people once lived for such a long time, the argument went, they could do so again; indeed, a life span of 50 or 60 years is an aberration.

Some legends of immortality center on distant, mythical locales. The Greeks told of the Hyperboreans, who, somewhere beyond the north wind, lived to be one thousand years old, at which time they leapt into the sea (presumably because they'd had enough). As in the legend of Shangri-la, outsiders might stumble into the land of the immortals by accident, but no map marked its location. Many explorers set out to find these long-lived peoples, but none succeeded.

Allied with the quest for long-lived populations was the quest for the source of immortality. The "fountain of youth" legend first appeared as the Hindu "pool of youth" and the Hebrew "river of immortality."

In the Hindu legend, the king gives the aged Cyavana his daughter Sukanya as a wife to atone for the behavior of her brothers. Cyavana and Sukanya encounter two demigods who try to woo the beautiful young woman away from her aged husband, but she remains loyal to him. Longing to be as young as his bride, Cyavana offers to reveal certain religious secrets to the demigods in exchange for the secret of rejuvenation. The agreement is made and the demigods take him to the Pool of Youth, from which all emerge "divinely fair, all of them and youthful." The Hebrew legend is recorded in biblical references to the River of Immortality, which confers eternal life on those who bathe in it. The tale inspired other legends of waters that brought immortality, an idea that appeared also in medieval romances. Searching for the fountain of youth, the Spanish explorer Ponce de Leon found Florida, which today attracts retirees to its gentle climate.

In recent times, inhabitants of three remote areas have claimed to live far beyond the normal life expectancy. In the 1950s more than 500 residents of the Soviet state of Georgia claimed to be between 120 and 165 years old. They attributed their longevity in part to a yogurt-based diet, sparking a boom in yogurt consumption in the United States. But authorities there kept no birth or baptismal records and it was accepted practice for residents to exaggerate their ages in order to inspire respect and honor. The supporters of Soviet leader Joseph Stalin, a native Georgian interested in the phenomenon of extreme longevity, found these claims politically useful, using them to predict a long life and rule for the dictator.

A village in Vilcambamba, a region of Ecuador, claimed nine centenarians in a population of 819, a rate more than a hundred times higher than in the United States. But as in Georgia, no written records backed up this assertion, which was further discredited when a researcher returning after five years found residents' claimed ages had jumped by up to 10 years during his absence. Similarly, a village called Hunza in the Pakistani region of Kashmir claimed to be home to many individuals over the age of 120, but the Hunzukuts offered no evidence at all to substantiate their contention.

Unfortunately for those seeking the key to a longer life, none of the many other claims of this nature have been proven—and many have been disproved. But other remote populations will no doubt continue to proclaim their longevity, and large numbers of people will continue to believe them. Hope, if not life, springs eternal.

Twentieth-Century Theory

The early 20th century saw the beginning of laboratory investigations on aging, as scientists learned to study cells in culture, outside the body. These early experiments, however, led investigators down what would turn out to be the wrong fork in the road. Alexis Carrel, a Frenchman who worked at the Rockefeller Institute (now Rockefeller University), initiated research that was continued until the mid-1940s. Carrel took cells from a chicken heart, cultured them and let them multiply, removing half when the culture became too large. Carrel and his coinvestigators claimed that they'd kept the same culture going for 34 years. This suggested that these cells—and by extension all cells—would keep dividing forever if nothing happened to stop them. They were immortal.

Carrel's claim had a profound effect on scientists' view of aging. If cells multiplied forever, then aging was not, as had been believed, a natural phenomenon but one that occurred because something outside the cell interfered with cell division. Thus, gerontologists turned away from what would otherwise have been an obvious avenue of investigation—the inner workings of the cell—and looked elsewhere for the causes of aging.

Carrel, however, was wrong. In 1959, Leonard Hayflick and Paul Moorhead began to study whether normal cells transformed themselves into cancer cells. In the course of this investigation, they made a seminal discovery: normal cells will only divide a fixed number of times, somewhere around fifty. This is now known as the Hayflick limit. This finding, which scientists were slow to accept, brought biogerontologists back to the study of how the workings of cells influence aging.

Current theories tend to interweave the idea of randomness with the idea of programmed aging: the process is programmed, but exactly how it manifests itself has at least a degree of randomness. A variety of theories describe the processes that very possibly play a role in aging.

Wear-and-tear theory   Wear and tear on the human body can occur on many levels; the cumulative effect is age-associated change. At the molecular level, notes Leonard Hayflick, "Important molecules might incur damage over time and not be replaced as quickly as they are lost or not at all." DNA repair systems in cells function less effectively and cells, tissues, organs and repair systems may gradually lose physiological efficiency, decline and ultimately fail. Jaime Miquel, a Spanish researcher, believes that molecular wear and tear may directly affect the mitochondria, the power plant of the cell, since the mitochondria apparently cannot repair damaged DNA.

Genetic Mutation Theory   Genetic mutations figure into the wear-and-tear theory. They occur naturally as cells function less efficiently. These mutations can be linked to age changes. Laboratory studies have shown that this is not the case with radiation-induced mutations, but that finding does not rule out a possible role for other mutations.

Free Radical Theory   Free radicals are molecules whose outer orbit contains an odd number of electrons. The molecule can become stable only by gaining or losing an electron and will try to unite with any available molecule. The effects on the target molecule are frequently detrimental. The free radical may cause the molecule to function improperly or may deactivate it entirely. These effects can be cancelled out by antioxidants, which prevent the free radicals from forming in the first place. If aging is a molecular process, antioxidants may slow it.

Error Catastrophe Theory   Another theory holds that aging is a product of cells' dwindling DNA repair capacity. DNA repair is not a perfect process and as it fails, copies of vital genes are lost. This affects protein synthesis, which is vital to physiological functioning. The body then begins to produce defective copies of essential proteins. Since a few enzyme molecules may produce thousands of copies of a protein, the effects of such an error could be dire. Laboratory studies have shown that old cells do not contain enough defective proteins to account for aging, but the theory nevertheless remains alive as a possible contributing cause.

Cellular Clocks   Biogerontologist Leonard Hayflick's cellular clock theory grew out of his early work on cell division. He argues that the same genetic process governs both the cessation of cell division and of cell function. People do not die because their cells reach their limit and stop dividing. Rather, as it continues dividing, the cell loses its capacity to function well. This decline is programmed, just as the limits on division are. The reduced function leads to changes in cells and those changes affect the whole body, making it more vulnerable to the diseases of old age. Hayflick believes, and research findings support his hypothesis, that the "cell clock" is located in the nucleus of the cell. Calvin B. Harley and others from McMaster University in Canada have identified one possible mechanism that would explain how the clock works: with each cell division, the repeated sequence of a part of the chromosome called "telomeres" is reduced at a fixed rate.

Neuroendocrine Theory   The neuroendicrine theory of aging links aging to programmed changes in hormone secretions and levels. These hormones are produced by the neuroendocrine system and have powerful effects on all systems of the body. According to this theory, changes in hormone secretions and levels are linked to age-related change.

Immune System Theory   According to this theory, age-associated changes and diseases occur because the aging immune system slowly loses its ability to recognize the host's own tissues. The body then begins rejecting its own tissues.

Waste Accumulation Theory   Age-associated changes may also be linked to waste accumulation at the cellular level. Just as kidney failure causes waste to accumulate in the blood and eventually kills the organism, so the built-up waste products in the cell might keep the cell from functioning properly, leading eventually to cellular death. Cells do accumulate waste as they age, but no evidence has yet connected this buildup to aging changes. For example, lipofuscin, known as age pigment, accumulates in cells, most commonly in nerve and heart-muscle cells. But even when large amounts are present the cells continue to function normally. Also, some cells found in old animals contain no age pigment or almost none, yet the animal is showing normal signs of aging. Still, waste accumulation remains a theoretically plausible explanation of some age-associated changes.

Cross-Linking   Collagen proteins, the glue that holds cells together, have also been implicated as a cause of aging. The molecular structure of these proteins resembles a ladder, with two supporting sides connected by rungs. Cross-linking occurs when additional links (rungs) form and connect separate ladder-molecules to each other. The phenomenon increases with age, making tissues less pliable. The theory proposes that cross-linking may block passage of nutrients and waste into and out of the cells, thus preventing normal cell metabolism and leading, eventually, to the death of the cell. Cross-linking could also damage the cell's DNA, causing mutations or cell death.

A Longer Life

Every man desires to live long; but no man would be old.
—Jonathan Swift

People have searched for ways to extend life for centuries, but none of their efforts has succeeded yet, in large part because the causes of age-associated change are still unknown. Humans do live longer, on average, than they did 100 or even 50 years ago. But the increase in life expectancy does not necessarily imply that the maximum potential human life span has increased, it simply means people have gotten better at avoiding death. Life expectancy will probably continue to increase as doctors learn to combat more diseases, but extension of the theoretical limits of human life is, at this point, unlikely.

The ancient Greeks would not have found this surprising. Hippocrates, Aristotle and Galen all believed that aging and death were natural and thus good, since "nature does nothing amiss." The idea that death was neither natural nor inevitable arose in Western thought in the 13th century, among alchemists. The English scholar Roger Bacon, a student of alchemy, gave four reasons why life was not inevitably short. The first was biblical: before the flood, people lived very long lives; and because the soul is immortal, corporal life can be extended to match. Bacon also believed that life was artificially short because people neglected hygiene and behaved immorally (probably an accurate assessment) and because the weaknesses acquired through bad habits were passed to the next generation (definitely not an accurate assessment). He also cited "secret arts," in which people had been rejuvenated after they were in contact with some substance, often gold.

But neither gold nor any other elixir concocted by alchemists could ward off death, and modern science has done no better. Through experimental manipulation of various factors scientists have successfully increased the life expectancy of some animals.

Parabiosis

Not an active field of research at present, parabiosis attempts to prolong life by exposing an older animal to the blood of a younger animal, thereby also exposing it to some presumed "youth substance." In 17th-century England, a Mr. Gayant was reported to have transfused the blood of a young dog into an old, infirm, almost blind dog, causing it to "leap and frisk" two hours later. Jean Denis, a French physician, first tried the technique on humans; he reported five such transfusions. When one of his patients died, however, the Faculty of Medicine in Paris banned further experiments and few attempts were made until the early 19th century.

In the 20th century, Frederic C. Ludwig of the University of California briefly revived interest in the technique of parabiosis. His experiment, which involved 500 pairs of rats, found that an old rat joined with a young rat lived significantly longer than an unpaired old rat. Both practical and ethical questions, however, make it unlikely that parabiosis will ever be used systematically to extend longevity in any species.

Older and Colder

Colder environments have been shown experimentally to increase longevity. At the cellular level, Leonard Hayflick observed that cells frozen and then thawed in tissue culture picked up where they'd left off when they resumed division. This finding perhaps helps explain the results of a 1917 experiment on fruit flies, in which Jacques Loeb and John H. Northrop found that the insects lived longer if kept in a cold environment. Experiments involving fish and other cold-blooded animals showed the same effect. However, subsequent studies showed that the relationship between cold temperatures and longevity is not as straightforward as it first seemed. In some cases, longevity was extended only if the organism was exposed at a particular stage in its development.

On Hold

Dormancy and hibernation have also been studied to see whether they affect aging. Organisms forced into a dormant state by harsh or extreme environmental conditions, like Hayflick's frozen cells, do seem to pick up their development where they left off. Warm-blooded animals kept in extended hibernation by artificially lowering the temperature of their habitat also live longer, while those prevented from hibernating have shorter lives. What, if anything, these findings mean for humans remains unclear: suspended activity would not increase the length of useful life, it would merely lengthen the elapsed time from birth to death.

Calorie Reduction

In the 1930s, Clive M. McCay of Cornell University first reported that a diet deficient in calories but not nutrients extended life. McCay's lean rats lived twice as long as the rats fed a normal diet. Subsequent studies showed that it was the reduced calories, not some substance present or absent in the diet, that accounted for this astonishing increase.

In the 1980s, Roy L. Walford added two significant pieces of data: rats lived longer even if the reduced-calorie diet was not started until midlife and, up to a point, the greater the reduction in calories the greater the added life span. (When calorie cuts exceeded 40 percent of the normal diet, however, the animals starved.) Encouraged by these findings, Walford himself cut his calorie intake radically to try to prolong his own life. Regardless of the outcome, his case will only be anecdotally interesting because he lacks a duplicate of himself to use as a control.

Still unknown is the mechanism by which the reduced-calorie diet prolongs life. One possibility is that lean animals remain more active and thus are able to avoid heart disease and other diseases we associate with an inactive old age.

Whether any reliable method will be developed to extend human life is an open question. For the moment, Leonard Hayflick's analysis stands: "In the field of aging, one fact stands out as incontrovertible: No one has ever shown unequivocally that, in humans, any medical intervention, lifestyle change, nutritional factor or other substance will slow, stop or reverse the fundamental aging process or the determinants of life span." Death, it seems, is something we'll just have to live with.

The Definition of Death

Defining death, once a simple matter of checking a pulse, has become medically, ethically and legally complex. With advances in medical technology, death as a moment has been replaced by death as a process. In most cases, that process is not lengthy. Death, for most people, is still a clear-cut phenomenon that suddenly follows an unexpected event—a heart attack, a car accident—or ends a long illness, such as cancer or AIDS. The heart stops and cannot be restarted, or if so, only briefly. The person is declared dead.

Two dramatic developments in medical technology lie behind the change in how we define death. One is organ transplant technology, the other is life-support technology. Both gained momentum in the 1960s and both, today, are routine. The modern age of organ transplants began in 1967, when Dr. Christian Barnard carried out the first successful heart transplant. With the development of increasingly powerful drugs that suppress organ rejection, survival rates increased.

Organ transplants, however, are most successful if the organs come from a "live" body: one in which the heart is still beating and blood is still circulating. With the development of life-support technology, it became possible to maintain "life" in what would otherwise be a cadaver. The practice requires that doctors, donors, recipients and families think of bodies as alive and dead at the same time.

Thus, the stopped heart no longer signals death, just as a beating heart does not necessarily signify life. A heart may stop and be restarted with cardiopulmonary resuscitation. A surgeon may stop the heart temporarily during a surgical procedure. A heart may continue to beat, although not indefinitely, in spite of irreversible brain damage. Life-support systems may maintain a body's breathing and heartbeat, both of which would stop were the machines switched off.

Death by Brain Criteria

Death is now understood not in terms of simple clinical death but in terms of brain death, technically known as "death by brain criteria." Different kinds of brain death fall along a continuum. The least extreme form is neocortical death, in which the upper part of the brain, where thoughts, pleasure, pain and volition reside, no longer functions. Cerebral death, the next step, comes when only the lowest centers of the cerebellum and the brainstem are still active. Death by whole brain criteria, when the brainstem itself has stopped functioning, is the only type of brain death recognized in the United States.

The difficulty with defining death as brain death is that the heart may function normally and circulation continue, at least for a limited time, when the brain no longer works. Thus, brain death does not necessarily occur when the EEG goes flat; the person must also have lost the capacity to live independent of mechanical intervention.

How to Recognize Death

Given the complications, physicians have developed formal guidelines for establishing death. Once a patient has sunk into a coma, physicians check six signs; no patient who tests negative for all of them has ever regained consciousness. The determination of brain death must be made by a disinterested team of physicians separate from those awaiting organs for transplant and those who have attempted to save the patient's life, either of whom might be accused of bias.

Physicians must first decide why the person is in a coma, an assessment that rules out any potentially reversible causes such as drug overdose, very low body temperature or severe chemical imbalance (as occurs in diabetic coma). In the absence of these causes, they then postulate structural damage to the brain severe enough to preclude recovery.

To see whether irreversible brain death has occurred, doctors carry out a series of tests to detect any functioning reflexes in the brainstem. Without these basic reflexes, a person cannot survive independently of a life-support system.

1. **The capacity to breathe independently.**
   Physicians first turn off the ventilator (if in use) and administer oxygen to see if the patient can breathe on his or her own. Carbon dioxide at times stimulates independent breathing, so doctors will try this as well.

2. **Coughing or gagging.**
   If the patient does not cough or gag when his or her airway is suctioned out, that reflex has failed.

3. **Pupils.**
   Doctors shine a light directly at the eye to see if the pupil constricts as it should.

4. **Blinking.**

A living person blinks when the cornea of the eye is touched; failure to blink suggests death.

5. **Grimacing.**

Doctors rotate the patient's head or flush the ears with ice water to check for the normal grimace reflex.

6. **Blood flow.**

In some European countries, such as Germany, Austria and parts of Scandinavia, physicians are also required to inject dye for contrast studies to prove that blood is no longer flowing to the brain.

Premature Burial

The reports of my death are greatly exaggerated.
—Mark Twain

Today the declaration of death occurs only when the last shred of brain function is gone, a determination made with the help of sophisticated and reliable monitoring equipment. In the past, however, people were declared dead when they seemed dead, resulting in occasional errors.

Premature burials were a terrifying fact of life. In the midst of an epidemic, when death was the usual conclusion to the illness, a person who looked dead was assumed to be dead. Some of these unfortunates revived while awaiting interment; others woke up on the way to the graveyard and panicked the mourners by banging on the insides of the coffin. Others were buried but were lucky enough to be targeted by grave robbers in search of their jewelry, who opened the coffin and let the "corpse" go (it seems likely that those so surprised never robbed another grave). The least fortunate of these premature burials were discovered after it was too late, when the tomb was opened to bury another relative or for some other reason.

People worried about premature burial could take steps to avoid it. One Londoner in the 19th century asked that his heart be cut out or his head cut off to avoid premature burial. The widow of the explorer Sir Richard Burton asked that her physician pierce her heart with a needle to make sure she was dead, after which she wanted to be embalmed.

In Belgium, a royal physician was so distressed when he heard the shrieks of a girl who was awakened from her trance by the sound of dirt falling on her coffin that he invented a system through which the person who was buried alive could summon help. His invention, patented in 1897, featured a tube that extended to the ground's surface and was attached to a ball on the person's chest. If the person breathed, causing the chest to move, the spring-loaded ball would be released and the tube would let light and air into the coffin. Above ground, a flag would appear, bells would sound and a lamp would light. It is not recorded whether such a coffin was ever built or ever summoned help.

The rise of the professional mortuary was partly based on the fear of premature burial. Mortuaries provided a holding area where living clients had the opportunity to make themselves known.

Although these physiological criteria determine whether a person is in fact declared brain dead, the medical establishment has not lost sight of the fact that meaningful life may be gone before brain death is declared. As the 22nd World Medical Assembly noted, "Clinical interest lies not in the state of preservation of isolated cells, but in the fate of a person. The point of death of the different cells and organs is not as important as the certainty that the process has become irreversible."

Evidence that brain death is indeed irreversible came from autopsies conducted in the 1960s, when unresponsive patients were kept on life support until their hearts stopped on their own. Pathologists found at autopsy that such patients had "respirator brains" that had become soft, dark green or totally liquefied after the cells had died days or weeks before. Conversely, patients with severe brain injuries die because the swelling of their brain puts pressure on the respiratory center of the brainstem and breathing stops.

The Moment of Death

The physiological changes that occur at the moment of death are straightforward: the heart stops pumping blood and cells no longer receive oxygen or nutrients, so they begin to die. What fascinates and worries most people is not as much the moment the heart stops as the prospect of knowing when their own death is imminent. It is not the moment that matters, but the moment before the moment.

Physically, that fleeting moment is characterized by the appearance of physical struggle, although the dying person cannot be aware of this struggle. What the dying person may be experiencing, recent research and analyses suggest, is a feeling of well-being and a sense not of dying but of travelling out of life. But there is also a physiological basis for this final activity.

Whatever the proximate cause, the ultimate cause of death is always lack of oxygen. Without oxygen, cells die. The body's ultimate response to the lack of oxygen is visible in what is called the "agonal moment" immediately before clinical death (heart stoppage) occurs. Like the word agony, agonal comes from *agon,* the Greek word that connotes struggle. The declining oxygen content in the blood may cause muscle spasms. Normal breathing may be replaced by gasps. A brief convulsion may wrack the body. Then it's over.

By the time the agonal moment arrives, even a person who has been anticipating death for months is not likely to be aware of the quick struggle. Whether a person is, at this moment, aware of anything is another question. The cause of death corresponds to the consciousness of death. Some people who die suddenly in accidents no doubt have no idea that their last conscious moment is their last. Those who experience a more prolonged death may indeed be aware that the moment is upon them.

The Dying Brain and the Near-Death Experience

The lack of oxygen that causes death may also produce the cluster of perceptions known as the near-death experience (NDE). People who appear clinically dead and then are revived report that during the interval of "death," they are aware of events in the immediate vicinity, in the mind or in some realm beyond.

When Raymond Moody first published his collected accounts of such experiences in 1977, most people viewed them as paranormal events that provided evidence of an afterlife. Recent analyses, however, explain NDE neurologically and suggest that the genetic basis for that last conscious moment is, in essence, imprinted in the right temporal lobe and limbic area of the brain. Under the right conditions, if death approaches not too slowly and not too quickly, the patient will experience this moment as a transition rather than as an end. Whether it is indeed a transition or merely the illusion of one is a separate question. Nor is it known how common this experience is, since most potential informants do not return with the data.

The new analyses suggest that the key factor in NDE is the gradual onset of anoxia (oxygen deprivation) in the brain. The effects of anoxia combine with whatever neural activity is going on when the anoxia strikes; both are superimposed on what might be termed a template, found in the right temporal lobe of the brain. The resulting activity may generate or at least correlate to the near-death experience.

Attempting to replicate Moody's findings, psychologist Kenneth Ring collected numerous accounts of NDE and discerned in them a "core experience" of five elements: entering the darkness (the tunnel effect), seeing the light, feelings of peace, body separation (out-of-body experiences) and entering the light. Every NDE did not include all of these elements, but most included at least two.

That such experiences occur is well documented, and many people believe that an NDE offers a glimpse of "the other side" of death. Some scientists, however, have analyzed the experiences to see whether they occur only near death and how else they might be explained.

Melvin Morse, a Seattle physician, began by investigating the near-death experiences of children, a population he believed would be relatively free of preconceptions on the subject. His first study compared 12 children who had cardiac arrests for a variety of reasons with 121 children who had been gravely ill but had no such brush with death. He found that only the first group, those who truly approached death, reported NDEs.

Morse's neurological explanation of NDE derives from the work of the neurologist Wilder Penfield. When operating on the brain, Penfield found that stimulation of an area called the Sylvian fissure, located in the right temporal lobe just above the right ear, produced sensations similar to some aspects of NDE. When he stimulated this area, patients reported out-of-body experiences, seeing dead relatives, seeing God and other elements of the core experience, with the exception of "the light." Morse and his colleagues theorized that NDE is in fact genetically imprinted in that part of the brain. When he published his analysis, he found that a group of Chilean researchers had independently arrived at the same conclusion.

The one aspect of NDE that Morse's theory does not account for is the light that many people report. This light is extraordinary, with a warm, enveloping quality that makes an extremely powerful impression on those who experience it. The light, too, can be explained in neurological terms. Susan Blackmore, a British psychologist, has analyzed NDEs in an effort to discover what physiological mechanisms might explain these apparently mystical experiences. She argues that neither paranormal nor spiritual explanations are necessary to account for the light or any other aspect of NDE. It's all right there in the brain.

Blackmore's explanation, amply supported by her own research and that of others, runs as follows. When brain cells become anoxic, they do not simply stop firing. Rather, what happens is what Blackmore terms "disinhibition," in which many cells that should not be firing start to fire. Under normal circumstances, neurons send chemical signals across the synapses, or gaps between them; these signals either excite the recipient cell or inhibit it. In anoxia, the inhibition function is lost first, hence the random firing. She argues that NDEs are triggered only under some types of anoxia, when onset is neither very fast nor very slow. Under these circumstances, rapid, disorganized firing of nerve cells over large parts of the brain could explain NDE.

The similarities between NDEs reported by different people—the tunnels, the out-of-body experiences, the light and the feelings of well-being—can be explained by the similarity of all human brains. The tunnel effect, Blackmore argues, arises from disinhibition in the visual cortex and relates to the way brain activity translates into images. Cells cluster at the center of the visual field, with fewer at the edges. If cells start firing randomly, more cells will fire at the center simply because there are more of them there. This activity translates into the visual image of a bright circle that appears brighter toward the center. The image will be round because that's how this kind of brain activity "appears." The "end of the tunnel" approaches, according to this theory, because as the "neural noise" produced by the firing cells increases, the light would appear to get bigger. The rushing sound that accompanies the passage down the tunnel likewise is a function of disinhibition.

The feelings of intense well-being reported in many NDEs, Blackmore and others argue, arises when the body releases endorphins, the opiates produced by the brain in response to stress. Investigations by other researchers strongly suggest that endorphins are released near death. Endorphins produce feelings of intense well-being. Interesting, if anecdotal, support for this theory comes from an account of an NDE reported by a 72-year-old man, whose experience of bliss while in a coma suddenly ended when beings of light were transformed into devils. It turned out that he had been given an injection of naloxone to try to rouse him. Naloxone is a potent opiate antagonist, which would have halted the release of the endorphins.

No paranormal explanation is necessary for out-of-body experiences (OBE), although many observers, including some scientists, continue to argue that OBE is a genuine paranormal experience. The literature on NDEs is full of accounts of people whose "spirit," when out of the body, saw and remembered seeing something that the person could not have known happened.

Raymond Moody, however, has concluded that no evidence supports the claim that "something" leaves the body during alleged OBEs. He and other investigators point out that too many nonparanormal explanations remain. These involve the conjunction of memory and information gathered by the five senses even in an apparently unconscious state. Indeed, a visual OBE has never been authoritatively documented in a blind person, whose "astral body" would presumably be sighted.

Endorphins also figure in the neurological explanation of the life review, in which one's whole life flashes before one as death approaches. The life review is not part of the core experience and is reported in only about one-third of NDEs. But since this review is often carried out by "beings of light," it is invoked as evidence that the NDE is indeed paranormal. Again, however, the dying brain theory provides a plausible, if complex, explanation that excludes the paranormal in favor of Wilder Penfield's studies of the temporal lobe. As Blackmore explains it, endorphins are released during stress. One of their effects is to lower the threshold for seizures in the temporal lobe (which Penfield showed to be the source of NDE-like experiences) and the limbic system, the part of the brain that governs feelings and emotions. In epileptics, seizure activity in this area can produce flashbacks and feelings of déjà vu. In NDE, abnormal activity in these areas causes flashbacks and the feelings of familiarity that may make the experience feel so real.

Harvesting and Storing Organs for Transplant

As soon after the moment of death as possible, any organs destined for transplantation must be removed. The removal of organs for transplant is like a routine surgical operation, except that the donor is not anesthetized. Known as "harvesting," the removal implies all the abundance and nourishment of a literal harvest, for it offers the recipient life.

Surgeons carry out the procedure in a sterile operating room in which the donor is hooked to life-support machines to keep the heart beating. Because of the life-support system, the organs are still receiving oxygen through the blood. The sequence of the operation depends on the number of organs the decedent is donating. If only one organ is being removed, the surgeons remove it and close the incision. When multiple organs are being removed, successive teams of surgeons move in and harvest the organs separately.

At times, the recipient of the organ waits, prepped for surgery, in a nearby operating room. More often, however, the organ must be packed up and transported as quickly as possible to the recipient's hospital. The need for speedy transport means that most donated organs go to people who live nearby. How long an organ remains viable for transplant depends on the organ. A heart-lung combination must reach the recipient in four to five hours, while in kidney transplants the interval may extend as long as 48 to 72 hours. A heart alone may be transplanted six to eight hours later and lungs alone up to 12 hours later.

Tissue donation is an equally important but less urgent process. A tissue may be removed after the physicians turn off the life-support system and kept for much longer before being transplanted. These include corneas, bones, skin, veins and heart valves.

Death, Disposal and Contagion

Any tissue that will not be transplanted from a corpse into a living recipient must be disposed of in some manner. Such disposal, and the manner in which it is carried out, for the most part serves more of a cultural than a public health function. Although many cultures and religions view dead bodies as unclean, today's dead pose no threat to the health of the living except in highly unusual circumstances.

The fear of contagion from corpses first prompted official action during the epidemic of bubonic plague in London in 1665. Without understanding precisely how, people knew that those who died of plague could infect the living. Accordingly, the corpse of a plague victim could not be laid out in a church, nor could friends and relatives accompany it on its final journey to the grave. Corpses were buried at night—perhaps because fewer people would be exposed—in graves at least six feet deep.

As the causes of disease became better understood, measures to avoid contagion from corpses became more specific. A house in which someone had died from an infectious disease might be quarantined. A pauper buried in a mass grave would be covered with a layer of lime powder. But in general, a corpse nailed in a wooden box was not viewed as a threat.

Nor do the dead pose many dangers to the living today. Although investigations have shown that some pathogens do survive in the body for significant periods of time after death, the chances that a person who has normal contact with the corpse might be infected are extremely low. One of the few circumstances in which the dead might infect the living would be if medical personnel accidentally jabbed themselves with a needle contaminated by the corpse with a pathogen such as the AIDS virus.

Although corpses pose almost no public health risk, morticians continue to argue that contagion remains a threat that must be eradicated by embalming. If this argument were valid, embalmers might be expected to have a higher than average rate of infection with diseases such as hepatitis B. In fact, they do not fall victim to such diseases any more often than the general public.

The developing world still faces some of the threats common in 17th-century London, sometimes from AIDS but more often from the lethal viruses such as ebola that emerge from time to time and kill a high percentage of their victims. Corpses of those who have died from these diseases pose no particular risk if handled with adequate protection—latex gloves, masks, rigorous standards of cleanliness. All too often, unfortunately, these forms of protection are not available.

The Sequel to Death

Life. A spiritual pickle preserving the body from decay.
—AMBROSE BIERCE

Depending on the manner of its disposal and, if applicable, on how much time elapses between death and cremation or embalming, a dead body undergoes a number of distinct changes. Those that take place soon after death are readily detectable by sight or with simple instruments. The dust-to-dust processes that we call decomposition are initially invisible to the naked eye, but soon become very evident indeed. The first three signs that life has fled (beyond cessation of heartbeat and breathing) are changes in body temperature, color and rigidity.

Algor Mortis

Body temperature drops after death in a phenomenon called algor mortis, or temperature of death. How quickly the body cools depends on how warm the living body was at death. If abnormal circumstances—immersion in freezing water, for instance, or high fever—suggest that a corpse's temperature is artificially high or low, a pathologist cannot accurately determine the time of death. Body temperature drops about one degree (Fahrenheit) per hour until it reaches that of the air surrounding it. If a person died with a normal body temperature of 98.6 degrees, the body will have a body temperature of about 96.6 two hours later.

Livor Mortis

The cessation of heartbeat stops the continuous mixing together of red blood cells and plasma, the two major components of blood. As a result, red cells settle to the lowest part of the body, such as the back if the corpse is lying on its back. This process is termed livor mortis, or color of death. The rest of the skin grows correspondingly pale as the red cells sink. After about two hours, the settling becomes visible; the skin becomes reddish where the red cells are concentrated. Eight hours after death, the red cells break down and the color becomes permanent. The resulting reddish-purple discoloration is known by morticians as postmortem stain.

Rigor Mortis

Familiar to readers of detective stories, rigor mortis, the rigidity of death, is the postmortem process that inspired the slang term "stiff" in reference to corpses. Immediately after death, the body relaxes completely. The face loses expression as muscles stop controlling the skin, which then sags. In normal circumstances, rigor begins to set in about two hours after death, sooner in a cold environment or if the person had been working hard just before death. The cause of rigor mortis remains uncertain. It may be the result of the coagulation of muscle proteins, to a shift within the muscle cells or to the metabolic processes that continue in some cells after death.

Rigor mortis occurs first in the face, then moves to the trunk, limbs and internal organs. The stiffness peaks after twelve hours before the body gradually becomes limp again as rigor fades, then vanishes entirely within 24 to 48 hours, depending on temperature and other variables.

Decomposition

Within 24 hours of death, often much sooner, most cadavers are turned over to the undertaker, who uses embalming or cremation to stop the process of decomposition. If, however, the body is not treated, a second round of changes becomes visible. (They do not make pleasant reading; squeamish readers are advised to proceed with caution.)

At the cellular level, autolysis (cell self-destruction) breaks the body down. Like the organism of which they are part, cells die in increments. The cell receives no nutrients after the heart stops beating; with no fuel, it produces no energy and cannot maintain its connections to other cells. The processes that controlled the passage of fluid into and out of the cell break down. The cell nucleus ceases to function and the cell itself swells. Some products within the cell clump together in the mitochondria (the structure powers the cell when it's alive). Packs of destructive acids break loose within the cell and finish it off.

The first visible sign of putrefaction (rotting) appears two or three days after death, when a greenish area of skin shows up first on the right lower quadrant of the abdomen and then spreads over the abdomen, chest and upper thighs. The discoloration and the very unpleasant smell that accompanies it are produced by the remains of decayed red blood cells and by intestinal gas, which contains sulphur. The gas, produced by intestinal bacteria, spreads next to the tissues, where it accounts for the bloated appearance of the body. Enough gas is produced to force the eyes and tongue to protrude and to push the intestines out through the vagina and rectum.

The greenish skin turns purple, then black. This discoloration spreads over the entire body after seven days, at which point large, foul-smelling blisters appear. The skin comes unglued as decomposition proceeds and the top layer will peel off in large sheets at the slightest pressure. More foul-smelling gas is produced when the organs and fatty tissues decay. By the time a second week has passed, the abdomen, scrotum, breasts and tongue are swollen and fluid seeps from the mouth and nose. If another week passes without intervention, hair, nails and teeth loosen. Most internal organs rupture and eventually liquefy, although the uterus and prostate may remain intact up to a year after death.

Within two to four weeks, what essentially remains of a dead body is a skeleton with skin.

The Autopsy

Whether performed shortly after death or after decomposition has progressed to a greater or lesser extent—or, indeed, even years later—the autopsy is the most important tool available for determining when and why a person died; it can also yield information that will save other lives. Nevertheless, autopsy rates in the United States are declining. Postmortem examinations (from the Latin for "after death") are in effect biographies; they tell how a human organism lived and died far more effectively than words ever could. Observations made during autopsy have in some cases saved thousands of lives or helped to characterize a new disease syndrome.

Autopsy Through the Ages

Anatomical studies have been carried out intermittently since classical times, but the first systematic dissections of the human body to determine the cause of death began in Bologna, Italy, around the beginning of the 14th century. In subsequent years, physicians most commonly carried out autopsies to try to find the cause of a particular disease. Thus, in the late 15th century, during an outbreak of plague, Pope Sixtus permitted medical students to open cadavers to try to find the cause of the disease. Similarly, the French explorer Samuel de Champlain ordered autopsies when scurvy hit his party. At times the reasons were religious: the first autopsy in the New World, done in Santo Domingo in 1533, was done to determine whether a pair of Siamese twins had one soul or two. The surgeon found that they were joined only at the liver, so priests determined that two souls were in need of posthumous baptism.

By 1769, autopsies had yielded enough information to allow the Italian physician Giovanni Batista Morgagni to publish the first text that correlated autopsy findings with clinical disease. This marked the beginning of anatomical pathology as a subspecialty of medicine. By the 1940s, American hospitals routinely autopsied about half the people who died while in the hospital.

Modern Autopsy

Today, autopsy follows only about 12 percent, on average, of routine hospital deaths. Except in cases of suspicious or criminal deaths, family members must give permission before a physician can order an autopsy. Families' reluctance to permit a postmortem accounts in part for the drop in autopsy rates; they may think that the person has "suffered enough" and besides, the doctor already knows the cause of death. At times, too, relatives may think that a grief-stricken spouse or parent would be further upset by an autopsy. Morticians may also counsel against autopsy because they think embalming will be harder and the cadaver rendered unfit for public viewing.

None of these objections is necessarily valid. Autopsies may, in fact, give a measure of comfort to families by reassuring them that the person could not have been saved. Nor is the diagnosis written on the death certificate immediately after death necessarily correct; a 1987 study found discrepancies between autopsy findings and diagnoses in one-third of the cases studied. Most morticians, too, now know that pathologists are sensitive to cosmetic issues. Whenever possible, they preserve the appearance of visible body parts and if the brain is autopsied, they insert tubes to replace dissected blood vessels so embalming may proceed.

Organ transplants complicate autopsies. Donated organs must be healthy, which rules out donations from people with diseases that cause organ degeneration. Organs that come from people who die suddenly or violently are often the best for transplant, but these deaths are generally coroner's cases, which means they are routinely autopsied. The transplants that succeed best come from bodies that have been mechanically kept "alive"—the heart beating and the blood circulating—until the organs are removed, after which, of course, pathologists cannot carry out a complete autopsy. Some jurisdictions have resolved the problem by ordering a pathologist to observe organ removal; in others, this problem has led to lost transplant opportunities.

The availability of a pathologist can also determine whether an autopsy is done. Many small hospitals employ no full-time pathologist; fewer autopsies are carried out in these facilities.

The Autopsy Procedure

When an autopsy is performed, determining the cause of death is usually a process of elimination. The kinds of autopsies and their various stages illuminate how pathologists conduct this process.

The average autopsy takes about two hours to perform. Medicolegal autopsies in which the death is unexplained, suspicious or criminal take longer; there is more to examine and more to exclude. Bullet wounds require more work than heart attacks because criminal charges are often involved and it is important to know precisely which wounds contributed to death. The complexity of the autopsy increases with the number of injuries.

The detail in which the cause of death must be described determines the type of autopsy the pathologist will conduct. A complete autopsy involves the entire body, including the brain. A limited autopsy excludes the head but includes the rest of the body. In a selective autopsy, the pathologist examines only relevant areas.

The normal autopsy takes place in four stages in which the pathologist moves from the highly visible evidence such as knife wounds to the microscopic and biochemical analysis of tissues and body fluids. The doctor first conducts a very careful examination of the body's exterior, looking for cuts, bruises, needle punctures or any other marks. As the examination proceeds, each step and observation is recorded on audio tape to make sure every detail of the process is preserved.

The internal examination generally begins with the "Y-cut" of incisions that begin in the shoulder area and meet beneath the breastbone, where a single incision continues down to the pubic area. After making this incision the pathologist removes the breastbone to reveal the organs. By examining the organs in situ (in place) the pathologist can see how they look in relation to one another and if a problem in one organ damaged others.

Next, the pathologist may remove the organs, close the incision and release the body to the mortician. Some religions, such as Judaism, require burial within 24 hours of death and this method allows the family to observe religious customs despite the need for a postmortem. However, in most cases the entire body stays in the autopsy room while the pathologist continues the procedure. The organs are removed, separated and studied individually. Very thin cross sections are cut and chemically fixed and studied under a microscope. The pathologist takes samples of body fluids for later microscopic study and, perhaps, laboratory culture or toxicology studies.

If the autopsy is to include the brain, the pathologist carries out that stage next. It starts with an incision across the back of the head (which will be invisible after the autopsy is complete), allowing the scalp to be folded down over the face. After opening the skull with a saw the pathologist examines the brain to verify or exclude brain lesions as factors in the death.

At this point, the pathologist has the raw material on which to base the autopsy's conclusions and the body can go to the mortician. Laboratory studies will continue to tell the story, providing more detail on whether the death was natural or unnatural, whether its cause was the one suspected, whether microbes or chemicals are present and whether cellular changes support or contradict the initial diagnosis.

Medicolegal autopsies are mandatory when death occurs under unexplained, suspicious or criminal circumstances. In criminal cases, a medicolegal autopsy may literally be an extension of the detective work carried out by the police. Pathologists determine how long the person has been dead as well as whether he or she died where the body was found or was moved there after death. The pathologist will look not only at the body itself, but also at related evidence: scrapings of skin found under a victim's fingernails, blood stains and the like. If poisoning is suspected as the cause of death, the pathologist can test for its presence. Molecular biology plays a growing role in pathological studies. With DNA typing, for example, a pathologist can help police to exclude or identify an assailant.

Anatomy Class

Where autopsy can determine an individual's cause of death, dissection can reveal the secrets of life. In the anatomy classrooms of medical schools, the dead teach the living. Since the mid-18th century, medical students have generally encountered their first cadavers in anatomy class. The meeting still has symbolic value and practical implications, as it brings an immediacy to the study of medicine that books cannot.

The Greek physician Galen was apparently the first to use cadavers to study anatomy. Cultural taboos kept him from using human bodies, so he dissected other animals, thus learning an anatomy that could not be applied directly to humans. Similar taboos existed in many other cultures and religions, although today most major religions permit cadavers to be used for study and education.

Until the early 14th century, the study of anatomy played little part in medical education, nor was it found in the chief medieval textbook on medicine. That changed in 1316, when Mondino de'Luzzi of Bologna published an anatomical text. For the next 200 years, anatomy was taught throughout Europe, with Italy remaining an important center, but it did not become common in English-speaking countries until the 16th century.

Until the mid-18th century, anatomy instructors carried out dissection on one cadaver while students watched and studied models and diagrams. Around this time, William Hunter introduced the so-called Parisian method, which allowed each student to dissect sections of a corpse.

The supply of cadavers for anatomical study was a problem in Britain and, later, the United States. In the 16th century, several governments agreed to provide medical schools with a certain number of the corpses of hanged criminals. This helped, but still demand exceeded supply and body snatching became common practice. Since the market was good, it attracted professional grave robbers, so-called resurrection men, but students and professors also took part. In some cities, the university system encouraged these acts by requiring medical students to provide their own cadavers for anatomy class.

In the American colonies, anatomical dissection apparently began in 1750; in 1762, William Shippen, Jr., began the first series of regular anatomy classes. As in England, the bodies of hanged men were often used, but the public often assumed that the schools got the cadavers from grave robbers and the dissections were considered scandalous.

Allegations of body snatching were not the only reason for public outcry over human dissections. Many people also saw them as a violation, disrespectful of the dead. Some medical schools, such as the University of Maryland, took extreme measures to protect the anatomy classes. In Maryland, the school built secret dissection rooms behind lecture halls and provided hidden passageways to the street so that students could enter and leave undetected.

Neither tunnels nor body snatching are necessary any more. Today, most of the cadavers used in anatomy classes are those of people who will their bodies to science. During a typical dissection, four students share each cadaver; two dissect one side of the body and two the other. They cover the hands and face with cloths soaked in preservative, both to preserve them and to keep the cadaver faceless until they become more accustomed, psychologically, to the dissection process.

The students begin by dissecting the back muscles, a part of the body that is both impersonal and large enough to give students the space to learn to use their dissecting tools. Over the course of the semester, they proceed through the rest of the body, turning to the head last. When they have completed their dissection, the bodies are cremated and buried in a mass grave.

Today, students of anatomy have an alternative: they can access "the Visible Woman" and "the Visible Man" on the Internet. These cybercorpses were created by researchers at the University of Colorado, who embedded bodies in gelatin, froze them, then sliced them crosswise into 5,200 ultrathin wafers. Photographs of each slice were assembled with other images produced by X ray, computerized tomography and magnetic resonance imaging, and recorded in digital form.

Freeze-Wait-Reanimate

If a body is not buried or cremated after death, nor dissected for autopsy, organ donation or scientific study, it may be held in cryonic suspension. This process freezes the recently deceased body at very low temperatures in order to preserve it, usually in the hope that medical science will conquer whatever killed the patient, who theoretically can then be thawed and reanimated. Although believers continue to arrange for their remains to be so treated, the chances today that they could be reanimated are zero.

Cryonics, as one early proponent observed, is based on the premise that the freezer is more attractive than the grave. In the process of cryonic suspension, the human body is frozen after death to be maintained indefinitely at very low temperatures. Those who choose cryonic suspension, and very few do, hope that one day, when the frontiers of medicine have pushed beyond whatever killed them, they can be thawed out and cured.

Those who wish to undergo cryonic suspension after death need sufficient funds and an advance plan. A prearranged plan is important because it is best to begin the cooling process as soon after death as possible; swift transport to the cryonics facility is essential. People planning their own cryonic suspension must secure the cooperation of survivors who might otherwise resist the notion, perhaps viewing cryonics as a scam or resenting the diversion of the decedent's estate away from them.

Indeed, cryonic suspension is expensive. At one of the three major cryonics societies, the minimum amount required is $120,000, of which $28,000 pays for the suspension procedures and the rest goes to long-term maintenance. Those who subject only their head to this process face lower but still substantial costs of $50,000. And this investment carries no guarantee that your remains will remain on ice indefinitely; more than one cryonics society has gone broke, and its patrons thawed.

The actual process of cryonic suspension involves several steps. As soon as possible after death, the body is transported to a cryonic suspension facility. In some cities, specially trained emergency technicians are dispatched to the deathbed; where they are not available a mortician must be engaged to replace the body's blood with the solution in which transplant organs are stored and transported.

Once the body arrives at the facility, technicians immediately "revive" it by hooking it up to a heart-lung machine. Since oxygen deprivation (an inevitable side effect of death) damages the body in multiple ways, they next administer drugs believed to counter some of this damage. Technicians also make a hole in the skull in which they place a brain probe and through which they observe the brain.

If only the head is to be suspended, technicians first replace the blood that circulates through the brain with preservatives. They next remove the head from the body at shoulder level. After that, the process continues much as it does for the rest of the body, the major difference being that heads are stored in uniform, commercial cryogenics units. Whole bodies are stored in more expensive and more difficult to transport custom-made units.

The cooling process then begins. The body is placed in a bath of silicon oil, where it remains for 36 to 48 hours. At the end of this stage, the body has been cooled to -108°F. Next, the body is wrapped and put in an aluminum pod. The pod is suspended in a vat filled with liquid nitrogen, which reduces the temperature to -321°F. After 24 hours, the body enters its final (interim) resting place, a large cylinder that holds one or two bodies. The cylinder is filled with liquid nitrogen and a plastic foam stopper plugs the top. At this point, aside from running out of money, nitrogen leaks represent the greatest threat to eventual reanimation, should it ever be possible. The long wait begins.

That wait may be very long indeed if prevailing scientific opinion proves true. The theory of cryonic suspension has multiple scientific problems. First, when the heart stops pumping blood cells die and their organization collapses. They do not wait like Sleeping Beauty, lifeless but intact. Medical scientists and cryobiologists both contend that reversing this process and reanimating whatever being is composed of these cells is an impossibility. It would be, as one scientist put it, like turning hamburger back into a cow.

The second problem is that the freezing process itself causes damage to cells and organs. A cell that has been frozen is not the same as a cell that has not been frozen. The vital organs will crack when subjected to the temperatures used in cryonics. The brain and the spinal cord, to remain viable, would have to be cooled far more quickly than is possible. Would it be worth waking up to find yourself paralyzed? The thawing process itself may further damage the body: successful thawing requires different conditions depending on the type of cell.

Proponents of cryonic suspension acknowledge these problems but believe in the process anyway. They argue that freezing does not cause enough damage to impede reanimation. They also have faith that technology will advance to the point that the problems will be resolved. Their arguments have swayed an extremely modest number of people. The largest cryonics society, Alcor, had only 26 clients (or their heads) preserved as of April 1993.

Beyond the practical impediments lie a host of ethical and societal questions. Cryonic suspension involves tampering with nature in a manner whose consequences cannot be predicted. Would people reanimated decades or centuries from now interfere with social and biological evolution? Should their genes be reintroduced into the gene pool or be left behind, as nature would have it?

The chances for reanimation today are zero. Nevertheless, a trickle of people will doubtless continue to forego "Rest in Peace" carved on a tombstone in favor of "Til We Meet Again" engraved on a large metal cylinder.

Immortality? Not Yet

Nothing can bring back the hour
Of splendor in the grass, of glory in the flower.
—WILLIAM WORDSWORTH

Humans have been seeking the key to immortal life throughout most of recorded history. They have not yet found it, and current scientific opinion holds that they never will. The reasons for scientists' pessimistic stance are several. First, although most biogerontologists favor one theory or another, most also acknowledge that aging (and death) are not products of a single mechanism. Thus, reversing mortality would require the reversal of multiple complex processes.

Second, a large and strong body of opinion among gerontology researchers holds that the human life span is fixed. That is, even if medical science cured all diseases and eliminated all pathologies, people would still die because they would wear out as nature intended. In support of this notion, scientists point to the great variation in life span among different species and the very consistent life span of each individual species.

Beyond the question of whether humans can achieve immortality is the equally important issue of whether they should. Imagine a world in which everyone lived forever. Such a world would have no room for change and renewal because birth rates would have to be maintained at artificially low levels. If the old never died, there would never be a time or place for the young to take over. And what if science eliminated death but not aging: could any society maintain an infinitely expanding population of people who required much care? Would such an infinite life be a life worth living, or would humans, like the Hyperboreans, feel like flinging ourselves into the sea after a thousand years?

The issue, perhaps fortunately, is moot. As physician Sherwin Nuland observed, "Whether it is the anarchy of a disordered biochemistry or the direct result of its opposite—a carefully orchestrated genetic ride to death—we die of old age because we have been worn and torn and programmed to cave in. The very old do not succumb to disease—they implode their way into eternity."

III
Mortal Statistics

The ageless human quest to understand death has prompted many scholars, scientists and other experts of various descriptions to devote their careers to gathering all manner of information on the topic. This data paints a vivid picture of how people die. Although death is a constant for everyone, it comes in many forms depending on a person's age, sex, occupation, place of residence, personal habits and other descriptive characteristics. Counted, measured, analyzed and added up, the details of human death can be condensed into statistics. Far from being dry and abstract, however, the numbers of death provide a revealing and fascinating glimpse into this universal human experience.

Life Expectancy Around the World

One of the great questions humanity has about death is: When will it occur? Today, demographic studies of life expectancy shed some light on the issue. Defined as the average number of years a person is expected to live, life expectancy figures differ widely around the world. The life expectancy average for the total world population for both men and women (estimated for 1995) is 65 years. Overall life expectancy for both men and women in developed countries is 75, while in less developed nations it is 62. According to the United Nations Fund for Population Activities' (UNFPA) report, *The State of World Population 1994*, the regions of the world with the highest life expectancy rates are North America (76) and Europe (75). Throughout most of Europe the figure is 76 years, except in Eastern Europe, where it is 71.

World regions with the lowest rates of life expectancy are Africa (53) and Asia (65). In eastern Africa, Uganda has a life expectancy rate of 42 years and

Zambia of 44, while in southeast Asia, the people of Cambodia and Laos have a life expectancy of 51 years. A region's figures for life expectancy increase with the decline of infant mortality rates that measure childhood deaths, as well as with the appearance of drugs to combat infectious diseases and the improvement of nutritional and sanitary conditions.

Race and sex make a significant difference in life expectancy rates. In the United States, for example, average life expectancy reached a high of 75.7 years in 1992. But while the figure for the white population hit 76.5 years, that for the black population only increased to 69.8 years. Several factors are believed to contribute to the 6.7-year difference, including higher rates of homicide, AIDS, tuberculosis and drug use among blacks, conditions usually associated with poverty.

In 1992 white males in America could expect to live to the age of 73.2 years and white females to 79.7 years. Black males could expect to live to 67.8 years and black females to 75.6 years, on the average.

Life expectancy calculations can also predict the average remaining life expectancy after a particular age has been reached. According to the 1992 figures for the United States, for example, at the age of 25 a male of any race has a life expectancy of 48.9 remaining years. A 25-year-old female of any race could expect to live another 55.1 years.

Life Expectancy Worldwide, 1990–95

Region/Country	Life expectancy (years)	Region/Country	Life expectancy (years)
World Total	65	Zambia	44
More developed regions	75	Zimbabwe	56
Less developed regions	62	**Middle Africa**	**51**
AFRICA	**53**	Angola	46
Eastern Africa	**49**	Cameroon	56
Burundi	48	Central African Republic	47
Ethiopia	47	Chad	48
Kenya	59	Congo	52
Madagascar	55	Gabon	54
Malawi	44	Zaire	52
Mauritius	70	**Northern Africa**	**61**
Mozambique	47	Algeria	66
Rwanda	46	Egypt	62
Somalia	47	Libya	63
Tanzania	51	Morocco	63
Uganda	42	Sudan	52

Life Expectancy Worldwide, 1990–95 *(continued)*

Region/Country	Life expectancy (years)	Region/Country	Life expectancy (years)
Tunisia	68	**South America**	**67**
Southern Africa	**63**	Argentina	71
Botswana	61	Bolivia	61
Lesotho	61	Brazil	66
Namibia	59	Chile	72
South Africa	63	Colombia	69
Western Africa	**51**	Ecuador	67
Benin	46	Paraguay	67
Burkina Faso	48	Peru	65
Ghana	56	Uruguay	72
Guinea	45	Venezuela	70
Guinea-Bissau	44	**NORTH AMERICA**	**76**
Ivory Coast	52	Canada	77
Liberia	55	United States	76
Mali	46	**ASIA**	**85**
Mauritania	48	**Eastern Asia**	**72**
Niger	47	China	71
Nigeria	53	Hong Kong	78
Senegal	49	Japan	79
Sierra Leone	43	Korea, North	71
Togo	55	Korea, South	71
LATIN AMERICA	**68**	Mongolia	64
Caribbean	**69**	**Southeastern Asia**	**63**
Cuba	76	Cambodia	51
Dominican Republic	68	Indonesia	63
Haiti	57	Laos	51
Jamaica	74	Malaysia	71
Puerto Rico	75	Myanmar	58
Trinidad and Tobago	71	Philippines	65
Central America	**69**	Singapore	74
Costa Rica	76	Thailand	69
El Salvador	66	Vietnam	64
Guatemala	65	**Southern Asia**	**59**
Honduras	66	Afghanistan	43
Mexico	70	Bangladesh	53
Nicaragua	67	Bhutan	48
Panama	73	India	60

Life Expectancy Worldwide, 1990–95 *(continued)*

Region/Country	Life expectancy (years)	Region/Country	Life expectancy (years)
Iran	67	Greece	78
Nepal	54	Italy	77
Pakistan	59	Portugal	75
Sri Lanka	72	Spain	78
Western Asia	**66**	Yugoslavia (former)	72
Iraq	66	Bosnia-Herzegovina	—
Israel	77	Croatia	—
Jordan	68	Slovenia	—
Kuwait	75	Yugoslavia	—
Lebanon	69	**Western Europe**	**76**
Oman	70	Austria	76
Saudi Arabia	69	Belgium	76
Syria	67	France	77
Turkey	67	Germany	76
United Arab Emirates	71	Netherlands	77
Yemen	53	Switzerland	78
EUROPE	**75**	**OCEANIA**	**73**
Eastern Europe	**71**	**Australia-New Zealand**	**77**
Bulgaria	72	Australia	77
Czechoslovakia (former)	73	New Zealand	76
Czech Republic	—	**Melanesia**	**59**
Slovakia	—	Papua New Guinea	55
Hungary	70	**USSR (FORMER)**	**70**
Poland	72	Armenia	71
Romania	70	Azerbaijan	70
Northern Europe	**76**	Belarus	72
Denmark	76	Georgia	72
Estonia	71	Kazakhstan	69
Finland	76	Kyrgyzstan	68
Ireland	75	Moldova	68
Latvia	71	Russian Federation	70
Lithuania	73	Tajikistan	70
Norway	77	Turkmenistan	65
Sweden	78	Ukraine	71
United Kingdom	76	Uzbekistan	—
Southern Europe	**76**		
Albania	73		

Note: Totals may not add because of rounding numbers.
United Nations Fund for Population Activities (UNFPA). *The State of World Population 1994.*

Leading Causes of Death in Many Nations

A review of statistics on life expectancy logically raises questions about the many means by which life can be cut short—the factors that define life expectancy. As of 1990, the four leading causes of death worldwide were:

1. infectious and parasitic diseases

2. diseases of the circulatory system (cardiovascular diseases)

3. malignant neoplasms (cancer)

4. diseases such as AIDS, diabetes and diseases of the digestive system, plus certain hard-to-define causes like senility

Taken together, the four main causes of death accounted for 39,964,000 deaths in 1990, out of a worldwide total of 49,936,000 for all causes.

Causes of Death Worldwide, 1990

Main cause of death	Estimated number	Rate per 100,000
Infectious and parasitic diseases	17,499,000	331
Circulatory system diseases[1]	11,931,000	225
Malignant neoplasms	5,121,000	97
External causes[2]	3,466,000	65
Perinatal causes	3,116,000	59
Chronic obstructive pulmonary diseases	2,888,000	55
Maternal causes	504,000	10
Other and unknown causes[3]	5,413,000	102
All causes	49,936,000	944

1. Includes heart diseases, cerebrovascular diseases, other diseases of the circulatory system, etc.
2. Includes accidents, suicide, etc.
3. Includes AIDS, diabetes, diseases of the digestive system, genitourinary disease, ill-defined causes including senility, etc.
World Health Organization, *Global Health Situation and Projections,* 1992.

In 1990, an estimated 17,499,000 people died around the world as a result of infectious and parasitic diseases. This represents a death rate of 331 per 100,000 people. An infectious disease is any illness caused by microorganisms such as bacteria, viruses or protozoa. Parasitic diseases may also be caused by microorganisms, but they are usually associated with larger life forms such as worms (tapeworms and hookworms), lice, ticks, leeches, fungi, flukes or mites that live either on or in the body.

According to the World Health Organization (WHO), one-fourth of all the deaths in the world are caused by the second largest killer, cardiovascular diseases (CVDs). Approximately 12 million people die each year throughout the world from heart attacks and strokes, a rate of 225 per 100,000 people. Because of advances in medical science, disease prevention and sanitation, CVDs and cancer take precedence over infectious disease as the main causes of death in industrialized countries. In the United States, for example, the infectious diseases pneumonia, influenza and tuberculosis were the top three leading causes of death in 1900, with heart attacks and strokes in fourth and fifth place, respectively. By 1940, heart disease, cancer and stroke were the top three causes of death, followed by infectious diseases as a whole.

Leading Causes of Death in the United States, 1970–92

Cause of death	Deaths in 1992	Death rate per 100,000		
		1970	1980	1992
All causes	2,177,000	945.3	878.3	863.3
Heart disease	720,480	362.0	336.0	282.5
Cancer	521,090	162.8	183.9	204.3
Cerebrovascular diseases	143,640	101.9	75.1	56.3
Pulmonary diseases	91,440	15.2	24.7	35.8
Accidents	86,310	56.4	46.7	33.8
Pneumonia and influenza	76,120	30.9	24.1	29.8
Diabetes mellitus	50,180	18.91	15.4	19.7
AIDS	33,590	—	—	13.2
Suicide	29,760	11.6	11.9	11.7
Homicide and legal intervention	26,580	8.3	10.7	10.4
Liver disease and cirrhosis	24,830	15.5	13.5	9.7
Kidney diseases	22,400	4.4	7.4	8.8
Septicemia	19.910	1.7	4.2	7.8
Atherosclerosis	16,100	15.6	13.0	6.3
Perinatal-related conditions	15,790	21.3	10.1	6.2

U.S. Dept. of Health and Human Services, National Center for Health Statistics, *Monthly Vital Statistics Report*, Sept. 28, 1993.

In the industrialized countries of the west, CVDs are responsible for as much as 50 percent of the death rate. Developing countries in Africa, Asia and South America, on the other hand, have a very low death rate from CVDs, about 16 percent. Such a difference in the death rates suggests the importance of lifestyle as a cause of CVDs. In addition to the faster pace of life and stress that comes with economic development, the pollution of air and water that accompanies industrialization leads to higher heart disease and cancer rates.

Cigarette smoking is also seen as a major factor in CVDs. As cigarettes are exported to the developing countries, death rates begin to reflect the ailments brought about by that habit. WHO predicts that by the year 2000 the death rate from CVDs in the developing countries will climb to 30 percent. Due mainly to antismoking campaigns and advances in medical technology, some developed nations are showing a marked decrease in deaths from CVDs, while others, such as Poland and Bulgaria, have shown increases in the 1970s and 1980s.

In the same period, deaths from CVDs dropped significantly in the United States, Canada, Australia and Japan. Other countries, such as Norway, Greece and Hungary, had stable death rates from CVDs. Finland, England and Wales have the highest death rates from CVDs, while Japan has the lowest. In the United States, between 1970 and 1987 there was a decline of 40 percent in deaths from CVDs for 34 to 74 year olds. For this age group, cancer is now the leading cause of death, rather than CVDs. Other Western countries are also showing declines of about 10 percent.

The importance of lifestyle over ethnicity as a determining factor in the development of CVDs can be seen in comparisons of death rates from CVDs for Japanese living in Japan with those for Japanese living in the United States. The CVD death rate for Japanese in the United States is six times greater than Japan's death rate from these diseases. Japanese who live in the United States fall between the Japan and United States rates for CVDs.

In 1990 the estimated number of deaths from cancer worldwide was 5,121,000, a rate of 97 deaths per 100,000 people. Before the 1990s are over it is predicted that 60 million additional people will die of cancer. More than 80 million people are expected to die of cancer in the first 10 years of the 21st century. From 1985 to 2015, WHO estimates an 18 percent increase in cancer deaths for the developed countries and a 141 percent increase for the developing countries. Lung cancer from smoking is expected to contribute significantly to the cancer mortality rate in developing countries.

The fourth leading cause of death worldwide is listed by WHO as "other and unknown causes." Each year there are 5,413,000 deaths (102 per 100,000) in this category. It includes AIDS, diabetes, diseases of the digestive system, genitourinary diseases and other causes that are difficult to define, such as senility.

Estimates made in 1994 suggest that 17 million people throughout the world have been infected with the HIV virus since the deadly infection surfaced in the United States in the early 1980s. One million of these are children, four million of the total have developed full-blown AIDS (even though only 985,119 cases were reported to WHO) and three to four million have already perished from the diseases associated with AIDS. Eighty percent of HIV infections and AIDS cases are in the developing countries, with 80 to 90 percent of HIV-infected children in Africa. Ninety percent of newly infected adults acquire HIV infection from heterosexual intercourse; by the year 2000, 30 to 40 million people are expected to test HIV positive.

AIDS Cases and Deaths in the United States, 1981–93

Year	Cases diagnosed	Cases diagnosed to date	Known deaths	Known deaths to date
Pre-1981	92	92	31	31
1981	315	407	128	159
1982	1,156	1,583	461	620
1983	3,084	4,647	1,502	2,122
1984	6,198	10,845	3,478	5,600
1985	11,775	22,620	6,929	12,529
1986	19,042	41,662	12,021	24,550
1987	28,560	70,222	16,270	40,820
1988	35,267	105,489	20,903	61,723
1989	41,681	147,170	27,449	89,172
1990	46,075	193,245	30,649	119,821
1991	54,778	248,023	34,746	154,567
1992	67,306	315,329	36,941	191,508
1993	46,180	361,509	29,084	220,592

Note: Delays in recording cases and deaths substantially impact data, particularly in recent years. In addition, through 1993 there were 273 people known to have died but whose dates of death are unknown.
U.S. Dept. of Health and Human Services, Centers for Disease Control and Prevention, *HIV/AIDS Surveillance*, March 1994.

In 1995 the health minister of Zimbabwe, Timothy Stamps, claimed that his country had the highest number of new AIDS cases in the world, and announced that one in every hundred Zimbabweans would probably die of AIDS-related diseases within 18 months. His report stated that each week at least 300 people died from AIDS-related ailments and that mortuaries were so congested with victims it was necessary to place more than one body at a time in the holding trays.

From a Bill of Mortality in London August 15–22, 1665:

The Diseases and Casualties this Week

Aged	54	Killed by a fall down stairs	1
Cancer	2	Murthered	1
Collick	1	Plague	3880
Consumption	174	Starved	1
Drownd	2	Teeth	113
Found dead in the Street	1	Ulcer	2
Gangrene	1	Wormes	18

The Illustrated Pepys, Robert Latham, ed., University of California Press, 1983.

Infant Mortality Worldwide

Hidden in the statistics on causes of death are the deaths of millions of young children each year. In demographic terms, infant mortality encompasses any infant who fails to reach his or her first birthday. The infant mortality rate gives the number of such deaths per thousand live births, and is calculated by dividing the number of infants who die before age one by the number of live births within the same year.

Nations with Highest and Lowest Infant Mortality Rates, 1994

Nation	Infant mortality rate[1]	Nation	Infant mortality rate[1]
Highest infant mortality		**Lowest infant mortality**	
Afghanistan	156	Iceland	4
Western Sahara	152	Japan	4
Angola	145	Finland	5
Sierra Leone	142	Liechtenstein	5
Malawi	141	Hong Kong	6
Guinea	139	Netherlands	6
Central African Rep.	137	Norway	6
Chad	132	San Marino	6
Mozambique	129	Singapore	6
Somalia	126	Sweden	6
Gambia	124	Taiwan	6
Bhutan	121	Austria	7
Guinea-Bissau	120	Australia	7
Rwanda	119	Belgium	7
Burkina Faso	118	Canada	7

Nations with Highest and Lowest Infant Mortality Rates, 1994 *(continued)*

Nation	Infant mortality rate[1]	Nation	Infant mortality rate[1]
Highest infant mortality		**Lowest infant mortality**	
Burundi	114	Denmark	7
Liberia	113	France	7
Yemen	113	Germany	7
Uganda	112	Ireland	7
Cambodia	111	Luxembourg	7
Congo	111	Monaco	7
Djibouti	111	Spain	7
Niger	111	United Kingdom	7
Zaire	111	Andorra	8
Benin	110	Aruba	8
Tanzania	110	Italy	8
		Malta	8
		Réunion	8
		Slovenia	8
		United States	8

1. Per 1,000 live births.
U.S. Bureau of the Census, *World Population Profile 1994.*

The worldwide infant mortality rate is 65 deaths per 1,000 live births, with the lowest rates (an average of 8) in North America and the highest (95) in sub-Saharan Africa. Among children under four years of age, there were nearly 13 million deaths worldwide in 1990, 27.6 percent from acute respiratory infections like pneumonia and 23.3 percent from diarrhea.

Infant Mortality Rates by Region, 1994

Region	Infant mortality rate (per 1,000 live births)
World	65
Developed regions	15
Developing regions	72
Sub-Saharan Africa	95
Asia	68
Near East and North Africa	60
Latin America and Caribbean	43
North America	8
Europe	9
Former USSR	34

U.S. Bureau of the Census, *World Population Profile 1994.*

Leading Causes of Childhood Deaths, 1990 (Birth to Four Years of Age)

Cause	Estimated number of deaths	Percent of total
World total	12,900,000	100.0%
Acute respiratory infections (mostly pneumonia)	3,560,000	27.6
Diarrhea (alone)	3,000,000	23.3
Birth asphyxia	860,000	6.7
Malaria	800,000	6.2
Neonatal tetanus	560,000	4.3
Acute respiratory infections-—measles	480,000	3.7
Congenital anomalies	450,000	3.5
Birth trauma	430,000	3.3
Prematurity	430,000	3.3

World Health Organization, *Global Health Situation and Projections,* 1992.

Death Rates in Different Countries

Not only does the infant mortality rate vary from region to region, so does the overall death rate for people of all ages. The death rate for any given population in any given year is expressed as the number of deaths for the year per thousand people at midyear.

Death Rates Worldwide, 1990–95

Region/Country	Death rate per 1,000	Region/Country	Death rate per 1,000
World total	9	Zambia	18
More developed regions	10	Zimbabwe	11
Less developed regions	9	**Middle Africa**	**16**
AFRICA	**14**	Angola	19
Eastern Africa	**16**	Cameroon	12
Burundi	17	Central African Republic	18
Ethiopia	18	Chad	18
Kenya	10	Congo	15
Madagascar	13	Gabon	16
Malawi	21	Zaire	15
Mauritius	7	**Northern Africa**	**9**
Mozambique	18	Algeria	7
Rwanda	18	Egypt	9
Somalia	19	Libya	8
Tanzania	15	Morocco	8
Uganda	21	Sudan	14

Death Rates Worldwide, 1990–95 *(continued)*

Region/Country	Death rate per 1,000	Region/Country	Death rate per 1,000
Tunisia	6	**South America**	7
Southern Africa	9	Argentina	9
Botswana	9	Bolivia	9
Lesotho	10	Brazil	7
Namibia	11	Chile	6
South Africa	9	Colombia	6
Western Africa	15	Ecuador	7
Benin	18	Paraguay	6
Burkina Faso	18	Peru	8
Ghana	12	Uruguay	10
Guinea	20	Venezuela	5
Guinea-Bissau	21	**NORTH AMERICA**	9
Ivory Coast	15	Canada	8
Liberia	14	United States	9
Mali	19	**ASIA**	8
Mauritania	18	**Eastern Asia**	7
Niger	19	China	7
Nigeria	14	Hong Kong	6
Senegal	16	Japan	7
Sierra Leone	22	Korea, North	5
Togo	13	Korea, South	6
LATIN AMERICA	7	Mongolia	8
Caribbean	8	**Southeastern Asia**	8
Cuba	7	Cambodia	14
Dominican Republic	6	Indonesia	8
Haiti	12	Laos	15
Jamaica	6	Malaysia	5
Puerto Rico	7	Myanmar	11
Trinidad and Tobago	6	Philippines	7
Central America	6	Singapore	6
Costa Rica	4	Thailand	6
El Salvador	7	Vietnam	9
Guatemala	8	**Southern Asia**	10
Honduras	7	Afghanistan	22
Mexico	5	Bangladesh	14
Nicaragua	7	Bhutan	17
Panama	5	India	10

Death Rates Worldwide, 1990–95 *(continued)*

Region/Country	Death rate per 1,000	Region/Country	Death rate per 1,000
Iran	7	Italy	10
Nepal	13	Portugal	10
Pakistan	10	Spain	9
Sri Lanka	6	Yugoslavia (former)	10
Western Asia	7	Bosnia-Herzegovina	—
Iraq	7	Croatia	—
Israel	7	Slovenia	—
Jordan	5	Yugoslavia	—
Kuwait	2	**Western Europe**	**11**
Lebanon	7	Austria	11
Oman	5	Belgium	11
Saudi Arabia	5	France	10
Syria	6	Germany	11
Turkey	7	Netherlands	9
United Arab Emirates	4	Switzerland	10
Yemen	14	**OCEANIA**	**8**
EUROPE	**11**	**Australia-New Zealand**	**8**
Eastern Europe	**11**	Australia	8
Bulgaria	12	New Zealand	8
Czechoslovakia (former)	11	Melanesia	9
Czech Republic	—	Papua New Guinea	11
Slovakia	—	**USSR (FORMER)**	**10**
Hungary	14	Armenia	6
Poland	10	Azerbaijan	7
Romania	11	Belarus	10
Northern Europe	**11**	Georgia	9
Denmark	12	Kazakhstan	8
Estonia	12	Kyrgyzstan	7
Finland	10	Moldova	10
Ireland	9	Russian Federation	11
Latvia	12	Tajikistan	7
Lithuania	10	Turkmenistan	8
Norway	11	Ukraine	12
Sweden	11	Uzbekistan	—
United Kingdom	11		
Southern Europe	**10**		
Albania	5		
Greece	10		

Note: Totals may not add because of rounding numbers.
United Nations Fund for Population Activities (UNFPA). *The State of World Population 1994.*

Likelihood of Dying from Various Causes

A given population group's likelihood of dying from specific causes may depend on age, race, sex and region.

Percentage Chances of Dying from Various Causes Worldwide, 1992

Cause of Death	Chance of Dying (%)
Infectious and parasitic diseases	35
Circulatory diseases	24
Malignant neoplasms	10
External causes	7
Perinatal causes	6
Pulmonary disease	6
Maternal causes	1
Other and unknown causes	11
Total of all causes	100

World Health Organization, *Global Health Situation and Projections*, 1992.

Leading Causes of Death in the United States, 1992

Cause of Death	Number of Deaths	Cause of Death	Number of Deaths
Heart diseases	720,480	Homicide and legal intervention	26,570
Cancer	521,090	Liver diseases and cirrhosis	24,830
Cardiovascular diseases	143,640	Kidney diseases	22,400
Pulmonary diseases	91,440	Septicemia	19,910
Accidents	86,310	Atherosclerosis	16,100
Pneumonia and influenza	76,120	Perinatal-related conditions	15,790
Diabetes mellitus	50,180		
AIDS	33,590		
Suicide	29,760		

U.S. Dept. of Health and Human Services, *Monthly Vital Statistics Report*, Sept. 28, 1993.

Fatal Occupations and Leisure Pursuits

An individual's likelihood of dying at any given moment in time is markedly greater for members of certain occupations or participants in certain recreational activities. The fatality profile of an occupation is often determined by the geographical location where the occupation is performed. A policeman working in a high-crime area may either be excluded or rated up by life insurers. Data from the National Traumatic Occupational Fatalities (NTOF) surveillance system published in 1991 ranks Alaska's occupational fatality rate of 33.1 per 100,000 workers as the highest rate in the U.S., more than 4.5 times the national rate of 7.2 deaths per 100,000 workers. A separate 1991 study conducted by the U.S. Occupational Safety and Health Administration (OSHA) detailed risks faced by workers in Alaska, Finland and other polar regions that share a harsh climate and rugged topography and rely on hazardous industries such as fishing, air transport and logging.

Alaskan Occupations with the Highest Fatality Rates (per 100,000)

Agriculture, Forestry, Fishing	132.3
Transportation, Communications, Public Utilities	59.2
Manufacturing	53.5
Construction	50.5

National Institute for Occupational Safety and Health, *Occupational Epidemics of the 1990s*, 1992 p. 18.

Aside from geography, another factor that contributes to the fatality profile of occupations is the degree of danger involved in the ordinary execution of their tasks. This might include people who work with explosives, for example. Conversely, about 30 workers in health-care occupations suffer fatal injuries each year, out of the total 150,000 occupational injuries in that field of work. Such injuries include accidental sticks from hypodermic needles containing blood tainted with contaminants such as HIV or the hepatitis B virus. This type of injury actually poses minuscule risk to health-care workers.

One of the most hazardous industries in the United States is agriculture, forestry and fishing. While only 2 percent of U.S. workers are employed in this sector, it has the fourth highest injury fatality rate (19.1 deaths per 100,000 workers) and ranks third in the number of deaths. Farming alone has a work-related injury death rate of 21.2 per 100,000 workers.

The likelihood of dying from cancer is three to five times greater than average for workers in certain industries. Mortality studies for several occupations reflect this.

- Cancers of the digestive system, respiratory system, brain and unknown sites, as well as lymphomas, occur more often than expected in workers exposed to vinyl chloride.

- Asbestos workers are at greatest risk of contracting lung cancer 25 to 40 years after exposure.

- In New York City, carpenters have a high rate of mortality from cancer of the stomach and cancer of the urinary bladder.

- Male workers in the rubber industry have an unusually high mortality rate from both stomach cancer and lymphatic leukemia.

- Three major studies of occupational cancer show that construction painters suffer significantly more lung cancer than the general population.

The National Institute for Occupational Safety and Health lists dozens of hazardous substances and chemicals used in the workplace. Occupations where exposure occurs suffer various leading work-related diseases and injuries, some of which are fatal. One category of illness, pneumoconiosis, includes diseases caused by the inhalation of different kinds of mineral dusts. Each year there are approximately 1,700 reported cases of pneumoconiosis and about 1,000 premature deaths from the disease in the U.S. Coal miners, for instance, are subject to "black lung" disease, a complex of respiratory disorders such as emphysema and tuberculosis. Silicosis, caused by inhalation of the silica dust in sand, different types of rock and quartz, affects workers involved in tunnel construction, stone cutting, blasting and quartz mining. It can become acute after only 10 months of high exposure.

Asbestosis is a chronic lung disease that falls outside the category of pneumoconiosis and is even more damaging. It affects those who mine asbestos, construction workers and those who manufacture asbestos products. More than a million workers have been exposed to hazardous levels of asbestos. They suffer breathlessness, failure of the respiratory system, lung cancer (especially among smokers), tuberculosis and tumors. There is no effective treatment for asbestosis and early disability or death is the usual outcome.

Life insurance companies will either exclude or rate up policies for people who engage in hazardous leisure activities, especially when engaged in competitively. Among these pursuits are:

Automotive motorcycling

Ballooning

Powerboat racing

Scuba diving (at depths of 66 feet or more)

Horse racing

Hang gliding

Bobsledding

Sky diving, parachuting

Mountain climbing

Snowmobile racing

Bungi jumping

Piloting (private sport)

The major life insurance companies keep large databases that show how many deaths from these activities they pay on each year. They exclude or rate up policies for people involved in these types of leisure activities based on actuarial studies.

Murder and Suicide Rates Around the World

Murder and suicide elicit greater fascination and horror among the living than does any other cause of death. Both have plagued humanity since prehistory, and both persist in every modern culture. Murder rates taken from Interpol's *International Crime Statistics* show the United States has the highest rate of all the developed countries. Northern Ireland for a time had a higher, fluctuating rate, due mainly to the civil unrest in that country. Ireland itself has a low annual murder rate of 1.08 per 100,000 population. In 1982, the murder rate in the United States was 13.82, which declined to 7.9 in 1987. A 1990 Senate Judiciary Committee report shows a rise to 10.5; in 1992 there was a 4 percent increase in the murder rate over the previous year. By comparison, the United Kingdom's 1990 rate was not quite 0.8 per 100,000, Japan's was 1.0 and West Germany's 1.2.

Murder Rates Worldwide, 1986

Rank	Country	Murder rate per 100,000 population
TOP 10		
1	Lesotho	53.19
2	Philippines	42.51
3	Bahamas	25.66
4	Zimbabwe	21.11
5	Lebanon	19.20
6	Thailand	16.56
7	Netherlands	12.26
8	Bermuda	10.79
9	Angola	10.30
10	Venezuela	9.93
UPPER MIDDLE		
11	Zambia	9.73
12	Dominican Republic	9.32
13	Papua New Guinea	9.23
14	Tanzania	8.67
15	United States	7.91
16	Seychelles	7.69

Murder Rates Worldwide, 1986 *(continued)*

Rank	Country	Murder rate per 100,000 population
17	Botswana	7.49
18	Trinidad and Tobago	6.76
19	Rwanda	6.71
20	Canada	6.33
21	Chile	6.26
22	Barbados	6.14
23	Denmark	5.77
24	Sweden	5.74
25	Finland	5.62
26	Italy	5.25
27	Luxembourg	5.25
28	France	4.63
29	Portugal	4.60
30	Ecuador	4.53
31	Kenya	4.53
32	Germany, West	4.51
33	Sudan	4.46
34	Malta	4.24
35	Hungary	3.72
36	Burundi	3.67
37	Australia	3.42
38	Belgium	3.27
39	Malawi	2.93
LOWER MIDDLE		
40	Fiji	2.89
41	Singapore	2.73
42	Jordan	2.72
43	Dominica	2.67
44	Colombia	2.54
45	New Zealand	2.54
46	Austria	2.44
47	Mauritius	2.33
48	Syria	2.25
49	Switzerland	2.24
50	Spain	2.16
51	Cyprus	2.06
52	Malaysia	1.97
53	Greece	1.83

Murder Rates Worldwide, 1986 *(continued)*

Rank	Country	Murder rate per 100,000 population
54	Israel	1.83
55	United Arab Emirates	1.79
56	Ivory Coast	1.78
57	Maldives	1.76
58	Qatar	1.71
59	Nigeria	1.69
60	Senegal	1.67
61	Hong Kong	1.64
62	Libya	1.60
63	Egypt	1.53
64	Japan	1.47
65	Turkey	1.41
66	United Kingdom	1.37
67	Korea, South	1.36
68	Saudi Arabia	1.15
BOTTOM 10		
69	Gabon	1.12
70	Ireland	1.08
71	Congo	1.06
72	Kuwait	1.06
73	Brunei	0.95
74	Norway	0.92
75	Indonesia	0.90
76	Morocco	0.78
77	Niger	0.21
78	Togo	0.18

INTERPOL: International Crime Statistics, 1987

The suicide rate in the U.S. falls somewhere in the midrange, between Ireland's low of 2.5 per 100,000 and Sweden's high of 21.6. In most countries, the suicide rate is much higher for men than for women. Women in the United States are one-third as likely to commit suicide as men; two-thirds of unsuccessful suicide attempts are made by women. From 1930 to 1970, the actual number of suicides in the United States rose by almost 5,000; by 1965, death by suicide was the 11th leading cause of death. Suicide rates for single people as well as divorced or widowed people are higher than for those who are married. For those under 65 years of age, the rate of suicide for divorced people is three times higher than for married people. In all age groups, the rate for singles is more than twice that of those who are married.

People with advanced education and prestigious occupations, such as doctors, lawyers and dentists, have much higher suicide rates than those with less education and more modest occupations. War and economic depression are also factors that influence suicide rates. During periods of prosperity, suicide rates generally decline. Overall, national suicide rates have remained fairly steady for the past three decades.

Comparison of Suicide Rates for Selected Countries

Country	Rate (per 100,000)
Ireland (1968)	2.5
Chile (1967)	2.8
Greece (1968)	3.6
Italy (1967)	5.4
Netherlands (1968)	6.3
Norway (1967)	7.0
Israel (1968)	7.6
United Kingdom (1968)	9.1*
Canada (1968)	9.7
Poland (1968)	10.6
United States (1967)	10.8
Australia (1968)	12.7
Japan (1967)	14.1
France (1968)	15.3*
Switzerland (1967)	17.3
Federal Republic of Germany (1967—excluding West Berlin)	21.3*
Sweden (1967)	21.6
Austria (1968)	21.9
Czechoslovakia (1967)	23.9
Hungary (1968)	33.7

* Provisional
Encyclopedia Americana, Grolier, 1992.

Death by Execution, Past and Present

Throughout the ages, another form of death that has both thrilled and terrified onlookers has been execution. This most drastic means of punishment was used frequently and for a wide variety of offenses. Ancient Romans routinely executed Christians either by crucifixion or by throwing them to the lions. In the Middle Ages, Vlad the Impaler—who was the inspiration for the fictional Count Dracula—crucified 25,000 Romanian peasants to punish them for a revolt. Kings and aristocrats in Europe and the rest of the world publicly tortured and killed their religious and political enemies. In 18th- and 19th-century England, the death penalty was used for major as well as minor crimes. The criminal was publicly hanged and then drawn and quartered to instill fear of the law in the onlookers.

In the United States, death by execution was used against cattle and horse thieves on the western frontier. Executions of bandits and political foes were common in Japan, China, South America, Mexico and Russia in the 19th century and the first half of the 20th century. It is estimated that Joseph Stalin was responsible for the execution of 20 million Russians whom he viewed as enemies of the Soviet system.

There has been a marked reduction in the rate of death from execution in the second half of the 20th century, due largely to the fact that many countries and states have abolished the death penalty. Some countries, like Belgium and Ireland, retain the death penalty but seldom, if ever, use it. Other countries, such as Israel and Morocco, strictly confine the use of the death penalty. In the United States the rate was on the decline even before a 1972 Supreme Court decision declaring the death penalty unconstitutional; since the reversal of that decision the rate of execution has remained small.

States and Countries That Practice Capital Punishment Today

Capital punishment has practically been abolished in western Europe and most of Latin America. In Africa, Asia and the Middle East, with the exception of Israel, capital punishment is still used for many crimes, although the frequency of its use varies.

In 1967 executions were suspended in the United States so that appellate courts could consider the constitutionality of the death penalty. In 1972, the Supreme Court ruled in Furman v. Georgia that the death penalty constituted "cruel and unusual punishment" for the crimes of rape or murder. The Court argued that the death penalty was used with "freakish" irregularity and, therefore, its use was "arbitrary" and "cruel."

In spite of the Court's ruling, most states enacted new death penalty statutes and in 1976 the Supreme Court in Gregg v. Georgia upheld them as constitutional. Capital statutes now typically authorize trial courts to impose death penalties or life imprisonment after a guilty verdict has been reached. Evidence is submitted at a postconviction hearing to establish what "aggravating" or "mitigating" factors were present in the crime. If "aggravating" factors prevail and the death penalty is imposed, then an appellate court automatically reviews the case.

In 1977, the Supreme Court ruled in Coker v. Georgia that death for rape was "grossly disproportionate and excessive." Thereafter, the only capital crime in the United States has been murder, except for such crimes as treason.

Some states do not use the death penalty: Alaska, Hawaii, Iowa, Kansas, Maine, Massachusetts, Michigan, Minnesota, North Dakota, Rhode Island, West Virginia and Wisconsin. Puerto Rico, the Virgin Islands and the District of Columbia also do not have the death penalty. As early as 1853 and 1854, Wisconsin and Michigan abolished the death penalty.

By 1991, 2,350 persons were on death row in 36 states. About 150 condemned persons, including one woman, have been executed since 1977. There is considerable debate over the merits of capital punishment in the United States and worldwide. Amnesty International monitors the use of the death penalty throughout the world and rates countries on its use.

Those who defend capital punishment feel that it is an appropriate penalty for murder. Opponents to the death penalty contend that "a life for a life" is not a sound principle and that society should not let the brutalities of criminal violence set the parameters for punishment. Another concern over the use of the death penalty is its racial and socioeconomic bias: it is more often pronounced upon poor and minority convicts. However, the Supreme Court refused in 1987 (McCleskey v. Kemp) to rule that the death penalty is racially biased against blacks convicted of murdering whites.

History's Most Lethal Wars

Humankind's proclivity for killing ourselves and each other, of course, extends far beyond individual deaths to encompass entire populations during times of war. Casualties from warfare in the ancient and medieval world were usually limited by the size of the communities, the duration of war, the size of civilian populations involved and the technology of warfare. From the warfare of ancient Greece and Rome to the Crusades, the Thirty Years' and Hundred Years' Wars of the Middle Ages to the American Civil War, war casualties usually numbered in the thousands or tens of thousands.

In the ancient world, civilian populations were often kept alive to be taken as slaves. The concept of "total war," defined by Karl Von Clauswitz in 1828, widened the idea of war to include the destruction of enemy civilian populations as a way of destroying the enemy's resources and will to fight.

In the 12th century the Chinese were using gunpowder for various types of firearms, and by the 14th century, the Europeans had developed the cannon as an effective weapon of war. By the 19th century, the development of explosives began to lead to much higher war casualties. It is estimated that from

650,000 to 750,00 people were killed in the American Civil War, the highest casualty rate for any war up to that time and until World War I.

The full extent of World War I casualties is difficult to assess, since people involved in the conflict died of many causes, such as frostbite, starvation, influenza and typhus. Estimates of the war's death toll have been taken from several different reporting sources.

Military Battle and Civilian Dead, World War I

Country	Military Battle Deaths	Civilian Deaths
ALLIES:		
France	1,357,800	4,266,000
British Empire	908,371	2,090,212
Russia	1,700,000	2,000,000
Italy	462,391	—
United States	50,585	—
Belgium	13,715	30,000
Serbia	45,000	650,000
Montenegro	3,000	—
Romania	334,706	275,000
Greece	5,000	132,000
Portugal	100,000	—
Japan	300	—
Allies total:	4,888,891	3,157,633
CENTRAL POWERS:		
Germany	1,808,546	760,000
Austria-Hungary	922,500	300,000
Turkey	325,000	2,150,000
Bulgaria	75,844	275,000
Central Powers total:	3,131,889	3,485,000
Grand Total	8,020,780	6,642,633

R. Ernest Dupuy and Trevor N. Dupuy, *The Encyclopedia of Military History*, rev. ed., Harper & Row, 1977.

World War II

While there is no exact data for the loss of lives in World War II, the estimates are considerably greater for this war than for World War I. It still stands as the costliest war in history, in terms of lives taken.

Between 15 and 20 million military personnel were killed in action. Among the Axis powers, Germany suffered about 3.5 million battle dead,

Japan 1.5 million and Italy 200,000. Among the Allies, the Soviet Union had the heaviest battle casualties, with a probably accurate estimate of 7.5 million dead. China lost 2.2 million soldiers, the United Kingdom calculated more than 300,000 dead, the United States lost 292,000 and France 210,000.

The estimate for civilian loss of life numbered about 25 million. The highest losses were by the USSR, which lost more than 7.7 million civilians, with China a distant second at perhaps 1 million civilian lives lost. France lost 400,000 civilians, the United Kingdom 65,000 and the United States 6,000 noncombatants. On the Axis side, Japan lost the most civilians—3.6 million—and Germany lost about 3.8 million civilians. In addition, about 6 million Jews and another 4 million Gypsies, homosexuals, mentally ill and disabled, mostly from Eastern Europe, were put to death by the Nazis.

Korean Conflict

The number of Chinese and North Korean casualties during the 1950–53 conflict is estimated at between 1.5 and 2 million, along with 1 million civilians. The UN forces lost 88,000 soldiers; of that number 23,300 were American. Total casualties for the UN (killed, wounded or missing) were 459,360, including 300,000 South Koreans. There were another 1 million civilians lost by South Korea.

Vietnam War

The war in Vietnam (1950–75) killed anywhere from 2 to 3 million Indochinese and 58,000 Americans. Three times as many U.S. bombs were dropped in this "limited war" as during World War II.

World's Worst Massacres and Genocides

War has often gone hand in hand with genocide. While the phenomenon of mass extermination of entire populations has darkened human history from the start, the term genocide (*genos,* group; *cide,* kill) was coined to describe the horrors that took place at Nazi death camps during World War II. Throughout history, massacres of large numbers of civilians have been carried out by invading armies and warring factions. Genocide, however, describes a thorough and systematic attempt to eliminate totally a national, ethnic, or other cultural group for political or ideological reasons. Modern times have seen the worst of man's inhumanity to man, not only in Europe but in Africa and the Middle East. Ethiopia, Somalia, Sudan and Rwanda have seen brutal civil wars in which tribes have tried to eradicate each other. Kurdish towns in Iraq have been bombed and gassed, causing hundreds of civilian deaths. These events continue a long history of massacre and genocide whose highlights include:

The fall of Baghdad, 1258: Mongol hordes led by the grandson of Ghengis Khan killed anywhere from 80,000 to 2 million people when they took over the city.

The Inquisitions: Brutal campaigns to ensure loyalty to Roman Catholicism raged through Europe for five centuries, claiming thousands of lives. The earliest, the Roman Inquisition, started in 1235. The Church used torture to force confessions and then burnt victims at the stake in order to weed out and suppress heresy. Led by Torquemada, a Dominican friar, the Spanish Inquisition struck terror in 15th-century subjects and continued after his death in 1498. In Toledo, Seville and Barcelona, the auto-da-fé, or burning of heretics, was used for mass executions of apostates and Jews who refused to convert to Christianity. In 1531, a Portuguese Inquisition began. A form of Inquisition continued into the 18th century, targeting women (especially older women) and accusing them of practicing witchcraft.

The St. Bartholomew's Day Massacre, 1572: Starting in Paris and spreading to other parts of France, Roman Catholics killed tens of thousands of minority Huguenots (French Protestants).

Balkan genocide, 1876–96: Twelve thousand Bulgarian peasants were brutally killed by the Turkish army of the Ottoman Empire in 1876. Between 1894 and 1896, the Ottomans conducted a massacre of Christian Armenians.

Armenian genocide: During World War I, Turkey targeted Armenia as an ally of Russia in what has been called the first modern genocide. The Turks rounded up the entire Armenian population of Turkey and deported them to Russia. The deportation, along with massacres by the Turkish army, led to the deaths of anywhere from 600,000 to 1 million Armenians.

The Holocaust, 1933–45: The murder of six million Jews by the Nazis during World War II represents the largest single genocide in history. In Nazi death camps, prisoners were efficiently gassed and cremated—if they didn't starve to death first. Other, smaller ethnic groups, such as Gypsies and Slavic peoples, also fell victim to Nazi genocide in smaller numbers; as did nonethnic targets such as homosexuals, the mentally retarded and political dissidents. The Nazis instituted their genocidal policies soon after gaining power in Germany and continued them until their defeat at the end of World War II. Many Nazi leaders were subsequently brought to trial in the Nuremberg War Tribunals and either executed or imprisoned.

Cambodian genocide, 1975–77: In April 1975, communist Khmer Rouge leader Pol Pot gained power in Cambodia and instituted a brutal dictatorship. Between two and four million Cambodians died of political violence and starvation as the Khmer Rouge forcibly attempted to collectivize agriculture.

Bosnian genocide, 1991–95: After the fall of the Soviet Union, ethnic conflict between the Serbians, Bosnians (Muslims) and Croatians of the former Yugoslavia resumed its centuries-old pattern. In a process termed "ethnic cleansing," largely carried out by the Bosnian Serbs, Bosnians and Muslims were evicted from their homes. An estimated 250,000 people died in the process, many shot by Serb soldiers. A peace accord was signed and war crimes trials were called for in 1995.

Deadliest Plagues, Epidemics and Natural Disasters in History

At certain moments in history, people's likelihood of dying had very little to do with who they were and how they lived their lives, and almost everything to do with simple geography. These were times of plague or other catastrophe, when everyone in a village, city, country or even continent faced grave risk of death simply by virtue of living and working where they did. Testifying to the terror summoned by a single disease—the bubonic plague—the term "plague" has come to refer to any widespread outbreak of ravaging or deadly communicable illness. Indeed, the bubonic plague stands as the definitive epidemic, probably because of the horror it brought to Europe and Asia from ancient times onward. Called the "black death," because it causes dark skin splotches or patches to erupt on the bodies of its victims, bubonic plague has been as nefarious throughout history as its nickname suggests. Some experts have suggested that the infamous Black Death of the 14th century, which killed 25 million, was in fact an anthrax epidemic that resembled the bubonic disease in its symptoms. Whether or not that was the case, mention of bubonic plague can send shivers down any spine.

Bubonic plague is spread by fleas who have lived off rats infected with one of two bacteria, *Yersinia pestis* and *Pasteurella pestis*. Some believe *Pasteurella pestis* was responsible for the 14th-century outbreak. The infected rats were carried from port to port in trading ships traveling between Asia and Europe. Flea bites first infected people along the coastal areas, then spread inland. In the 14th century the disease's effects were amplified by a concurrent outbreak of pneumonic plague, spread by the coughing of human carriers.

Some people who contracted bubonic plague survived the ravages of the disease, but most did not. The poor were especially hard hit by the contagion, since the rich were often able to flee areas of dense population where the epidemics raged. The symptoms of the disease are horrific, showing up two to five days after infection, when the victim begins to shiver with high fever and a severe headache. Hemorrhages take place within the skin, causing the dark patches, and blood poisoning may cause early death. If it does not, soon the "buboes" appear. These are red, smooth, oval-shaped swellings that appear in the groin, armpits, neck and other parts of the body, causing intense pain.

The urban, seagoing rats infected with the plague caught the disease from wild rodents. Plague still lurks in the world today, but it is more likely to be spread by wild rodents than urban boat rats. Vaccination against the plague is now possible in those parts of the world that may still be affected by it and antibiotics are successful in treating the disease, especially if it is caught at an early stage.

A greater problem in modern times has been cholera, which is caused by a bacterium, *Vibrio cholerae*. Its main symptoms are dehydration from diarrhea and vomiting, muscle cramps and blue lips. Until 1961 most cholera occurred in Asia (a 9th-century Tibetan manuscript written in Sanskrit described the disease), but since then it has become pandemic, spreading from Indonesia to Africa, other parts of Asia, the Mediterranean and coastal areas of North America. Treatment today consists of antibiotics and measures to rehydrate the body. Vaccines are available for short-term protection. The disease can be controlled mainly by cleaning up the water supply or not drinking the water in affected areas.

Pandemics of various killer diseases have often been accompanied or brought on by other epidemics or natural disasters. Catastrophes such as earthquakes, volcanic eruptions, famine from crop failures, flood or fire often lead to contamination of water supplies and other sanitary disasters, encouraging the spread of disease. History's great epidemics have taken many forms. Shortly after Columbus's arrival in the Americas, Europeans began to succumb to sexually transmitted diseases. In the 17th and 18th centuries there were severe epidemics of smallpox throughout Europe. Cholera epidemics raged in the ancient world and are still a threat today. Yellow fever, influenza, tuberculosis and, more recently, AIDS are some of the other infectious diseases that have caused plagues.

430 B.C.E.: Bubonic plague broke out in Athens in the early part of the Peloponnesian war (431–404). It was thought to have traveled from Ethiopia to Greece, first appearing in Piraeus. It reached Athens when the Spartans drove the population from the surrounding countryside into the city, causing overcrowding during the heat of the summer. The Greek historian Thucydides both recorded the war and fought as an Athenian soldier. He contracted the plague but was able to survive and describe its symptoms. He wrote about the burning head fevers, reddened and inflamed eyes, bleeding from the throat and tongue, fetid breath, vomiting and spasms and finally the outbreak of pustules and ulcers on the skin. While the bodies of up to one-quarter of the Athenians piled up in the streets, widespread looting and rape took place.

24 August, 79 C.E.: The resort town of Pompeii was buried under volcanic ash when the nearby volcano, Vesuvius, suddenly erupted without warning. The entire population of the town was destroyed; the number of deaths was in the thousands.

500–650: Called the Plague of Justinian, episodes of bubonic plague raged throughout the Roman empire during this period, killing 100 million people. In Constantinople (542 C.E.) the plague destroyed half of the city's population. Reports placed the death rate at 16,000 a day. Of the 400,000 people in the city, 230,000 are thought to have perished from the plague. This plague was believed to have begun in Egypt before reaching Constantinople.

1347: Bubonic plague appeared in southern Russia and the Crimean ports. It then began to spread to the Mediterranean countries, moving steadily to the west by merchant ships trading from Asia to Europe. By 1348 hundreds of thousands of Europeans began to die from the plague as it struck every country on the continent, traveling from one to another. The Black Death wiped out one-third of the European population, about 25 million people.

1494: Called the "French pox," syphilis began to kill thousands of people. Although it was recognized as a disease transmitted by armies and associated with sexual intercourse, there was no control or treatment for the disease.

1545: Spanish conquistadors brought smallpox to Mexico, killing 800,000 locals. The death rate of indigenous Mexicans was much higher than that of the Spanish, because they had not built immunities to the disease.

1630: Bubonic plague struck northern Italy, killing about one million people. Southern France was also affected. It was believed that invading armies brought the plague with them. The plague continued to hit Europe every 10 to 15 years; doctors could do no more than quarantine those who were stricken.

1650: The Thirty Years' War, plague and famine continued to blight Europe and spread to the Americas. It is estimated that the plague wiped out as many as 95 percent of the Native Americans who came into contact with Europeans.

1664: London experiences its worst epidemic of plague, which kills an estimated 100,000 people. Bills of mortality kept close record on the number of dead, but physicians were still unable to cope with the disease except by the use of quarantine. One out of ten victims survived the illness.

1666: On top of the plague, the great London fire destroyed 13,000 houses and 87 churches, leveling 400 acres of the city. Only nine fatalities were attributed to the conflagration, despite the great property loss.

1713: European sailors spread smallpox to South Africa, killing many native inhabitants.

1721: In Massachusetts during a smallpox epidemic, Cotton Mather, an early pioneer in smallpox inoculation, ordered a Boston physician to inoculate 240 townspeople; 234 of those inoculated survived the disease. Smallpox epidemics usually killed as many as 40 percent of the victims, and there was no known way of dealing effectively with the illness once it was contracted. Mather had learned about the effectiveness of inoculation from his African slave.

November 1, 1775: The Lisbon earthquake claimed 50,000 lives, caused huge losses of property and destroyed art treasures and libraries.

1817: Cholera, a problem in Asia since at least the 9th century, made its entrance into Europe through Russia. It drastically reduced the populations of Moscow and St. Petersburg and caused millions of deaths in a series of epidemics. At the first signs of an outbreak, the rich were able to escape the cities, leaving the urban poor the main victims.

1845: In the century that preceded the worst potato blight in Ireland, there were more than 20 others of major proportions. The famine of 1845 was most devastating, though, because by then four million Irish and two million English had come to depend wholly on the potato for their sustenance. The famines led to thousands of deaths and the mass emigration of the Irish to North America. It is estimated that one out of every six who left Ireland died on the trip because of crowded and harsh conditions aboard ship.

1853: In New Orleans, 11,000 people died in an epidemic of yellow fever.

1878: Fourteen thousand people in the southern United States died of yellow fever.

August 28, 1883: In Krakatau, Java, Indonesia, a volcano erupted, killing 30,000 people. The eruption caused a tidal wave 120 feet high. Coastal towns in Java and Sumatra were flooded by the wave. Volcanic ash rose 17 miles into the atmosphere, hiding the sun and plunging the area into two days of darkness that made rescue efforts difficult. The blast of the volcano was heard in Australia 2,200 miles from the eruption.

April 19, 1906: More than 1,000 people were killed in an earthquake that leveled much of San Francisco and caused thousands of others to flee from their homes.

1918–19: World War I killed 10 million people, but in its aftermath the so-called "Spanish flu," a virulent form of influenza, became pandemic and is believed to have killed as many as 20 million.

September 1, 1923: The Tokyo earthquake destroyed 500,000 houses and drove a million people from their homes. The death toll in the city was 132,807. Damage to surrounding areas raised that number to 300,000, with up to 2.5 million left homeless.

1925: Amidst chaos and social disorder, famine raged in China. A continuous problem, famine this year struck Szechwan and resulted in the deaths of three million people.

1984: Researchers identified HIV, the human immunodeficiency virus, which causes AIDS.

November 13, 1985: Twenty thousand people were killed in a volcanic eruption in Columbia. Ten thousand are killed in a Mexican earthquake the same year.

1988: Floods in Bangladesh left 20 million homeless. An earthquake in Armenia killed about 20,000 people.

Samuel Pepys' Accounts of London's Plague

A particularly devastating outbreak of plague began in London in the spring of 1665 and lasted until the summer of 1666. More than 100,000 people died. Samuel Pepys kept a diary of the period, making the notes below:

April 30, 1665 Great fears of the sickeness here in the City, it being said that two or three houses are already shut up. God preserve us all. . . .

August 12, 1665 The people die so, that now it seems they are fain to carry the dead to be buried by daylight, the nights not sufficing to do it in. And my Lord Mayor commands people to be within at 9 at night, all (as they say) that the sick may have liberty to go abroad for ayre. . . .

September 3, 1665 Up and put on my coloured silk suit, very fine and my new periwigg. . . but darst not wear it because the plague was in Westminster when I bought it. . . nobody will dare to buy any haire for fear of the infection that it had been cut off of the heads of people dead of the plague. . . .

October 16, 1665 But Lord, how empty the streets are, and melancholy, so many poor sick people in the streets, full of sores and so many sad stories overheard as I walk, everybody talking of this dead and that man sick and so many in this place and so many in that. And they tell me that in Westminster there is never a physitian and but one apothecary left, all being dead but that there are great hopes of a great decrease this week: God sent it.

Note: Pepys did not die from plague. A combination of heart disease, arteriosclerosis and uremic poisoning killed him in 1703 when he was 70 years old.

Catastrophic Accidents

Nature and violence have not been the only causes of mass death. As technology and science have advanced in the 19th and 20th centuries, the world has felt the impact of devastating accidents caused by human blunders or negligence. Among the more notable are the following.

The Johnstown Flood

In 1889, Johnstown, Pennsylvania, witnessed a flood that was a product of human tampering with nature. Located near Pittsburgh in a coal-mining region, it was the leading steel-producing town in the United States. Its location in a mountainous area with heavy rainfall, near the headwaters of the Conemaugh River, made it vulnerable to flooding. Upstream, a dam created an artificial fishing, swimming and boating lake for wealthy families seeking a summer retreat from Pittsburgh. The owners knew of its structural defects but did not want to give up their vacation spot. On May 31, 1889, the dam burst after a prolonged period of rain. An estimated 20 million tons of water rushed towards Johnstown, drowning more than 2,300 people and causing property damage of 10 million dollars.

The *Titanic*

On April 15, 1912, the luxury liner *Titanic* sank in the North Atlantic Ocean after hitting an iceberg. More than 1,500 passengers and crew drowned; about 800 were rescued. It is believed that the captain of the ship ignored warnings of icebergs in the area in order to set a record time crossing from the United States to Europe. Because of its 16 watertight compartments, the *Titanic* was considered an unsinkable ship. False confidence may have caused sloppiness on the ship's maiden voyage.

Major Train Accidents

Up until 1853, railroad accidents were few and the number of deaths was low. Early trains traveled slowly, were few in number and rarely ran at night, nor did they travel long distances. From 1853 until 1915 there were fewer than one hundred deaths related to major train accidents. Since 1915 there have been a number of train wrecks with fatalities numbering in the hundreds.

Major Railroad Accidents, 1915–93

Year	Country	Deaths
1915	Scotland	227
1917	France	550
1918	United States	101
1926	Costa Rica	300
1944	Italy	521
1949	Poland	200
1957	West Pakistan	300
1970	Argentina	236
1972	Mexico	204
1981	India	268
1990	Pakistan	210

1995 Information Please Almanac, Houghton Mifflin.

Aviation Crashes

The airline industry proudly boasts that air travel is statistically far safer than travel by car, but airplane crashes have always attracted enormous attention for their drama. With the advent of widespread air travel in aircraft carrying hundreds of people, crashes became even more sensational.

March 3, 1974, Paris: A Turkish DC–10 jumbo jet crashed in a forest shortly after takeoff; all 346 passengers and crew were killed.

March 27, 1977, Santa Cruz de Tenerife, Canary Islands: Pan American and KLM Boeing 747s collided on runway. All 249 passengers on the KLM plane and 333 of the 394 people aboard the Pan Am jet were killed. The fatality total of 582 is the highest for any type of aviation disaster.

January 1, 1978, Bombay, India: An Air India 747 with 213 aboard exploded and plunged into the sea minutes after takeoff. Everyone was killed.

May 25, 1979, Chicago, Illinois: The left engine of an American airlines DC–10 dropped off seconds into the flight. The crash killed 272 on the plane and 3 on the ground, making it the worst aviation accident in U.S. history.

November 28, 1979, Mt. Erebus, Antarctica: An Air New Zealand DC–10 crashed on a sightseeing flight; 257 were killed.

March 18, 1980, USSR: Fifty people are killed at the Plesetsk Space Center when a Vostok rocket exploded on its launch pad while taking on fuel.

June 23, 1985, airborne: An Air India Boeing 747 exploded over the Atlantic Ocean off the coast of Ireland; all 329 people aboard were killed.

August 12, 1985: A Japan Airlines Boeing 747 crashed into a mountain, killing 520 of the 524 aboard.

December 12, 1985: A chartered Arrow Air DC–8, bringing American soldiers home for Christmas, crashed on takeoff from Gander, Newfoundland; all 256 aboard died.

January 28, 1986, Cape Kennedy, Florida: The space shuttle *Challenger* exploded 73 seconds after liftoff, killing all seven crew members, including New Hampshire teacher Christa McAuliffe, the first American civilian to attempt space travel.

July 3, 1988, Persian Gulf: The U.S. Navy cruiser *Vincennes* shot down an Iran Air A300 Airbus, killing 290 persons after mistaking the plane for an attacking jet fighter.

December 21, 1990, Lockerbie, Scotland: A New York-bound Pan Am Boeing 747 exploded in flight when a terrorist bomb blew up. The jet crashed into the Scottish village, killing all 259 aboard and 11 persons on the ground. The passengers included 38 Syracuse University students and many U.S. military personnel.

July 11, 1991, Jedda, Saudi Arabia: A Canadian-chartered DC–8 carrying Muslim pilgrims home to Nigeria crashed after takeoff, killing 261 persons.

April 26, 1994, Nagoya, Japan: A China Airlines airbus 300–600R from Taiwan crashed near the runway while attempting to land, killing at least 261 people and injuring 10 others.

May 11, 1996, Miami, Florida: One hundred miles into a flight from Miami to Atlanta, a Valujet DC–9 turned back because of smoke in the cockpit. Air traffic controllers lost radio contact and the plane crashed in the Everglades, killing all 109 people aboard.

July 17, 1996, New York: TWA flight 800 bound for Paris exploded over the Atlantic Ocean just south of Long Island, thirty minutes after takeoff from Kennedy airport. The reason for the explosion is unconfirmed at this writing. All 230 people aboard died.

Industrial Accidents

The advance of technology has created great potential for industrial accidents with far-reaching effects. Accidents such as these can cause extensive human casualties both when they occur and as their aftermath unfolds.

December 6, 1907, Monongha, West Virginia: 361 people died in a coal mine explosion.

April 16–18, 1947, Texas City, Texas: After a freighter carrying ammonium nitrate exploded, most of the city was destroyed in fire and 516 people died.

December 3, 1984, Bhopal, India: An explosion at a Union Carbide chemical factory released toxic gas into the air, killing a minimum of 2,352 and injuring about 150,000, some of whom may yet die as a result.

April 26, 1986, Chernobyl, USSR: An explosion and fire in the graphite core of one of the nuclear power plant's four reactors released radioactive material. The direct number of people who have died from the accident is calculated at 250, but it is expected that it will be responsible for another 100,000 cancer-related deaths.

May 10, 1993, Bangkok, Thailand: In history's worst factory fire, 187 people died and another 500 were injured when a doll factory burned.

Largest Mass Graves

Accidents, genocide, warfare and natural catastrophe have filled mass graves around the world from time immemorial. Mass graves have also been used for the burial of the destitute since Roman times, as they still are in large cities. In Rome, cities sometimes built gardens atop these sites. Up through the 19th century large paupers' mass graves were common; one in Paris was so large it could hold over 1,500 bodies. It usually took three years to fill these graves, which remained open with bodies laid out in crude coffins before they were closed. An English workhouse, St. Pancras Guardians, did not close its mass grave so that the dead could be buried in it twice a week. In northern China, the mass graves used in times of disaster carefully separated men from women. New York City's Potters Field is one of the largest mass graves in the world. The number of people who have been buried there is not known, but a marker is used now for every 150 bodies.

The Black Hole of Calcutta was a mass grave for 146 anti-British Indian rebels who were thrown into a ditch by a fortress and then buried alive.

One of the largest wartime mass graves in the 19th century was at Andersonville, Georgia, where 13,000 Union soldiers perished from starvation and disease in a prisoner of war camp. They were buried in a nearby cemetery in trenches that held 100 bodies each.

During World War II, a river in Peking became the mass grave for 20,000 Chinese soldiers and civilians killed by the Japanese. When the Russians entered Chinese territory at the end of the war, the Japanese used a large pit to hide thousands of Chinese they had killed in medical experiments. For their part, the Russians killed 4,000 Polish officers during the war and buried them near Smolensk in the Katyn Forest in a mass grave.

By far the largest mass graves were used at the close of World War II to inter the tens of thousands of unburied victims of the German concentration camps. Using bulldozers and tractors, the former guards and liberating troops removed large piles of dead bodies to their final resting place.

Satellite photography has identified the sites of recent mass graves in Bosnia and investigators have further confirmed the existence of these graves.

Oldest Graveyards

Those lucky enough to have died in less anonymous circumstances than mass plagues, abject poverty or raging warfare have often found their final resting place in the sanctified ground of a cemetery. One of the oldest cemeteries still in use is the Mount of Olives graveyard in Israel. It is a highly valued site of burial for certain Orthodox Jewish people because important religious scholars are buried there. Lots are valued by their location near these graves in the belief that these will be the first people resurrected on the Day of Judgment. Grave sites can fetch as much as $20,000.

In the United States and Europe, many graveyards of the past are noted for their impermanence. Old churchyard graveyards, unless they were quite large, generally became fixed as historic sites. But many others have been recycled, turned to other uses as circumstances demanded. As population density increased, old graveyards were sometimes relocated to new sites far out of town. For example, in 1785 the Cimetière des SS. Innocents—dating back to Roman times—was located in the center of Paris. It was closed down and paved over while some of the remains were sent to other locations.

In England by 1840, the crowded conditions of church graveyards within the city limits raised questions of sanitation. People worried about the health dangers of placing coffins one on top of the other in the same grave. In 1855, an act was passed to restrict burial grounds to the outside of the city. Even before the Burial Act of 1855, the famous Kensal Green Cemetery was laid out around the outskirts of the city by a private company.

In New York City, Potters Field was used for burying the poor. It moved to several different locations starting at Madison Square in 1794 until it reached its present location on Hart's Island. One of the oldest graveyards to be laid out in a pattern of grid streets lies in Connecticut, where New Haven's Evergreen Cemetery first opened in 1796. Mount Auburn Cemetery in Massachusetts is the oldest garden cemetery in the United States and dates from 1831. Indian mounds going back over a thousand years can be found in Appleton Cemetery located in Wisconsin.

A mansion stands in Arlington National Cemetery in Washington, D.C. Built in 1802 by George Washington's adopted son, George Washington Parke Custis, the mansion gave up its 1,100 acres of grounds to create a military cemetery in 1864. The site is still used today to bury distinguished Americans such as President John F. Kennedy.

Largest Cemeteries

Some of the world's largest cemeteries resemble parks, filled with winding paths, sculpture in various styles, meticulous landscaping and an atmosphere of peace and eternity. In New York City, such cemeteries include Greenwood and Woodlawn cemeteries; Chicago has Graceland, Indianapolis has Crown Hill and Massachusetts has Mt. Auburn in Cambridge. In Albany, New York, there is Albany Rural Cemetery; Cincinnati has Lake View; Laurel Hill is in Philadelphia; in Milwaukee there is Forest Home; and in Pittsburgh Allegheny Cemetery.

One of the largest nonprofit cemeteries in the United States is in Ohio. It was opened in 1845 and features 733 acres and 426 types of trees. Forest Lawn Memorial Parks, the first cemeteries to be termed "memorial parks," are four cemeteries located near Los Angeles and have a total area of 1,273 acres. Wisconsin has a 200-acre cemetery located in the center of Milwaukee. Many of these large cemeteries are the burial grounds of the rich and famous.

IV

The Fate of the Body

Ay, but to die and go we know not where;
To lie in cold obstruction and to rot;
This sensible warm motion to become
A kneaded clod; and the delighted spirit
To bathe in fiery floods or to reside
In thrilling regions of thick-ribbed ice;
To be imprison'd in the viewless winds,
And blown with restless violence round about
The pendant world.

—WILLIAM SHAKESPEARE,
Measure for Measure

Once death comes, the dead themselves cease to have any needs. The fate of the body is a concern strictly of the living. Communities must dispose of corpses for psychological, aesthetic and sanitary reasons; loved ones universally feel the need to honor the dead, set them on the right path to the afterlife or merely to express their grief. A multitude of variations on the theme have evolved throughout time, but humankind has generally stuck to a few basic approaches to dealing with dead bodies.

Burial may be the most ancient technique for disposing of human bodies. This ancient custom can be traced to Neanderthal communities of more than 250,000 years ago. The burial procedures of the Neanderthals appear to have been formalized and were not haphazard. Instead of simply dumping bodies into a hole in the ground, the living carefully positioned the corpse in a fetal or supine pose. Neanderthal graves contained tools, weapons or other artifacts and the bodies were laid in an east–west orientation so the head of the deceased always faced the east.

In the course of time, as human cultures were established, people developed techniques to mummify the dead. Bodies were treated with smoke to "cure" them, dressed in their best clothes and often remained in the homes of their relatives. A Chilean practice that goes back at least six thousand years involved stuffing bodies with plants and other materials after first cleaning out the cavities. The skin, which was removed before the stuffing process, was later used to cover the mummy. Wigs and masks of clay were then placed over the head and face.

The great mummy makers of history, of course, were the Egyptians. When they first developed mummification five thousand years ago, they used it mainly for pharaohs. By 400 B.C.E., mummification became a more standard burial practice for the rest of Egyptian society.

For the Greeks, burial of the body was important in order to allow the souls of the deceased to enter the lands of the afterlife. Heroes and warriors who died in battle entered the Elysian Fields. As illustrated in two great works of Greek literature, an enemy could exact revenge on the dead by preventing a proper burial. In Homer's *Iliad*, Achilles violated protocol requiring that Hector's body be returned to his relatives. Instead, he "humiliated" the body of Hector by tying it to his chariot and riding it around the walls of Troy for Hector's family to see. In Euripides's play *Antigone*, Creon vengefully refuses to bury one of his nephews, who had unsuccessfully fought with another of Creon's nephews—who was favored with a proper burial. Creon's niece Antigone, sister to the warring brothers, defies Creon and buries the ill-favored brother's body, even though doing so dooms her to death at Creon's command.

The ancient Romans also believed that proper burial allowed the deceased to enter the land of the dead. An unburied body would have to travel very far along the river Styx before being able to cross over to the land of the dead. It was the Romans' custom to throw dirt over any abandoned, unburied body they came across to help the soul find its resting place. If they knew that a relative had not been buried, they built a temple in which to make sacrifices, ensuring that the living would not suffer as a result.

Along with earth burial, cremation was also used in prehistoric and ancient times. Cremation is mentioned in the Bible and in some areas it was regarded as a regular community activity. About 1000 B.C.E., the Greeks began to use cremation for those who died of the plague, as well as for their enemies, to release the soul from the body and for the wealthy. Romans started using cremation about 750 B.C.E. as a way to honor some of their dead. During this period of Greek and Roman cremation, the Egyptians continued to practice mummification in the belief that cremation would make an after-life impossible for the dead.

Letting Nature Take Its Course

Bodies that are not cremated, preserved or protected from the elements in any special way will decay in response to various environmental factors. Forensic investigators study murder cases by considering the decay factors near unprotected bodies in order to narrow down the time and manner of death. There are a number of variable decay factors they take into consideration, such as temperature, the degree of exposure of the corpse, the surrounding insect, rodent and plant populations, the presence of other carnivores or scavengers and the amount of rainfall, ice or snow.

Heat accelerates decay; cold slows it down. Warm weather invites insects and scavengers (vultures, other carrion-eating birds or animals), thus reducing the body to a skeleton fairly quickly. Animal and insect activity diminishes in cold weather.

Chemical changes in the body proceed more rapidly in warm temperatures. Enzymes break down the digestive system and other chemical actions add to the rot and putrefaction of the body. In cold weather, insect activity declines and maggots are slower to develop. At freezing temperatures, flies and maggots on the surface of the body die, but within a frozen body maggots may still live. In 1991, a body of a prehistoric hunter over five thousand years old was found in the Alps in an excellent state of preservation. Both his body, clothes and weapons were in surprisingly good condition since they were preserved by the ice crevice he had fallen into. His age was estimated at thirty.

A human body buried in a pit or a grave without any coffin or embalming treatment will wear down to a bare skeleton within 12 years or even sooner—especially if it is a baby's body, which will take half the time of an adult's body. If the body remains in a coffin, whether of wood or some other material, after several hundred years it will become a mass of unrecognizable remains with a marked odor of decay. Dry, hot climates may mummify certain parts of the body. Skin and tendons around the bones turn to a leathery parchment while the internal organs decompose. In peat bogs, bodies have been preserved for five thousand years because of the special chemicals in the bog water and the absence of air. These "bog people" have been found throughout Europe as well as other places in the world.

How well embalming slows down the body's decay from the elements depends on how thoroughly the embalming job was carried out. The tendency has been to embalm heavily the parts of the body the relatives will see (neck, hands, face). The rest of the body does not generally receive enough embalming to make a difference in slowing down decomposition. Insects, as well as fish in the case of water burial, will be repelled by the embalming fluid, slowing decay. A good embalming job can slow decay for long periods of time, even for centuries.

The body decomposes much faster in a water burial than on land, almost four times as fast. Sometimes, however, if the water is the right temperature (from cool to cold), a chemical action known as adipocere will transform the body from its proteins into a fatty-wax. This substance markedly slows down the activity of the bacteria of decay. Bodies that have been preserved by the process of adipocere have their internal organs preserved as well.

A body slowly exposed to the vacuum of outer space would probably begin to mummify as it lost moisture. This type of mummification would be similar to the freeze-drying that takes place in the manufacture of some instant foods.

Call of the Wild: Animals and Excarnation

Many cultures throughout human history have allowed wild animals to devour their dead. This method of body disposal is called excarnation. People have used this approach from prehistoric times to the present in regions including Northeastern India, Bali, Tibet and Mongolia.

In ancient Africa and Egypt, dead slaves were cast into the desert to be eaten by jackals, wolves and hyenas. Closer to the Nile, crocodiles were used for the disposal of corpses. In Afghanistan, dogs were kept to devour the dead as well as the enfeebled elderly who were still alive. Dog owners of Central Asian nomadic tribes, usually people of means, used their dogs at their own funeral, basing their personal honor on the number of dogs that came to feast. The practice has also been observed in Siberia, where dogs are kept for this purpose, but the bones are buried. In South Africa castaway bodies have been left for the hyenas and jackals to devour.

The Zoroastrians are a notable example of the current use of excarnation. Originating in ancient Persia, they eventually settled in India and became known as Parsees, a word that means "Persians." While most cultures and religions abhor the devouring of the flesh of their dead by wild animals, the Parsees have an elaborate belief system surrounding excarnation. They see the earth as a sacred vessel. In death, the human body becomes inhabited by demons. To burn the body whole would therefore pollute the air and to bury it would pollute the earth or water. They also believe it is worthy to feed wild animals, who represent the goodness of creation.

Parsee custom calls for placing the body on a hill where either vultures or wild dogs will quickly strip the flesh of the corpse. The bones are then removed and buried. In Bombay, India, there are special towers erected to hold corpses so vultures can strip them to the bone in about an hour. The bones are swept down a shaft. These structures are called "Towers of Silence." Parsees who emigrate to Great Britain, the United States and other countries that do not allow the practice of excarnation use cremation as their funerary practice instead.

Until recently in Indochina and Australia, it was the custom of some tribes to expose dead bodies in trees, using coffins to hold them in place. After a period of time, any remaining parts would be placed on an ant hill; finally, the dry bones would be buried. Using wild animals to dispose of the dead has also been practiced by Native American peoples, especially tribes of the Great Plains, Central America and Alaska.

Christians and Lions: After the Execution

It wasn't exactly natural, but a version of excarnation appeared in the mid-3rd century B.C.E., when Rome launched a soon-to-be popular form of public spectacle: gladiator fighting. These fights to the death, pitting slaves against each other, were often held at funeral festivals. Wild animals, mostly lions and dogs, also played a role in the gladiatorial contests, which took place in large public arenas in Rome and other cities. By the time of Christ, criminals, condemned slaves and Christians entered the Roman circus of torture, violence and mass execution.

By 80 C.E., the Rome's great Coliseum amphitheater roared with the bloodlust of crowds of 50,000. When the empire's fury turned against the Christians, the religious dissidents were accused of cannibalistic and incestuous rites. Some Christians were thrown to the leopards, dogs and bears as well as to the lions in the Coliseum. Rumors cropped up, however, that some Christians seemed magically protected. The story of Androcles and the lion originated at this time, as did the story of Blandina, a young Christian girl who was tied to a stake but whom the wild animals refused to touch.

Bite Me: The Rituals of Cannibalism

Wild animals, of course, are not the only creatures who take an occasional taste of human flesh. Cannibalism has been a part of human history from the beginning, appearing in many parts of the world, such as the Pacific Islands,

Polynesia, Australia, New Zealand, South America and Africa. Not only has it served a ritual function during wartime, cannibalism can still appear during periods of acute famine. Moreover, throughout the developed world there have been contemporary instances of serial killers with a perverse appetite for human flesh.

As a cultural phenomenon, cannibalism has served symbolic purposes. Some people have believed that eating the flesh of a dead enemy warrior transferred his power to the cannibal. The same principle applied to the consumption of dead relatives; either way it showed respect to the dead.

The Greek historian Herodotus related several instances of ritual cannibalism used to honor dead relatives. According to this scholar, certain groups in Europe ate their dead fathers. One custom was to hold a feast in which the flesh of sheep was mixed with human flesh for the banqueting family members and near relatives. The skull of the dead father was afterwards given a gold setting and each year was presented for a commemorative ceremony. Herodotus also wrote of another group who killed their elders and then boiled their bodies for a large feast.

The natives of Australia and New Guinea thought it necessary to eat relatives' bodies as a way to pay respect and prevent their ghosts from returning. These funerary feasts, however, were not pleasurable. On the contrary, attendees were gloomy, regurgitated their food and showed many other signs of disgust. In one New Guinea tribe, the Gimi, women ate the decomposed corpses of male relatives in the male sanctums they normally were not allowed to enter. Living male relatives afterwards gave them parts of a pig corresponding to the human body part they had eaten. During their wedding ceremonies, women imitated ritual cannibalism they had performed.

Cannibalism may have been part of the Aztecs' elaborate system of ritual sacrifices. These sacrifices were made to placate the gods and to enable warriors to commune with them. Some estimates claim that 250,000 Central Americans were sacrificed each year up through the 15th century. First the hearts of sacrificial captives—men, women and children—were torn out of the chest and their bodies were cast down the sides of the pyramids. Warriors or other celebrants waiting below supposedly cut the bodies into pieces, placing slabs of raw flesh atop bowls of maize and passing them around. The neighbors of the Aztecs followed similar practices. Some historians, however, dispute the assertion that the Aztecs cannibalized their sacrifices.

And Now for Something Completely Different. . .

A fellow who wanted to go out with a bang reportedly asked that his cremated remains be packed into shotgun shells. His friends were to shoot his ashes over his favorite target-practice sites.

A woman who never missed an episode of her favorite soap opera wanted to continue the tradition after death. She asked to be buried with a television tuned to the appropriate channel.

Summum, a nonprofit organization in Utah, claims a membership of the only certified mummifiers in the U.S. Trained at Lynn University in Boca Raton, Florida, members also learn traditional mortuary science and work throughout the country. To date, 135 people have either used their services or have signed up to do so when they die.

People often store the ashes of loved ones in highly personalized containers. A columbarium in San Francisco reports interring cookie jars, cameras and tobacco humidors filled with cremated remains.

At a pet cemetery in Illinois, pet owners whose furry loved ones precede them to the great beyond can purchase companion plots in which their own ashes can be buried.

Ashes to Ashes: Cremation Through the Ages

Cremation has been used throughout human history, by many cultures and many faiths. For some groups it is the primary means of disposing of the body, while for others it is strictly forbidden. In a number of societies, such as ancient Greece and Rome, Tibet and Mongolia, cremation was reserved for the wealthy. By contrast, all devout Hindus in India use cremation as the centerpiece of elaborate funeral ceremonies.

The Teutons and Vikings believed in cremation. The Vikings built special burial ships for their leaders, who were placed aboard with their possessions and, often, their sacrificed servants. Mourners set fire to the boats and pushed them out to sea. The Scandinavians practiced cremation until the 11th century, when they converted to Christianity. Pre-Christian Russia also used cremation, switching to burial after converting. Today, Jews, Greek Orthodox Christians, Southern Baptists and Moslems largely disapprove of cremation, but in 1963 the Roman Catholic Church removed its ban. Of all the developed countries, Japan has the highest rate of cremation. The women of a family have the responsibility of burying the loved one's remains in the family cemetery plot.

Funeral Pyres

The funeral pyre, used since ancient days, consists of a pile of wood and sometimes a platform, upon which the body is placed and set afire. The use of funeral pyres continues today throughout Asia and other undeveloped parts of the modern world. By their very nature, cremations involving funeral pyres are quite public, and are important religious ceremonies for the groups that still engage in the practice.

Bodies placed on funeral pyres are usually covered in some way. Aboriginal Australians painted bodies with red ocher. The Babylonians covered bodies with cloth that could easily catch fire and then placed them in clay coffins inside the funeral pyres. The epic Anglo-Saxon poem *Beowulf* attests to the practice of cremation in that medieval culture:

> They built for Beowulf the band of the Jutes
> A funeral pyre; 'twas firmly based.
> They hung it with helmets as he had bidden,
> With shining byrnies and battle-shields.
> In the midst they laid, with loud lament,
> Their lord beloved, their leader brave.
> On the brow of the cliff they kindled the blaze,
> Black o'er the flames the smoke shot up;
> Cries of woe, in the windless air,
> Rose and blent with the roar of the blast,
> Till the frame of the body burst with the heat
> Of the seething heart. In sorrowing mood
> They mourned aloud their leader dead.

In India, Hindu widows were expected to grieve in an especially dramatic way, by throwing themselves upon their husbands' funeral pyres in a ritual suicide known as *suttee*. Women rarely wanted to perform *suttee*, but they were forced to do it by their husbands' relatives. British colonial rulers abolished the practice in 1829. Modern Hindu women perform a kind of figurative *suttee* by lying on their husband's pyre until it is lit.

Modern Cremation

Within the past 20 years, the rate of cremation among Americans has risen from less than 5 percent of 2 million funerals to 20 percent of the 2.2 million who died in 1992. In California, 42 percent of the dead were cremated in that period. The increased popularity of cremation in the United States may have several reasons. Cremation has a purity and simplicity that appeals to the American taste for cleanliness and economy. It also costs much less than full interment. Burial space is becoming harder to find, thus boosting costs even more and making Americans wonder how permanent any burial site really is. It is projected that by the year 2010, 40 percent of America's dead will be cremated.

The latest cremation techniques involves placing the body in a crematorium furnace, or retort, either in a wooden or metal casket that meets specific environmental standards or wrapped in a body bag or sheet. Most crematoriums use natural gas for the flame, but some use oil, propane gas or electricity. There are two burners at either side of the body and one below.

To keep smoke to a minimum, the temperatures are set anywhere from 1,100°F to 1,300°F. The burning of the coffin and body can raise the oven temperatures to as high as 2,500°F. In order to reduce the amount of smoke produced, drafts introduce air to complete combustion, although very heavy bodies will still emit black smoke and flames. The smoke and gases from the cremation process are continually recirculated to cut down on pollution.

As a further measure against air pollution, the ovens are outfitted with afterburners and scrubbers, which add to the time taken for complete cremation. Modern equipment for cremation reduces the time necessary to cremate a body, generally half an hour. It does not require preheating it can cool completely within an hour after use. Crematoriums using older equipment can do the job in about three hours.

The ash and bone fragments are collected at the bottom of the retort. The remains, or cremains, weigh about three to nine pounds (the average weight is 6.5 pounds, with a volume of 200 cubic inches), depending on the sex of the deceased. The color will vary from gray to white to yellow. Coloration may also be affected by the composition of any metal casket in which the body was placed. The remains are swept out of the retort, processed and placed in a plastic or other temporary receptacle and returned to the family.

Processing refers to reducing the remains to a granular size. If the body was cremated in a casket with metal fittings, those will be removed from the remains. Gold and surgical metal do not melt at these temperatures; large pieces such as prostheses will be removed and discarded in processing, while small pieces such as dental posts or staples stay mixed with the remains. Dental metal that contains little gold usually evaporates in the high heat or flows into cracks in the retort. If the deceased wore a pacemaker, it must be removed before cremation, because burning the device can cause an explosion.

Disposal of Ashes

Since ancient times, cremated remains have often been placed in urns and stored in columbariums. A columbarium may be an elaborate building or a simple structure suitable for the permanent housing of cremated remains. The Assyrians used urns and the Etruscans oversized pots placed on pedestals.

Columbariums are found in Italian, Grecian and Roman catacombs. Some have been discovered inside hills in such places as Mexico and Nicaragua, where the ashes are kept in a chamber called a *mogotes*. Modern Buddhists keep them on altars built into their homes.

Today, cremated remains are often cast to the winds at a favorite location designated by the deceased or chosen by survivors. Alternately, urns containing the remains may be kept by a loved one or buried in a cemetery. Modern columbaria can hold thousands of urns, labeled and stored in recessed niches. A French columbarium with 25,000 niches, built in 1887, has filled 15,000 of them. Some of these niches hold the remains of famous people from the past, such as Isadora Duncan. A San Francisco columbarium built in 1898 has been restored in San Francisco and has become a tourist attraction; weddings are held there.

Preserving the Body: Mummification and Embalming

In many religious and cultural traditions, preservation of the body after death has been seen as an essential component of respect for the dead or as a requirement for the well-being of the soul in the afterworld. Cremation, excarnation or other post-mortem methods of disposal are not options for people whose customs call for bodily preservation. In such societies, mummification or embalming, followed by some form of burial, have been the norm.

Mummy's the Word: The History of Mummification

Mummies are dried up corpses, skin over skeleton. Generally thought of as the products of human labor, they can result from natural phenomenon as well. Cold dry air, such as that in certain mountains and caves, can produce mummies, as can burial in hot, dry sand. Before the Egyptians started mummifying their pharaohs, they buried their dead in the hot sand to generate the mummy effect. Natural mummies have occurred throughout the world as a result of unusual, often accidental burial conditions. Some religious figures experienced this transformation after death, prompting outpourings of religious fervor on their behalf.

Masters of every aspect of death, the ancient Egyptians perfected the craft of artificial mummification. Actually a type of embalming, Egyptian mummification entailed the removal of the internal organs, saturation of the body cavities with oil and spices and dehydration of the body with a sodium carbonate compound called natron. Insofar as they enter a state of complete dehydration, the body parts are not really preserved. They can crumble like dust or become tough and leathery.

In their top-line mummification procedure, the Egyptian mummy makers started by removing the brain. Then they cut open the body and removed the abdominal contents, washing the internal organs with palm wine and permeating them with aromatic herbs. Next, the body cavity was filled with a number of different spices, such as myrrh and cassia. After the technicians sewed up the gut, the body was set aside for 72 days, covered by natron to further the mummy's dehydration. This substance was not used on the head and neck because it discolored the skin.

Internal organs were preserved in special jars, but the brain was discarded as useless. Believed to be the organ of intellect, the heart was left in the mummy to assist the deceased on the journey to the land of the dead. A great many cosmetic procedures were used to beautify the body during the process of mummification. Sometimes the substances used, such as hot pitch, harmed the parts of the body which the mummy makers were trying to preserve. After the drying period, the body was washed and wrapped from head to foot in fine linen smeared with a gum that acted as a glue. The mummy then went back to the relatives, who placed it in a wooden sarcophagus in a human shape. Finally, the mummy case was placed upright in a sepulchral chamber.

For Egyptians who wanted a less expensive mummification process, cedar oil was injected into the anus and forced up the intestines, thus bypassing the disembowelment process. After a 70-day drying out period the oil was allowed to flow out of the body, along with the dissolved digestive tract. In the meantime, the natron dissolved the flesh and other body parts, leaving nothing but the skin and bones. The mummy was returned to the relatives without cloth coverings or any other amenities.

In a third and still cheaper kind of mummification, the cedar oil was replaced by an enema which was used to rid the body of the digestive tract. The body was dried in natron and returned to the relatives.

Calculated in current dollars from Egyptian records, the finest mummification ran about $1,200, the mid-priced service about $300 and the economy version about $75. These costs would go up with the addition of services such as removing the fingernails and sewing gold in their place. Mummification has to a limited extent been practiced by the Chinese, the Tibetans and in Mexico, where the soil of graves naturally mummifies buried bodies.

Bodily Fluids: The History of Embalming

All human things are subject to decay,
And, when fate summons, monarchs must obey.
— JOHN DRYDEN, *Mac Flecknoe*

The earliest method of embalming entailed covering the body with fragrant substances and sap from plants. The Persians, Syrians and Babylonians preserved their dead with honey and different spices. The Incas used resinous substances, Native Americans filled the skin of the corpse with sand, Aleutian Islanders tied the body tightly in a fetal position after cleaning it out, early Mongols used musk and rose water and the Chinese used camphor and spices for three years before cremating the bodies.

The Egyptians, experts in mummification, were also the great pioneers of embalming. They began to use embalming and mummification for religious purposes about five thousand years ago. They used preservative fluids and spices on the inside and outside of the body, rather than injecting them through the arteries. They removed the internal organs and wrapped the body in special cloths and shrouds.

Evidence gathered from the 2,500-year-old mummified corpse of a Chinese woman indicates that her embalmers packed her in an airtight coffin filled with a preservative liquid. The box was enclosed in six others and buried 60 feet underground, packed in tons of charcoal and clay. When the body was found in the 1970s, it was in an excellent state of preservation. It weighed 76 pounds, the flesh and hair were in good condition and there was still flexibility in the joints. All the organs were preserved, but except for the brain they were shrunken.

While there are some biblical references to embalming, the early Christians with few exceptions refused to use embalming, because they felt it was a pagan practice and violated the corpse. An exception to this rejection was the embalming of Charlemagne in 814. Some medieval monks also maintained the practice of embalming royal corpses, with varying degrees of success. These embalmers used more than 50 different substances—some effective, some not—hoping to preserve the body long enough to move it from the field of battle or other location to the burial site. In the 16th century, surgeons (who were also barbers) were the only ones allowed to practice embalming in England. In 17th-century New England, undertakers buried the body as quickly as possible and only embalmed it if it had to be transported, by removing the internal organs and draining body fluids.

By the mid-19th century morticians developed the skill to inject embalming fluid into the blood vessels. This technique replaces the body's fluids arterially with embalming fluids, to reduce the presence of microbes and slow down the natural decomposition of the body. Embalming fluids are also designed to give the body a lifelike appearance. Odors from modern embalming substances repel insects and other invasive animals.

The Modern Embalming Process

It was not until 1867, with the discovery of formaldehyde, that embalming entered its modern age. The next great breakthrough was the injection of the formaldehyde into the arterial system of the corpse. Today, there are many derivatives and other fluids that are used instead of formaldehyde, but formaldehyde provides the chemical basis for many of these substances. The modern embalming process depends on the replacement of the body's fluids with chemicals that both disinfect and preserve the body tissues.

The embalming process involves many techniques, materials and tools. In addition to ordinary scalpels, tissue scissors, dissecting forceps, separators, aneurysm needles and syringes, the embalmer has many specialized tools at his or her disposal.

- Embalming table, either stainless steel or porcelain. The body is laid out on the table and stripped of clothing and valuables, which are returned to the family.

- Disinfectants, either sprayed or spread in solution over the body to kill insects, maggots or mites and to reduce odor.

- Nasal suction, to remove fluids. Fluids are drained from the body, or their flow is cut off.

- Positioning of the body, lifting the head and chest to assume a "restful" position. Glue is used to keep the fingers together.

- Soaps and germicidal solutions, to wash the body and destroy bacteria and viruses. The hair is washed and dressed. Blood spots are removed from the hair and the rest of the body. Often a professional beautician or hairdresser is called in for this step.

- Mouth formers, trocar buttons (used to fill up holes in the body), eye caps and trocar (long hollow needle used to remove fluids and inject embalming fluid). Used to add further cosmetic touches, especially to the head, face and neck.

- Needle and thread, used to close the mouth. Care must be taken with how the mouth is closed, to give it a pleasant rather than a tight appearance. Barbed wire inserted through the gums is also used for this procedure.

- Embalming fluids, used according to four possible methods:

  1. arterial (fluid goes into blood vessels)
  2. cavity (fluid injected into abdomen and chest)
  3. hypodermic (fluid placed under the skin in certain areas)
  4. surface (liquid or gel chemicals applied directly over the surface of the body)

A new subcategory of embalmers has emerged in recent years, reviving the ancient techniques of the Egyptians, the world's first embalmers. In 1975, a Salt Lake City company started to promote a modern method of mummification designed to outdo the Egyptians. The charge for the mummification starts at $40,000 and can reach $75,000 with all the extras. Special chemicals complete the dehydration process and the mummy is sealed in layers of fiberglass and a resin made from an epoxy-like substance. Optional add-ons include welding into a thick, molded and decorated bronze shell, the counterpart of the Egyptian wooden sarcophagus.

Six Feet Under: The History of Burial

The grave's a fine and private place,
But none, I think, do there embrace.

—ANDREW MARVELL

More common than excarnation, cannibalism or, indeed, any other method of body disposal has been simple earth burial. Over the eons, people have devised any number of ways to bury their dead. In one method, known as "burial by fragments," "disarticulate burial" or "secondary burial," the body was buried in pieces. Practices that leave the body whole may lay it out flat of flex it at the knees. Also common is the fetal position, in which the body is folded over and tied tightly. Fetal bodies might be buried seated, lying down or standing.

In the Middle East as early as the 14th century B.C.E., bodies were placed in ceramic vessels and rudimentary coffins. Later, the bones from were moved to caves closed off by large boulders. This kind of cave burial was common in Europe as well as the Middle East. The earliest cave burials left the body exposed. As the practice was refined bodies were shrouded with fabric, placed in cedarwood coffins or earthenware and finally placed in sarcophagi made of stone. Some cave burials took place in labyrinthine catacombs.

Burials of more than one person in a grave have been common throughout history. A man and wife or a mother and child might be buried this way. In the modern world, private graves in crowded cemeteries may hold up to three coffins, while the unclaimed or indigent may be laid to rest in common graves such as those at Potter's Field in New York.

Before governments started requiring that bodies be buried in officially designated cemeteries, burials might take place anywhere. Some people buried their dead under church floors, discomfiting living worshippers with the smell of dead bodies. If the floors themselves rotted, body parts might become visible.

Churchyards were common places for burial until the early part of the 19th century, when they became so crowded and ill-kept that their use was discontinued. Some people, such as Gypsies, buried their dead under bushes or at the meeting of roads, a place where criminals were hanged as well. Suicides and criminals were also buried at crossroads in the belief that the intersections would confuse their spirits and the passage of traffic would suppress their movements.

Most cultures have made special burial provisions for suicides, unbaptized children, divorced people, murderers, sex offenders and other problematic individuals. Likewise, burials of leaders and military or civic heroes have been honored by coffins draped with flags, honor guards and soldiers firing rifles.

Graves, Tombs, Crypts, Catacombs, Mounds, Pyramids and Craters

In the past, families or friends of the dead dug their graves, but by the 16th century, laws required the use of official grave diggers. Grave diggers also had the job of taking care of the graveyard, registering the deaths, ringing the death bell and other related duties. The size and depth of graves was an important issue; the cost of a grave depended on these factors. Before the advent of the backhoe, grave digging was an arduous task, taking many hours to complete. Single gravesites were used to bury successive generations of corpses. The bones of the predecessor were tossed out to make room for a new burial, or they were placed in charnel houses.

In modern times, cemeteries are designed to give the appearance of permanence. Grave markers are often placed flush to the ground and a park-like atmosphere with grass and landscapes contrasts with the gloomy appearance of the old graveyard. With the premium on choice real estate sites, it remains to be seen if these gravesites will withstand the changes of time.

Tombs can be placed either above or below ground. Buildings used to bury the dead are called tombs or mausoleums. Unlike graves, they have the advantage of being above ground, and much greater care is taken to preserve the entombed body. The Taj Mahal is an example of a tomb; it contains crypts, or burial vaults, for the family of its builder.

Catacombs, a sort of cemetery built underground, comprise tunnels and recessed rooms where coffins or tombs are placed. The catacombs of ancient Rome were used by the early Christians not only as a burial place but as a hiding place from their persecutors.

When the ancient Greeks used urns to store the cremated remains of the deceased, they called them craters. Some of these funerary urns have survived as great works of art, beautifully crafted and decorated with painting or sculpture. Mythological characters and scenes convey the attitudes the Greeks had about both life and death. Echoing the practice of the Greeks, many cemeteries and memorial parks today provide special space for urn burials of cremated remains.

Prehistoric mound-building cultures used earthen structures as tombs. The Egyptians progressed from simple mounds and tombs to the age of great pyramid building. The Great Pyramid of Cheops was built with over 5 million tons of stone. It covers more than 13 acres and stands 481 feet high. It took more than 20 years to build, requiring the labor of upwards of 400,000 workers, mostly slaves. Pyramids were designed to provide the ultimate security against grave robbers, but over the centuries invading armies were able to make a considerable dent and looters found their way in.

Evolution of the Burial Ground

Because of concern about sanitary conditions, ancient Romans, Jews, Egyptians and Chinese built their burial grounds outside of their main cities. These large burial sites were referred to as "cities of the dead." Christians, on the other hand, did not exhibit the same concern. In their early catacombs and later churches, they worshipped right alongside the dead. By the 6th century, the overcrowding of catacombs became so bad that Christians, too, started using burial grounds outside the city. They continued to use church property within the cities until the 18th century, when these plots became hopelessly overcrowded.

One advantage of church graveyards was that families had access to the grave sites at no expense as long as they were members of the congregation. The disadvantage was that churches took in no money for the care of these cemeteries. Today's cemeteries are also nonprofit, but the town or city that owns the land or the association that takes care of it charge fees for the plots to cover maintenance.

In London, legislation was passed in 1855 prohibiting churchyard burials. About this time large cemeteries were built outside the city and a major effort was made to curtail burials in town. The out-of-town burial remains the standard practice in most major cities throughout the world.

Early settlers in America buried their dead on their farms. Later, the church became the focus for burials. In the 17th and 18th centuries important leaders of the community were buried beneath the churches themselves. Church graveyards in small towns were ill-maintained and had an unsavory reputation among those who buried the dead. Boston was the first American city to gain a detached graveyard, which opened in 1832. Philadelphia soon followed; Greenwood cemetery was established in New York in 1842. From 1860 on, churchyard burials have been few and exceptional.

Potter's Field: Burying the Poor and the Anonymous

Into the early 19th century, English authorities sometimes refused burial to debtors in order to pressure his or her survivors to pay the debts. Records going back to the 16th century show many incidents of bodies being held for the purpose of debt collection, but there are no records showing if these attempts met with success. It was an unpopular practice and was made illegal. Similarly, in the U.S. most states passed laws forbidding the interruption of a burial or the seizure of a body as collateral for a debt. Mortuaries have been known, however, to hold embalmed bodies for long periods of time when they could not collect payment for their services.

For centuries, pauper's graves were common throughout Europe; some contain the bodies of great geniuses, like Mozart, who died poor. The U.S. has also had its potters fields, some of which have become building sites or parking lots. Along with those of executed criminals, the bodies of the poor have also been used by medical schools for dissection.

Mass graves appear during times of crisis, such as natural disasters, famine, plague and war. Confronted with large numbers of anonymous or unclaimed corpses, the living need an efficient means of disposal. Mass graves have also been used for burial of the poor. Rather than cremate their poor (it was considered the burial of choice for the wealthy) the ancient Romans buried them in mass graves outside the walls of the city. These mass graves were far from sacred and were often turned into parks and gardens. Some British workhouses in the mid-19th century saved money by stockpiling the bodies of dead inmates for mass burial.

Pet Cemeteries

In ancient Egypt cat cemeteries were common, for the cat was worshipped as a sacred animal and was mummified after death. The rise of Christianity consigned dead pets to oblivion, both because animals were believed not to have souls and because they were central to so many pagan traditions. In the modern world, pets have assumed an honored place in developed countries. They are beloved, but they have a shorter life span than their owners, so bereaved pet owners must decide what to do with Fido's or Fluffy's body.

A growing number of Americans have turned to pet cemeteries. Pet cemeteries illustrate the tremendous love people have for their pets. Caskets and gravesites are carefully selected. Pet graves have headstones that may contain a picture of the pet, the pet's name, its date of birth and death, the owner's name and an epitaph, often in rhyme. The public has been horrified when scandals arise around pet cemeteries, as when the owners are discovered to be throwing bodies away or selling them to scientific laboratories or rendering operations that reduce animal bodies to tallow.

The Men in Black: Morticians and Their Craft

In Western civilization, the task of ushering the body from deathbed to grave has fallen to specialists referred to as morticians or undertakers. The undertaker's job has evolved from ancient Rome, where a special temple sold funeral supplies and managed the slaves that worked on the body. In 1675, William Boyce opened an undertaker's shop in England, one of the first to provide the services now recognized as the funeral director's job. By the mid-18th century, many English families used private undertaking businesses. Undertakers often operated on a part-time basis, while furniture makers made coffins. Others specialized in services like grave digging and transport of coffins in carriages. In 1768, Blanche White of New York set up a business that provided both upholstering and undertaking services; in 1820 Mrs. Benjamin Birch launched a combined cabinet-making and undertaking venture in Montreal, Canada.

After the American Civil War the advent of arterial embalming with formaldehyde elevated the undertaker's profession. Business people who knew embalming or could afford to hire embalmers had access to specialized skills and could operate on a full-time basis. The National Funeral Directors Association was organized in 1882. Early in the 20th century, the term mortician replaced undertaker, a title in use since the late 17th century. The term funeral director came into use in the late 19th century to describe those who oversee the body's passage from deathbed to grave. By 1920, the NFDA boasted 10,000 members.

Changes continue to occur in the funeral industry as it adapts to changing attitudes about disposal of the body and learns to satisfy demanding customers who know their rights. Today's funerary professionals prefer to be called funeral directors. The funeral director stores the body, issues the death certificate and other documents, arranges to have the body cleaned and embalmed and sells the casket to the survivors. He or she also helps work out the details of the manner of body disposal, negotiates with the cemetery owner for a burial plot or a niche in a columbarium. Funeral directors arrange the funeral service, placing a death notice in the paper, planning the viewing of the body and the service itself, scheduling the hearse and supervising the procession to the cemetery.

Funerals Really Are Big Business

Based in Houston, Texas, Service Corporation International (SCI) is the largest chain of funeral homes in the world. SCI runs 1,471 funeral homes—771 of them in the United States—and also owns 204 cemeteries and 68 crematoriums in the U.S. The typical SCI funeral home performs 250 funerals annually, although in "peak periods" a facility might handle four funerals in a single day. With total volume of a quarter-million funerals per year, SCI pulls in annual revenues of $1.1 billion.

V

The Great Beyond

Seekers ask: What is the purpose of life, given the certainty of death?
—The Katha Upanishad

Dying is a sacred act, for individuals and societies worldwide. All major religions honor death in specific ways to remind believers of the impermanence of this life, and to affirm that what lies beyond death is infinitely more meaningful. The purpose of earthly identity (and its inevitable demise) have absorbed human thinking since the beginning of time. For the preservation of a tribe, a culture, the human species and, indeed, for the planet as well, the meaning of death is a vital focus of life.

Why do humans die? How did death first become a part of the human condition? From stories told around small tribal fires to sermons preached in cathedrals, the reasons for death center on eight primary concepts, according to religious scholar, Th. P. Van Baaren. In these paradigms, the most obvious reason—that organic life is finite; that matter decays and decomposes—is brushed aside. Humans need more than scientific description.

1. Death is a natural act, or at least it is in accordance with the will of the gods and therefore must be accepted.

2. Man is fated to die as a result of a god's dying first, establishing a precedent for mortals.

3. A conflict among gods caused death, with man taking the consequences.

4. Man has been cheated or duped by the carelessness of a god, and death is the result.

5. Human shortcomings—inherent weakness—account for death.

6. Death is the result of wrong choices or bad judgments made by man.

7. Some form of guilt, due to the nature of man (sin, or a quality such as disobedience or curiosity) has caused death.

8. Because man himself has desired death, it is his fate to die.

The Immortal Soul: Timeless Essence

Once the "reason" for death has been established, the wise and the holy (as well as ordinary folk) move on to the next question: "Then what?" The nearly universal belief in immortality of the soul reflects human desire to know the unknowable, to have the assurance that one's existence, in some form, continues forever. Philosophical and religious traditions offer a wide range of possibilities. Devotional practices, rituals, prayers, meditations and everyday acts of righteous living show the way to eternal life. Since ultimately the afterlife is a mystery, faith is a vital ingredient.

From earliest times, humans have left archaeological traces of their interest in the soul. Megalithic grave designs from the Bronze Age indicate a belief that some element of the deceased has continuity beyond the grave. Spiral petroglyphs indicate the movement of the stars through the night sky or the rippling of waters moving outward infinitely. The petroglyphs are positioned so that they are struck by rays of the sun, particularly on the solstices, coming through cracks in the structure. Resembling the pattern of the sun's sinking into the sea each evening and rising again each day, the spirals relate (it has been hypothesized) to a notion of death and resurrection.

Soul is often defined as that which gives life to any animate thing. It is the inner, noncorporeal, essential part of an animate entity. Soul is often connected to "breath." Plato expanded earlier Greek philosophies to define *pneuma* (wind) as the "breath of the universe." He identified this, on a microcosmic level, as the psyche of a human being.

In Islamic Shi'ism, *ruh* is the pure breath of all matter, a spiritual substance immortal by nature. In Hindu traditions, it is believed that each person has a definite number of breaths per lifetime. When that number is up, death occurs. An old story in this tradition tells of a great spiritual teacher who asked his assistant if a good day to die was coming up. When the teacher learned that a sacred day was to occur three days hence, he slowed his breathing to extend his time. On the sacred day, he died with a smile on his lips. For the Chinese, *ch'i* (breath, energy) has a timeless quality. When one is alive, the ch'i is focused or concentrated. When one dies, the ch'i is dispersed into the universe.

In Judaic biblical works, the coming of the Messiah, resurrection of the dead and immortality of the soul form the basis of conceptual teachings about the soul. There is, as within all major religions, great variation in Jewish thought. The Hasidim and the Cabalistic forms of Judaism espouse belief in reincarnation. Exactly how divine will manifests is a question scholars have pondered for centuries. Many contemporary Jews see their religion as completely this-worldly, believing that one lives on through his or her work, and through offspring. However, a majority of Jews affirm that their religion is both this-worldly and otherworldly, seeing that life is good in itself but receives its ultimate meaning as preparation for the soul's eternal existence with God.

Christians do not believe that immortality is a natural consequence of perfecting human nature, but rather a gift granted by God for those who are transformed by the Holy Spirit through Jesus Christ. Christians developed a particular notion of a dichotomy between body and soul, with the soul deemed immortal and the body related to sin. Over time and transformations, the Christian afterlife has become a vision of the eternal soul reunited with a transformed body, in the presence of God, after the Final Judgment of humankind. A fundamental notion of Christianity is that through the death and resurrection of Jesus, humankind was offered salvation, or freedom from death: the wages of man's sins.

Within each religion, fundamental concepts reflect a wide range of beliefs. The notions of personal resurrection and "one soul/one body" generally preclude the idea of reincarnation, but many Christians, influenced by Eastern religions and psychology, incorporate this idea in their beliefs. The Chinese concept of two souls (which dates from the 11th century to 256 B.C.E.) is still practiced in limited form among some groups. The yin, or feminine soul, *p'o*, was believed to follow the body into the underworld, known as Yellow Springs. Its masculine complement, the yang soul, *hun*, moved out of the body into the universe and could be venerated as an ancestor. The p'o protected the body after death. Specific rituals to preserve the body were necessary to insure that the p'o did not leave the body, that it was not invaded by negative forces, and did not bring ill fortune to the living. Offerings and prayers assured the well-being of the p'o soul of an ancestor. In China, from about 400 B.C.E., it was also believed that some men had achieved immortal status. These immortals (*hsien*) died like everyone else but left their tombs. Hsien were transformed into birdlike beings who were free to wander the earth, advising humans; they could fly among the stars in a perfect spectral body for eternity.

The secret of death, according to the holy book of Hindu culture, The Katha Upanishad, is to realize the Supreme Self, which goes far beyond an individual soul. The Supreme Self lives at the heart of all beings as the True Self, the deathless Self. Specific yogic and meditation practices, as well as divine grace, comprise the path to this deathless death (dying into the One).

Similar in many ways to the Hindu religion from which it evolved, Buddhism regards the ultimate goal of existence to be a quality of no-soul, or *anatta*. Enlightened beings have evolved beyond the personal soul, into the One. This process is much too difficult to achieve in one lifetime, thus a soul must go through an almost endless cycle of births, deaths and rebirths (*samsara*). *Karma*, the natural laws of cause and effect, determines how a soul will reincarnate into a new bodily identity. Evolving through one's karma by the actions performed in that lifetime (*dharma*) leads eventually to release from the cycle, freeing the personal soul to its *Atman* (True Self). Atman unites with Brahman, the One, the Ultimate Ground of existence, a quality of pure essence beyond any condition of personal identity.

The ancient Egyptian concept of the soul delineated specific types of spiritual aspects. Each person was believed to have:

- *kaò,* a vital force that leaves the body at death and travels to meet its heavenly double in the kingdom of Osiris, dwelling forever in both the tomb and in paradise.
- *baò,* the conscience, or heart, which faced the final judgment.
- *akh,* the transfigured spirit.
- *ba,* the power of animation after death.

Near-Death Experiences: The Previews

The near-death experience, a set of phenomena which can occur after clinical death (see Chapter 2), has been cited as evidence for life after death and immortality of the soul. Accounts of near-death experiences date back hundreds of years, recorded by philosophers such as Plato and modern writers such as Melville and Tolstoy. The near-death experience was first studied scientifically by 20th-century physician Elizabeth Kübler-Ross, who saw a great need to prepare the dying for death. Interest in near-death studies resulted in the establishment of the International Association for Near-Death Studies in 1981.

Kübler-Ross conducted a study of approximately 20,000 people and compiled a list of the common themes of near-death experiences. Her findings were later corroborated by Dr. Raymond Moody, author of *Life After Life*, Robert A. Monroe, who wrote *Journeys Out of the Body*, and others. To rule out cultural, age or religious background biases, Kübler-Ross studied a wide range of individuals. The youngest subject was 2 years old, the oldest, 97. They hailed from the United States, Australia, Canada and other countries. Subjects reflected a broad range of cultural and religious backgrounds, including Inuit, ethnic Hawaiians, Australian Aboriginals, Hindus, Buddhists, Protestants, Catholics, Jews, agnostics, atheists and others with no religious views.

The near-death experiences documented by Kübler-Ross were preceded by various life-threatening events, including accidents, murder attempts, suicide attempts and lingering deaths. All of the experiences reported occurred when there were no measurable signs of brain activity, no signs of life whatsoever. Commonalities found among near-death experiences (not all share all traits) are:

- Separation of a spiritual essence from the body, with an absence of pain.

- A sense of physical wholeness in this out-of-the-body self, even if the body one has just "left" is disfigured or disabled.

- The out-of-body spirit hovers over the scene of death, watching in a detached manner.

- Awareness of the entire scene, including the people working on the body: their thoughts, conversations, behavior and attire, with no negative feelings about the situation.

- The experience of physical perfection; what Kübler-Ross calls the "temporary, ethereal body". Amputees report having legs, deaf-mutes give exact reports of the speech and sounds heard, the blind can describe in accurate detail what they see.

- Being surrounded by loving guides, angels or beloved deceased family members and friends.

- A quality of timelessness and complete spaciousness. In this existence one can be anywhere he or she chooses, at the speed of thought.

- Travel through a passageway, often described as a tunnel, sometimes as a river or a gate. (Kübler-Ross assumes this symbolic transition is culturally determined.)

- Approaching a source of incredibly beautiful, unforgettable light; a cosmic consciousness.

- Absolute unconditional love in the presence of this light, which most people in the western hemisphere called Christ or God, understanding and compassion. It is in this presence that the subject becomes aware of his or her potential, of what he or she could be like.

- A review and evaluation of one's total existence, with the sense of being all-knowing and all-understanding.

- Leaving the ethereal, simulated body and resuming the form one had before birth, the form one will have when merged with the source, with God, when one's destiny is completed.

- The being of light instructs the dying person to return to his or her body, to return to life. Reluctantly, the subject chooses to do so for the sake of loved ones who would be left behind.

- Upon return to the physical body, subjects lead very different lives. They no longer fear death and realize the importance of love in ways never before experienced. With a sense of connectedness to all living things and other people, appreciation of the true meaning of life guides them.

Critics of the spiritual nature of near-death experiences argue that medications or disturbances of brain functioning, among other things, can account for the near-death visions. Supporters of the out-of-body thesis respond that the dying patients register flat EEGs (electroencephalograms), meaning that all brain activity has stopped. Also, near-death experiences occur in people who have not received hallucination-producing medications, or, often, any medications at all, as in cases of sudden injury.

Although not the norm, horrifying experiences while out of the body have been reported. According to Tibetan spiritual teacher Sogyal Rinpoche, near-death experiences parallel some stages of death as outlined in the Bardo Thödol. Sogyal asserts that people probably forget the negative experiences upon return to the body.

Flowers and Trees and Death

Many Buddhists believe that a person's soul is transported upon a lotus flower.

Aztecs called their otherworldly paradise Xochitlicacan, the "place of flowers." The Huichol Indians of Mexico also believe in a paradise filled with flowers. To reach this paradise while still alive, Huichols ingest peyote buds and in a near-death experience say that they travel to meet with their ancestors.

Greeks and Romans believed that amaranth, a sacred flower, granted immortality.

Christians associate willows, cedars and evergreens with death and everlasting life. These trees are commonly planted in American cemeteries.

Among Hindus, sandalwood is used for making incense, for embalming and for constructing funeral pyres.

One-Way Ticket: The Passage Between Worlds

Since prehistoric times, cultures and religions have created art and stories, mythic maps of the afterlife, to guide souls to their destination and assist the vital life force on its journey "home." The passage must be carefully navigated, and rigorous procedures must be observed. The symbols of flight, movement and crossing over are used to describe the passage from this life to whatever lies beyond. Images of boats and bodies of water predominate in cultures located near water. A common feature of these journeys is a moment of judgment.

The question of judgment after death, particularly in Christian traditions, has a twofold meaning. On the one hand, each individual is judged after death, based on the merits of his or her personal life. The mass of humanity will also be judged collectively, on the Day of Judgment, or the Last Day. This is when Christ will appear on earth (the Second Coming) and take the righteous into Heaven. For Catholics, a priest gives the sacramental Last Rites to commend the soul of the dying person to God, through prayer.

In the Egyptian Books of the Dead, judgment took place in the underworld Hall of Maat, the goddess of justice. When the soul confessed that it had no sins, its ab, or heart, the seat of conscience, was weighed against a feather. Horus, the Sky God, attended the balance; and Thoth, Scribe of the Dead, acted as an impartial witness. A crocodile-headed monster, the Devourer of Souls, waited under the scale to swallow any heart heavy with sin. Those whose hearts passed the judgment were led by Horus to join Osiris in the paradise of the Happy Fields.

Early Grecian mythology held that the soul, upon leaving the body, crossed the River Styx to get to Hades. Charon, the ferryman, is portrayed as a cantankerous, shrewd, eccentric man who decides which souls will be allowed passage. Virgil's *Aeneid* gives an explanation for Charon's choices when Sibyl tells Aeneas:

> *Those who are taken on board the bark are the souls of those who have received due burial rites; the host of others who have remained unburied are not permitted to pass the flood, but wander a hundred years, and flit to and fro about the shore, till at last they are taken over.*

A vital part of the myth is that souls must bring a coin for Charon as payment for transport. This accounts for the burial practice of laying two coins on the deceased's eyes or one under the tongue.

Prominent in Zoroastrianism, a Persian religion, is the Chinvat Bridge, the site of the final judgment. On the bridge, the soul of the deceased is judged for the thoughts, words and actions of the life just lived. Based on the judgment, the soul is then either led into heaven or hurled into hell beneath the bridge.

In some Native American stories, the spirit must walk a narrow wooden beam to gain access to the great beyond. Because the soul is believed, in some traditions, to linger near the body soon after death, a holy person must perform rituals and prayers to assist lost souls on their journey.

In Tibetan tradition, at the burial site a shaman projects his spirit into the otherworld to guide souls away from the living and onto the right path to the next world. Hindu and Buddhist religions detail at least seven heavens and as many hells, which are transitory states of existence between incarnations. The Bardo Thödöl (which means "liberation through hearing on the after-death plane"), better known as The Tibetan Book of the Dead, is the ancient Buddhist text which guides the dying toward salvation. The Tibetan Book of Dying gives specific instructions for those attending a dying person. It also characterizes the intermediate (bardo) plane, including vivid descriptions of the demons and gods one will encounter at one level. The soul, on its journey, must regard these heavenly and hellish experiences as illusory and pass through them. Once the soul leaves the bardo, it reincarnates into a new body. The Tibetan Book of Dying also provides the means for seeking salvation.

Prior to the introduction of Buddhism from India, the Chinese heaven and hell were thought of geographically, as regions beyond China's borders. With the advent of Buddhism, the majestic Mount T'ai to the west was regarded as both the place where life began and where the dead came to be judged.

Why is That Done at Funerals?

Undertakers, mourners, and pallbearers wear black to show their grief and as a disguise to protect themselves from malevolent spirits and ghosts that might be hovering nearby.

Don't wear new clothes, especially new shoes, to a funeral. The dead might become envious. That's why, traditionally, mourners wore sackcloth and ashes and went barefoot.

Why does traffic halt for a funeral procession? Because any delay in transporting a soul might make it into a restless ghost, intent on tarrying in this world rather than passing over into the next.

In England, the dead were always carried out of the house feet first. Otherwise, the spirits might glance back into the house and beckon family members to accompany them to the grave.

Funeral wreaths reflect pagan beliefs. Their circles are designed to keep the dead person's spirit within bounds.

Afterworlds: Good, Bad, Indifferent

The soul's passage to the next world brings it, in the majority of religions, to a place of eternal reward or eternal punishment. Most religions assume a three-part universe of heaven, earth and hell. Heaven is located above the earth, perhaps because the spirit is considered to rise; and since bodies—often the locus of sin—are generally buried in the ground, hell is depicted as below the earth. Heavens are vast, light, airy; hells are dense, dark and extremely hot or icy cold (or a torturous combination of both). Descriptions of existence in heaven and hell are quite vivid. For those traditions that view the afterlife as a judgment for the dead, heaven is a place where one's goodness is rewarded; hell is an abode of suffering for sins. The primary distinction of religious traditions is whether heaven and hell are final destinations, or temporary passages toward another, more essential existence.

Paradise: The Ultimate Reward

For religions that believe in a final abode for righteous souls, that setting is described abundantly. Paradise reflects what each culture or religion values most highly here on earth. The greatest reward of every paradise, however, is the attainment of eternal bliss in the presence of the divine.

Christians view heaven as the realm of reward for one's earthly existence. Belief in Jesus Christ as Lord and Savior is the primary foundation for ascension into heaven, where one's soul dwells with God in eternal peace. Christian images reflect a blissful state where good souls commune with God and the angels, amid white clouds, flowers and birds. The white rose, in Western tradition, symbolizes perfect and pure love. Winged angels, golden paths and pearly gates symbolize heavenly bliss. In his *Paradiso*, the Italian poet Dante Alighieri described nine heavens, advancing in importance and magnificence, that await those who have earned entrance on their merits. Beyond the nine heavens is the realm of God and the saints, where there is no time or space, only pure light.

Ancient Egyptian Books of the Dead described a paradise quite similar to the best of earthly life: fertile fields, great harvests.

Tibetan images of paradise include the lotus flower—pristine, delicate, many-petaled—unfolding in the sun.

Native Americans envisioned a happy hunting ground, with plentiful game and food.

Hell: Penance Down Below

The landscape of hell was described in rich detail by Dante in his *Divine Comedy*. Working within the Christian tradition, Dante envisioned nine concentric circles, progressively smaller and more intense in terms of the sins and punishments, ending in a conical point where the ice-cold monster—Lucifer, Satan, the Devil—resides. The torments of the soul on its agonizing descent are neither quick nor easy.

The Hebrew Gehinnom (Greek: Gehenna), found in postbiblical Judaic works and in the New Testament, is the Jewish denotation of hell. Its name is derived from the Valley of Ben Hinnom where children were burned in fire in the worship of Moloch. Although there are lurid descriptions of torment, and of fire and ice, hell is primarily considered as a metaphorical concept, rather than as a literal place of torture. Hell is generally considered in terms of "the remoteness of the souls of the most wicked from God."

In Islam, the Koran gives vivid descriptions of both heaven and hell as final destinations for the righteous and the damned, based on God's judgment of each individual's life deeds. Upon judgment, each man and woman passes over the bridge of al-Aaraf. Infidels fall into hell; the faithful sail into heaven. Replete with all the worst and the best that mortals can imagine, hell is a realm of eternal torture and heaven is a lush and sensuous abode of everlasting bliss.

Purgatory: A World of Its Own

The Greek notion of "afterdeath" is quite different from the Christian concept, with Hades being the final repository of souls. It is not a place of torment and punishment, as is the Christian hell, but rather a quasilife, devoid of meaning, where souls wander aimlessly forever, as shadows of their former selves.

For Roman Catholics, purgatory is an intermediate realm between heaven and hell, where souls who are not extremely good or evil go for purification. The Catholic concept of purgatory seems to have been influenced by the Persian Zoroastrian tradition. Its main elements are purification by a temporary punishment, so that the soul may enter heaven unblemished. Dante described the Roman Catholic purgatory in his *Purgatorio*, portraying the arduous penance souls must accomplish to pass through a wall of flames into the realm of the saved.

In close relation to the Catholic purgatory is the concept of limbo, a temporary realm for the souls of babies who have died unbaptized. These infant souls enter heaven after a very brief stay in limbo. The prayers of the living assist the souls' movement.

Beyond the Great Beyond: Other Fates for the Soul

Resurrection: A New Life

For some Christians, God's incarnation as the flesh-and-blood Jesus Christ, culminating in his crucifixion and resurrection, offers believers escape not only from figurative, spiritual death but, ultimately, from physical death as well. The resurrection from the dead of Jesus Christ, part human, part divine Savior, demonstrates for Christians the reality of eternal life and extends to them the promise of the same. Christians believe in the concept of personal resurrection and the transformation of the whole self after death. Biblical teachings refer to the resurrection of believers in two distinct ways. Individual resurrection occurs after death and personal judgment, with the souls of the righteous ascending to heaven and those of the damned descending to hell. A collective resurrection of humanity is also foretold. Upon the Second Coming of Christ, signaling the end of all time, the righteous will be taken into heaven to live with God for eternity.

These concepts have been studied and interpreted by church scholars for centuries. One question is: What will be resurrected? Conservative Christians believe the body in its most perfected form (as it was, or would have been, before death) will be resurrected. Others adhere to a belief that the spirit of each individual will exist in eternity.

Eschatology, "the science of the last things," relates to resurrection as a component of the end to the known world. Each religion's cosmology includes the end as well as the beginning of creation. Beliefs about the end include visions of the kingdom of God; a new heaven and a new earth; the restoration of paradise as it was before the Fall of Man. Nihilistic beliefs conceive the end as the twilight of the gods; the end of the world; extinction.

In Old Testament terms, the resurrection of the chosen people relates to the nation of Israel. Orthodox Jews believe that with the coming of the Messiah, the faithful will be resurrected from the dead. As with Christians, ambiguities exist for Jews around the notion of what is resurrected: the body or its spiritual manifestation. Furthermore, the integral connection of body and soul influences beliefs about burial. Orthodox Jews (as well as certain Christian denominations) do not support the practice of cremation, believing that it denies the doctrine of bodily resurrection.

For Muslims, resurrection of the body is an essential element of Islamic teaching. On the Day (*yawm*) of the Awakening (*ba'th*) the dead will rise to their feet for their final judgment. This prayer from the Koran is recited at mosques on the Sabbath (Friday). It expresses the Muslim belief in immortality, and the belief that on the day of judgment true life will begin.

Reincarnation: Many Bodies, One Essence

Some religions conquer death via reincarnation, the rebirth of the deceased's soul in another physical shell. The notion of reincarnation is founded on that of transmigration, the idea that after death some spiritual or ethereal part of the person migrates and enters another body (human or animal). Transmigration is essential to ancestor worship traditions, which believe that the spirit of a deceased ancestor reenters the community through the body of a newborn descendant.

In Hinduism and Buddhism, transmigration is related to the cycle of samsara (going through, wandering) whereby the soul passes through successive lives in accordance with karma—the impersonal laws of natural cause and effect—and dharma, the deliberate acts of a lifetime (which include yogic practice and meditation). Samsara can also mean everyday life in the world. It is not possible to achieve perfection in one lifetime. Thus, the soul is bound to the wheel of life: a succession of births, deaths and reincarnations. When a soul evolves to the point of liberation (*moksha*) it becomes Atman, the True Self, merging with Brahman, the Ultimate Ground of existence, beyond any personal identity.

Reincarnation, for Hindus, is based on a hierarchical caste system wherein there is no upward mobility within a lifetime. Early Buddhists rejected the notion of caste, believing instead that anyone not achieving enlightenment would be reborn as a god, a human, an animal or a ghost (*preta*). Reincarnation, as one Buddhist teacher described it, can be understood by contemplating "the image of lighting one candle from the flame of another."

We've Got Contact

Many people believe that the living and the dead are not forever separated once the dear departed reach their postmortem destinations. Such beliefs may be formalized in religious form or may assume the shape of superstitions that combine religious, cultural and scientific elements.

Ancestor Worship: Veneration and Continuity

Many societies believe that the dead who live on in the netherworld continue to influence earthly events. Tribes and cultures that worship ancestors believe the wisdom of deceased elders and leaders can be sustained to guide and unite the entire community. The term "worship" can be problematic, as the practices and beliefs of ancestor-worship traditions are often similar to those of other cultural and religious groups that otherwise honor and remember deceased relatives. The Bantu-speaking peoples of Africa, for instance, dis-

Suicide: Whose Life Is It?

What is worth living for is worth dying for.
—ALBERT CAMUS

Most often, religion delineates the fate of the soul after death in accordance with the events of earthly life, but the manner of death—especially when suicide is involved—can also have repercussions for the soul's eternal destiny. Suicide, the voluntary act of ending one's life, is a complex ethical and moral issue. The practice of and attitudes toward suicide greatly depend on individual and societal views on the afterlife.

The Dialogue of a Misanthrope with His Own Soul, an Egyptian text, is the first known document that seems to deal with suicide. This work views death as attractive, since it leads to a better existence. Most religions do not condone suicide if an individual is considered to be of sound mind. Judaism generally asserts that the taking of one's own life denies that life is a divine gift, and that suicides will not share in the World to Come. Christianity takes the position that one's life is not one's own, but rather belongs to God. It is God's decision when life will end. In the Middle Ages, Christians who committed suicide were prosecuted posthumously and their bodies were ejected from cemeteries.

Religions do, however, support suicides that are motivated by altruism and martyrdom: those who passively accept death as divine will, in service to God. Some religious traditions integrate a form of self-willed death as a spiritual act. *Sallekhana* is a specifically approved form of suicide, sanctioned by Jainists, followers of the saint Mahavira. Through this act of faith, one can free himself from the cycles of karma. Sallekhana is a gradual starvation process supervised by a monk. When a person is seriously ill or debilitated by old age, sallekhana is considered to be the culmination of spiritual striving and meditation.

Still, religiously motivated suicides involve complex issues, and they are not universally supported. The Jonestown, Guyana, mass suicide in 1978 brought reactions of shock and horror. Jim Jones, founder of The People's Temple, led 60 of his followers to their voluntary death, promising they would enter a new and better world where they would not be persecuted and would enjoy the rewards of God's elect.

Now quite rare, a kind of religiously motivated suicide dating from medieval times is the Hindu custom of *suttee,* in which the widow of a warrior was expected to throw herself upon her husband's burning funeral pyre. The purpose of this self-sacrificial practice was the woman's atonement for her own sins as well as those of her husband.

In opposition to religious belief, humanists have argued throughout history that the decision to end one's life is a basic individual right. The ancient Roman philosopher Seneca was a proponent of the individual's right to choose death. In recent times, suicide as a personal decision has been espoused by Minnesota pediatrician Dr. Jack Kevorkian, who has medically assisted individuals in ending their lives. Kevorkian claims that religious leaders impose what they consider a "universal medical ethic" on secular institutions. He contends that so-called medical ethics are actually religious ethics. In a 1994 speech he stated, "So, if you meet a physician who says, 'Life is sacred,' be careful. We didn't study sanctity in medical school."

tinguish between ancestors who are a real force in the community, called *vidye,* and the ordinary dead, called *fu,* who become ghosts or shadows. While fu are honored at grave sites and given ritual attention at family shrines, the vidye influence the culture as a whole and are invoked for many generations.

Far Eastern religions (Shinto in Japan, Confucianism in China and some Buddhist sects) are the most prevalent examples of ancestor worship. It is also practiced among some African tribes. Each society's concept of the afterlife determines the forms, rituals and meanings of ancestor worship. Some cultures elevate ancestors to the status of gods. The Boshongo, for example, a central African Bantu tribe, describe the world's creation as the work of the deity Bumba, who is also a tribal ancestor.

Other faiths simply set aside time to remember and honor the dead. The Japanese create altars at which they offer prayers and perform ceremonies. The altars are adorned with special objects and offerings to the deceased ancestors. Offerings can serve to make the existence of ancestors in the afterlife more pleasant. The Chinese offer spirit money to the gods of the underworld to alleviate an ancestor's suffering. Deceased relatives are also believed to have powers of intervention in the affairs of the living, and thus must be treated with reverence to assure good fortune.

Necromancy

Practitioners of necromancy believe the living can make direct contact with the dead to benefit from their wisdom. Deriving from the Greek words *nekros* (dead) and *manteia* (divination), this occult practice dates back to ancient Persia, Egypt and Rome and is still practiced in some cultures. Although divination is a universal phenomenon throughout the world, necromancy is often associated with magic, sorcery or witchcraft. It does not include using mediums (as does spiritualism or spiritism) or encounters with souls through shamanic journeys. Apparitions of ghosts also are not a part of necromantic process.

The dead, believed in necromancy to have great prophetic powers, are summoned forth to provide information, usually about the future, or about unknown causes. The spirit of the dead person is summoned, but sometimes the corpse is also called back to life. One occult theory is that some of the dead person's body energy remains in the astral corpse after the soul leaves the body. This astral corpse may be evoked to return to the physical plane by the power of magic.

If the deceased was murdered, his or her spirit can be called forth to reveal the identity of the murderer. Without the limitations of mortality, dead spirits are believed to be all-knowing and all-seeing. In Western occult tradition, necromancy is believed to be most effective when performed within twelve months of a person's death, as this is thought to be the time period that the soul hovers near its grave.

Although there are numerous accounts of necromancy in the Bible and in the Talmud, the practice was usually condemned in Judeo-Christian tradition as sinful, the work of the devil. One of the best-known biblical necromancers was the Witch of Endor, who summoned the spirit of the dead prophet Samuel from the realm of Gehenna for King Saul. In the late Middle Ages and early Renaissance, necromancy was a crime that brought death to many during the Inquisition and witch-hunts.

However, one of Roman Catholicism's earliest popes practiced necromancy with the aid of a wizard. Additionally, a monk named Albert de Saint Jacques explained in his 1675 book, *Light to the Living by the Experiences of the Dead*, how clergymen gained knowledge of the afterworld by consulting those who dwelt in it.

Necromancy is often found in legends, myths and literature. In Greek mythology, Odysseus, while alive, visited Hades to consult Tiresias. In Nordic lore, sagas about Odin, the god of the dead, tell of the awakening of a dead prophetess.

Spiritualism

Belief in the possibility of communicating with spirits is nearly universal in human civilization. Philosophies similar to Spiritualism have echoed through time and cultures worldwide. As with all spiritual developments, communication with the dead has a long history, dating back to prehistoric shamanism. In the miracles of world religions, communication with dead spirits is a common theme. But Spiritualism is defined as a separate religion by its followers, and its tenets include scientific proof of life after death. Spiritualists believe that the personality lives on after death in a spiritual body, rather than in a new physical body. This is the point upon which some Spiritualists split off into a group called spiritists. The spiritists believe in reincarnation into a new physical body.

Spiritualists do not believe in the concepts of paradise, heaven or hell; nor in a last judgment or resurrection of the physical body. They assert that the soul remains near the earthly plane for a period of time before advancing in the knowledge and moral qualities which allow it to proceed to higher planes, until finally it becomes pure spirit. Certain souls who have mastered spiritual wisdom (master teachers) remain in a disembodied state to communicate with ordinary humans through mediums.

The physical phenomena accompanying contact with the dead, one element of Spiritualist's beliefs and practices, include rapping sounds, telekinesis, levitation and automatic writing. Spiritual healing, another core of Spiritualist practice, includes the laying on of hands and absent healing, whereby the medium works with a spirit doctor to heal someone not present. Mental mediumship phenomena include crystal gazing, clairvoyance, dowsing and trans-speaking.

Modern Spiritualism originated in the United States in 1848 with the Fox sisters, Maggie and Katie, who communicated with spirits through rappings. As mediums, they became quite popular and conducted elaborate séances throughout the country. Their fame encouraged other mediums, and by the mid-1850s Spiritualism had a large following in the U.S. and Europe, attracting such people as Arthur Conan Doyle (who later wondered if he had been the victim of a great cosmic, spirit-world joke).

The Theosophical Society, an outgrowth of the Spiritualist movement, was cofounded in 1875 by a Russian, Madame Helena Petrovna Blavatsky, and the American Spiritualist Henry Steel Olcott. Blavatsky was renowned for the supernormal phenomena that often occurred in her presence. Theosophy focused on the secret laws of nature; its goal was to unite Eastern spirituality with Western thought and science.

New Age mediums, now called channels, go into a trance state and a teacher spirit takes over the channel's body. Channels most often communicate with highly evolved souls who give messages about the meaning of life and death, whereas 19th-century mediums focused more often on messages from departed relatives proving the reality of life after death. Channeling is in many ways a blending of Theosophy and Spiritualism, although channels are not a part of either group. Edgar Cayce (known as the Sleeping Prophet), Jane Roberts and Ruth Montgomery are a few prominent individuals who practiced channeling before the movement became popular.

Hanging Around: The Dead Among Us

Ancient cultural and religious beliefs hold that some of the dead, usually those who have suffered greatly in life or endured an unnatural passing, reside among the living either in ethereal or physical form. These creatures are generally objects of horror, representing as they do unhappy or cursed souls who don't belong on earth.

Ghosts

The term "ghost" has been used to mean soul, spirit, breath, the immaterial part of human beings, the moral nature, a good or an evil spirit. Generally, ghosts are understood as the soul of a deceased person appearing in visible form: an apparition or a specter. Although "giving up the ghost" was one way of describing death in early biblical texts, no official position is taken in Christian doctrine about the existence of ghosts. In fact, the existence of ghosts is generally not supported by religious doctrine. Still, shadowy phantasms continue to be seen, felt and heard in graveyards or near the places of their death, usually at night or in the early dawn hours, throughout the world. Often, these lost souls need to be appeased with prayer, sacrifice or ritual so they will not haunt the living.

The Ashanti people of Ghana tied powerful charms on the bodies of criminals who were executed to prevent their ghosts from returning to harm the executioners. Shaving the head of the deceased criminal and painting it red, white and black was another precaution. In this way, the criminal would be recognized if he prowled about as a ghost.

Ghosts and demons in India are believed to haunt cemeteries or live in trees. Sometimes they appear, in either a beautiful or an ugly form, seeking food or blood. The monkey god Hanuman is the Hindu guardian against ghosts. Offerings of coconuts and oil and red lead poured over his image protect the living from ghosts.

The Irish *fetch* and the Scottish *wraith* refer to dead spirits, but can also describe the immaterial appearance of a living person to forewarn his or her death. A phantom, from the Greek *phantasma,* is sometimes an unreal or dream-image, but can also be the mind of one human affecting the mind of another by means beyond the normal senses. Ghouls (from the Arabic *ghul*) are monsters that haunt cemeteries and feed on dead bodies. The French *revenant* (one who comes back) has been used in English to denote visits from the dead. In Ireland, *banshees* sometimes ride in the death coach, a phantom carriage driven by a headless driver and drawn by black horses. Wherever the death coach stops, someone in that house will die the next day.

In China a ghost (masculine, *kuei* and feminine, *yao*) is the spirit of someone who has died an unusual death, usually from a criminal act. Ghosts of bandits were believed to linger close to the site of their execution. If a pregnant woman passed this spot, the ghost might later try to wrest out the child's soul during birth and be born in its place. In Japan, the most dangerous ghosts are those of people who have died violently or who die in disgrace. They become angry spirits (*onryo*) exacting revenge. Onryo can bring a series of harsh disasters onto the entire country.

Hollywood films such as *The Exorcist, Ghostbusters* and *Poltergeist* portray encounters with the spirits of the dead as breathtaking, horrifying and action-packed. Real-life ghost hunters claim that their work is quite often boring.

Ninety-eight percent of ghostly investigations turn up very mundane explanations. It's that fascinating, unexplainable 2 percent that keeps believers attuned to the world of spirits.

Ghost hunters John and Anne Spencer categorize apparitions in the following ways:

- Recordings of past events reveal ghosts as voices or as holograph-like images. Recordings made at the site of a death, often a traumatic or violent death, can record the event again much like an ethereal movie. Living people at the location may be unaware of the otherworldly echoes transpiring around them. If a person stands in its way, a ghost will walk right through or pass close by without being noticed.

- Anniversary ghosts return at the time of their death, repeating the scene. The problem with anniversaries is knowing exactly when the ghost will appear, since it's impossible to know: are they on daylight savings time? What about leap year? Anniversary ghosts appear some time close to the date of their death, and weather conditions (approximating those at the time of death) seem to precipitate an appearance.

- Interactive ghosts are those most in tune with mediums and channels. They bring messages and insights from the other side and seem to know things about the deceased that one would not know unless he or she was a "real" spirit. A presence is felt, rather than heard or seen directly. People report that they feel watched in a particular room, as if someone is there.

- Poltergeists are not considered true ghosts by serious ghost hunters, since ghosts are apparitions in haunted places, and poltergeists are haunted spirits. A poltergeist focuses on a particular person and cannot be seen by uninvolved others. Poltergeist activity—moving heavy objects, hurling items across a room—lasts for several months only.

- Ghosts of the living—doubles, doppelgängers, vardogers and bilocators—are all instances of living people who seem to be in two places at the same time. Doubles are seen in two locations at the same time. Doppelgängers appear close to the actual person, as though a living shadow. Vardogers are forerunners in time. Bilocators are a special kind of double, a divided self doing two different things at the same time.

- Crisis apparitions are ghosts which leave the dying body to warn others of danger. Or, at the moment of death, these ghosts may appear to relatives or friends to explain the death.

The Grateful Undead: Zombies

In Haiti, Voodoo practitioners claim to be able to bring the soulless body of a dead person back to life. According to ethnobiologist Wade Davis, however, zombies (from the African word *nzambi,* meaning "spirit of the dead") are actually live people who had been drugged to make them appear dead. The victims were given a strong poison containing toxic animal and plant products, which induces a deathlike state, and were then buried alive. The Haitian Voodoo magician then opens the grave and uses other substances—such as a potion called "zombie's cucumber"—to revitalize the victim. Having experienced extreme physical and psychological abuse, the victim is disoriented and afraid. Zombies are given a new name and become virtual slaves to the sorcerer. They need minimal nourishment but cannot be fed salt, so it is said, or they will instinctively want to reenter their tombs.

A sorcerer may also practice "spiritual zombiism," by catching the souls of the departed. Like his or her physical counterpart, the spiritual zombie then "lives" under the spell of the magician.

Vampires: A Case of Bad Blood

In a series of novels called the Vampire Chronicles, Anne Rice let vampires have their say. With all their fear and sorrows, Rice's vampires seem almost human. Perhaps there's one secret even *Interview with the Vampire* didn't reveal. Ealine Marieb and John Mallatt described an unusual condition in their 1992 book, *Human Anatomy.* Those who cannot get a decent night's sleep or a real tan may in fact suffer from a bad skin disorder known as porphyria (from the Greek *porphyra* meaning "purple"). This rare, inherited skin disease is exacerbated by sunlight:

> When exposed to sunlight, the skin of the porphyria victim becomes lesioned and scarred, and the fingers, toes, and nose are often mutilated. The teeth grow prominent as the gums degenerate (the basis of large vampire fangs?). Rampant growth of hair causes the sufferer's face to become wolf-like and the hands to resemble paws. One treatment for porphyria is the injection of normal heme molecules extracted from healthy red blood cells. Since heme injections were not available in the Middle Ages, the next best thing would have been to drink blood, as vampires were said to do. The claim that garlic keeps vampires away may stem from the fact that garlic severely aggravates porphyria symptoms.

Long before science ascertained that blood carried life, humans were aware of its power. The life literally drained out of animals and people in streams of blood. Often, blood was drunk as a way of transferring this vitality to oneself. Vampire tales have been a part of myths and folklore for centuries, long before Count Dracula supposedly took his first bite.

Count Dracula, the hero of Bram Stoker's famous novel, is said to be based on Prince Vlad V of Wallachia (1431–76), known as the Impaler and as Dracul or Dracula, a word meaning both devil and dragon. Prince Vlad was not a bloodsucker, but he was, most likely, a sadist. His most memorable military exploit, in June of 1462, was to impale 20,000 Turkish soldiers on tall poles. When invading Turk forces came upon the site, they made a hasty retreat.

In the late 17th century, Hungary, Poland and the surrounding regions suffered from epidemics of smallpox. The thousands of dead bodies that piled up probably helped inspire the sudden surge of vampire tales. One appeal of vampire stories is their challenge to the firm distinction made between "alive" and "dead." Another lure is the tantalizing connection between two of life's greatest mysteries: sex and death.

Superstitions: None of This is True (Knock on Wood)

You'll reach a dead end if you're hell-bent on giving someone the evil eye, but you might be in seventh heaven (if you don't make enough noise to raise the dead) when an owl or butterfly graces your presence. Superstitions about death abound in all cultures. Most involve live creatures, natural elements and, knock on wood, ordinary acts of everyday life. All agree, it's tricky business keeping body and soul together.

Mirrors. The ancients believed that any object which reflected a person's spirit was divine. Thus evolved the custom of covering a mirror when someone in the family dies, to prevent the departing soul from getting trapped in the mirror and not making it to heaven. And of course, beware of anyone whose image does not reflect in a mirror: You're looking at a vampire. If you break a mirror, take heart. There is a way to reclaim those seven years of bad luck. Gather all the broken pieces together and throw them into a stream.

Robins, the harbingers of spring and of new life, can also foretell the opposite. A robin flying into a church or tapping on a house window signals death.

Killer bees have been around a long time. From Wales comes the belief that if a swarm of bees settles on the ground someone will die. If they light on a tree branch in your yard, guess who it will be?

Sneezing prompts automatic benedictions from complete strangers, who immediately say, "God Bless You," or "Gesundheit." This tradition goes beyond simple manners. The underlying belief is that sneezing expels evil spirits from the soul. By accident, the soul could leave the body along with the demons, so a blessing is invoked, just in case.

Snakes. Early Egyptians worshipped snakes and considered them immortal. The symbol for eternity is a snake with its tail in its mouth. Medieval folk saw the slithering creature differently, believing that a snake could put its tail in its mouth, roll after a person, knock him down and kill him,

Holidays of the Dead: Soul Food

Humankind's commingled fear of and fascination with death, forces that gave rise to religious belief and cultural practice, form the foundation for various death-related holidays and celebrations held around the world. These events allow people to look death in the face, either with awe and respect or humor and irreverence.

Days of the Dead

Prior to the arrival of Spanish conquistadors, the Aztecs of central Mexico celebrated harvest and death rites honoring Mictlantecuhtli, the god of death, at the end of October. The Spaniards introduced All Saints' Day and All Souls' Day and a fusion of the two celebrations occurred.

Seasonally, in Mexico, autumn brings signs of rebirth. It is the time between the wet and dry seasons when the countryside is lush with blooming flowers. Also, thousands of monarch butterflies migrate to the forests of central Mexico at this time of year. For many centuries, Mexicans have believed the returning butterflies bear the spirits of the departed. Images of butterflies are carved into many Aztec monuments.

To celebrate the Days of the Dead, Mexicans strew marigolds along the paths to their houses so the dead can find their way home. Altars are created, decorated with special foods, mementos of the dead, flowers, candles and photographs of departed loved ones. Stories are told and prayers are said. Families go to cemeteries, clear and clean the graves, arrange flowers and light candles for the returning spirits. This is a time to remember and honor the dead and to rejoice in life.

As with Halloween in the United States, the Mexican Days of the Dead are also festive and death is mocked. Children dressed as ghosts, ghouls and mummies run through the streets shouting *calaveras!* (skulls!) for money and candy. Special foods are prepared in the images of death: marzipan coffins, white chocolate skeletons. *Pan de muertos* (bread of the dead), with "bones" decorating the crust, is placed on the altar. If a child thinks he or she has seen the ghost of dead grandparent, parents might say, "The dead only die if they die in our hearts."

Halloween

Halloween, in terms of religion, is the eve of All Saints' Day in the calendar of the Roman Catholic church. However, the holiday has its roots in pre-Christian times. Originally, it was celebrated by pagan Celts as the eve of Samhain. Samhain was New Year's Day for the Celts, the time when The Lady, who ruled the earth for half a year, went to sleep and God took over. Samhain was also a day of the dead, when the souls of those who had died during the year were allowed access to the land of the dead. On November 1, the gates separating the worlds of the living and the dead were opened. The barriers between this world and the world of spirits went down and spirits wandered. The graves of dead fairies open and they dance with the living. Sometimes human musicians are captured on this evening so that the fairies will have music for their ball.

It is also the night when the grand Puck, a famous fairy, travels down from the mountains and curses all the blackberries. After November 1, none of the blackberries in Ireland are fit to eat. This reflects the fact that the festival represented the first day of winter, when the crops should be harvested and animals brought in from distant fields. These customs were widely practiced in ancient Ireland, but when the country was converted to Christianity in 300–400 C.E., the Catholic Church encouraged the redefinition of traditional customs into Christian terms and concepts.

All Saints' Day, November 1, is the day to pay homage to all the saints who do not otherwise have a feast day in their name. November 2 was designated as All Souls' Day, to embrace the pagan festival. This is the day set aside to recognize the souls of all the faithful departed who had died during the previous year. The celebration for All Saints' began the night before, to subsume the pagan tradition (since pagans believed that the eve of Samhain was when the dead wandered). Thus, on October 31 people laid out food offerings and drink, wore masks and costumes, and lighted bonfires. There was also a custom, similar to modern trick-or-treating, called "souling" or "soul-caking," in which poor people would go about begging for currant buns.

The practices of the eve of Samhain were incorporated into Christian teaching as the Eve of All Saints, or the Even of All Hallows, or Hallow Even, and thus, Hallowe'en. The church also redefined Celtic beliefs, declaring that the spirits of Samhain, once thought to be wild and powerful, were manifestations of the Devil, who misled people to worship false idols.

Halloween in the United States does not have the sacred connotation of honoring the dead. In the United States, Halloween reflects a playful attitude toward death. It is a time of merriment, costumes, sweet treats and mischief. Masks, skeletons, haunted house tours, ghoulish music, pumpkins carved for candles, witches, devils, angels and vampires mock death and celebrate life. Secular U.S. holidays for honoring the dead—such as Memorial Day—occur at other times of the year.

Life and Death Celebrations Worldwide

Festivals that recognize death or the supernatural are universal; throughout the year, all cultures celebrate aspects of life and death as they correspond with earth's seasonal rhythms. The natural cycles of the beginning and ending of the growth season, the sun's movement toward the earth, bringing light, and away from the earth, bringing darkness, are reflected in societal and cultural rituals everywhere.

Easter is the spring feast of the Resurrection of Christ, celebrated on the first Sunday after the full moon of the vernal equinox. The festival was originally a Saxon rite to honor Eastre, the goddess of spring: Emperor Constantine declared it a Christian holiday in 325. Seasonally, Easter is a time of rebirth for the plants and trees that have been dormant all winter. Eggs are an important part of Easter rituals, denoting new life.

In the United States, Memorial Day, originally a day of tribute to Civil War dead, has become a day to honor veterans of all wars. Cities hold parades featuring veterans, graves are tended and decorated with flowers, and observers attend church services and family picnics.

In China, the spring festival is a time of purification and regeneration; an important part of this is the care and honoring of the dead through prayers and sacrifices. In a practice called "saluting the tomb," red-colored rice and peeled eggs (symbols that the old gives way to the new) are left on top of graves. November is the month for Ghost Day celebrations. People burn paper money as offerings for dead relatives. The Winter Dress Festival, held during October and November, is when the Chinese visit the graves of their ancestors. As gifts, they burn imitation garments made of paper at the tombs.

Each February, Panama City stages a mock funeral called the "Burial of the Sardine" during Carnival, just before Ash Wednesday. With great ceremony, a dead fish is dumped into the ocean. In late summer and early autumn, Nepalese celebrate Gokarna Aunsi, a day to honor all fathers, both living and dead. Special meals and sweet treats are prepared.

For three days in the middle of summer, the Japanese celebrate the Bön festival, dedicated to the spirits of their ancestors. Graves are cleaned, household altars and special foods are prepared. This is traditionally a time to go home, as Thanksgiving is for Americans, and the feasting goes on all night. In some parts of Japan, people conduct formal closing rituals on the third day. At dawn, paper boats holding lanterns, flowers and fruit are placed in rivers and lakes to carry away the souls of the dead.

Throughout the Western world, May 1 and November 1 are days of traditional significance. These dates six months apart represent the beginning and the end of the growing season and are celebrated in many different ways.

Rituals and holidays that honor the memories of dead heroes serve to keep a society's overriding philosophies alive, giving cohesion and purpose to the culture itself. In the United States, a formal holiday honoring slain civil rights leader Dr. Martin Luther King, Jr. is one example of a nation proclaiming that death could not put an end to the ideal of racial equality. The commemoration of Veterans' Day celebrates the nation's commitment to fight for freedom. Thus the dead live on as emblems of a culture's values.

VI

The Culture
of Death

From the mythology of ancient Egypt to the movies of modern Hollywood, death has always inspired human imagination. Social, scientific and religious beliefs and practices fused in the creative mind, generating stories, imagery and iconography. Customs and philosophies evolved and continue to evolve, just as human feelings about death continue to find expression in traditional literary and art forms as well as the classical and modern literature and arts of Western civilization. These community and creative activities seek to contain death, to define its role and meaning in human life. So too does popular culture, the everyday beliefs and values that people call upon when the topic of death comes up. Attitudes about death form a core part of every culture.

What a Way to Go: The Agents and Victims of Violent Death

People have been killing each other for as long as they have walked the earth. As civilizations have evolved, violent death of various sorts has assumed a permanent place in human culture. Attitudes toward those who kill and those who are killed depend on the reasons for their actions or fate; some killing is seen as justified or even righteous, while some is repugnant or ignoble. Likewise, those who die by human hands may earn honor or infamy in doing so.

Murder: The Universal Taboo?

Nearly all societies have some sort of taboo against killing. This serves both to acknowledge the value of life and to prevent the total mayhem that would doubtless ensue if people killed each other whenever they had the impulse. Interestingly, exceptions are as universal as the prohibition.

In Judeo-Christian tradition, the Old Testament's Eighth Commandment says "Thou Shalt Not Kill." Yet the Bible has other passages that seem to justify killing under some circumstances, such as war and vengeance. In practice, devout Christians have sanctioned plenty of killing, even in this century: The Vatican, for instance, has never excommunicated Adolf Hitler for the extermination of more than 10 million people during World War II.

Islam has a taboo against killing, but allows exceptions; the Koran warns, "slay not the life which Allah has forbidden save with right." In Hindu, Buddhist and Jain tradition, there is a principle of *ahimsa*, or nonviolence, but Hindus have often exempted warriors from ahimsa. Buddhism considers killing acceptable to protect one's faith; even Buddha himself slew some heretics. Self-defense is also allowed. Jain has tended to take ahimsa the most seriously, forbidding the killing of anything with more than one sense. Thus, though it is permissible to kill plants, Jains cannot seriously pursue agriculture because working in soil can kill insects. However, even some Jains can fight wars under some circumstances.

Secular laws reflect these attitudes. All societies provide harsh punishments for murder, often death or lifetime imprisonment. However, most punish some less harshly than others—the category of manslaughter, for instance, distinguishes between murder and less morally reprehensible killing. Manslaughter generally applies to reckless accidents, or to circumstances not entirely within the perpetrator's control. Interestingly, it has also been applied to survivors of suicide pacts.

Different cultures disagree on what is murder and what is not. In the United States, for instance, people are horrified by infanticide—it tends to be punished as murder, and a mother who kills her baby is reviled by press and public alike. In India and many other cultures, however, female babies have routinely been killed soon after birth; this is an ancient practice that continues to this day. In England, killing infants is not looked upon as murder. Under the law it is considered manslaughter and society tends to pity, rather than condemn, a mother who kills her baby.

Dowry Death

Dowry death is a form of murder that still occurs in India, where it has been practiced for centuries. A bride may be killed if her dowry does not satisfy either her husband or his family. The payment of dowries was outlawed by the Indian government in 1961, but many families still demand dowry, and continue to demand more after the marriage has taken place. Dowry deaths ravage all castes of Indian society. Women's families submit to the extortion to ensure a "decent marriage" for their daughters. Often it is the mother-in-law who urges that the bride be killed, so that the son can remarry and collect another dowry.

In 1994, 5,582 dowry deaths were recorded, marking an increase from 1990's total of 4,836. In that four-year period, 20,537 women were killed by their husbands or in-laws, often by being set on fire. Some husbands have been tried for the murder of their wife, but many escape because of friendly connections with the authorities or the indifference to abuse toward women. Women have held demonstrations and formed support groups that keep records of dowry deaths and seek to protect wives. With all this concern, the attitudes of parents of female children is so negative that they allow themselves to become the victims of these dowry demands in their urge to have their daughter have a "decent marriage." In the newspaper advertisements the term "decent marriage" is the code phrase for those looking for dowry marriages.

Vengeance and Honor

Vengeance is retribution for a wrong, often in the form of blood payback. Historically, it has been closely intertwined with notions of honor, integrity, pride and dignity, often upheld by formal codes professed by nations, tribes, families and individuals. Only a few contemporary societies are governed explicitly by codes of honor and traditions of vengeance, but vestiges of these practices live on nearly everywhere.

In ancient Greece, vengeance was a fact of life and could make a man a hero. It is central to the Greek creation myth, as well as to the plots of *The Odyssey*, *The Iliad*, *The Oresteia* and many other works of Greek literature.

Islam's Koran cautiously sanctions revenge: "Whoso is slain wrongfully, we have given power unto his heir, but let him not commit excess in slaying!"

The Old Testament, not surprisingly, offers mixed messages on this subject. The book of Leviticus commands "Thou shalt not avenge," yet in Genesis God says "he that sheds the blood of man, for that man his blood shall be shed," and Exodus states "Thou shalt give life for life, eye for eye, tooth for tooth, hand for hand, foot for foot."

The New Testament stands more definitively against vengeance. Jesus directly rejects Exodus: "You have learned that they were told 'eye for eye, tooth for tooth.' But what I tell you is this, 'Do not set yourself against the man who wrongs you. If someone slaps you on the right cheek, turn and offer him your left.'" However, the biblical God is vengeful throughout, and

Christians have been able to justify many acts of vengeance by claiming they are God's agents, carrying out his will.

Vengeance has often been institutionalized by feuds—states of ongoing hostility between families, tribes or other groups. This phenomenon is as old as historical and archaeological record. In medieval Europe feuds proliferated and often served as the most organized system of justice. Feuds are often socially sanctioned, even encouraged through ritual. In Albania, Corsica, Somaliland and southern Greece, funeral dirges urge a murdered person's male family members to avenge the death; kinsmen who fail to follow through on these exhortations are likely to be ostracized by the community. Feuding continues today in the Middle East, parts of Italy, the southern United States, gang-ridden inner cities and elsewhere. These are based as much on codes of honor and collective desires for vengeance as any in medieval Europe.

Sardinia is still governed more by a well-established and elaborate code of individual and group vengeance than by the state; the Mafia, both in Sicily and in the United States, is similar. In Texas, though there is no clear code of collective vengeance, individuals protect their own honor fiercely. Feuds raged there during the Civil War and Reconstruction, and even today the law allows a man to "stand his ground" (most U.S. state laws say he has to back up as far as he can before trying to kill in self-defense).

Even apart from such "cultures of vengeance," vengeance today has a certain degree of mainstream social acceptance, as scholars Pietro Marongiu and Graeme Newman point out in their 1987 examination of the subject, *Vengeance: The Fight Against Injustice.* Both the law and the public, on occasion, show sympathy toward people who act violently out of vengeance. Indeed, our criminal justice system is founded on these values; punishment has always been motivated far more by vengeance than by the relatively modern notion of rehabilitation. This has been evident in the recent increase in executions in the United States—and in political support for them.

Dueling

A duel is a fight over honor and a performance that lets the world know one would die to save one's reputation. In fact, throughout history only a minority of duels have been fought to the death. Unlike literary, mythic or cinematic duels, real-life duels usually peter out after a few gunshots or sword swipes. The custom grew out of a French tradition called the wager of battle, in which a man accused of something shameful fought his accuser under judicial supervision. This practice was abolished in the mid-1500s; the duel replaced it almost immediately and later spread to England and other European countries.

A duel generally starts when one person impugns another's honor. When the offended party challenges his offender to fight, the challenged person must accept or lose his honor. The two agree to follow very specific procedures; at least one outsider usually observes to make sure these agreements are adhered to.

Dueling persisted despite adamant opposition from organized religion; as early as 887 Pope Stephen VI denounced it. Later, Protestant churches also tend to oppose it. In the U.S., the last famous duel was in 1804, between Aaron Burr and Alexander Hamilton, resulting in Hamilton's death. The practice is now illegal in most countries, but variants on the tradition still exist, in urban gangs, for instance, or among mobsters.

Capital Punishment

There is plenty of Old Testament support for the death penalty; the Exodus command "Whoever strikes another man and kills him shall be put to death" is only one of many pro-capital punishment passages. Execution is also frequently justified in terms of vengeance or retribution. The 18th-century philosopher Immanuel Kant wrote that even if a society were to agree to dissolve itself, it should first make sure to put all the murderers to death "in order that everyone might receive his desert." Advocates of capital punishment also say that death is the only way to ensure that hardened murderers will not kill again. If they only get life imprisonment, they might be paroled or even kill a guard or fellow inmate while in prison. These advocates also argue that the death penalty serves to deter potential criminals. Public or well-publicized executions make an example of an offender, showing that one cannot expect to get away with crime.

Yet opponents of the death penalty point to the Bible, too, particularly to the Eighth Commandment ("Thou shalt not kill"), to Jesus's intervention in the stoning of an adulteress and to his comments on vengeance. Early Christians tended to oppose capital punishment (of course, this may have had less to do with subtle scriptural interpretations than with the fact that they were a persecuted minority and thus very likely to be put to death), as do many Christians today.

Opponents of capital punishment point out that in a racist society, the sentence can never be applied fairly: Statistics show blacks are far more likely to get the death penalty than whites. Other research has shown no evidence that capital punishment actually prevents crime. Some argue that rehabilitation of criminals is often possible, that the death penalty wastes human potential, while others feel the state's moral authority is weakened by capital punishment—how taboo is killing, really, if the state does it? Many point out the possibility of error; innocent people can be executed. In the United States, opponents of the death penalty also cite the Eighth Amendment to the Constitution, which forbids cruel and unusual punishment.

Since the 18th century, when Italy's Cesare Beccaria, France's Voltaire and others argued against it, execution has been decreasing internationally. Though there is currently a resurgence of enthusiasm for capital punishment in the United States, more than half the nations in the world have abolished it in law, while about a hundred are rid of it in practice.

Crimes Punishable by Death

Capital punishment originated in ancient times and was first used to mollify offended gods when someone committed a particularly egregious sacrilege. Since then it has been imposed for murder and an astonishing range of other crimes. Below are some examples.

Adultery: in many societies for thousands of years; today in a handful of countries, including Iran, Pakistan, and Afghanistan.

Sodomy/homosexuality, bigamy/polygamy, bestiality, incest and rape: at many points in history, since antiquity.

Arson: until the late-19th century in Great Britain and some U.S. states; for arson in British government dockyards, until the 20th century.

Kidnapping: under traditional Jewish law.

Assaulting parents: in 16th-century Switzerland and 17th-century Sweden. Cursing parents, and being a "rebellious son" in Massachusetts Bay Colony, mid–1600s.

Lese majesty (any offense against the ruler of a state): often, throughout history.

Robbery: in Great Britain for centuries; today in a number of African countries, including Gambia and Nigeria.

Illegal drug possession or dealing: in contemporary Singapore; in the United States, drug trafficking can also be a capital crime, as can possession of over 50,000 pounds of marijuana, though at the time of this book's publication, the U.S. had executed no one for this offense.

Political dissent: in many countries today.

Treason and military/war crimes: in some contemporary societies, such as South Africa, where they are the only offenses punishable by death.

Petty crimes (forgery, poaching, rioting, picking pockets, stealing turnips, socializing with gypsies, bearing arms in a rabbit warren, stealing letters [applicable only to Post Office employees], damaging a fishpond, etc.): as recently as the turn of the 19th century under English law; in 1801 a 13-year-old boy was hanged for breaking into a house and stealing a spoon.

Religious crimes (heresy and blasphemy, terms that can refer to almost any kind of dissent from prevailing religious beliefs): in many cultures since ancient times. Many saints have been executed for these offenses, including, most likely, Jesus himself. Religious executions continue to this day; in the Muslim state of Iran adherents to the Baha'i faith are routinely killed. Witchcraft, sorcery and devil worship have all, at times of particular religious anxiety, been capital crimes. In the early 14th century hundreds of thousands of suspected witches or Satan-worshippers were executed all over Europe. This lasted through the 18th century, but was especially brutal from 1400 to 1500. In the American colonies, 20 suspected witches were killed in Salem, Massachusetts, in 1691–2. Idolatry and breaking the Sabbath have at times been punished by execution, in 17th-century Massachusetts Bay Colony, for example. Christians have historically persecuted and killed atheists; Islamic states do so to this day.

The Cost of War

The range of religious beliefs and secular attitudes toward war are shaped by diverse societies' views on life, death and killing, as well as on the political needs and historical circumstances of nations.

In ancient times a military death was seen as a good death. Dying in war was considered the noblest death among the ancient Norse; warriors slain in battle went to a different, and far more festive, afterlife than other dead people—Valhalla, an enormous dining hall. Though ancient Greek philosophers had much to say both for and against war, it is clear that military death was valorized as a way to gain immortality—a fallen warrior becomes a hero, and is thus remembered after death. It is worth noting that, though Ares, the god of war, is generally portrayed in an unpleasant light, Athena, who is also associated with war, is the goddess of wisdom.

Eastern religions for the most part eschew war. Both Confucianism and Taoism, China's major religions, have tended to regret war and see it as a last resort, though neither are pacifist traditions by any stretch. Confucius said "Military weapons are like fire; if you do not lay fire aside, it will burn you." But he also said "If you want peace, prepare for war." Both traditions disapprove of starting wars, but see defensive war as inevitable. In India, the concept of doing no harm, or *ahimsa,* is important to Hinduism. Mahatma Ghandi popularized the notion of ahimsa in the form of non-violence and won followers in India and all over the world—one of the most famous of whom was Martin Luther King, Jr. Yet Hindus have waged war throughout history, not only to defend their own territories but to invade those of others. Since Ghandi, non-Hindus have tended to view Hinduism as being more peace-loving than it really is. Jains adhere much more rigidly to ahimsa than Hindus do. They have been committed to peace for thousands of years; Ghandi was influenced as much by their teachings as by Hinduism. Jains forbid offensive war altogether; there is disagreement about defensive battles. Some Jains see them as acceptable, others feel that killing is unacceptable in any form.

Though Buddhists, too, have a tradition of ahimsa, war has been an equally important part of their history. In Japan, Korea, India and Tibet, Buddhists have fought fiercely, sometimes against governments, sometimes against other monasteries. Indeed, in Japan from the 10th to the 16th century the most devoutly Zen generals were often the most vicious killers. Buddhism, Confucianism, Christianity and the country's native religion—Shinto—all nourished Japan's extreme militarism. Warriors were highly venerated and the emperor has been regarded almost as a god, lending a divine intensity to the state's defense. However, a trend toward pacifism has developed in Japan over the past 30 years. This has partly been forced upon the country, as their military was dismantled by the Allies after World War II. However, it is also related to the nuclear tragedies the Japanese suffered during that war: millions of people died after the U.S. dropped its nuclear bombs on Hiroshima and Nagasaki.

The highly local religions of clan-based societies have tended to take a pragmatic view of war. African tribes and nations have a long history of fighting both European colonialists and each other, but values about war and peace vary widely throughout the continent. Most societies have, or had, gods of war, but many also have gods of peace. Some tribes believe that war is sent by offended gods as a punishment. Likewise, Native Americans have always fought wars, both intertribal and with white settlers. At the same time, peace—within oneself, with the universe, between two people, among tribes and nations—has been a long sought-after ideal. Of course, Native American cultures vary widely in this as in most matters (there being more than two thousand different tribes). Some, like the Plains Indians, were quite aggressive, while others, like the Pueblo and the Inuit, actively favored peace over war.

Each of the world's three major monotheistic faiths contain contradictory beliefs about war. Peace-loving and militarist strains exist side by side in Judaism's rich and sometimes contradictory teachings. Jerusalem has long been idealized as a city of peace, yet fought over bitterly. Today, however, many Jews worldwide support an end to the centuries-old warfare between Israel and Palestine, and are working and praying for peace. *Jihad*, or holy war in defense of the faith, is central to Islamic tradition. Such wars continue to this day. Yet there are many Muslims who do not support all the conflicts that are waged in the name of Islam; many also point out that the Koran's teachings advocate peace as well as war.

Christianity boasts plenty of scriptural teachings against war and a strong pacifist tradition that endures to this day (pacifists oppose all forms of violence). The latter is particularly strong in sects like the Quakers, Brethren and Mennonites. However, Christians have also long supported the idea of the "just war." Almost from the faith's beginnings, as it spread through Europe, Christians fought people of other religions—as well as each other. Many observers have noted that Christianity appears to stand against war in general, but to favor war in particular. During the Cold War, the decades-long nuclear arms race between the United States and the USSR, many Christians in the west supported interventions worldwide against Russia on the grounds that Communism was antireligious. Some even believed that they had no reason to fear nuclear holocaust because biblical Armageddon was close at hand anyway.

Today in the United States, both prowar "hawks" and antiwar "doves" have been influenced by Judeo-Christian tradition. The peace movement has always involved only a minority of the U.S. population, though it has been a vocal presence. Its ranks have included internationalists, people opposing specific conflicts on moral grounds, antinuclear activists and pacifists. In the 20th century, Americans overwhelmingly favored involvement in World Wars I and II but were more ambivalent about Vietnam. Generally, wars tend to boost a U.S. president's popularity, particularly in times of economic hardship.

Personal Decisions: Individual Control Over Mortality

Different cultures around the world and throughout history have accorded varying degrees of control to the individual over his or her own spiritual, social and physical fate in life. When it comes to the beginning and ending of life—to birth and death—these values can become at the same time quite stringent and quite muddy. Suicide and abortion have challenged philosophers, clerics, rulers and ordinary people at every turn of human history.

Views of Suicide

French novelist Albert Camus wrote, "There is only one serious philosophical problem, and that is suicide." It is certainly true that few subjects bring into sharper relief human feelings about death, dying and life itself.

Different cultures and religious traditions have varied radically in their views.

Traditional China and Japan approved suicide in certain circumstances, while Islam has generally taken a strong position against it. In ancient Greece and Rome, the morality of self-killing depended on an individual's circumstances. In Rome under some political regimes, if an aristocrat lost face or fell out of favor with the emperor, suicide was practically obligatory. The Stoics thought poor health, economic hardship, slavery, madness or the protection of one's family or state could justify a suicide. Plato, however, saw male self-killing as a deprivation to the community, writing "the man who kills himself does not know his place. Like a fugitive slave he steals himself."

Christianity did not have a strong stance on suicide until North African theologian St. Augustine wrote that suicide was an act of cowardice, an easy way out of suffering. Augustine was also concerned about his contemporaries' enthusiasm for martyrdom, and worried about the belief that confession absolved one from all past sins. He fretted that people might just want to confess, kill themselves, skip earthly suffering and go straight to heaven.

After Augustine, Christianity continued to take a strong stand against suicide. Medieval Catholics were particularly intolerant of it as a subversion of God's will. The 18th-century Enlightenment, a period in which individual rights were strongly emphasized, was more indulgent of self-killing. Both of these contradictory views influence popular Western attitudes to this day.

In many religions, suicide committed out of religious devotion has been allowed. Jain, for instance, an Eastern religion that adheres strictly to the principle of nonviolence, generally opposes suicide along with nearly all other killing. Yet particularly holy Jains—including the religion's founder—have starved themselves to death out of piety, and this is completely acceptable.

In some cultures, the ethics of suicide have depended, in part, on gender. For instance, in ancient Greece it was permissible for a woman to kill herself out of grief over a son or lover's death, but for a man to give in to such personal despair would have been considered weak. Until recently in India, widows were frequently expected to burn themselves to death on their husbands' funeral pyres in a ritual called *suttee*. Needless to say, men were not expected to do this if their wives died.

Modern mental health professionals have tended to view suicide not as a choice, as moral philosophers and theologians have, but as something that happens to a person as a consequence of mental illness. Many see a suicide attempt as a cry for help rather than an actual desire to end one's life. Nineteenth-century sociologist Emile Durkheim thought it was an outcome of social forces beyond the individual's control. The taboo against discussing suicide is lifting, but slowly; silence about death is pervasive enough, and suicide has long been considered shameful, if not sinful. Some contemporary thinkers, however, see suicide as an ideal death, because it gives one complete control over one's last moments.

The law has dealt with suicide in a variety of ways. English and French law used to mete out severe punishments for suicide attempts; France eased up after the 1789 revolution, but England took until 1961. Today in the United States, nearly all states have decriminalized suicide attempts, but courts still tend to uphold the involuntary confinement of suicidal people.

Euthanasia and Physician-Assisted Suicide: An Ancient Debate

For the past twenty years, the physician's role in ending a patient's life has become a subject of raging public debate in the United States. Euthanasia, translated from the Greek, means "dying well." In current debates it refers to mercy killing of the hopelessly ill. It can take many forms.

- Active euthanasia involves an act that results in death.

- Passive euthanasia allows a patient to die naturally, without medical interference.

- Voluntary euthanasia requires the patient's consent or that of his or her designated representative.

- Involuntary euthanasia is carried out without the consent of a patient or his representatives.

- Physician-assisted suicide loosely refers to any of the above, when a doctor takes part in a patient's self-deliverance.

In 1976, the euthanasia issue was hotly debated when 22-year-old Karen Ann Quinlan, after two respiratory arrests, became permanently brain-dead by some, but not all, medical definitions. She was kept on life support in a hospital, with no hope of any recovery. A lengthy court battle ensued and her father was eventually granted the right to order an end to her medical treatment. Michigan physician Dr. Jack Kevorkian (popularly known as "Dr. Death") has reignited the debate. His assisted suicides, including one of a woman who had lost her ability to play bridge, but played tennis with her son the day before her death, were much publicized, and have inspired a variety of conflicting statutes and court rulings nationwide.

Most states have laws against physician-assisted suicide, but several courts have challenged them. The issue is expected to come before the United States Supreme Court soon. All states currently have some sort of right-to-die law empowering patients to decide whether they wish to receive medical treatment when they are no longer competent to make decisions. Physician-assisted suicide is legal in several countries—Germany and the Netherlands, for instance.

One of the arguments in favor of physician-assisted suicide is best expressed by the title of a popular movie on the subject *Whose Life Is It Anyway?* Advocates believe people have the right to control—and to choose to end—their own lives. Others argue from a "quality of life" perspective: when a person's life is no longer worth living, either because of extreme pain or because he or she can no longer do the things that have made her life meaningful, it is only merciful and humane for doctors to allow him or her to die. Still others believe it is permissible only when a person is nearly brain-dead and shows no possibility of recovery. Medical advances have made this scenario all too common; some states have broadened their definition of death accordingly.

Opponents of the right to die argue from a variety of positions. Some believe that killing is always wrong; others, citing the Hippocratic oath, say that doctors in particular are professionally bound always to side with life, never death. Some worry about abuses: Can depressed people with terminal illnesses be trusted to act in their own best interests? And what if their representatives stand to gain handsome inheritances after their deaths? Some advocates for the elderly and disabled have objected to the way "quality of life" arguments have been framed; they argue that instead of worrying so much about the right to die, society should reexamine the attitudes that make people feel they cannot lead rewarding lives if they are aging or have lost some of their physical capabilities.

Assisted suicide may be a new question for lawyers and policy-makers, but for doctors it goes back to antiquity. The Hippocratic oath specifically forbade doctors to give patients fatal poison, even if requested. When Hadrian, a Roman emperor, asked a doctor to help him commit suicide, the doctor, in distress, killed himself instead. However, later on, in the first century, it became more acceptable for doctors to help patients to end their lives, a situation that continued for several hundred years.

Death in Popular Culture

Death's prominence in daily life has given rise to a wide range of social phenomena, from street slang to superstitions. Indeed, so large has death loomed in every culture at every moment in history that the living could accurately be described as obsessed with death. But this obsession has yielded a rich store of colorful speech, imagery and lore.

Speaking of Death: Euphemisms, Colloquialisms and Slang

Death is so frightening that over the centuries people have gone to great lengths to avoid speaking of it directly. Sometimes they seek refuge in muted euphemism—the neutral "passed away" or "passed on," for example. Even more often, however, death language reflects the need to create vivid metaphor and humor out of fear.

The theater has been a rich source of death idioms, yielding such expressions as "curtains," "final curtain," "curtain call," "last (or final) call," "lights out," "last bow," "blackout" and "fade-out." A dying person is also said to "drop (or ring down) the curtain," to "bow out" or to "take the last cue from life's stage."

The imagery of gambling and games has long pervaded the language of death. When someone dies, "his number is up" or "all bets are off." Other game-related idioms include "going to the races," "handing in one's chips", "crapping out," "playing one's last hand (or card)," "throw up the cards," "throw sixes," "tossing in one's marbles," "losing the race," "cashing in," "getting one's ticket punched" or "dropping the cue" (from billiards). Suicide has been called "solitaire."

The sea and sea-faring tradition, because so many people lost their lives to it, has offered many a death metaphor. Some terms for drowning include: "being spilled in the drink," "feeding the fishes," "going to Davy Jones's locker," "making a hole in the water" and "taking one's last drink." People also use expressions from this tradition to describe other kinds of death. A dead person may be "all washed up" or "catching the tide."

Suicide has been euphemized as "the Dutch act," "dousing one's lights," "kissing oneself good-bye" and "undoing Nature's work." Suicide by hanging is known as "the rope cure." Killing oneself by lying on railroad tracks and waiting for a train á la Anna Karenina has most ignobly been dubbed "greasing the tracks" or "taking the hobo short line."

Some language emphasizes death's democratic nature: unlike Santa Claus, death comes to everybody. Death has been called the equalizer, as well as the Great Leveler; when people die they join the majority.

Other expressions focus on the afterlife: one "goes to one's eternal reward," "meets one's maker," "crosses over Jordan," "goes home," "rides into the sunset," "heads for Cloud Nine," "pays St. Peter a visit" or "goes to the great beyond."

Humorous synonyms for dying include: "taking the big dirt nap," "becoming a landowner," "buying the farm," "calling it a day," "calling it a job," "laying down one's knife and fork," "counting (or pushing up) daisies," "going out the back door," "becoming filling for a casket," "breaking one's clay pipe," "biting (or kissing) the dust," "cheating the gallows," "coiling up one's cable," "shuffling off," "going for a Burton" (after Burton ale), "handing in one's dinner pail," "going to grass," "going belly up," "eating dandelions by the root," "stepping off the carpet," "pulling in at the last terminal," "putting out one's nightlight," "swallowing one's birth certificate," "going blooey," "hanging up one's harness and tack," "hanging up one's hat," "jumping off the deep end," "stalling the engine," "taking a powder," "taking a dirt bath" and "being put to bed with a shovel."

Terms for death include: "the way of all flesh," "pale horse," "final summons," "fold-up" and "extreme penalty."

Morbid Humor

It has been called "black humor" and "gallows humor"; jokes are an important way for people to deal with death's disturbing, disruptive nature. Yet poking fun at death also feels taboo—it is an outlawed topic, but when mentioned, it is supposed to be taken "seriously." A few famous cracks at death follow:

We're all cremated equal.

—JANE ACE

They say you shouldn't say anything about the dead unless it's good.
He's dead. Good.

—MOMS MABLEY

Guns aren't lawful
Nooses give
Gas smells awful
You may as well live.

—DOROTHY PARKER

One classic genre is the dead baby joke:
Q: What's turning brown and knocking on the window?
A: A baby in a microwave.
Q: What's easier to unload, a truck full of bowling balls or a truck full of dead babies?
A: The second—you can use a pitchfork.

Death in Legend and Folklore

Oral folk tradition offers a window onto a culture's oldest and most widely shared values. Many deathly themes in folklore are cross-cultural, reflecting humanity's common struggle to make sense of its destiny.

Many tales demonstrate the inescapability of death. In one Persian story, a young man working for the Sultan sees Death lurking around the premises. He flees to Teheran to escape, but Death asks the Sultan the boy's name. When the Sultan tells him, Death says, "I thought it was him. But I was surprised to see him here, because I have an appointment with him in Teheran later today." Similarly, numerous cultures—such as ancient Greece—created stories about the inflexibility of one's appointed hour of death.

Another tradition offers hope that death can be outwitted. In the Puerto Rican tale of Tia Miseria (Aunt Misery), a magician grants Tia a wish. The neighborhood boys are always climbing into her pear tree and tormenting her, so she wishes whoever climbs the tree will get stuck there at her command, to be freed only at her will. Tia is an old woman, and before long Death comes for her; she tricks him into climbing up to get some pears, then leaves him up there for weeks. She lets him down only when her best friend, who is tired and sick and wants to die, pleads with her to release him. But Tia first makes Death promise that he'll never come back for her. He did promise, and that is why there will always be Misery in the world. A similar story exists in Portugal. Other tales of tricking death have been found throughout the United States, Italy and elsewhere.

Other stories explain how death came to be—often as a punishment for human failings. In one Polynesian fable the hero rapes a goddess; among the Melanesians, five brothers have an argument. Greek, Fiji, Maori and Sudan traditions also describe death as a payback for human disobedience to the gods, as do the Luba people of Zaire. Another common death tale is the one in which the lover makes a journey into the afterworld to rescue his or her beloved; Greece, India and other traditions share this story.

The tale of Gilgamesh, from Mesopotamia, is highly unusual in its message: Immortality is flatly impossible for humans. Gilgamesh grieves passionately over his friend's death, pleading, "What is this sleep that holds you now? You are lost in the dark and cannot hear me." Facing the horror of his own death, he then goes to the gods to find out how he can live forever—they tell him that there is no hope. Finally they relent, and tell him where he can find a plant that will give its bearer eternal life. Gilgamesh tracks it down, but a sea serpent makes off with it before he can take it home. He then goes home and engraves this story on stone tablets—the only way he can truly attain immortality.

Famous Deaths

Famous death scenes, whether literary or real, play an important part in cultural mythologies. They help people to imagine how they will face their own death, and to think about how they will, in their own hour of death, make sense of their lives. A celebrated death scene also provides a window on how one culture views death.

An example is the death of Socrates. A philosopher and troublemaker, he was convicted by an Athenian jury of irreligion, plotting against the state and, more unusually, "corrupting youth." He drank poison in prison after delivering a lengthy discourse on the fate of the soul after death. He was surrounded by grieving friends, much to his irritation, as he thought death was not to be feared and "a man should die in peace."

Christ's death may be the most familiar in Western art. His body on the cross is, in some representations, racked with pain; in others, it is calm and almost undamaged. The mourning of his disciples, his mother Mary and Mary Magdalene, and Christ's own anguished cry "My God, my God, why hast thou forsaken me" all set the scene for the Christian tradition's deeply troubled relationship to death.

In contrast, at his own death Buddha, like Socrates, scolds a follower for weeping, saying, "it is in the very nature of things most near and dear to us that we must divide ourselves from them." He sent for all the villagers, and when they came, he asked if they had questions about his teachings. They had none. He then entered *nirvana*, or absence of self, liberation from desires or thoughts, but since he had entered that state before, while living, death had no power over him. His disciples honored his body for six days. On the seventh day, the body was placed on a funeral pyre. According to tradition, when the last follower came to pay his respects, the pyre spontaneously combusted and burned to the ground.

Saints' death scenes are often particularly memorable. John the Baptist was beheaded by King Herod, his head later served up on a dish to his wife's daughter, the dancer Salome; both his execution and the presentation of his head have been favorite artistic subjects. Even more popular is the Virgin Mary's physical ascent to heaven, referred to as the Assumption. Christian martyrs are often sainted partly because of their gruesome deaths; thus these scenes take on legendary power. St. Sebastian's nude body was pierced full of arrows and he was left for dead. Actually, though, he was still alive, and rather than escape, he confronted Diocletian, the cruel ruler who had ordered his death. Diocletian then ordered him beaten to death with cudgels.

Ghost Stories

Ghostly tales of the returning dead have been told for thousands of years all over the world, from China to Zimbabwe. They exist in both oral and literary form; the first, obviously, is much older. Many traditional tales now have been written down, but they often retain a different character than those composed as written stories: they are intended to be performed and include key points at which the teller is supposed to jump at the listeners in order to startle them.

An example of the blending of oral and written ghost stories is Mark Twain's retelling of "The Golden Arm." In that story, a woman has a golden arm, and when she dies her husband steals it as he is lowering her into the ground. It is a windy night and he hears a faraway voice crying "Where's my golden a-a-a-rm?" This refrain is repeated over and over again, getting closer and closer. The voice follows him through his door, up his stairs into bed, finally answering its own question: "YOU GOT IT!"

At this point, of course, the teller should jump at the audience to scare the daylights out of them—the original purpose of the oral ghost story.

The best-known ghostly literary traditions in the English-speaking world are the Victorian and Gothic. Henry James's novella *The Turn of the Screw* is one of the most famous. Another, *The Legend of Sleepy Hollow*, features a headless horseman who rides through the night. And of course there are the works of Edgar Allen Poe, including *The Tell-Tale Heart*.

Other genres have carried on the tradition as well. Two examples of ghostly opera are Wagner's *The Flying Dutchman* and Mozart's *Don Giovanni*.

Macabre Characters: Death Personified

Popular culture has often anthropomorphized death, sometimes in comic form and sometimes with downright frightening effect. Often depicted as a skeleton or a skull with a clothed human body, Death has been called "the Grim Reaper," "reaper man," "ol' Man Mose (or Mr. Mose)," "bold one," "bony one," "clean and peeled one," "frugal one," "grave one," "shaky one," "Great Whipper," "Grim Monarch," "Old Floorer" and "Old Mister Grim." Though most often male, Death is sometimes female. It has also been imagined as bucktoothed and skinny, or has taken on numerous other physical attributes.

Emily Dickinson thought of Death as a courtly sort; "Because I could not stop for Death/He kindly stopped for me." Some think he might even be sexy: another poet, Margaret Widdemer, imagined Death embracing the dying, saying "I am the Dark Cavalier; I am the Last Lover/My arms shall welcome you when all other arms are tired."

Other depictions are darker. A famous biblical Death-figure is one of the four Horsemen of the Apocalypse (the other three being Pestilence, War and Famine). Death rides a pale horse and the Greek god of death, Hades, rides close behind him. Still older is the Angel of Death in Jewish tradition, also known as Samael. He is the Angel who harbors the most hatred toward man.

In one traditional story, God hides Moses so Samael cannot get his soul.

Often Death is clever or crafty, playing games with people. Ingmar Bergman's eerie film *The Seventh Seal*, one of the few motion pictures in which Death makes a personal appearance, features a chess game with Death. This scene is fabulously spoofed in "De Duva," a comic short featuring a badminton game with a Death who is klutzy, all limbs.

Dead Letters: Death in Literature

Second perhaps only to the topic of love, death has fascinated writers through the ages. Poets and novelists have contemplated its meanings, form and impact in some of history's greatest works of literature. Here are a few of the highlights.

One of the most dramatic death scenes in classical literature is that of Dido in Virgil's *The Aeneid.* After Aeneas leaves her, the lustily grieving Phoenician queen commands her unsuspecting sister to build a sacrificial pyre with some of his effects on it. The next day, Dido climbs the pyre and stabs herself in front of her entire household, passionately denouncing Aeneas and begging the gods to take her away to the underworld.

Dante Alighieri's *Divine Comedy,* written in the early 14th century, remains the West's most daring literary attempt to imagine, in detail, the afterlife. It may also, after the biblical book of Revelations, be the most elaborate expression of the Christian fear of divine judgment after death.

Shakespeare's *Romeo and Juliet,* like his other tragedies, reflects the notion (a relatively new one in his time) that death represents a terrible loss. It also explores avoidable death caused by human misunderstanding and pettiness. The play incorporates the classic theme of the union of love and death.

Arden of Feversham, attributed to William Shakespeare, was a popular Elizabethan domestic tragedy that drew upon the facts of the murder of Thomas Arden, the mayor of Feversham (in Kent), who was killed by his wife's lover. The culprit, Thomas Morsby, was hanged; Alice Arden was burned to death for conspiracy and adultery.

Some of the 19th century's most famous death scenes are extravagantly emotional, sometimes even patently sentimental; the dying person, often female, takes on an implausible saintlike quality, as does Eliza in Harriet Beecher Stowe's *Uncle Tom's Cabin*, Beth in Louisa May Alcott's *Little Women* and Nell in Charles Dickens's *Death of Little Nell.*

Though written in the 19th century, Leo Tolstoy's *The Death of Ivan Illich* provides an early description of the contemporary attitude toward death—that it must be denied. Illich is kept in the dark about the gravity of his illness and his imminent death. Everyone around him, to his rage, pretends it is not happening: he wants to cry out "'Enough lies, we all know that I am dying!' . . . but he never [has] the courage to do this."

The Mystery of Marie Rogêt by Edgar Allan Poe is based on the celebrated, unsolved strangling of Mary Cecilia Rogers in New York in 1841. This story was Poe's first commercial success. The author theorized that Rogers had been pregnant and was killed by an abortionist; it was eventually found that she was, indeed, pregnant. Some believe that Poe, who knew the victim, committed the murder himself.

Joseph Conrad's 1910 *Heart of Darkness* savagely captures "intense and hopeless despair" in the face of death. The dying man's last words are "The horror! The horror!"

To write *An American Tragedy*, Theodore Dreiser sat, taking notes, throughout the 22-day trial of Chester Gillette, who was found guilty of drowning his pregnant girlfriend, Grace Brown, in 1906 in upstate New York. Gillette changed his story several times while appealing his conviction, but was finally executed in 1908. Dreiser published the brilliant novel based on this sad tale in 1925.

The Stranger, written in 1958 by existentialist novelist Albert Camus, begins: "Today mother died. Or was it yesterday . . ." The narrator shows complete indifference toward his mother's death, and toward his own life. Eventually he commits a murder and on the eve of his execution rejoices in his life, knowing he is about to lose it. This, like James Agee's novel, *A Death in the Family* (see below), is a profoundly modern view of death: it is experienced alone, apart from the rituals, social units and philosophical structures that once helped people to make sense of it. Now the individual has to create his or her own meaning for death—as for life.

In Nigerian writer Chinua Achebe's 1959 novel, *Things Fall Apart*, white missionaries come to an African village and irreparable conflict ensues, much of it over the topic of death. Whites and villagers clash over the spirits of the dead and the proper treatment of dead bodies, while the villagers struggle among themselves over vengeance—whether to kill the white men, whether their traditional life is worth dying for. In the last scene, the main character has killed himself after killing one of the white men, and the white commissioner is baffled by the villagers' beliefs about the body of a suicide.

James Agee's *A Death in the Family*, written in 1957, is a fictionalized reflection on his own father's death. The work describes with heartbreaking accuracy the inability of family members to understand each other's reactions to a death.

Toni Morrison's *Beloved*, in which a slave mother kills her children to keep them from being taken away from her, explores maternal love, killing and the relationship of the living to ghosts.

The Macabre Period

Death has always been a subject of fine art, of course, but sometimes events outside the art world affect its content. In Europe's Macabre period, in the 14th and 15th centuries, death becomes a virtual obsession: skulls, bones, decaying bodies and faces covered with snakes or toads appear in paintings throughout this period. This is partly (though not entirely) the legacy of the black plague. Similarly, today, death is a frequent subject of paintings, photographs, prints, multimedia pieces and sculpture, in part because so many artists and their loved ones are dying of AIDS.

Death in Film

A number of film genres have grown out of the 20th century's repressed cultural fascination with death. Mystery films such as those directed by Alfred Hitchcock nearly always revolve around an unsolved death. Thrillers and action movies usually have more complicated plots, but narrative tension more often than not depends on our fear of death—witnessing main characters come close to and usually avoid death. Horror and "slasher" films play off the same premise, but usually a more gruesome and supernatural death is involved—and it is not always avoided. A more recent form is the "'hood" genre that includes the films of Spike Lee and John Singleton, among others. These directors explore life against a constant backdrop of urban violence and its deadly impact on young African-Americans. True-life murder cases have also inspired numerous box-office favorites.

In the continuing controversy over representations of violent death in popular culture, the so-called "snuff" film has become a kind of metaphor. In these porn films, according to legal scholar Catharine MacKinnon, the deaths of women and children are not only depicted, they are real; the makers literally kill people in the process of making the films. There is little conclusive evidence to support the existence of the snuff film, but the idea reflects a real 20th-century fear that the imagery of death in movies, pornography or TV will somehow cause real death.

But cinematic exploration of death has hardly been limited to these genres. Below are some of the best-known Hollywood movies about death.

Death Takes a Holiday (film), directed by Mitchell Leisen. In this 1934 comedy starring Frederick March and Evelyn Vinable, Prince Cirki—who is actually Death incarnate—decides he needs a vacation. While he's catching up on his R&R, nobody on earth dies.

M (film), directed by Fritz Lang. This early German "talkie" starring Peter Lorre immortalized the truly twisted "Monster of Düsseldorf," Peter Kurten.

Beginning at age 16, the sexual sadist engaged in a long career of murdering children and young women, whom he raped before, while and/or after strangling, stabbing or beating them. The city of Düsseldorf was terrorized by Kurten for 14 months in 1929 and 1930 when he escalated the frequency of his killings. He was caught at age 47 with the help of a woman who had escaped his rape attempt, and was sentenced to death nine times and beheaded in 1931.

They Made Me a Criminal (film), directed by Busby Berkeley. Former world middle- and welterweight boxing champion Charles "Kid" McCoy (Norman Selby) provided the plot for this 1939 hit. Apparently his live-in girlfriend, Theresa Mors, had second thoughts about becoming his tenth wife; drunk and angry, he murdered her. McCoy was convicted of the 1924 slaying and sentenced to 122 years in San Quentin, but was released after serving only eight; in 1940 he took a lethal overdose of sleeping pills. The actor John Garfield won critical acclaim for his portrayal of the homicidal pugilist.

Double Indemnity (film), directed by Billy Wilder. This 1944 *film noir* recounts a sordid story of greed. In February of 1927, Ruth Snyder took out a double-indemnity life insurance policy on her husband, Albert. She and her lover, Henry Judd Gray, then proceeded to bash the sleeping Albert over the head with a weight, chloroform him and strangle him with picture wire. Gray then tied Snyder up to make the killing look like a burglary, but the two were eventually tricked by police into confessing. At her electrocution at Sing Sing in 1928, Snyder was surreptitiously photographed by a man with a camera strapped to his ankle; this picture became one of the most famous tabloid exclusives ever. Gray was executed in the same chair minutes later.

Monsieur Verdoux (film), directed by Charlie Chaplin. Chaplin wrote and starred in this 1947 black comedy inspired by the antics of serial killer Henri Désiré Landru. Between 1915 and 1919, Landru enticed an unknown number of women to his house just outside Paris by placing classified ads in newspaper matrimonial columns. He stole his "fiancées'" money and possessions and hacked up their bodies, burning the pieces in his furnace. The "Bluebeard" was arrested when neighbors complained about the foul smoke emanating from his chimney, convicted of eleven murders and guillotined in 1922.

Bonnie and Clyde (film), directed by Arthur Penn. Wildly successful, this movie drew criticism for romanticizing Bonnie Parker and Clyde Barrow's vicious crime spree of 1932–4. The outlaws traveled around the Midwest, Texas and Oklahoma, committing petty robberies and numerous pointless murders, but were confronted and killed at a Louisiana roadblock in 1934. Warren Beatty and Faye Dunaway played the title roles in the 1967 film.

Looking for Mr. Goodbar, by Judith Rossner (novel). The 1973 rape and stabbing of a 28-year-old Manhattan teacher, Roseann Quinn, inspired Rossner to write this best-seller, later made into a movie starring Diane Keaton. Quinn had picked up a man, John Wayne Wilson, in a bar across the street from her West 72nd Street apartment; the two argued and he killed her. With the help of his male companion, police quickly apprehended Wilson in Indianapolis and returned him to New York. He committed suicide by hanging himself with a bed sheet while awaiting trial.

Ordinary People (film), starring Mary Tyler Moore and Timothy Hutton, portrays a family falling apart after a son's death.

Terms of Endearment (film), starring Debra Winger, Shirley Maclaine and Jack Nicholson, is about a middle-aged woman dying of cancer.

Philadelphia (film), starring Tom Hanks and Denzel Washington, was the first mainstream feature film about AIDS. It addressed an aching popular need to contemplate an all-too-common contemporary way of death. Though it broke new ground in many ways, it followed thousands of years of tradition in marrying love with death—the one scene between Tom Hanks and his lover (played by Antonio Banderas) that is at all erotic, or even romantic, is the death scene.

Pulp Fiction (film), starring John Travolta and Samuel Jackson, is an ironic treatment of violence in the movies, which hilariously parodies the gratuitous killing found in action films.

Natural Born Killers (film), directed by Oliver Stone, focuses on two serial killers who, seized upon by the media, become internationally popular celebrities. Stone's intention was to point out that American culture is obsessed with violent death, but many felt that he simply exploited the issue without making any new points. One of the most graphically violent movies ever made.

Death on TV

Despite the staggering amount of violence argued over by parents and politicians, there is actually very little death on TV. Children's television contains almost no death, and death from natural causes is rare any time of day. Even on soap operas, people are generally killed by freak accidents or violence, rarely disease or age. This may be changing somewhat, with the rise of more realistic hospital dramas like "ER" and with the evolving presence of AIDS on TV.

Over the past 20 years TV violence has been repeatedly raised as a matter of concern by the American Medical Association, the National Parent-Teacher Association (PTA), the American Psychological Association (APA) and the National Coalition on Television Violence (NCTV). These groups and many others have worried that TV violence is linked to high teen homicide rates. Some are concerned that people imitate acts they see on TV; others fear that kids who grow up watching violence will become insensitive to it. Concerns have been raised that TV violence will shape viewers' values, leading them to approach the world with a more defensive, potentially violent attitude. In a careful review of the major studies on this subject, media scholar Nancy Signorielli found that there was no conclusive evidence yet to support the first two fears, but the third concern could not be dismissed.

Who dies on TV? The most likely people to die violently are elderly women, followed by lower-class men and elderly men.

Television has begun to recognize the reality of death from AIDS. Because in its early years the disease was associated with stigmatized groups (gay men, poor people, drug users), and because fatal diseases of any description are rare on TV, progress has been slow. However, in the past few years *And The Band Played On* and several other movies on AIDS have been made for TV. The subject has also been addressed on soaps and prime-time shows. TV news coverage has been as frequent as that of newspapers, though generally not as informative.

Suicide is a frequent cause of death on soap operas, and teen suicide is a common topic of made-for-TV movies as well as talk shows. As with newspaper stories, there is reason to be concerned that TV suicides inspire imitation; however, it is also believed that, portrayed sensitively, they can inspire people at risk to get help. Some stations have run suicide hotline numbers and other helpful information along with shows on suicide.

Death in Music

In Western classical music, the requiem is the most common piece of commemorative music. The most famous requiems have been composed by Brahms, Berlioz, Faure, Mozart and Verdi. Some other well-known compositions about death are Bach's Cantata 106, titled *God's Time is the Best,* Schubert's *Erlking,* and Strauss's *Four Last Songs.*

Folk music has a long-standing fascination with death. Tragic ballads in which a lover kills his or her beloved, like "Banks of the Ohio," or "Frankie and Johnny" are common.

Rock music has, since its inception, been associated with danger, taboo and sex, all, in popular tradition, close cousins of death. Although the topic of death is not explicitly addressed in rock music lyrics any more than in other media, many rock stars have died tragic, untimely deaths that have inspired virtual cults of death—witness Elvis Presley, Jimi Hendrix, Jim Morrison, Janis Joplin, John Lennon and Kurt Cobain. Morrison's grave in Paris, for instance, is covered with graffiti and constantly surrounded by somber young mourners even to this day. Young people, who tend to be encouraged by the culture to avoid thinking about death, very often find in such pop music icons the freedom to face their own mortality. The death of favorite stars is seen as a kind of breaking of social taboo.

It is worth noting that young people are not the only ones fascinated by dead pop music stars. Tabloids continue to report sightings of an Elvis returned from the dead, and numerous fanzines, mostly written by middle-aged people or retirees, are dedicated to the notion that his death was faked and that he is literally still alive. Though many of these people probably cannot be believed, their ideas are not as marginal as one might think. In 1991, a Time/CNN poll found, in a random sample of one thousand adults, that 16 percent thought it was "possible Elvis might be alive."

Rap, especially gangsta rap, tends to be rife with references to murder and guns. It has come under fire from parents' groups and public figures like Tipper Gore; as a result the genre has faced censorship from radio and video stations, and albums are often sold with warning labels. Like the controversies over television violence, this issue raises an important question: Do words and images kill people? The musicians themselves argue that their music merely reflects the reality of urban life; to suppress it simply leaves the general public unaware of the danger and death city youths face daily.

Death and Material Culture

The psychological and spiritual impact of death, as well as the religious and social practices surrounding mortality, have inspired the creation of a wide array of useful and decorative objects. These artifacts reflect both death's place in the everyday life of a society and its attitudes toward the end of life.

The Decorative Arts

Ancient Romans carved skeletons onto bronze bowls and depicted them on mosaic floors. Death, especially as a Horseman of the Apocalypse, appears on the occasional cathedral frieze. But death imagery really took the Western decorative arts by storm in the 16th and 17th centuries. In this period, people liked to adorn their homes with objects that reminded them of death—skeletons, hourglasses, scythes, grave digger's shovels and clocks were all common motifs. Portraits often featured these objects in the background, or in a subject's lap. Cabinets, desks, mantelpieces or dishware might be decorated with such symbols. This iconography began to taper off in the 18th century.

Portable Memento Mori

Memento mori are objects that remind one of death; at many points in history people have carried such things around with them so as not to forget their mortality. In ancient Egypt or Rome, miniature coffins might be passed around at a party to let guests know they should fully enjoy the moment. Egyptians might also carry small wooden mummy figures. In the West in the 16th and 17th century, one might carry around a small death's-head carved of bone, or, in odd continuity with the ancients, a pocket-sized coffin.

Shrouds and Palls

In Jewish tradition a body is buried in a white linen shroud. This custom goes back to ancient Roman times, when Jews buried their dead in shrouds to protest the extravagance of Roman burial clothing. In Islamic tradition, the body is wrapped in white cotton. During the early Middle Ages in Europe, the deceased might be wrapped in a gold cloth, or fabric dyed in red, blue and green. Later, a burial cloth (pallium, or pall) might be black, decorated with deathly symbols, and the dead person's initials, or coat of arms. After the 13th century in most of Western Europe, a linen shroud covering the corpse from head to toe, especially its face, was common.

Coffins

Ancient Egyptians carved their mythology on the walls of coffins; the Coffin Texts are one of the major sources of information about this culture. Orthodox Jews bury their dead in a simple pine box; Muslims also use a plain wooden coffin. Christians in Europe, before the 13th century, made coffins of stone; after that point they switched to wood, the material used today.

Ghana has a more colorful tradition, burying chiefs in elaborately carved and painted coffins representing the highlights of the chief's life. The practice has spread to ordinary folk, who are often buried in coffins representative of their profession: a fisherman in a giant crab, a baker in a loaf of bread, a farmer in an ear of corn. The coffins can become quite complex, as with the truck-shaped number for a lorry driver, complete with battery-powered horn, head-lights, radio and cassette player.

Hearses

Early hearses were ostentatious silver and black vehicles; today one cannot always tell them apart from regular limousines.

Graves and Tombs

Ancient Roman and Christian tombs tended to bear inscriptions about the deceased's life, with an image of him which was not an accurate likeness so much as a representation of his personality (a bookish type might be depicted reading at a desk, for instance). Around the 5th century, floral or abstract ornaments replace portraiture and inscriptions.

From the 13th century on, one of the images most commonly found on Western, especially French, tombs is that of the mourning procession—pall-bearers wearing hooded cowls, carrying a body. Another is a praying figure. From 14th- to 16th-century Western Europe, the decomposing dead body, or *transi,* is also common. On Italian tombs of this period, one finds statues of the deceased. Another common image from the early Middle Ages through the 16th century is that of a figure lying down; in the 16th century it became common to combine praying and prone figures. Another common 16th-century image is a portrait of the dead person holding a skull. It is also important to note that in the 15th century crosses on tombs and graves became ubiquitous in the West, as they are to this day.

In 17th- and 18th-century Europe an increasing number of people were buried in cemeteries as opposed to inside churches, with simple headstones. This tradition was exported to the American colonies. Gravestones in New England were often decorated by a death's-head with wings, or by a skull and crossbones. In the 18th century these creepy images were replaced by a more cheerful cherub.

U.S. cemeteries got more elaborate in the 19th century and an increasing number of commemorative statues appeared, as well as classical ornamentation such as wreaths and columns.

The Catafalque

In Western Europe from the 13th to 20th centuries, an enormous platform called the catafalque is used in funeral ceremonies; the coffin is placed under it. In the 14th century it was swathed in brocade fabrics; through at least the 16th century it was surrounded by torches and candles; the 17th century added lavish ornaments.

Items Buried with the Dead

The 500-year-old corpse of an Inca woman was recently found buried with statues wearing feather headdresses. During China's Great Tomb period, people were buried with paintings of the boats that were to ferry their souls to the afterworld. Ancient Egyptians buried their dead with amulets, often on a necklace, as well as ceremonial daggers and numerous other objects.

Other Deathly Objects

Chinese households keep altars for honoring deceased ancestors. Each has a wooden tablet inscribed with the names and death dates of family members. The family places incense on the altar, as well as food offerings, with chopsticks, on special days. Another important Chinese object is the earthen Heredity Jar, carried in a funeral procession; children compete to see who can stuff the most food for the deceased into it.

In the 15th and 16th centuries, at funerals of European heads of state it was common to carry a wooden or wax effigy in place of the actual body.

The Fashions of Death

Always a banner of social mores, clothing has a close relationship with death. Depending on a culture's attitudes toward death, it may call for dressing the deceased or the mourners in specific garb. Everyday fashion may also show death's pervasive influence, in styles and accessories meant to protect the wearer or make a statement.

Corpse Style   The clothing of the dead has varied drastically throughout history. Lindow Man, a human sacrifice from the first century BCE, was buried naked with two sheepskin capes rolled up at his feet. (In case he got cold? No one knows.) Another recently discovered human sacrifice, the 500-year-old corpse of an Inca woman found in the Peruvian Andes, was wrapped in wool.

The ancient Greeks and Romans went in for expensive, lavish burial clothing. Hindu ritual simply calls for new or clean clothes. In the 20th century it is common for Westerners to bury the dead in their "Sunday best" or a favorite garment.

Mourning   In Chinese custom, mourners wear unbleached, unhemmed white clothing. In Western Europe, mourners wore red, green and blue through the 14th century, except in Spain, where they wore black at least as far back as the 12th century. Philippe Ariés, a scholar of Western attitudes toward death, estimates that the custom of wearing black emerged in the late Middle Ages and became widespread in the 16th century.

In the first half of the 20th century, Western women in mourning wore crepe and enormous veils; middle-class children were often dressed in violet. Today it is unusual for anyone to wear such conspicuous funeral clothing, or even to wear mourning for any length of time after a burial. A black armband on the day of the funeral will do; many Americans no longer wear black at all to funerals, choosing instead any "good" clothing.

Mourning jewelry comes in and out of vogue. In the 17th century, rings decorated with a skull and crossbones would be handed out like party favors at New England burial services. The 18th century saw a variation on this theme: commemorative jewelry, which is meant to honor the deceased long after death—pendants shaped like coffins and filled with the dead person's hair, or tiny tombs with weeping women etched into them (also decorated with hair). In the 19th century the jewels became simpler and less explicitly deathly; lockets contained a portrait and a lock of hair.

Everyday Death

At some points in history, people have worn accessories with death symbols to remind themselves of their own mortality. In France and England in the 16th and 17th centuries, for example, death's-heads and miniature coffins decorated rings, hats, watches and coffins. Today, many young people wear jewelry shaped like skulls because death is viewed as subversive: there is such cultural silence surrounding it that to wear its emblems is an act of rebellion.

VII

Death's Leading Lights

The old cliché about death and taxes is at least half right: No one escapes death. . . . At least, no one that we know of. Some of us, however, go out (or help others out) with more fanfare than others, achieving a kind of immortality at the brink of the grave. The following pages contain a selection of some of history's most improbable deaths, most heinous murders and serial killings, most intriguing last words and other bits of grisly gossip.

Famous Cemeteries and Their Residents

Some cemeteries are famous as the final resting places of large populations of famous dead people. Among the notable are:

Arlington National Cemetery, Arlington, Virginia. Residents include: Omar N. Bradley, William Jennings Bryan, William O. Douglas, John Foster Dulles, James Forrestal, Dashiell Hammett, John Fitzgerald Kennedy, Robert Kennedy, Jacqueline Kennedy Onassis, William Howard Taft, Earl Warren, the Tomb of the Unknown Soldier and George Westinghouse.

Christ Burial Church, Philadelphia, Pennsylvania. Residents include: William Rush, Benjamin Franklin and many other colonial and Revolutionary War leaders.

Forest Lawn Memorial Park, Glendale, California. Residents include: Gracie Allen, Wallace Beery, Humphrey Bogart, Clara Bow, Joe E.

Brown, Nat "King" Cole, Walt Disney, Theodore Dreiser, W.C. Fields, Errol Flynn, Clark Gable, Samuel Goldwyn, Sydney Greenstreet, Jean Harlow, Gabby Hayes, Buster Keaton, Ernie Kovacs, Alan Ladd, Carole Landis, Charles Laughton, Stan Laurel, Harold Lloyd, Carole Lombard, Marjorie Main, Chico and Harpo Marx, Mary Pickford, Clifford Odets, Dick Powell, George Raft, Will Rogers, Casey Stengel and Spencer Tracy.

Hartsdale Cemetery, Westchester County, New York. Residents include: Bela Bartok, Joan Crawford, Judy Garland, Karen Horney, Jerome Kern, "Moms" Mabley, Thelonious Monk, Otto Rank, Basil Rathbone, Paul Robeson, Richard Rodgers, Sigmund Romberg and Ed Sullivan.

Hollywood Memorial Park Cemetery, Hollywood, California. Residents include: Bugsy Siegel, Louis Calhern, Cecil B. DeMille, Douglas Fairbanks, Sr., Peter Lorre, Adolphe Menjou, Paul Muni, Rudolph Valentino and Nelson Eddy.

Los Angeles Calvary Cemetery, Los Angeles, California. Residents include: Ethel, John and Lionel Barrymore, Jack Benny, Ben Blue, Eddie Cantor, Jeff Chandler, Lou Costello.

Mount Auburn Cemetery, Boston, Massachusetts. Residents include: Edwin Booth, Charlotte Cushman, Mary Baker Eddy, Felix Frankfurter, Charles Dana Gibson, Oliver Wendell Holmes, Winslow Homer, Henry Cabot Lodge, Henry Wadsworth Longfellow, Amy Lowell, James Russell Lowell, Josiah Royce and Charles Sumner.

Woodlawn Cemetery, New York, New York. Residents include: Nora Bayes, Arde and Joseph Bulova, Ralph Bunche, George M. Cohan, Duke Ellington, Jay Gould, W.C. Handy, Victor Herbert, Fritz Kreisler, Samuel Henry Kress, Fiorello H. LaGuardia, Herman Melville, Marilyn Miller, Adam Clayton Powell, Joseph Pulitzer, Joseph Stella and Frank Winfield Woolworth.

Say What?: Famous Last Words

Today most people die in hospitals, usually surrounded by machines, doctors and nurses, but in the past people most often expired at home, among friends and family. It was these loved ones who took the time and trouble to record the final words of the dying. Here is a selection of interesting, amusing, famous, or otherwise remarkable last words.

Allen, Ethan (d. 1789). On being told that the angels were waiting for him: "Waiting, are they, waiting are they? Well, let 'em wait!"

Antony, Mark (d. 30 B.C.E.). To Cleopatra, on his suicide: "You must not pity me in this last turn of fate. You should rather be happy in the remembrance of our love and in the recollection that of all men I was once the most powerful and how at the end have fallen not dishonorably, a Roman by a Roman vanquished."

Baba Meher (d. 1969). The guru spoke his last words in 1925 and lived in silence for the next 44 years: "Don't worry, be happy."

Barnum, Phineas T. (d. 1891). A huckster to the end: "How were the circus receipts tonight at Madison Square Garden?"

Barrymore, John (d. 1942). To an interviewer while fatally ill: "Die? I should say not, dear fellow. No Barrymore would allow such a conventional thing to happen to him."

Beethoven, Ludwig von (d. 1827). The deaf composer had at least one reason for optimism: "I shall hear in Heaven."

Bonaparte, Elisa (d. 1820). Napoléon's sister, on being told that nothing was as certain as death: "Except taxes."

Bouhours, Dominique (d. 1702). A prominent French grammarian, correct as always: "I am about to—or I am going to—die. Either expression is correct."

Chopin, Frédéric (d. 1849). In the days before embalming, being buried alive was a common fear; the composer wrote down his last request: "The earth is suffocating. Swear to make them cut me open, so I won't be buried alive."

Churchill, Sir Winston (d. 1965). Been there, done that: "Oh, I am so bored with it all."

Crosby, Bing (d. 1977). A duffer to the last: "That was a great game of golf, fellers."

Curran, John Philpot (d. 1817). When the Irish wit's doctor noted, "You are coughing with more difficulty," he replied: "That is surprising, since I have been practicing all night."

Diogenes (d. 4th century B.C.E.). On being asked why he wished to be buried face down: "One brother anticipates the other: Sleep before death. Everything will shortly be turned upside down."

Disraeli, Benjamin (d. 1881). Upon hearing that Queen Victoria wished to see him, the British politician inquired: "Why should I see her? She will only want me to give a message to Albert."

de Fontenelle, Bernard (d. 1757). The 100-year-old French scholar was a master of understatement: "I feel nothing except a certain difficulty in continuing to exist."

Fox, Henry (first Baron Holland) (d. 1774). The Baron's friend Selwyn was known for his interest in corpses and executions: "If Mr. Selwyn calls again, show him up. If I am alive I shall be delighted to see him and if I am dead he would like to see me."

Gipp, George (d. 1920). "The Gipper," a football star, left his last request in a note to Knute Rockne, Notre Dame's coach: "One day, when the going is tough and a big game is hanging in the balance, ask the team to win one for the Gipper. I don't know where I'll be, Rock, but I'll know about it and I'll be happy."

Hale, Nathan (d. 1776). Before being shot as a spy by the British: "What a pity it is that we can die but once to serve our country."

Heath, Neville (d. 1946). Before his hanging, the murderer requested a last drink: "Ah. . . you might make that a double."

Hegel, Georg Wilhelm (d. 1831). This philosopher's last words may still be true: "Only one man ever understood me. And he didn't understand me."

Jefferson, Thomas (d. 1826). On his deathbed, late on the evening of July 3, Jefferson was trying to hold out until the fourth. He asked his granddaughter's husband, N.P. Trist: "Is this the Fourth?" Trist nodded yes. Jefferson actually did survive until early in the afternoon on the fourth. At the same time, John Adams, his close friend and political rival, also lay dying. His final words, spoken either minutes before or minutes after Jefferson's death: "Thomas Jefferson still survives."

Kafka, Franz (d. 1924). Asking Max Brod to destroy all of his work: "There will be no proof that ever I was a writer."

Kath, Terry (d. 1978). The rocker was playing Russian roulette: "Don't worry, it's not loaded."

Kierdorf, Frank (d. 1958). While dying of burns, this professional arsonist was being questioned by a police official, who put his ear to Keirdorf's mouth with the request that he try to speak louder: "I said. . . go fuck yourself."

Saint Lawrence (d. 3rd century). While being burned to death: "This side is roasted enough, oh tyrant great, assay whether roasted or raw thou thinkest the better meat."

Machiavelli, Niccolo (d. 1527). The political philosopher was quite the cynic: "I desire to go to hell and not to heaven. In the former place I shall enjoy the company of popes, kings and princes, while in the latter are only beggars, monks and apostles."

Mao Tse Tung (d. 1976). Two contradictory versions of his last words exist: "Act according to the principles laid down," or "Act in accordance with past principles."

Marx, Karl (d. 1883). On being asked by his housekeeper if he had any last words: "Go on, get out! Last words are for fools who haven't said enough."

Maugham, W. Somerset (d. 1965). Some words of wisdom from the novelist: "Dying is a very dull, dreary affair. And my advice to you is to have nothing whatever to do with it."

Mayakowski, Vladimir (d. 1930). The Russian poet left a final bit of advice in his suicide note: "I don't recommend it for others."

Mozart, Wolfgang Amadeus (d. 1791). In bed ill, shortly before his death, with sheets of his unfinished *Requiem* scattered around him, he asked his wife: "Did I not tell you I was writing this for myself?"

O'Neill, Eugene (d. 1953). The playwright realized he had come full circle just before his death in Boston's Hotel Shelton: "I knew it! I knew it! Born in a hotel room and, goddamn it, dying in a hotel room!"

Orwell, George (d. 1949). The final entry in his notebook: "At fifty, everyone has the face that he deserves."

Paine, Thomas (d. 1809). Replying to his doctor, who commented, "Your belly diminishes": "And yours augments."

Roosevelt, Franklin Delano (d. 1945). In poor health for years, the president probably didn't exaggerate his last words: "I have a terrific headache."

Ross, Robert (d. 1918). Oscar Wilde's companion parodied Keats's epitaph ("Here lies one whose name was writ in water"): "Here lies one whose name was written in hot water."

Rothstein, Arnold (d. 1928). When asked who shot him, the gangster answered: "Me mudder did it!"

Runyon, Damon (d. 1946). Dying of throat cancer, the writer penned a last note to his friends: "You can keep the things of bronze and give me one man to remember me just once a year."

Sedgewick, General (d. 1864). During the battle of Spotsylvania, the Civil War general looked over a parapet toward the enemy: "They couldn't hit an elephant at this dist. . . "

Shaw, George Bernard (d. 1950). An hour before his death, he remarked to a friend: "Well, it will be a new experience anyway."

Stein, Gertrude (d. 1945). Her last conversation was tape recorded: "What is the answer?" Receiving no answer, she laughed, "In that case, what is the question?"

Strachey, Lytton (d. 1932). Still a critic with his last breath: "If this is dying, I don't think much of it."

Switzer, Carl (Alfalfa) (d. 1959). The Little Rascals' "Alfalfa" was in a bar with the man who shot him; both were drunk: "I want that fifty bucks you owe me and I want it now!"

Vanderbilt, William Henry (d. 1885). It's difficult to feel sympathy for this dying millionaire: "The care of 200 millions of dollars is too great a load for any brain or back to bear. It is enough to kill a man. There is no pleasure to be got out of it as an offset—no good of any kind. I have no real gratification of enjoyment of any sort more than my neighbor on the next block who is worth only half a million."

Queen Victoria (d. 1901). Queen Victoria looked forward to joining her beloved husband, who preceded her in death in 1861: "Oh that peace may come. Bertie!" Prince Albert, on the other hand, had somewhat less romantic last words for his wife and queen: "You have not forgotten the important communication to Nemours? Good little woman."

Voltaire (d. 1778). As the lamp beside his bed flared: "What? The flames already?"

Wagner, Richard (d. 1883). In typical Wagnerian fashion: "I am fond of them, of the inferior beings of the abyss, of those who are full of longing."

Wilde, Oscar (d. 1900). About a month before his death, while at a café sipping absinthe, the ailing playwright still had his renowned sense of humor: "My wallpaper and I are fighting a duel to the death. One or the other of us has to go."

Young, Brigham (d. 1877). The Mormon leader summed it all up: "Amen."

Once is Not Enough: All-Star Serial Killers

The most famous serial killers, while certainly guilty of horrible crimes, are not necessarily the most prolific. David Berkowitz—"Son of Sam"—was responsible for a comparatively paltry six deaths and Jack the Ripper only boasts five confirmed slayings, though many more are often attributed to him. What follows is a rogues' gallery of the world's most diabolical murderers.

Barbosa, Daniel. Raped and murdered 71 girls and women in Colombia and Ecuador in 1985.

Bianchi, Kenneth and Angelo Buono, Jr. "Hillside Strangler." Together strangled ten women in Los Angeles between October 10, 1977, and February, 1978. Bianchi killed two more in Bellingham, Washington, in January 1979 and was apprehended there. Found sane, pled guilty and sentenced to life. Buono arrested, tried, sentenced to life without parole.

Bundy, Ted (Theodore Robert). Murdered at least 30 women and girls between 1974 and 1979 in Washington, Utah, Colorado and Florida. Arrested February, 1979 in Pensacola, Florida. Tried and convicted of two Florida killings. Electrocuted January 24, 1989.

Burke, William. Nineteenth-century body-snatcher who decided it was easier to kill people than to dig them up. Estimated to have murdered 32 people, mostly male, around Edinburgh. Hanged January 28, 1829.

Chikatilo Andrei Romanovich. See page 180.

Corll, Dean Allen. Two accomplices, Elmer Wayne Henley and David Brooks steered boys and young men to Corll for five to ten dollars apiece. Corll got his victims drunk to unconsciousness, then tied them naked, handcuffed and spreadeagled on a plank. Tortured victims until they died, sometimes for more than 24 hours. Twenty-seven known victims killed between 1970 and 1973. Corll shot to death by Henley on August 8, 1973. Brooks sentenced to life, Henley to 594 years.

Corona, Juan V. Twenty-five bodies of men dug up in area of Yuba City, California, in May 1971 after farmer found a recent grave on his land. Most were stabbed and their heads battered by a machete after homosexual assault. Corona convicted January 1973, sentenced to 25 consecutive life terms.

Dahmer, Jeffrey. See page 180.

de Brinvilliers, Marie. Poisoned and killed dozens of patients in a Paris hospital in mid-1600s. Poisoned her father in 1666, then two brothers. Also killed numerous strangers. Arrested March 29, 1676, beheaded, then burned. Victims totalled close to 100.

de Jesús Gonzalez, Delfina and Maria. Enslaved girls and women in their brothel, Rancho El Angel, in western Mexico. Killed them if they became pregnant, sick, old or uncooperative. Arrested 1964. Remains of 50 to 80 bodies found, including newborn babies and 11 men. Each sister sentenced to 40 years.

de Salvo, Albert Henry. "Boston Strangler." Killed 13 women in Boston area between 1962 and 1964. Talked his way into their homes, raped and strangled them. Always tied ligature in a bow under victim's chin. F. Lee Bailey defended him, got him committed to a mental hospital. Never tried for murders, but did confess to them while in hospital. Sentenced to life in 1967 for other sex offenses. Committed suicide in prison, November 1973.

Fernandez, Raymond and Martha Beck. "Lonely Hearts Killers." Convicted of killing two women and one baby, probably killed 17 other women. Victims were members of lonely hearts clubs. Fernandez courted women, Beck posed as his sister. Conned many women out of money, killed those who resisted. Both electrocuted at Sing Sing Prison, New York, on March 8, 1951.

Gacy, John Wayne, Jr. In late 1970s, brought young men to his home on the pretext of giving them a job. Sexually abused, tortured and killed 33 victims. Arrested December 1978, tried, executed by lethal injection May 10, 1992.

Graham, John Gilbert. Convicted of one murder—his mother, Daisy King—but killed 43 on November 1, 1955. Planted homemade bomb in mother's luggage on airplane. Bomb exploded in midair shortly after takeoff from Denver. Was seen buying life insurance policies on mother from airport vending machines. Executed in gas chamber January 11, 1957.

Grossman, Georg Karl. Raped and murdered approximately 50 women in Germany during World War I. Apprehended 1921. Committed suicide in prison.

Guay, Joseph Albert. "The Love Bomb Murder." Murdered 23 people on an airplane by planting a bomb that exploded 20 minutes after takeoff from Montreal. Heavily insured wife was on the flight. Convicted February, 1950. Guay and two accomplices hanged.

Haarmann, Fritz. "Ogre of Hanover." From 1918 to 1924, raped and strangled homeless boys in Hanover, Germany. Bit victims through the throat. Sold body parts to unsuspecting public as meat. Apprehended in 1924, admitted to 30 to 40 killings, though may have been responsible for up to 50, convicted of 24. Beheaded January 1925.

Harvey, Donald. Murdered at least 50 patients by poisoning while working as an orderly in hospitals in Kentucky and Ohio. Arrested in Cincinnati in 1987 and convicted of 37 slayings. Sentenced to 20 life terms.

Hoch, Johann Otto. In late 1800s, married women in Europe and the U.S. for their money, then slowly poisoned them. Hanged for one slaying in Chicago February 3, 1906. Thought to have murdered more than 50.

Hooijaijers, Frans. Injected patients in Dutch nursing home with lethal overdoses of insulin in late 1960s and early 1970s. Convicted of five killings, sentenced to 13 years. Total murders estimated at up to 259.

Kearney, Patrick Wayne. "Trash Bag Killer." From 1975 to 1977, murdered 32 young gay men in southern California. Put nude, mutilated corpses in trash bags and dumped them by the sides of highways. Turned himself in to police in Redondo Beach, California, July 1, 1977. Pled guilty to 21 slayings and sentenced to life.

Kiss, Béla. Murdered his wife and her lover in Budapest in 1912. Advertised for new wives, killing 21 women who responded. Vanished during outbreak of World War I when his crimes were discovered.

Kraft, Randy (Randolph). "Freeway Killer." In 1982 and 1983, seduced and killed approximately 63 men in New York, Michigan, Ohio, Washington, Oregon and California. Tortured and castrated victims, several of whom were Marines. Arrested in southern California May 14, 1983. Tried and sentenced to die in gas chamber at San Quentin.

Kurten, Peter. See page 156.

Landru, Henri Désiré. See page 157.

Lopez, Pedro. Killed three fellow prison inmates in 1967. After release, raped and strangled numerous Indian girls, aged 8 to 12, in Peru. Caught and deported to native Colombia. Continued killing girls until arrest in April 1980. Fifty-three graves were found, but Lopez claimed to have murdered about 110 in Ecuador, 100 in Colombia and over 100 in Peru.

Lucas, Henry Lee. Stabbed mother to death in 1960. Between 1975 and 1983, sometimes with his lover, Ottis Toole, roamed the country, randomly raping (before and after death), torturing, mutilating and killing people by strangling, stabbing, shooting or beating. Occasionally cannibalized victims. Apprehended in Texas June 11, 1983. By June 1985 convicted of several murders, sentenced to death. Execution stayed, Lucas transferred to Florida prison for further trials. Confessed to 360 slayings. Actual number unknown, thought to be 147.

Lüdke, Bruno. Killed, then raped approximately 85 women in Germany between 1928 and 1943. Caught in January 1943 and sent to Nazi hospital in Vienna. Died from medical "experiment" April 8, 1944.

Mudgett, Herman Webster. Murdered approximately 200 young women in his home, "Murder Castle," in Chicago in the early 1890s. Also slew several other women, men and children in various locations. Caught in Boston by an insurance investigator and sent to Philadelphia for trial. Hanged May 7, 1896

Nelson, Earle Leonard. "Gorilla Murderer." Killed—mostly by strangling—and raped (before and after death) at least 20 women and one baby from February 1926 to June 1927. Victims were found across the U.S. and Canada. Apprehended in Canada near U.S. border, returned to Winnipeg for trial. Convicted of one murder and hanged January 12, 1928.

Nesset, Arnfinn. In Norway from May 1977 to November 1980, injected poison into 22 elderly patients at nursing home he managed, killing them. Actual number of victims may be as high as 62. Arrested March 9, 1981. Tried and convicted, sentenced to 21 years plus up to 10 years "preventive detention."

Nilsen, Dennis. In London between 1978 and 1983, picked up young gay or homeless men, invited them back to his apartment. Drank heavily, had sex if they were gay, then stabbed or strangled victim. Used butchering skills to cut up corpses after they were decomposing. Boiled some pieces and put them down the sink or toilet, kept large parts like heads in plastic bags. Plumber called to fix building's drains and Nilsen arrested February 19, 1983. Judged sane, sentenced to life. Fifteen known victims.

Panzram, Carl. Confessed to killing (and often sodomizing, before and after death) 20 men and boys. Sentenced to life for burglary and one murder September 1928. Beat prison laundry foreman to death in 1929. Hanged September 5, 1930.

Petiot, Dr. Marcel. Convicted of slaying 27 people in Paris in the early 1940s by injecting them with poison. Locked victims in a small room and watched through a peephole as they died. Arrested in 1944 and confessed to 63 killings. Guillotined May 26, 1946.

Pomeroy, Jesse. In Boston in the 1870s, killed at least 27 children. Sentenced to death in 1881, but sentence later commuted to life. Killed three other inmates in escape attempt. Died in state farm for criminally insane in 1932.

Sutcliffe, Peter. "Yorkshire Ripper." Arrested Jan 2, 1981 in Sheffield, Yorkshire while having sex with a prostitute in his car. Convicted of murdering 13 women (who had been stabbed and mutilated) and the attempted murder of seven. All but one victim were prostitutes. Sentenced to life and served three years in jail, then transferred to a psychiatric hospital.

Tessov, Ludwig. Between 1898 and 1901 killed an estimated 30 children across Germany. Strangled, then dismembered victims. Tried and executed.

Williams, Wayne. In late 1970s and early 1980s, numerous teenage black men were reported missing and/or found murdered around Atlanta. By spring 1981, 20 bodies had been found, six more men were missing. Williams was arrested, convicted of two murders in March 1982 and sentenced to two consecutive life terms. Total number of victims estimated at 24.

Noblesse Horrible

History is littered with examples of bloodthirsty aristocrats. Their special, sometimes divine, status seems at various times to have been a license to kill. The Roman emperor Caligula, for example, enjoyed watching his henchmen torture and kill people while he dined. Historians generally agree he went mad, probably after a severe illness several months into his reign. Declaring himself a god, Caligula banished or murdered most of his relatives, including his adopted Gemellus, and named his favorite horse a consul. But he sowed what he reaped, and was assassinated in 41.

Gilles de Rais, a 15th-century baron and Marshal of France who fought with Joan of Arc, was another nobleman with extremely sadistic tendencies. Between 1431 and 1440, he was responsible for the deaths of over eight hundred people. Most of his victims were boys, whom he enjoyed seeing tortured and mutilated, sometimes on a stage as a form of theatrical entertainment. He also organized hunting parties—the prey being young shepherds—and may have used some victims as Satanic sacrifices. De Rais was arrested and tried in 1440 and he and a number of his servants were hanged.

History's most notorious mass murder, known as Vlad Tepes, Vlad the Impaler, Vlad Dracula or just Dracula (c. 1431–77), was the prince of Wallachia, an area just south of Transylvania. Though he is famous for having impaled thousands of enemies on wooden stakes, he also engaged in other atrocities such as cutting off limbs and organs, decapitation, burning, roasting, breaking on the wheel, forcing people to commit cannibalism, and skinning, burying or boiling people alive. And while he did not fly around biting people on the neck, he is said to have dipped his bread in blood. Dracula was never held accountable for his murderous ways, but was instead ambushed and killed by Turks in a forest near Bucharest.

The Hungarian "Blood Countess," Elizabeth Báthory (1560–1614), who caused an estimated 650 deaths, may have been a descendant of Dracula. In 1600, she began slaughtering young, virginal women by having their throats cut, then draining their blood into vats to bathe in; she believed that these literal bloodbaths would make her look younger. She was apprehended, tried and convicted in 1611. While the servants who procured her victims were hanged, Countess Báthory herself was allowed to live, walled up in her room at her castle, with a small opening for food to be passed through. She died there in 1614.

All Together, Now: Cult Murders and Suicides

Cult killings and suicides are often particularly brutal and pointless, usually carried out by people who have fallen under the spell of a charismatic (and sometimes insane) "spiritual" leader. A few of the most dreadful of these mass deaths follow.

Los Angeles, California, July 27—August 26, 1969: Several members of the Family, on orders from their leader, Charles Manson, went on four separate killing sprees, brutally murdering nine people. The second and worst of these bloodbaths took the life of five people, including actress Sharon Tate, eight months pregnant. (Tate was the wife of film director Roman Polanski.) The group shot and repeatedly slashed and stabbed their victims and even dismembered one. The words "Healter Skelter" (*sic*) were written in blood on the wall of the house where the seventh and eighth victims lived. Manson and 20 Family members were arrested in September, 1969, on suspicion of car theft; police only discovered that they were responsible for far worse crimes when one member told a cellmate about their activities. Manson and four followers were convicted and sentenced to life imprisonment. While the exact number of other Family victims is unknown, Manson told officials that he had single-handedly killed 35 people. In 1975, "Squeaky" Fromme, one of Manson's closest adherents, was apprehended after attempting to assassinate President Gerald Ford.

Jonestown, Guyana, November 18, 1978: Following an investigatory visit by California congressman Leo J. Ryan and several newsmen, Peoples Temple leader Jim Jones ordered the suicide of his entire group of followers living at the settlement in the South American jungle. A few members were murdered, but most patiently lined up to take cyanide mixed with a fruit-flavored drink variously reported to be Kool-Aid or Fla-Vor-Aid. Jones used a gun to kill himself and his wife rather than suffer the pain and convulsions brought on by the poison. A handful of residents survived the massacre by hiding in the dense undergrowth, but the next day Guyanese troops found over 900 people—276 of them children—dead, lying facedown on the ground and already decomposing. Also dead, shot earlier by Jones's "police" at the nearby airstrip, were Congressman Ryan and four members of his group.

Matamoros, Mexico, April 11, 1989: Mexican federales and U.S. customs officials entered Rancho Santa Elena—a compound just south of the border town—on a drug raid and found much more than they bargained for. Along with the remnants of a recent marijuana shipment were the accoutrements of *Palo Mayombe*, a satanic form of Santeria: an altar, candles, the remains of goats and chickens, pieces of human scalps—and a cauldron in which floated a charred turtle, a goat's foot and pieces of human brain. Outside, in a corral, were the graves of 14 people who had been tortured, dismembered, mutilated and sacrificed. One of the bodies was identified as Mark Kilroy, an American college student whose March 13th disappearance had finally sparked an investigation into the vanishing of several Mexicans in the area and whose case had appeared on the TV show *America's Most Wanted*. The man responsible for this cult of drug dealing and ritual slaughter was "El Padrino," Adolfo de Jesus Constanzo, a Cuban from Miami who had set up headquarters in Mexico City. When police tracked him down in the capital city, however, Constanzo ordered his right-hand man to shoot him and his lover, adding two more corpses to the count.

New Orleans, Louisiana, November 7, 1990: Yahweh Ben Yahweh (Hulon Mitchell, Jr.) was arrested on charges of murder, conspiracy and racketeering; 13 of his closest aides were also apprehended at various other locations. Yahweh was the founder of the Nation of Yahweh, a large, wealthy and powerful Miami sect whose members were commonly referred to as "Yahwehs." Though it appeared that he was leading a group dedicated to black empowerment (his followers did establish some worthy programs to help southern Florida's poor black community), Yahweh had actually been engaging in his own reign of terror since the cult's founding in 1979, ordering the murders of random whites and of people with whom he had disagreements. He was eventually convicted on some of the charges and sentenced to 18 years in jail. The death toll as a result of his activities is unknown, but it is at least in the dozens, if not higher.

Waco, Texas, April 19, 1993: A 51-day standoff between the Branch Davidians—a radical offshoot of the Seventh Day Adventists who had lived at Ranch Apocalypse since 1930—and federal agents ended in carnage. The ordeal had begun on February 28, when the federal Bureau of Alcohol, Tobacco and Firearms attempted to raid the compound and arrest the sect's leader, David Koresh (Vernon Wayne Howell), on firearms charges. The ensuing gun battle resulted in the deaths of four agents and six Davidians. The raid failed because the Davidians knew what was coming and were prepared with firepower far greater than the feds'. The FBI attempted to end the siege by tear-gassing the compound on the morning of April 19, but the residents, who had gas masks and were prepared to die, simply stood their ground and shot at the agents. At around noon, an FBI surveillance plane reported several small fires burning within Ranch Apocalypse; the flames soon engulfed the entire complex and stockpiled ammunition went up in huge explosions. After the conflagration died down, 76 burned bodies were recovered, including 25 children. Not all had died from the fire, however: Koresh and 18 others had died of bullet wounds—some self-inflicted—and one 2-year-old had been stabbed. Eight cult members managed to escape.

Cheiry and Granges-sur-Salvan, Switzerland and Quebec, Canada, October 5, 1994: Three separate locations of the Solar Temple, a quasireligious New Age group, exploded in intense fireballs. Fifty-four people were later found dead. Many had succumbed not to fire but to gunshots or stabbing before the incendiary devices were detonated. The evidence suggests that while most of the dead were participants in a planned mass suicide, others had been unwilling victims. The remains of the sect's leader, Luc Jouret, were among those found at Salvan.

Last Suppers: Notorious Cannibals

Some of the names—Ed Gein, Alfred Packer, Jeffrey Dahmer—are familiar, notorious. Others, like Joachim Kroll or Liver-Eating Johnson, are not as well known, but no less chilling. They come from different countries and different centuries, but they all have one thing in common: a predilection for dining on human flesh. Herewith, a repast of murderous cannibalism, with a little necrophilia on the side.

Sawney Bean: He lived in the 16th century in a cave near Galloway, Scotland, with his wife and clan, totalling 46. The group ambushed, robbed, killed and ate an estimated 1,500 passersby during a 25-year period. They were eventually discovered and the entire family was burned at the stake, without a trial.

The Donner Party: A group of 89 settlers led by George Donner struck out for California in 1846. Following some bad advice, they took a short cut that slowed them down and prevented them from reaching the Sierra Nevadas before winter set in. The weather was particularly brutal and they were trapped by snow for four months. Lewis Keseberg, one of 49 survivors, was found beside a boiling pot containing Mrs. Donner's liver. He claimed that he and the others resorted to cannibalism only after fellow settlers' natural deaths, but there was evidence of murder. Keseberg was tried and released; he later ran a steak house.

Alfred Packer: This gold prospector led five men on an expedition into the San Juan Mountains near Salt Lake City in 1873. He returned alone, but with the others' money and equipment, saying that the men had abandoned him. The five were found later, murdered and stripped of flesh. Packer was sentenced to 40 years hard labor (he served 17). During the sentencing, Judge Melville Gerry spat out, "There were only seven Democrats in Hinsdale County and you ate five of them, you depraved Republican son of a bitch!"

John "Liver-Eating" Johnson: A Montana trapper of the 1880s, he butchered Crow Indians and ate their livers. Johnson became sheriff of Coulson, Montana in spite (or perhaps because) of his activities.

Albert Fish: In New York circa 1910–34, this sadomasochist tortured, raped, killed and ate at least 15 people, mostly children, for sexual gratification. He had spent time in and out of prisons and psychiatric hospitals, but was judged "harmless." Finally facing the electric chair, Fish said, "It will be a supreme thrill—the only one I haven't tried." He had to be electrocuted twice at Sing Sing in 1936, the first attempt having short-circuited.

Edward Gein: By profession a Wisconsin farmer, this necrophiliac was considered "eccentric" by his neighbors. Gein robbed graves after his mother's death in 1945, eating some body parts and using others—particularly female genitalia, skin, scalps, faces, heads and skulls—as knickknacks or clothing.

From 1954 to 1957 he killed at least 15, continuing his bizarre interior decorating and trussing up bodies like deer. Police found body parts in the freezer, furniture upholstered with skin and four skulls adorning his bedposts. He was incarcerated in the state mental hospital until his death in 1984.

"Uncle" Joachim Kroll: Kindly "uncle" to neighborhood children, he killed and mutilated, then raped and often ate, at least 14 girls and women in Germany between 1955 and 1976. He was caught when a fellow boarder found their building's common toilet stopped up with human tissue and organs. Kroll explained that he ate some victims because meat was expensive. He was tried and sentenced to life in prison.

Edmund Emil Kemper III, "Co-ed Killer": This sexual sadist from Santa Cruz, California, started his career by killing and mutilating cats as a young teen. At 15 he killed his grandparents, but he was paroled at 21. Between May 1971 and April 1972 Kemper killed several young women by shooting or stabbing them; he cut off his victims' hands and heads and had sex with the corpses. The heads were kept wrapped in plastic and used later for sex; flesh from the legs of at least two was cooked in a casserole. His final killing was of his mother, after which he turned himself in to police. Kemper was tried on eight counts of murder and is serving a life sentence. He explained that he cannibalized his victims because he "wanted them to be part of [him]."

Andrei Romanovich Chikatilo, "Rostov Ripper": An impotent Russian teacher and clerk, he viciously stabbed over 50 people to death in Russia, the Ukraine and Uzbekistan from 1978 to 1990. Using children, vagrants and prostitutes for sexual gratification, he cut slits in some corpses in order to have intercourse. He often bit or cut off and ate body parts—tongues, lips, noses, breasts, genitals—sometimes while the victim was still alive. Chikatilo also boiled flesh or cooked it over a campfire. He was arrested in Rostov after a massive police investigation, judged sane, tried and executed by firing squad in 1994.

Jeffrey Dahmer: This lonely, homosexual necrophiliac admitted killing 17 boys and men between 1978 and 1991 so they wouldn't leave him. He usually picked up his victim at a bar, brought him home for a drink, drugged him, then strangled or stabbed him to death. He then had sex with the corpse, dismembered it and took Polaroids; sometimes he saved parts, especially hearts and genitals, in formaldehyde or in the refrigerator. Dahmer also boiled some heads and saved the skulls. During his cannibalistic meals, he reportedly experimented with various condiments, including A1 steak sauce. He also attempted to lobotomize some sedated victims by pouring acid into holes drilled into their head. Dahmer was arrested in his Milwaukee apartment when one victim, Tracy Edwards, escaped and flagged down police. Dahmer was declared sane, convicted by a jury and given 16 consecutive life sentences, but he was beaten to death by a fellow inmate in 1994.

Outrageous Fortune: Three Despicable Killings

Sometimes a shockingly pointless murder—whether of someone famous or not—captures attention and sparks outrage throughout the world. Here are three such cases.

At about 3:20 A.M. on March 13, 1964, Catherine "Kitty" Genovese, 27, returned to her home in an affluent neighborhood in Queens, New York, after closing the bar she managed. As she parked her car, she noticed a man lurking in the shadows. Alarmed, she headed not for her apartment building, but for a well-lit nearby street. The man followed her and assaulted her with a knife. Genovese screamed that she had been stabbed and several windows opened; someone shouted, but no one came to help or called the police. The assailant walked away, the windows closed and Genovese struggled to her building. The man returned and stabbed her a second time; again she called out and again windows opened and closed. Genovese managed to crawl inside her building's vestibule, where the attacker found her and stabbed her yet a third time. At 3:50 A.M., about half an hour after Genovese's first cries for help, a man finally phoned the police. It was too late: Kitty Genovese was dead, murdered while 38 people watched. The officers questioned her neighbors, receiving a variety of excuses for their inaction: "[I] thought it was a lovers' quarrel," "I was tired." The killer, Winston Mosely, was arrested on March 19 and received a death sentence—later commuted to life—for two murders. The name Kitty Genovese has become a symbol of the dangers of apathy in modern society.

John Lennon once joked that the Beatles were "more popular than Jesus." This angered Mark David Chapman, a "pathological narcissist with a 'grandiose sense of self-importance,'" who had been in and out of mental institutions. He decided that Lennon was the Antichrist. On December 5, 1980, Chapman left his home and wife in Hawaii and travelled to New York, armed with a snub-nosed .38. At around 5 P.M. on the eighth, shortly after posing for photographer Annie Liebovitz's famous *Rolling Stone* cover, John Lennon left his apartment in the Dakota on West 72nd Street, gave his autograph to Chapman and went to a recording session. When he returned just before 11 P.M., Chapman was still there; he shot the former Beatle five times. Lennon bled to death before reaching the hospital. The world mourned and tens of thousands of fans held vigils outside the Dakota and, later, in New York's Central Park and in Liverpool, England, Lennon's home town. Mark David Chapman is serving a sentence of 20 years to life. Lennon's murder crystalized growing fears of celebrity stalking.

In Chicago, on May 21, 1924, two brilliant, wealthy young students, Nathan Leopold and Richard Loeb, committed what they believed to be the perfect crime and what was later to inspire Alfred Hitchcock's 1949 classic, *Rope.* It was, for them, simply an intellectual exercise. After weeks of careful planning, they abducted 14-year-old Bobbie Franks, a distant relative of Loeb. In their rented car, while Leopold drove, Loeb stabbed the boy several times in the head with a chisel; Franks bled to death. The two waited for nightfall, eating at two restaurants to kill time, then stripped the corpse, poured acid over it and hid it in a culvert. After typing a ransom note, the murderers meticulously rid themselves of all incriminating evidence, burying their victim's clothes in Indiana and tossing pieces of their typewriter into two separate lagoons. Bobbie Frank's body was soon found, however, along with Leopold's glasses, and the "flawless" plot began to unravel. Leopold and Loeb broke down under police questioning and confessed; they pled guilty, were defended by Clarence Darrow and received life sentences for murder and 99 years each for kidnapping. Nathan Leopold served 33 years; after his release in 1958, he moved to Puerto Rico, where he died of a heart attack in 1971. Richard Loeb was killed in prison in 1936. The names Leopold and Loeb still symbolize wanton, senseless murder.

Media Circus of the Macabre: Tabloid Sensations

Most everyone knows more than they ever wanted to about the 1994 murders of Nicole Brown Simpson and Ronald Lyle Goldman. Surrounded by the most overblown media feeding frenzy to date, actor and football legend Orenthal James "O.J." Simpson was tried and acquitted for the slashing and stabbing of his ex-wife and her friend. For months, the world witnessed all-O.J. television: the events leading to the trial and the trial itself could be viewed on any number of TV stations, at any time of the day or night. In addition, there was daily coverage of the affair in American and many international newspapers. But while this may be the most extreme example of media sensationalization of a tragic death, it is certainly not the first.

Sensational journalism is not a 20th-century invention. If Lizzie Borden were alive today, she could tell us all about being convicted by the press. On

August 4, 1892, Borden's father, Andrew, and stepmother, Abby, were found in the family home in Fall River, Massachusetts, brutally hacked to death with a hatchet. Lizzie was arrested for the killing, but before her trial, a newspaper published the now-famous lines, "Lizzie Borden took an ax,/And gave her mother forty whacks;/And when she saw what she had done,/She gave her father forty-one." (In fact, Andrew Borden had 10 wounds and his wife, 19.) The evidence against Lizzie was slim, however, and she was acquitted. There has, of course, been much speculation over the past century about who the actual murderer was; while a few still believe she was guilty, others suspect the family's maid, Bridget Sullivan. But it was Lizzie Borden who bore (and still bears) the stigma, until her death in 1927.

Silent-movie star Roscoe "Fatty" Arbuckle caused one of Hollywood's greatest scandals when he allegedly murdered actress Virginia Rappe on September 5, 1921. While a wild party raged in another part of his hotel suite, Arbuckle took the woman into his bedroom; soon screams were heard. She was found bleeding, with her clothes torn off, saying "I'm dying. Roscoe did it." She died three days later. Arbuckle's studio did its best to cover up the details and succeeded to a degree. Various theories were presented—that Rappe's bladder ruptured when the obese Arbuckle raped her, that he inserted a jagged piece of ice or a champagne bottle into her vagina—but none were ever proved. The star was tried three times, resulting in two hung juries and, finally, an acquittal. The third jury even issued a formal statement, calling the accusations "a great injustice." But because he was also tried in the media, Fatty Arbuckle's career never recovered and he died of a heart attack in 1933.

In a real-life locked-door mystery, Isadore Fink was shot three times and killed on March 9, 1929, inside his one-room hand laundry in New York. The door was bolted from the inside and the window was barred—the only possible means of escape was a tiny transom. No gun was ever found, so suicide was ruled out. The coroner determined that Fink had died instantly, so he could not have entered the room and locked the door after himself. The story provided fodder for the imagination of Alfred Hitchcock (who considered turning the story into a movie, but never came up with an ending) as well as for dozens of tabloids, but the how and why of Fink's murder remain unknown to this day.

Elizabeth Ann Short, a beautiful aspiring actress, was found in a vacant lot, horribly murdered, in Los Angeles on January 15, 1947. Her nude torso had been cut in two at the waist with surgical precision; she had rope marks on her wrists and ankles and slashes and cigarette burns over her entire body, which had been drained of blood and scrubbed clean with a brush. The letters "B.D." were carved in her thigh. In investigating the killing, a Los Angeles

Herald-Express reporter discovered that Short had the habit of dressing entirely in black and that at the drugstore soda fountain she frequented she had been dubbed the Black Dahlia. When the story—containing the mysterious sobriquet—was published, wire services and papers throughout the country picked it up and the name "Black Dahlia" instantly became synonymous with "vicious sex murder." The case was never solved.

Issei Sagawa must be the strangest media darling ever. In Paris in 1981, this Japanese painter decided to act on his fondest fantasy: he ate a beautiful white woman. He first shot his Dutch victim, Renee Hartevelt, in the back of the neck, then had sex with her corpse as a prelude to dining on her flesh (he later compared her raw thigh to tuna sushi). Apprehended due to his own incompetence, Sagawa was sentenced to an indefinite stay in a mental hospital, where he was diagnosed as "an untreatable psychotic." Strangely, however, this is where his story begins in earnest. While in the French hospital he began a correspondence with Japanese playwright Juro Kara, who published a bestselling fictionalized novel (*Sagawa-kun kara no Tegami—Letters from Sagawa*) based on these letters. The Rolling Stones then got in on the act, with their song "Too Much Blood" on *Under Cover* and Sagawa wrote his own wildly successful book about his cannibalistic fetish, *Kiri no Naka* (*In the Fog*). Within a year of his incarceration, however, Sagawa's wealthy, influential father managed to get his son transferred to an institution in Tokyo, where he remained for a mere 15 months. Upon his release in 1985, the murderer found himself deluged with offers for interviews and became a major celebrity in Japan and Europe; he was even pictured in the food section of a magazine eating barbecue at a restaurant. Sagawa continues his life in Tokyo today, still painting and writing and still a prominent media figure.

Stranger Than Fiction: Weird, Gruesome and Improbable Deaths

The human fascination with death, particularly out-of-the-ordinary exits, seems innate, secretly or openly shared by all. One category of particular allure comprises the bizarre, the accidental and the truly ironic; those with a morbid sense of humor may find some of them quite amusing.

A passenger on a crowded bus in Barcelona escaped the crush by climbing onto the roof, where he found an empty coffin. It started to rain, so he laid down in the coffin and closed the lid. Meanwhile, two more passengers made their way to the roof. When the man inside the coffin asked the other two if the rain had stopped, they were so startled that they jumped off the bus; one was killed.

Miami construction worker Jose Rodrigues was killed when a toilet on casters was blown off the fourth floor of an unfinished building and fell on him.

Three burglars broke into a factory in Norway in 1977, set a charge to blow open the safe, stepped back and detonated the explosives. Part of the factory was destroyed and all three men were killed; the safe had contained dynamite.

Ulm, Germany saw the first recorded case of murder by cancer in April, 1978. During the previous year, Siegfried Ruopp, a chemistry teacher, had been mixing a liver-destroying carcinogen into his wife's jam. As she lay in pain in her hospital bed, he gave in to temptation and brought her yet another jar of the poisoned jam. Ruopp was discovered and apprehended; his wife, Ingeborg, died that July.

A woman in Warsaw, Poland, became distraught when her husband announced he was moving in with another woman. After he left their 10th-floor apartment, the woman attempted suicide by jumping from the balcony. She landed on her wayward husband as he exited the building, killing him; the wife survived.

Demonstrating the danger of following popular fads, a man in Sydney, Australia killed his girlfriend, 62-year-old Gwen Owen, with the pet rock she had given him.

Food seems to be more hazardous to the health than one might think. At a factory in Baltimore, John Ramsey fell into a coleslaw blender and was mixed to death. In a Pennsylvania cookie-baking plant, Robert Hershey fell into a vat of melted chocolate and drowned; Nazar Zia of Michigan suffered a similar fate, drowning in a vat of gravy. Charles W. Doak, owner of the Wilson Candy Company, was murdered by being beaten with a nine-pound candy cane. At the National Institutes of Health in Bethesda, employee Shirley Foster was electrocuted by a frozen yogurt machine. And a woman in Napier, New Zealand was stabbed to death by her husband in 1984; the weapon was a frozen sausage.

Hemorrhoids fatal? In October, 1982, Norik Hakpisan, 24, of London, attempted to cure himself of a bad case by applying gasoline. (Paraffin was apparently an old family remedy, but, inexplicably, he used gas instead.) The fumes were ignited by a nearby hotplate, causing a flash fire and the young man's death.

Australian snooker expert Ray Priestley died while attempting a difficult shot. Hanging upside-down from a rafter over the snooker table, he slipped and smashed his head on the concrete floor.

Three New Jersey workmen tried to free a skunk from a length of irrigation pipe by banging it down on its end. When they hoisted the pipe up it hit an overhead power line, electrocuting two of the men. (The fate of the skunk is unknown.)

Antoine Blisonnette of Montreal yawned one day while on the job at a factory and discovered that her mouth would not close. She succumbed during corrective surgery, possibly becoming the only person ever to literally die of boredom.

In Belgium in 1966, eleven students in an auto safety class were killed when a truck ran into them.

Iranian Ali-Asghar Ahani was shot in the head and killed in April, 1990, by a snake he was attempting to capture. The hunter held the snake's head to the ground with the butt of his shotgun, but the clever serpent coiled itself around the gun and pulled the trigger.

In a case right out of a James Bond movie, Georgi Markov, a Bulgarian defector and broadcaster for the BBC, was killed in London on September 7, 1978, by a still-unknown man. Markov was walking across Waterloo Bridge when he felt a sharp pinprick in the back of his leg. When he turned around, he saw only a man picking up an umbrella. Forensic scientists later discovered that Markov had been shot by a tiny gun built into the tip of the umbrella. The bullet, a metal pellet the size of a pin head, contained a lethal dose of ricin, a particularly deadly poison.

Robert Stevens was killed while working at a cosmetics plant in Deer Park, New York when a vat of hot, molten lipstick was accidentally poured over him.

Money trouble killed Hrand Arakelian, 34, of California, while he was on the job in a Brink's armored car. He was guarding the cargo—$50,000 in quarters—when the truck, cruising down the San Diego Freeway, swerved; the boxes of coins shifted and crushed him to death.

In England, Dr. Alice Chase, author of *Nutrition for Health*, died of malnutrition.

While boating off the coast of Spain in June, 1983, Marie Cista caught a small fish. After she released her struggling catch from the hook, it leapt out of her hands and straight up into the air. Cista watched as the fish arced over her head and began its descent; it landed in her open mouth, choking her to death.

Two Boy Scouts were killed in Frankfurt, Germany in June, 1995 when the rope broke during a game of tug-of-war.

A Michigan man died of stupidity in March, 1995, while trying to fix a truck. In order to find the source of a noise, James Burns hung upside-down underneath the truck while a friend drove it down a highway. Burns was killed when his clothes caught on something and pulled him into the drive shaft.

Bobby Leach, an early-20th-century Evil Knievel, survived trips over Niagara Falls in a barrel but met his match on an orange peel in Christchurch,

New Zealand in 1926. He slipped on the peel and broke his leg so badly that it had to be amputated; Leach died of complications following the surgery.

A welder in Birmingham, England died of severe burns after urinating off a railway bridge onto an electric cable carrying 25,000 volts.

Proving that what goes around comes around, Henri Villette of Alençon, France died while attempting to kill a cat. The pet-murderer tied the cat in a bag and tossed it into a river, but slipped and fell in after it. He drowned, but the cat escaped and swam to safety.

Which Way Did They Go?: Remarkable Deaths of Remarkable People

It's not just ordinary people who sometimes die peculiar deaths; occasionally famous people make rather strange exits as well.

Aeschylus, one of ancient Greece's greatest playwrights and author of such classic tragedies as the *Oresteia* trilogy and *Prometheus Bound*, is reputed to have met a most peculiar end. An early biography relates that in Gela, Sicily, c.456 B.C.E, an eagle mistook Aeschylus's bald head for a rock. The airborne raptor dropped a tortoise on him, hoping to smash the hapless reptile's shell and feast upon its innards. Unfortunately, the playwright's skull was not as sturdy as a rock and he was killed.

At least two English kings have been hastened to their demise by their own doctors. On the morning of February 2, 1685, Charles II suffered a seizure, due, it is now thought, to Bright's disease, a terminal illness. His doctors, using the most modern medical procedures, bled him, gave him emetics and enemas and blistered his shaved head. The following morning they removed another pint of his blood. He died around noon.

King George V's death was brought about by euthanasia, a detail revealed in a magazine article 50 years after the fact. The king lay dying, in the final stages of a lung disease, on January 20, 1936. Prince Edward (later King Edward VIII) had told his father's physician, Lord Dawson, that he and his mother, the queen, did not wish the king's life to be artificially prolonged. Late on the evening of the twentieth, it became apparent that the king might linger for hours, "little comporting with that dignity and serenity which he so richly merited and which demanded a brief final scene," as Dawson wrote. The doctor also felt that the news of the king's death should be carried in the morning papers, rather than in the "less appropriate" evening editions. With this and the prince's sentiments in mind, Dawson took matters into his own hands and injected into the king's jugular vein ¾ gram of morphine and 1 gram of cocaine. The king died a few minutes before midnight and the news appeared in the morning papers.

One afternoon in August, 1876, Wild Bill Hickock sat down at a poker game in a saloon in Deadwood, South Dakota. He did not have his back to the wall, as was his customary practice. While borrowing some money, a drunk named Jack McCall snuck up behind Hickock and shot him in the head, shouting, "Take that!" Wild Bill died immediately. The cards he had been holding were scattered around him; they were aces and eights—the aces of spades and clubs, the eights of spades and clubs and the jack (or queen) of diamonds. This hand is now called the "Dead Man's Hand."

For reasons unknown, a number of prominent architects have died rather unusual deaths; Stanford White was no exception. White, who was married, was known as the greatest American architect of his time, having designed, among other buildings, Madison Square Garden. He carried on a very public affair with the much-younger Evelyn Nesbit, a beautiful model. Eventually, however, Evelyn married millionaire "Mad Harry" Thaw who was, by all accounts, completely mad. After the marriage, Evelyn continued to see White from time to time and Thaw was irate. On the night of June 25, 1906, White, Evelyn and Harry were all in attendance at the opening of a musical at a theater located on top of Madison Square Garden. During the finale, as the chorus was singing, "I challenge you to a duel," Mad Harry approached White and shot him in the face, then twice more, killing the architect atop his own masterpiece.

Other prominent architects who suffered similarly bizarre fates include Pliny the Elder (24–79), who was buried in lava in Pompeii when Mt. Vesuvius erupted; Andrew Jackson Downing (1815–52), who died in a steamboat explosion; Pierre Jeanneret (1896–193?), Le Corbusier's cousin and collaborator, who was killed in a skydiving accident over Algeria; and Louis Kahn (1901–74), who collapsed and died in a men's room in New York's Penn Station, had his wallet snatched by a bum, was mistaken for a bum himself and remained in the morgue, unidentified, for days.

The Mad Monk, Grigori Yefimovich Rasputin, probably the most difficult man in history to kill, died a protracted and particularly gruesome death. While some of the details of his murder remain in question to this day, certain facts related by Prince Feliks Yusupov (the main perpetrator) and by the sister-in-law of one of the Prince's servants are widely accepted. What is abundantly clear is that, in 1916, the Russian monarchy was in a state of chaos. Rumors that Rasputin controlled the czar and czarina by some evil, charismatic power abounded; hence, the assassination plot. (Rasputin's daughter, Maria Grigorievna, however, claimed that Yusupov's motive was anger at being repulsed in his sexual advances toward Rasputin.) Yusupov and his coconspirator, V.M. Purishkevich, a political activist, enlisted the help of three other men: Captain Ivan Sukhotin, Grand Duke Dmitri Pavlovich and Dr. Stanislas

Lazovert. Late on the evening of December 16, 1916, Rasputin went to Yusupov's palace at his invitation. His host took him to a room in the basement, where Rasputin drank port liberally mixed with cyanide (provided by Dr. Lazovert) and may have eaten cakes and candies laced with cyanide as well!. When the poison had no effect on the monk, Yusupov went upstairs to confer with the others; they decided to shoot Rasputin and Yusupov returned to the basement with his revolver. According to Yusupov's account, he then shot the monk in the back. The story told by the servant's sister-in-law, however, differs radically. In this version, all four of the other murderers went to the basement with Yusupov, gang-raped Rasputin, shot him in the head, kicked and punched him and then castrated him. In any event, Dr. Lazovert arrived on the scene at some point and declared Rasputin dead. But when Yusupov returned to the basement room about an hour later, he thought he saw the monk's eyelid moving. He shook the body to make sure it was dead, but Rasputin jumped up and grabbed the Prince, who fled upstairs in terror. The monk dragged himself upstairs, out into the courtyard and through the snow toward the palace gates. Yusupov and Purishkevich, either in pursuit of Rasputin or being pursued by him, shot him in the head and shoulder and kicked and punched him. Two of the others arrived and continued the beating (and possibly stabbing) and finally subdued the Mad Monk. The four tied Rasputin up, took him to the nearby Moika Canal and dropped him through a hole in the ice. The body was found two days later; the autopsy revealed the cause of death to be not poisoning, gunshot wounds, beating, or stabbing, but drowning.

Etched in Stone: Intriguing Epitaphs

Carving poetic, descriptive or amusing epitaphs on gravestones was a common practice in past centuries, one which has since gone out of style. The following are just a few masterpieces from a bygone era.

The majority of epitaphs, of course, are appropriately touching, like this one discovered by Nathaniel Hawthorne:

Poorly lived,
And poorly died,
Poorly buried,
And no one cried.

—Lillington, Massachusetts

But many epitaphs had a lighter tone, intentional or not. Rhyming was once *de rigeur*; some people went to great lengths in composing verse for their loved ones' memorials:

Underneath this pile of stones
Lies all that's left of Sally Jones.
Her name was Briggs, it was not Jones,
But Jones was used to rhyme with stones.

—SKANEATELES, NEW YORK

Here lie the remains of Thomas Woodhen
The most amiable of husbands and excellent of men.
N.B. His real name was Woodcock, but it
Wouldn't come in rhyme.—His widow.

—DUNOON, SCOTLAND

The death of a baby is no laughing matter, but some memorials seem to take exception. Perhaps these grieving parents were simply straining for a rhyme, too:

Beneath this stone our baby lays,
He neither cries nor hollers,
He lived just one and twenty days,
And cost us forty dollars.

—BURLINGTON, VERMONT

Since I was so very soon done for,
I wonder what I was begun for.

—NEW HAVEN, CONNECTICUT

Other accidentally funny epitaphs crop up all too frequently; these people were simply in need of an editor:
Here lies the dust of Louisa Orr, whose soul is now a little angle in Heaven.

—GERMANTOWN, PA

Erected to the memory of
John Philips
accidentally shot as a mark
of affection by his brother.

—SARATOGA, NEW YORK

Sacred to the memory of three twins.

—STOWE, VERMONT

Intentional humor, in the form of puns and wordplay, sometimes found a rather strange home in cemeteries:

Here lies Ann Mann;
She lived an old maid and
She died an Old Mann.

—BATH ABBEY, ENGLAND

This tombstone is a Milestone;
Hah! how so?
Because beneath lies Miles who's
miles below.

        —YORKSHIRE, ENGLAND

Here lie I bereft of breath
Because a cough carried me off;
Then a coffin they carried me off in.

        —GRANARY BURYING-GROUND, BOSTON

Descriptions of death by foolishness appear as a warning to future generations on these markers:

Here lies the body of Susan Lowder
Who burst while drinking a Seidlitz powder.
Called from this world to her Heavenly Rest
She should have waited till it effervesced. 1798

        —BURLINGTON, NEW JERSEY

In memory of
Mr Peter Daniels
1688–1746.
Beneath this stone, this lump of clay,
Lies Uncle Peter Daniels,
Who too early in the month of May
Took off his winter flannels.

        —MEDWAY, MASSACHUSETTS

Fear God,
Keep the commandments,
and
Don't attempt to climb a tree,
For that's what caused the death of me.

        —EASTWELL, KENT, ENGLAND

A gruesome reminder of the cause of death was another popular type of epitaph:

Here lie I and no wonder I'm dead,
For the wheel of the waggon went over my head.

        —PEMBROKESHIRE, ENGLAND

Here lies I—
Jonathan Fry—
Killed by a sky-

Rocket in my eye-
Socket.

—FRODSHAM, CHESHIRE, ENGLAND

The pale consumption gave the fatal blow,
The fate was certain although the event was slow.

—ITHACA, NEW YORK

Freedom from a shrewish wife was once a common theme on mens' headstones:

Sacred to the memory of Anthony Drake,
Who died for peace and quietness sake;
His wife was constantly scolding and scoffin'
So he sought for repose in a twelve dollar coffin.

—BURLINGTON, MASSACHUSETTS

Here lies my wife, a sad slattern and shrew,
If I said I regretted her, I should lie too!

—SELBY, YORKSHIRE, ENGLAND

But sometimes the wives had their (posthumous) say, too:

Here lieth
Mary—the wife of John Ford
We hope her soul is gone to the Lord
But if for Hell she has changed this life
She had better be there than be John Ford's wife
1790

—POTTERNE, WILTSHIRE, ENGLAND

She lived with her husband fifty years
And died in the confident hope of a better life.

—BURLINGTON, VERMONT

Certain inscriptions on tombstones of the "Wild West" do nothing to dispel the movie myth of outlaw gunfighters with itchy trigger fingers:

Here lies
Lester Moore
Four slugs
from a 44
no Les
no more

—TOMBSTONE, ARIZONA

He called Bill Smith a liar.

—CRIPPLECREEK, COLORADO

Played five aces,
Now playing the harp.

—BOOT HILL CEMETERY, DODGE CITY,
KANSAS

Some have used gravestones for billboards:

Sacred to the memory of
Jared Bates
who died Aug. the 6th 1800.
His widow, aged 24, lives at 7 Elm
Street, has every qualification for a
good wife and yearns to be comforted.

—LINCOLN, MAINE

Here lies Jane Smith, wife of Thomas Smith, marble cutter. This monument was
erected by her husband as a tribute to her memory and a specimen of his work.
Monuments of the same style 350 dollars.

—SPRINGDALE, OHIO

Many old epitaphs are quite terse; the bereaved may have been trying to
save a little money on the engraving.

JOHN BURNS.

—*Oswego County, New York*
He was.

—HORSHAM, ENGLAND

Some, however, spared no expense in venting their spleens:

M.S. Donald Robertson
Born 1st of January 1785
Died 4th of June 1848
Aged 63 years.
He was a peaceable man and, to all appearance a sincere Christian. His death
was very much regretted—which was caused by the stupidity of Lawrence
Tulloch of Clotherton who sold him nitre instead of Epsom salts by which he was
killed in the space of three hours after taking a dose of it.

—CROSS KIRK, SHETLAND, ENGLAND

To the memory of Mary Gold,
Who was gold in nothing but her name,
She was a tolerable woman for an acquaintance

But old Harry himself couldn't live with her.
Her temper was furious
Her tongue was vindictive
She resented a look and frowned at a smile,
And was sour as vinegar.
She punished the earth upwards of 40 years,
To say nothing of her relations.

—MASSACHUSETTS

Composing one's own epitaph has long been a popular pastime among famous and literary types. These found their way to grave markers:

Good friend, for Jesus' sake forbeare
To digg the dust enclosed heare;
Bleste be the man that spares thes stones,
And curst be he that moves my bones.

—WILLIAM SHAKESPEARE, HOLY TRINITY
CHURCH, STRATFORD-ON-AVON,
ENGLAND

Life is a jest and all things show it;
I thought so once and now I know it.

—JOHN GAY (POET AND DRAMATIST),
WESTMINSTER ABBEY, LONDON

Here lies One
Whose Name was writ in Water.

—JOHN KEATS, PROTESTANT CEMETERY,
ROME

Other equally worthy epitaphs were never carved in stone:

Excuse my dust.

—DOROTHY PARKER

I've played everything but a harp.

—LIONEL BARRYMORE

I would rather be in Philadelphia.

—W.C. FIELDS

And then there is this inscription which simply defies explanation:

Here lies the body of John Eldred,
At least, he will be here when he's dead;
But now at this time he is alive,
The 14th of August, Sixty-five.

—OXFORDSHIRE, ENGLAND

Part Two

VIII

Surviving the System

Death is not the greatest loss in life. The greatest loss is what dies inside us while we live.

—NORMAN COUSINS

Countless challenges face people as they cope with the process of dying, whether as patient or loved one. Dying and death, and all the attendant concerns, are emotionally, physically, legally and financially difficult in modern society. Lingering or sudden, anticipated or not, death is seldom welcome or easy, all the less so for the impersonal nature of contact with medical professionals, the struggle with the red tape of the health-care system and the legal and financial transactions required during this extremely stressful time. Nonetheless, preparation and knowledge can lighten the burdens of death and dying.

The Patients' Bill of Rights

When an individual is admitted to a hospital that is a member of the American Hospital Association, they will be given a copy of the Patient's Bill of Rights, below:

A Patient's Bill of Rights

The American Hospital Association presents "A Patient's Bill of Rights" with the expectation that the observance of these rights will contribute to more effective patient care and greater satisfaction for the patient, his physician and the hospital organization. Further, the association presents these rights in the expectation that they will be supported by the hospital on behalf of it's [*sic*] patients as an integral part of the healing process. It is recognized that a personal relationship between the physician and the patient is essential for the provision of proper medical care.

The traditional physician-patient relationship takes on a new dimension when care is rendered within an organizational structure. Legal precedent has established that the institution itself also has a responsibility to the patient. It is in recognition of these factors that these rights are affirmed.

1. The patient has a right to considerate and respectful care.

2. The patient has a right to obtain from his physician complete current information concerning his diagnosis, treatment and prognosis in terms the patient can be reasonably expected to understand. When it is not medically advisable to give such information to the patient, the information should be made available to an appropriate person in his behalf. He has the right to know, by name, the physician responsible for coordinating his care.

3. The patient has the right to receive from his physician information necessary to give informed consent prior to the start of any procedure and/or treatment. Except in emergencies, such information or informed consent should include, but not necessarily be limited to, the specific procedure and/or treatment, the medically significant risks involved, and the probable duration of incapacitation. Where medically significant alternatives for care or treatment exist, or when the patient requests information concerning medical alternatives, the patient has the right to such information. The patient also has the right to know the name of the person responsible for the procedures and/or treatment.

4. The patient has the right to refuse treatment to the extent permitted by law and to be informed of the medical consequences of his actions.

5. The patient has the right to every consideration of his privacy concerning his own medical-care program. Case discussion, consultation, examination, and treatment are confidential and should be conducted discreetly. Those not directly involved in his care must have the permission of the patient to be present.

6. The patient has the right to expect that all communications and records pertaining to his care should be treated as confidential.

7. The patient has the right to expect that within its capacity a hospital must make reasonable response to the request of a patient for services. The hospital must provide evaluation, service and/or referral as indicated by the urgency of the case. When medically permissible, a patient may be transferred to another facility only after he has received complete information and explanation concerning the needs for and alternatives to such a transfer. The institution to which the patient is to be transferred must first have accepted the patient for transfer.

8. The patient has the right to obtain information as to any relationship of his hospital to other health-care and educational institutions insofar as his care is concerned. The patient has the right to obtain information as to the existence of any professional relationship among individuals, by name, who are treating him.

9. The patient has the right to be advised if the hospital proposes to engage in or perform human experimentation affecting his care or treatment. The patient has the right to refuse to participate in such research projects.

10. The patient has the right to expect reasonable continuity of care. He has the right to know in advance what appointment times and physicians are available and where. The patient has the right to expect that the hospital will provide a mechanism whereby he is informed by his physician or a delegate of the physician of the patient's continuing health-care requirements following discharge.

11. The patient has the right to examine and receive an explanation of his bill, regardless of source payment.

12. The patient has the right to know what hospital rules and regulations apply to his conduct as a patient.

No catalog of rights can guarantee for the patient the kind of treatment he has the right to expect. A hospital has many functions to perform, including the prevention and treatment of disease, the education of both health professionals and patients, and the conduct of clinical research. All these activities must be conducted with an overriding concern for the patient, and, above all, the recognition of his dignity as a human being. Success in achieving this recognition ensures success in the defense of the rights of the patient.

Planning Ahead: Practical Considerations

In an age when health care has become a maze of technological, legal, ethical and economic gray zones, it is essential to be prepared for the many complexities of modern death, whether one's own or that of a loved one. Even the young and healthy are advised to familiarize themselves with the issues at hand and to draft the wills, powers of attorney and other documents that can protect them and their loved ones in the event of accident, prolonged illness or sudden death.

For better or worse, ongoing advances in medical technology have expanded the boundaries of human life. Doctors can save more lives, but they also face new quandaries about when to prolong life artificially and when to allow nature to take its course. Their commitment to the Hippocratic Oath, which requires them to save life when possible and to "do no harm," presents them with dilemmas they did not have to face even a few years ago. The professional obligations of doctors and hospitals sometimes conflict with the needs and desires of patients and their families, with the result that the law plays a much larger role in medicine than it ever has before.

Any patient who wants to have a say in his or her own care must express these wishes in detail to loved ones, doctors and hospitals. Careful reflection on one's own beliefs, values and desires (perhaps with the advice of a clergy member or other counselor) and review of one's many options (with the assistance of an attorney or ombudsman) will free the patient and his or her loved ones from the need to make difficult choices in times of stress. To ensure compliance with a patient's preferences, they should be put in writing in legally enforceable form. Loved ones and health-care providers need only refer to these documents to resolve murky situations that may arise. In order for written requests to be honored, however, doctors and loved ones must know of their existence. Patients should inform their primary physician and their next of kin that they have assembled such documents and should outline their contents and location.

Whether a patient wishes to be kept alive at all costs or allowed to die with a minimum of intervention, a number of end-of-life documents can help him or her clarify any desires about medical treatment and postmortem arrangements. It is advisable to assemble as many of these as possible to increase the chances of one's wishes being honored:

1. living will

2. health-care proxy

3. durable power of attorney

4. Department of Health Nonhospital Do Not Resuscitate (DNR) Order with DNR bracelet

5. organ and/or anatomical donor card for transplant, research and teaching

6. advance health-care directive

7. informational document

8. declaration regarding final arrangements

Living Will

This document provides instructions directly to the doctors, hospitals or other health-care providers involved in one's treatment. It may detail the circumstances (e.g. coma, terminal condition) under which treatment should be discontinued, which treatments or medications to suspend (e.g. invasive surgery, artificial nutrition or hydration, measures that serve no purpose but to delay inevitable death), which to maintain (e.g. pain medication, kidney dialysis) and what sorts of "heroic measures" (e.g. emergency surgery, CPR) should and should not be used. A living will may also indicate other preferences regarding organ donation, autopsy, alternative treatments and the designation of an agent to carry out these wishes if the patient is incapacitated.

Almost all of the 50 states accept the validity of living wills; those that do have various requirements that living wills must meet. Standard state forms are published for completion by individuals and their attorneys. Following is a generic living will statement; different states may allow for or require a variety of other provisions.

LIVING WILL DECLARATION

Declaration made this _____ day of _____ , 19 _____ .

I, Jane Q. Doe, being of sound mind, willfully and voluntarily make known my desire that my dying shall not be artificially prolonged under the circumstances set forth below, do hereby declare:

If at any time I should have an incurable injury, disease, or illness certified to be a terminal condition or a permanently unconscious condition by two physicians who have personally examined me, one of whom shall be my attending physician, and the physicians have determined that my death will occur whether or not life-sustaining procedures are utilized, or that I will remain in a permanently unconscious condition, and where the application of life-sustaining procedures would serve only to artificially prolong the dying process, I direct that such procedures be withheld or withdrawn, and that I be permitted to die naturally with only the administration of medication or the performance of any medical procedure deemed necessary to provide me with comfort care.

If I have a condition stated above, it is my preference to NOT RECEIVE artificially administered nutrition and hydration (food and fluids) procedures, except as deemed necessary to provide me with comfort care.

If I have been diagnosed as pregnant and that diagnosis is known to my physician, this document shall have no force or effect during the course of my pregnancy. However, if at any point it is determined that it is not possible that the fetus could develop to the point of live birth with continued application of life-sustaining procedures, it is my preference that this document be given effect at that point.

If I am unable to make health care decisions for myself, I hereby appoint John Q. Doe, currently residing at 123 Main Street, Anytown, State 99999, as my Attorney-in-fact/proxy for the purpose of making decisions relating to my health care in my place.

If any provision in this document is held to be invalid, such invalidity shall not affect the other provisions which can be given effect without the invalid provision, and to this end the directions in this document are severable.

In the absence of my ability to give directions regarding the use of such life-sustaining procedures, it is my intention that this Declaration shall be honored by my family and physician(s) as the final expression of my legal right to refuse medical or surgical treatment and accept the consequences from such refusal.

I understand the full import of this declaration and I am emotionally and mentally competent to make this declaration.

_____

Signature

Jane Q. Doe
Anytown
Anywhere
State

The Declarant has been personally known to me and I believe him or her to be of sound mind. I did not sign the Declarant's signature above for or at the direction of the Declarant. I am not related to the Declarant by blood or marriage, entitled to any portion of the estate of the Declarant according to the laws of Intestate

Succession or under any will or codicil of the Declarant, or directly financially responsible for the Declarant's medical care. I am at least 19 years of age.

Witness Signature: _____

Witness Name: _____

Witness Address: _____

_____

_____

Witness Signature: _____

Witness Name: _____

Witness Address: _____

_____

_____

Health-Care Proxy or Power of Attorney

Another state-specific end-of-life document is the health-care proxy, in which the patient designates who shall make medical decisions for him or her in the event he or she loses the ability to reason or communicate. Like a living will, this document may contain instructions on the kinds of care to be refused or requested, or make various provisions about treatment to be received. The proxy outlines the specific responsibilities and authority of the designee, and indicates any limitations on his or her power. Patients should select their proxy carefully, choosing someone they trust to honor their wishes even in the face of pressure from relatives or medical personnel. States may impose restrictions on who may serve as a health-care proxy; in some cases the attending physician or other hospital employees may not act as proxy unless related to the patient by blood. It is advisable that the patient name one or more replacement representatives to serve as health-care proxy in case the primary designee cannot fulfill his or her obligations. Following is a generic health-care power of attorney authorization that assigns power of attorney in health-care matters to a proxy.

HEALTH CARE POWER OF ATTORNEY

1. DESIGNATION OF HEALTH CARE AGENT. I, Jane Q. Doe, of Anytown, State, appoint:

Agent Name:	John Q. Doe
Agent Address:	123 Main Street Anytown, State 99999
Phone:	Home: (999) 555-1234 Work: (999) 555-5678
Relation, if any:	spouse

as my Agent to make health care and personal decisions for me if I become unable to make such decisions for myself, except to the extent I state otherwise in this document.

NOTICE: Generally you should not appoint any of the following persons as your Agent:

(1) your treating physician or health care provider;
(2) an employee of your physician or health care provider unless the person is your relative;
(3) your residential care provider; or
(4) an employee of your residential care provider unless the person is your relative.

2. CREATION OF HEALTH CARE POWER OF ATTORNEY. By this document I intend to create a Health Care Power of Attorney. This power of attorney shall take effect upon my disability, incapacity, or incompetency, and shall continue during such disability, incapacity, or incompetency.

3. GENERAL STATEMENT OF AUTHORITY GRANTED. Subject to any limitations in this document, I grant to my Agent full power and authority to make health care decisions for me to the same extent that I could make such decisions for myself if I had the capacity to do so. In making any decision, my Agent shall attempt to discuss the proposed decision with me to determine my desires if I am able to communicate in any way.

In exercising this authority, my Agent shall make health care decisions that are consistent with my desires as stated in this document or otherwise made known to my Agent. If my desires regarding a particular health care decision are not known to my Agent, then my Agent shall make the decision for me based upon what my Agent believes to be in my best interests.

4. STATEMENT OF DESIRES CONCERNING LIFE-SUSTAINING CARE, TREATMENT, SERVICES AND PROCEDURES. I specifically direct my Agent to follow any "living will" executed by me.

5. INSPECTION AND DISCLOSURE OF INFORMATION RELATING TO MY PHYSICAL OR MENTAL HEALTH. Subject to any limitations in this document, my Agent has the power and authority to:

a. Request, review and receive any information, verbal or written, regarding my physical or mental health, including, but not limited to, medical and hospital records;

b. Consent to the disclosure of this information to others.

6. SIGNING DOCUMENTS, WAIVERS AND RELEASES. Where necessary to implement the health care decisions that my Agent is authorized by this document to make, my health care Agent has the power and authority to execute on my behalf any of the following:

    a. Documents to authorize my admission to or discharge (even against medical advice) from any hospital, nursing home, residential care or assisted living or similar facility or service;

    b. Documents titled or purporting to be "Consent to Permit Treatment" or "Refusal to Permit Treatment"; or

    c. Any necessary waiver or release from liability required by a hospital or physician.

7. AUTOPSY, ANATOMICAL GIFTS, DISPOSITION OF REMAINS. I authorize my Agent, to the extent permitted by law, to make anatomical gifts of part or all of my body for medical purposes, authorize an autopsy, and direct the disposition of my remains.

8. DESIGNATION OF ALTERNATE AGENT. If the person designated as my Agent is not available or unable to act, I designate the following persons to serve as my Agent to make health care decisions for me as authorized by this document, who serve in the following order:

FIRST ALTERNATE AGENT

    Agent Name: Mary Q. Doe

    Agent Address: 456 Main Street
                              Anytown, State 99999
    Phone: Home: (999) 555-0000   Work: (999) 555-1111

9. NOMINATION OF GUARDIAN. If a Guardian of my person is to be appointed for me, I nominate my Agent (or Alternate Agent) to serve as my Guardian.

10. DURATION. I understand that this power of attorney exists indefinitely from the date I execute this document unless I establish a shorter time or revoke the power of attorney. If I am unable to make health care decisions for myself when this power of attorney expires, the authority I have granted my Agent continues to exist until the time I become able to make health care decisions for myself.

11. PRIOR DESIGNATIONS REVOKED. I revoke any prior Health Care Power of Attorney.

12. HOLD HARMLESS. All persons or entities who in good faith endeavor to carry out the terms and provisions of this document shall not be liable to me, my estate, my heirs or assigns for any damages or claims arising because of their action or inaction based on this document, and my estate shall defend and indemnify them.

13. SEVERABILITY. If any provision of this document is held to be invalid, such invalidity shall not affect the other provisions which can be given effect without the invalid provision, and to this end the directions in this document are severable.

14. STATEMENT OF INTENTIONS. It is my intent that this document be legally binding and effective. If the law does not recognize this document as legally binding and effective, it is my intent that this document be taken as a formal statement of my desire concerning the method by which any health care decisions should be made on my behalf during any period which I am unable to make such decisions.

(YOU MUST DATE AND SIGN THIS POWER OF ATTORNEY)

I have read and understand the contents of this document and the effect of this grant of powers to my Agent. I am emotionally and mentally competent to make this declaration.

Signed on _____ day of _____ , 19 _____ .

_____
                                                          Signature

Jane Q. Doe
Anytown
Anywhere
State

READ AND CAREFULLY FOLLOW THE WITNESSING PROCEDURE. IT REQUIRES TWO WITNESSES AND A NOTARY TO FORMALIZE THIS DOCUMENT.

STATEMENT OF WITNESSES

I declare that the person who signed or acknowledged this document (the "Principal") has identified himself or herself to me, that the Principal signed or acknowledged this document in my presence, that the Principal appears to be of sound mind, and under no duress, fraud or undue influence. I am not the person appointed as Agent or Alternate Agent by this document, nor am I a provider of health or residential care, an employee of a provider of health or residential care, the operator of a community care facility, or an employee of an operator of a health care facility.

I further declare that I am not related to the Principal by blood, marriage, or adoption, and to the best of my knowledge, I am not a creditor of the Principal or entitled to any part of the estate of the Principal under a will now existing or by operation of law.

Witness Signature: _____

Witness Name: _____

Witness Address: _____

_____

Date: _____

Witness Signature: _____

Witness Name: _____

Witness Address: _____

_____

_____

Date: _____

State of _____ ,

County of _____ ss:

On this _____ day of _____ , 19 _____ , Jane Q. Doe, known to me (or satisfactorily proven) to be the person named in the foregoing instrument, personally appeared before me, a Notary Public, within and for the said State and County, and acknowledged that he/she freely and voluntarily executed the same for the purposes stated in the document.

My commission expires:

_____   _____
                                 Notary Public

Durable Power of Attorney

Not specifically a medical document, the durable power of attorney confers the authority to make a wide variety of legal decisions. Most people give this power to an attorney or a spouse; in any event the designee should be able to keep a clear head about the patient's best interests even if family squabbles, religious strictures or financial pressures intrude. It takes effect when the grantor loses the capacity to make decisions, either by virtue of unconsciousness or mental disability. The durable power of attorney may place limits on the rights and responsibilities of the designee and may instruct the designee on the patient's medical and other preferences. Again governed by state law, which may restrict the identity or role of proxies, durable powers of attorney are available as standard legal forms.

Department of Health Nonhospital Do Not Resuscitate (DNR) Order

Most states allow patients to request that they not be revived if their heart stops. Patients can make this request official via a standard Do Not Resuscitate (DNR) Order. The order accompanies the patient's chart; patients may also wear a hospital bracelet alerting medical personnel to the existence of the DNR order.

Organ and/or Anatomical Donor Card for Transplant, Research and Teaching

In some states, licensed drivers can fill out a form on the back of their drivers' license indicating if they wish to donate their organs for transplant or medical research in the event of their death. Nondrivers, or those whose licenses do not include an organ-donor form, should complete a uniform donor card and keep it in their wallet. Organ and anatomical donation instructions detail which organs and body parts may be used for which purposes, which should be reserved and if the entire body should be made available to a university or medical school for teaching or research purposes. It is important to note, however, that even when an organ donor card exists, the final decision regarding donation must be made by the decedent's family. With or without the card, doctors should solicit organ donation from relatives in the following order:

1. spouse
2. adult son or daughter
3. parent
4. adult brother or sister
5. legal guardian

The consenting relative must sign an "instrument of anatomical gift" to finalize the donation process. Individuals who wish to donate their organs after death should make their wishes known to their relatives and discuss the matter with them to ensure that their request is carried out.

Only one in five Americans carry organ-donor cards permitting their body parts to be used for transplantation or research in the event of their death. Yet the need for organs is acute, outstripping the supply by many times. According to the United Network for Organ Sharing (UNOS), more than 40,000 people currently await organ transplants; more than 3,000 people die each year while waiting for an organ. Doctors have developed techniques that make possible the transplantation of many different organs, and in the face of shortages have even learned how to use tissue from other animals and how to create artificial organs. Their success with organ transplantation has escalated world demand, placing even greater strain on the supply of the genuine organs that remain the best option for transplants. The organs most needed by patients throughout the world are:

pancreas

liver

kidney

heart

lung

skin

bone marrow

cornea

cartilage

Organizations such as UNOS and The Living Bank provide information and donor registration materials to those who wish to contribute their organs after death for transplantation, therapy, research or medical and anatomical study. Donors choose one of two donation options:

1. Discrete organ donation,

in which designated organs are used separately for transplant into one or more recipients. This form of donation potentially allows a single donor directly to save many lives if he or she donates many different organs.

2. Whole-body donation,

in which the entire body goes to a medical school or other institution for teaching or research purposes.

Organs donated for transplantation must be healthy and viable. If the donor has died from certain diseases, such as cancer, only the eyes may be donated because the other organs have been compromised. Likewise, bodies donated to science must be free of communicable disease, excessive obesity, marked deterioration and amputation and must not have been subject to autopsy. Some institutions will not accept mutilated bodies or those missing an important organ. The age of the body and the exact cause of death may also be considerations. Families of donors whose bodies or organs are rejected should have other plans in place so as not to face that confusion in their time of grief.

Organ-donor bodies are generally kept on minimal life support to keep the organs viable while recipients are located and transportation arrangements are made. Once the donation process is set in motion, the organs are harvested and transported to their destination as rapidly as possible—often by air—in special carriers. Sometimes the organs go to an organ bank while a recipient is located; some organs go directly to those in need of transplantation.

Bodies donated for research or teaching may or may not be transported by the receiving institution. If not, the donor's family must engage a hearse or ambulance to deliver the body. In recent years the business of body-brokering has emerged to supply medical schools with cadavers, which are in very short supply. Brokers may purchase bodies from families or institutions and resell them for up to $1,500. The practice may seem gruesome, but cadavers are invaluable medical tools which are becoming increasingly more difficult to obtain. In the past they were more abundant because far greater numbers of paupers and vagrants died without families with resources to provide for burial. Now the medical profession relies far more heavily on voluntary donation by compassionate individuals and families.

Advance Health-Care Directive

Although not legally binding, a separate document outlining a patient's beliefs and preferences about medical care can offer guidance to loved ones or health-care professionals as they make decisions about the patient's care. This advance health-care directive or values statement consists of a general statement regarding the prolongation of life and the conditions of care, and any instructions on how these values should be honored. It may go into greater detail than a living will concerning specific medical conditions and procedures. Following is a generic advance health-care directive; this sort of statement can include any other information of relevance to the patient.

ADVANCE HEALTH CARE DIRECTIVE

If I, Jane Q. Doe, of 123 Main Street, Anytown, State 99999, am not able to make an informed decision regarding my health care, I direct that my instructions and wishes as stated in this document be followed.

1. DESIGNATION OF AGENT. I recognize that if I am unable to make an informed decision regarding my health care, it may become necessary for some other person to act on my behalf. I designate

Agent Name:	John Q. Doe
Agent Address:	123 Main Street
	Anytown, State 99999
Phone:	Home: (999) 555-1234 Work: (999) 555-5678
Relation, if any:	spouse

as my Agent to make health care decisions for me, if I am not able to make an informed decision for myself, except to the extent that I state otherwise in this document.

If I revoke my Agent's authority, or if my Agent is not willing, able, or reasonably available to make a health care decision for me, I designate the following person as my alternate Agent:

Agent Name:	Mary Q. Doe
Agent Address:	465 Main Street
	Anytown, State 99999
Phone:	Home: (999) 555-0000 Work: (999) 555-1111
Relation, if any:	None

If the person that I designate as Agent or an alternate Agent is or ever becomes my spouse, he or she shall be ineligible to serve as my Agent if we are separated, or if our marriage is annulled or we are divorced.

By the use of the term "health care decision" I mean an informed decision to accept, maintain, discontinue or refuse any care, treatment, intervention, service or procedure to maintain, diagnose or treat my physical or mental condition, subject to any statement of my desires and any limitations included in this document.

By the use of the term "health care" I mean all medical treatment, the provision, withholding or withdrawal of any health care or medical procedure, or service to maintain, diagnose, treat or provide for a patient's physical or mental health or personal care, unless such authority is otherwise limited by this document.

By the use of the term "Agent" I mean any health care decision-maker such as a Patient Advocate, Health Care Representative, Health Care Proxy, Power of Attorney for Health Care, or Health Care Surrogate.

2. AUTHORITY OF AGENT. My Agent is authorized to make any and all health care decisions for me that may be deemed appropriate by my Agent, subject to my wishes and the limitations (if any) as stated in this document. My Agent shall request and evaluate information concerning my medical diagnosis, the prognosis, the benefits and risks of the proposed health care, and alternatives to the proposed health care. My Agent shall con-

sider the decision that I would have made if I had the ability to do so. If my Agent does not know my wishes regarding a specific health care decision, my Agent shall make a decision for me in accordance with what my Agent determines to be in my best interest. In determining my best interest, my Agent shall consider my personal beliefs and basic values to the extent known to my Agent.

My Agent must try to discuss health care decisions with me. However, if I am unable to communicate, my Agent may make such decisions for me. To the extent deemed appropriate by my Agent, my Agent may discuss health care decisions with my family and others, to the extent they are available.

I authorize my Agent to:

a. Request, receive and review any information, verbal or written, regarding my physical or mental health including medical and hospital records, and to consent to the disclosure of such records to others.

b. Execute on my behalf any releases or other documents that may be required in order to obtain any information, verbal or written, regarding my physical or mental health.

c. Make all necessary arrangements for health care services on my behalf, including the authority to select, employ and discharge health care providers.

d. Make decisions regarding admission to or discharge from, even against medical advice, any health care facility or service.

e. Sign any documents titled or purporting to be "Consent to Permit Treatment" or "Refusal to Permit Treatment", necessary waivers or releases from liability required by a hospital, physician, or other health care provider.

3. EFFECTIVITY. This document shall become effective upon a determination by appropriate medical personnel that I am unable to make and communicate informed decisions regarding my own health care. The authority conveyed by this document shall not be affected by my subsequent disability or incapacity. I expect to be fully informed about and allowed to participate in any health care decision for me, to the extent that I am able.

I am to be considered incapable of making or communicating health care decisions if two physicians have personally examined me and signed a written opinion that I have a condition that means that I am unable to receive and evaluate information concerning my medical diagnosis, the prognosis, the benefits and risks of the proposed health care, and alternatives to the proposed health care, or I am unable to communicate decisions to such an extent that I lack the capacity to make my own health care decisions. This power exists only when I am unable, in the opinion of such physician(s), to make health care decisions for myself.

A copy of this statement must be attached to this document. A copy of this written determination shall be made a part of my medical record, and shall be reviewed not less than annually.

All the powers conferred to my Agent shall be suspended if I regain the ability to make or communicate health care decisions. The powers granted to my Agent shall become effective again if I am later determined unable to participate in health care decisions in the manner described above.

4. TERMINAL CONDITION. If I have a "terminal condition", I direct that my Agent make decisions concerning withdrawal or withholding of health care. If based on my previously expressed preferences, the diagnosis and prognosis, and my Agent is satisfied that certain health care is not or would not be beneficial, or that such health care is or would be excessively burdensome, then my Agent may express my will that such health care be withheld or withdrawn, even if death may result.

If my physician believes that any life sustaining procedure may lead to a significant recovery, I direct my physician to implement the treatment for a reasonable period of time. If it does not improve my condition, I direct that the treatment be withdrawn even if it shortens my life. I also direct that I be given medical treatment to relieve pain or to provide comfort, even if such treatment might shorten my life, suppress my appetite or my breathing, or be habit-forming.

By the use of the term "terminal condition", I mean that my death from an incurable or irreversible condition is imminent, and even if life sustaining procedures are used there is no reasonable expectation of my recovery.

5. COMA. If I am in a "permanent coma", I direct that my life not be extended by life-sustaining procedures; such procedures shall be withheld or withdrawn.

If my physician believes that any life sustaining procedure may lead to a significant recovery, I direct my physician to implement the treatment for a reasonable period of time. If it does not improve my condition, I direct that the treatment be withdrawn even if it shortens my life. I also direct that I be given medical treatment to relieve pain or to provide comfort, even if such treatment might shorten my life, suppress my appetite or my breathing, or be habit-forming.

By the use of the term "permanent coma", I mean that I am not conscious and am not aware of my environment, I show no behavioral response to the environment, I am not able to interact with others, and there is no reasonable expectation of my recovery within a medically appropriate period.

6. LIFE SUSTAINING PROCEDURES. By the use of the term "life sustaining procedures", I mean any procedure, treatment, intervention, or other measure that has the primary effect of prolonging my life and is not necessary to provide for my comfort or freedom from pain.

7. ARTIFICIAL NUTRITION/HYDRATION. I authorize my agent to determine whether artificial nutrition or hydration should be withheld or withdrawn.

By the use of the term "artificial nutrition or hydration", I mean food and fluids that are provided to me by artificial means such as a nasogastric tube or tube into the stomach, intestines or veins.

8. SPECIFIC MEDICAL PROCEDURES. Notwithstanding any other provision of this document, it is my general desire to (i) RECEIVE the following procedures or treatment that are so marked, if such procedures are deemed appropriate by my attending physician and any agent that I may have designated to make health care decisions for me, and (ii) NOT RECEIVE the following procedures or treatment that are so marked, although such procedures are deemed appropriate by my attending physician.

	RECEIVE	NOT RECEIVE
Artificial or mechanical respiration		X
Cardiopulmonary resuscitation		X
Blood or blood products	X	
Any form of surgery or invasive diagnostic procedures		X
Kidney dialysis		X
Antibiotics	X	
Chemotherapy		X
Radiation		X

For any item that I have marked "RECEIVE", I do not wish to receive such procedure or treatment, if I have a terminal condition or am in a permanent coma, except to the extent necessary to provide comfort for me and freedom from pain.

9. PREGNANCY. If I have been diagnosed as pregnant and that diagnosis is known to my physician, this document shall have no force or effect during the course of my pregnancy with respect to the withholding or withdrawal of life sustaining procedures and/or the withholding or withdrawal of artificially administered nutrition and hydration. However, if at any point it is determined that it is not possible that the fetus could develop to the point of live birth with the continued application of life sustaining procedures, it is my preference that this document be given effect at that point. If life sustaining procedures will be physically harmful or unreasonably painful to me in a manner that cannot be alleviated by medication, I request that my desire for personal physical comfort be given consideration in determining whether this Advance Directive shall be effective during any period that I am pregnant.

10. DONATION OF ORGANS. Notwithstanding the other provisions of this document, if I have been determined to be dead according to law, I direct my attending physician to maintain my organs on artificial support systems only for the period of time required to maintain the viability of and to remove the organs and/or tissues which are to be donated. I hereby make this anatomical gift, if medically acceptable, to take effect upon my death. I give any needed organs, tissues or parts to be donated for any purpose permitted by law.

11. AUTOPSY. My Agent may give consent to or refuse an autopsy.

12. NOMINATION OF GUARDIAN/CONSERVATOR. If it becomes necessary for a court to appoint a guardian or conservator of my person ("Conservator"), I designate my Agent (or alternate Agent) be appointed as the guardian or conservator of my person.

No bond shall be required of my Guardian/Conservator in any jurisdiction. Any decisions concerning my health care to be made by my Guardian or Conservator of my person, shall be made in accordance with my directions as stated in this document.

By the use of the term "Guardian" or "Conservator of my person", I mean a person or entity appointed by a court to provide for my care and physical well-being. Such term does NOT include the appointment of a person or entity to manage my financial affairs.

13. HOLD HARMLESS. All persons or entities who in good faith endeavor to carry out the terms and provision of this document shall not be liable to me, my estate, or my heirs for any damages or claims arising because

of their action or inaction based on this document, and my estate shall defend and indemnify them, except for willful misconduct or gross negligence.

14. SEVERABILITY. If any provision in this document is held to be invalid, such invalidity shall not affect the other provisions which can be given effect without the invalid provision, and thus the directions in this document are severable.

I recognize that different states and jurisdictions have somewhat different statutes regarding advance directives. I direct that this document be interpreted in any applicable jurisdiction under both present and future law in a manner that gives the broadest interpretation to my desires.

If any provision is not legally enforceable, it is my intent that this document be taken as a formal statement of my wishes and desires concerning health care decisions, and the method by which any health care decisions should be made on my behalf during any period in which I am unable to make such decisions.

I hope that my health care providers and other persons responsible for my care will regard themselves as morally bound by these provisions.

I have read and understand the contents of this document. I am emotionally and mentally competent to make this declaration. It is my intention that this document be honored by my family and health care providers as the final expression of my legal right to refuse medical or surgical treatment and to accept the consequences from such refusal. I do not intend any direct taking of my life, but only that my dying not be unreasonably prolonged. It is not my intent to authorize affirmative or deliberate acts or omissions to shorten my life, rather, only to permit the natural process of dying.

Date: _____

_____
Signature

Jane Q. Doe
Anytown
Anywhere
State

WITNESS SIGNATURE BLOCK

Under the penalty of perjury I declare that the Declarant and each witness signed this document in each other's presence. Based upon my personal observation, the Declarant appears to be a competent individual, and is aware of the nature of this document. The Declarant is personally known to me or has satisfactorily proven to be the person who voluntarily signed this document and did not appear to be under or subject to any duress, fraud, constraint or undue influence. To the best of my knowledge, I am not

(1)   related to the Declarant by blood, marriage, or adoption,
(2)   designated as Agent or alternate Agent under this document,
(3)   entitled to any portion of the Declarant's estate according to the laws of intestate succession or under any will or codicil of the Declarant,
(4)   the attending physician of the Declarant or an employee of the attending physician or an

owner, operator, officer, director, or employee of a hospital or care or residential facility in which the Declarant is a patient or resident,

(5)   an employee of the Declarant's life or health insurance provider,

(6)   directly financially responsible for the Declarant's medical care,

(7)   entitled to a present claim against any portion of the Declarant's estate, or

(8)   entitled to any financial benefit by reason of the death of the Declarant.

I am at least 19 years of age, and did not sign this document for the Declarant.

Witness Signature: _____

Witness Name: _____

Witness Address: _____

                       _____

                       _____

Date: _____

Witness Signature: _____

Witness Name: _____

Witness Address: _____

                       _____

                       _____

Date: _____

Informational Document

Stored in one or more readily accessible locations, this document contains information on the patient's other end-of-life documents. Along with a list of the various documents pertaining to health care and where they can be found is a summary of other vital papers—wills, life insurance policies, and so on—that loved ones will need to locate in the event of the patient's incapacitation or death. Copies of the informational document may be kept by the patient's attorney, spouse, doctor or other appropriate person.

Declaration Regarding Final Arrangements

Healthy or ill, anyone concerned about their final days of life and what happens to them after death should discuss these issues with loved ones and prepare a written statement making any nonmedical requests. Desires about organ donation, cremation versus burial, memorial services and the like can be outlined in this document. Individuals may wish to designate the funeral home and type of casket they prefer, or what kind of music or flowers they would like at their funeral. Anything of significance can be covered in an informal final statement, ensuring that the decedent's wishes are honored and removing the burden of choice from survivors' shoulders. An example of a declaration regarding final arrangements follows.

DECLARATION REGARDING FINAL ARRANGEMENTS
OF
Jane Q. Doe

I wish to describe my desires and to facilitate the making of arrangements at the time of my death. My family and friends will be in the best position depending upon the circumstances to do what is right. To assist them in the process of making arrangements, I am providing the following information:

1. NOTIFICATION. I desire that my clergyperson, Thomas Q. Public of Local Church at Church Address, Anytown, be contacted immediately in order to offer assistance and comfort to my survivors.

2. FUNERAL HOME/DIRECTOR. I desire that Susan Q. Public, of Local Funeral Home, Funeral Home Address, Anytown, be consulted in making the arrangements requested in this document, and modifying these arrangements as may be appropriate at the time of my death.

3. DONATIONS/ANATOMICAL GIFTS. I desire that any of my organs which may be useful to others be taken for anatomical gifts, if possible. I have completed the appropriate form to make these gifts.

If my organ donation is not possible, then I desire that my body be donated to Local Charity Hospital, Hospital Address, Anytown.

If for any reason it is impractical to donate my body or my body is rejected for medical science studies, I desire that my body be disposed of as indicated below.

4. TREATMENT OF BODY. I desire that my body be buried in Local Cemetery, Cemetery Address, Anytown.

5. POSTMORTEM EXAMINATION. I do authorize a postmortem examination (autopsy). I desire that my family or other appropriate person(s) request that no autopsy be performed so that my body may be donated to medical science. However, I understand that in some instances an autopsy will be required by law.

6. SERVICES. I desire that the following service(s) be held:

a.   A funeral service at Local Funeral Home, Funeral Home Address, Anytown for anyone desiring to attend. The body shall be present.

b.   A wake at Local Funeral Home, Funeral Home Address, Anytown for anyone desiring to attend. The body shall be present.

7. MUSIC. I would like the following musical selections to be performed at my funeral:
        -a classical instrumental piece

8. READINGS. I desire that John Q. Doe be asked to read at my funeral. I would like the following to be read:
        -a poem

9. SPEAKERS. I would like the following person(s) to speak at my funeral if they would feel comfortable doing so:

-Mary Q. Doe

10. FLOWERS/MEMORIAL. I request that donations be made to organizations listed below in lieu of flowers.

I request that a memorial fund be established with donations to be made to the following organizations:

-Local Charity

11. CASKET/CONTAINER I desire that my family or other appropriate person making my arrangements select a casket/container that is consistent with my tastes. I desire that my casket be made of mahogany.

I do desire an outer burial container. I understand that the cemetery may require one and therefore, would prefer the outer burial container to be a burial vault.

12. PALLBEARERS. I would like the following persons to serve as pallbearers:

-family members

If any of the persons named are unable to serve for any reason, I would like the following persons to serve as alternate pallbearers:

-friends

13. OTHER WISHES. I also desire that visiting hours be arranged. I do want a marker. I request the following information be inscribed on the marker:

-epitaph

I would like an obituary notice to be published in:

-Local Newspaper

Biographical information is attached to this declaration.

I have given careful thought and consideration to these instructions. I understand that this declaration is not legally binding, and that the ultimate decision will be made by my family and other appropriate person(s) based on the circumstances at the time of my death. I hope that my desires will be fulfilled, to the extent possible.

I have discussed these instructions with my family and all appropriate person(s).

Dated this _____ day of _____ , 19 _____ .

Name: Jane Q. Doe

Address: Anytown. State 99999

Home, Hospice or Hospital? Choosing Where to Die

Throughout most of human history, people died at home surrounded by loved ones. Disease and injury killed quickly, unhindered by effective medical intervention. Childbirth, which took place at home, in particular killed large numbers of women and infants. Doctors, medicines and hospitals were primitive at best and downright dangerous much of the time. Medical care—if any was available—was most often delivered at home. Death and dying were an integral part of daily life, highly visible and far less mysterious.

With the advent of modern medicine, death moved to the hospital, fading from everyday awareness and becoming more abstract. With industrialization, the causes of death changed as well. Where infectious diseases such as diphtheria, influenza and pneumonia once claimed most lives, cancer and heart disease took over. These painful, lingering diseases required sophisticated care that could not be delivered at home. Sequestered in an institutional setting, out of sight of their loved ones, today's dying patients stay alive longer than ever before, and the longer they struggle the more intensive medical attention they require. In the hospital, death has become an exercise in technology.

In recent years, growing numbers of patients have expressed dissatisfaction with the isolated, impersonal hospital system. The American hospice movement emerged from this discontent, as well as from the high cost of hospital care. Hospices attempt to bridge the gap between home and hospital, providing a level of personal care to the dying without artificially prolonging life. Staffed by nurses, psychologists and social workers, these establishments provide a physically and emotionally supportive setting in which patients can prepare for death. Hospices also relieve loved ones who cannot provide the high level of care required but who wish to honor the patient's need for human warmth and solace. Hospices accept death as a natural part of life and work with the patient to achieve a dignified, pain-free demise.

Heart and Soul: Social and Psychological Concerns

The Stages of Death

Dying people and their loved ones experience a roller coaster of emotions as death approaches. In the early 1970s, Dr. Elizabeth Kübler-Ross conducted a pioneering study of the psychology of death and determined that there are five mental stages of death:

1. denial and isolation
2. anger

3. bargaining

4. depression

5. acceptance

Experts have widely accepted this model and generally agree that it transcends cultural, racial, socioeconomic and gender differences. The duration of each stage may vary from person to person, but anyone experiencing a close encounter with death passes through the phases in the order identified by Kübler-Ross. The final acceptance allows the patient to die in peace and the survivors to go on with their lives.

The Role of Religion

For those who know their death is imminent, as well as for their family and friends, a variety of religious rituals offer solace and provide a reassuring sense of the meaning of death. Informal visits from clergy members, for prayer or counseling, allow believers to prepare their souls, address their fears and resolve unfinished personal business. Some faiths also conduct formal rituals in preparation for death. For instance, the Roman Catholic and Eastern Orthodox churches administer last rites or extreme unction to the dying person to ready the soul for admission to heaven.

Deathbed Etiquette

Candor and receptiveness are the best policy when speaking with a dying person. According to Dr. Elizabeth Kübler-Ross, the question is not whether to tell someone he or she is terminal, but how to share the experience with them. As the patient becomes aware of approaching death and struggles to accept it, friends and family can offer strength and understanding. It is important for dying people to be told about their condition. Where doctors often choose not to reveal the prognosis to a terminal patient, believing ignorance will sustain hope, such secrecy in fact makes the patient feel isolated, cut off from his or her caretakers.

If, on the other hand, the patient shares a sense of partnership with the doctor and knows he or she is being kept abreast of developments, the patient gains a crucial sense of dignity. Doctors and loved ones alike can offer realistic hope about new procedures, alternative treatments or the power of prayer. Honesty about a dying person's condition allows him or her to participate in medical decisions, express opinions and desires about pain management and optimal care, make choices concerning "heroic efforts" and life support and prepare for the eventuality of death.

Kübler-Ross suggests, however, that patients not be told how much time they have left. Patients who have a timetable in mind may focus on surviving until a certain date and then give up hope, often dying soon thereafter. Hope not only lengthens life but sustains the spirit, allowing the patient a measure of peace and optimism.

Those gathered at a loved one's deathbed also benefit from gentle honesty. Visitors can do grieving friends and family no greater honor than to listen. There is little anyone can say to ease the suffering of someone about to lose a parent, spouse, child or close friend, so it is best not to intrude with false hope, trivial conversation, medical anecdotes or other attempts to divert the emotional process. Acknowledge the realities of the moment and offer support and sympathy to distraught family and friends. If they need a shoulder to cry on, a cup of coffee or just a companionable silence, oblige their wishes.

Psychologists have found that loved ones need to feel a strong connection with the dying person. To that end, they can benefit from recalling past events they shared with their loved one in a process psychologists term "rehearsing." Reminiscences about the dying person's habits, personality traits and life history, and the part he or she played in family lore, can transform private grief into a larger experience of love. Recalling the dying person's special characteristics confers a kind of immortality on his or her memory.

The Right to Die: Options for the Terminally and Chronically Ill

In recent years, the suffering person's "right to die" has been the subject of wide public debate and discussion. Religious beliefs or other moral systems define the thinking of many people, for and against the right to die. Faiths such as Roman Catholicism place the sanctity of human life above all other concerns, thereby repudiating the notion that in certain circumstances death may be preferable to life. For those who believe in a supreme being, no human has the prerogative to "play god" and decide who will live or die.

Other, more humanistic, codes define human life in qualitative rather than quantitative terms, contending that people have the right to die when their quality of life falls below some minimum standard. In this view, the freedom to choose the time, place or manner of one's death enhances the value of life. "Death with dignity" allows the individual to end life before the effects of irreversible illness or injury become too demeaning. When the suffering person can no longer express his or her wishes, the power to prevent further physical or mental degradation may also extend to loved ones with an intimate knowledge of his or her views on the matter. Whoever makes the decision, it may be accomplished in several ways: by refusing or suspending certain kinds of medical care, by committing suicide or by requesting euthanasia, also known as "mercy killing."

Of course, wide acceptance of euthanasia poses risks. Advocates for the disabled and the mentally ill argue that mercy killing could be abused to eliminate "unproductive" or "undesirable" members of society without their consent. Outside the health-care system, loved ones burdened by caring for a declining relative may decide to end that person's "suffering" for their own reasons. A more immediate concern, however, is that raised by the highly publicized activities of Dr. Jack Kevorkian. Dedicated to advancing the right-to-die cause, Kevorkian has helped several ill people to kill themselves. Some observers have questioned whether all of these patients were in fact close to death or suffering unduly. Clearly, the parameters of the right to die are far from well defined.

Self-Deliverance

Not so long ago, suicide was a taboo subject as well as illegal in most countries and in all 50 states. Religious prohibitions had a greater impact on attitudes than they do today, and general morality made fewer allowances for gray areas of behavior. Now, however, mainstream thinking about suicide for the seriously ill has begun to shift. Growing numbers of people have come to believe that the quality of life matters as much as does the quantity of life, and that intolerable pain, loss of faculties or severe, irreversible disability can make life not worth living. Most of the antisuicide laws still stand, but the authorities are increasingly likely to look the other way when people severely compromised by illness or injury are involved. Those in unbearable pain, incapable of basic physical functioning or doomed to lose their mental competence have a variety of self-deliverance options.

The decision to end one's own life is not one to be taken lightly. Judgments about death can be clouded by any number of distractions, anxieties, beliefs and external influences. Financial pressures due to the high cost of health care may sway the decision, as may the feelings of loved ones. But the decision should rest on the patient's own needs, desires and prospects.

Doctors can be of great help to the patient at this point. They can best assess just how the patient is and can let him or her know if self-deliverance would be premature or ill advised. A doctor will make sure the patient is fully informed of his or her medical status and of all the treatments available. A doctor can also determine if the patient cannot make a proper decision because of depression or other emotional disturbance or because the patient's judgment is clouded by medication or disease. Further assistance in making the decision can be found in a number of publications readily available in libraries and bookstores or from self-deliverance organizations (see Resources section beginning on page 304). Support groups affiliated with some of these organizations or operating independently can also help the dying patient with this decision.

Some publications (see bibliography) contain explicit instructions on how to take one's own life with the least amount of pain and the greatest chance of success. The most common technique is to ingest three times the minimum lethal dose (MLD) of barbiturates before securing a plastic bag over the head with a rubber band around the throat. This formula ensures that even if the drugs do not kill the patient they will render him or her unconscious long enough to suffocate without instinctively removing the bag.

When a doctor prescribes drugs to a patient knowing he or she intends to use them for self-deliverance, the act represents indirect euthanasia. To protect themselves, doctors who assist dying patients in this manner often ask that their patients tell no one how they obtained the prescriptions. A doctor may write either a single prescription for a lethal dose, write several prescriptions for nonlethal drugs that will have the desired result when combined or may instead write a series of small prescriptions for the patient to fill over a period of time. The latter approach also gives the patient the opportunity to reflect on the choice to die. The recommended drugs for indirect assisted suicide are secobarbital (brand name Seconal), pentobarbital (Nembutal) or amobarbital (Amytal or Tuinal).

Several steps that require forethought and planning should precede the actual suicide. The dying person should assemble documentation of his or her desire to die, such as a living will, put his or her worldly affairs in order and inform friends and family. A place and time should be chosen, and if desired loved ones may be invited to be present. Unless confined to a hospital, most self-deliverers choose a private and comfortable place such as their home and ask their closest loved ones to be present. It is legally advisable that they do not actively participate in the actual process, as they may be prosecuted for murder.

Some patients, however, may require assistance and may prefer that a loved one rather than a medical professional be involved. In this case, the patient should take care to select someone trustworthy to serve as helper. The patient's doctor should remain available to the helper by telephone should anything go wrong. When obtaining the necessary prescriptions, the patient should ask the doctor for detailed instructions on how to take them and should find out exactly how they will act. If administered properly, orally ingested drugs should induce deep, irreversible coma within an hour and death within several hours.

Physician-Assisted Suicide

For the terminally or chronically ill person in unbearable physical and emotional pain, physician-assisted suicide may offer the best prospect of relief. Physician-assisted suicide is one form of euthanasia, a term that combines the Greek prefix *eu-*(good) and the root *thanatos* (death). A chosen death qualifies as euthanasia if it relieves great suffering in a physically ill person who has exhausted every medical option without success. If certain death lies weeks or months away, if a serious chronic condition will only worsen, if a longer life will only mean greater pain, degradation and loss of dignity, physician-assisted suicide can indeed be a good death.

A felony in the United States, euthanasia is illegal in every country but the Netherlands, where it has been legal since 1973, although not for foreigners. Nevertheless, a large percentage of American doctors believe in the practice, and many discreetly administer euthanasia. Those who offer this service must take a number of precautions because of the law.

A declining patient may seek several types of physician aid-in-dying. For those already on artificial life support, a doctor may oversee passive euthanasia, which takes the form of practices such as "pulling the plug" and abstaining from "heroic measures" to save a life. At present, the removal of life support or compliance with a do not resuscitate order generally poses few legal problems if a patient has prepared for it by drafting a living will and a durable power of attorney for health care. Most doctors and hospitals honor these documents, although their legality is still in debate in some places.

Active euthanasia takes the form of assisted suicide, either indirect (see above) or direct. Patients who lack the physical or emotional resources to take their own life may opt for direct euthanasia. In this situation, a doctor administers a lethal dose of drugs and then monitors the death process itself. This puts the physician at greater legal risk but greatly reduces the very real risk of medical failure.

If a patient has decided to end his or her suffering via physician-assisted suicide, among the most important decisions he or she faces is finding the right doctor to help. Euthanasia should be administered by a physician with whom the patient enjoys good rapport, easy communication, a similar ethical outlook and mutual respect. The doctor should also have a sympathetic nursing staff and be affiliated with a reputable hospital that has proven its tolerance of physician-assisted suicide.

In open dialogue, the patient should express any concerns and desires and be satisfied that the doctor will take them into account and honor them. Doctor and patient should discuss the various ways in which death can be hastened, and should agree on the most humane and appropriate approach. No patient should entrust his or her last act of self-determination to a doctor who is morally or ethically offended by euthanasia, who is a relative stranger or who is not familiar with every aspect of the patient's medical condition and history. The patient must feel confident that the doctor will allow a change of mind at any time and that the doctor will confirm the patient's desire to die immediately before administering the fatal dose.

Those who have no close friends or family, or whose loved ones are unable to help for emotional, religious or other reasons, may find that a doctor is the only one who can see them through the process. Some patients are afraid of botching the task on their own, and a doctor has the advantage of professional training and skills. A doctor can make the necessary medical preparations and will follow procedures to make the process easier. He or she has lawful access to lethal drugs and knows which will work best and how they should be administered.

Doctors face a range of ethical considerations when deciding whether or not to help someone end his or her suffering. A doctor cannot grant this request unless the patient is clearly suffering badly and has repeatedly and consistently expressed the wish to die (preferably in writing, with a witnessed signature). The doctor in this position should seek the opinion of at least one other doctor to corroborate that the patient will probably die within a few months or that the chronic condition can only get worse. It is also the doctor's responsibility to make sure loved ones have had an opportunity to express their views, although the decision ultimately rests with the patient.

When evaluating the medical justifications for hastening death, doctors should take into account all indicators of a patient's discomfort and distress. Relevant physical symptoms include:

sleeplessness, fatigue and exhaustion

respiratory difficulties

nausea and vomiting

constipation or incontinence

hunger or thirst

weight loss

bedsores

perspiration and itching

chronic hiccups or coughing

fungal infections of the mouth

other infections

catheterization or intubation

lack of bodily control

Relevant symptoms of emotional distress include:

confusion, disorientation or forgetfulness

grief or anxiety

dependence on 24-hour nursing or care by others

overall sense of degradation and loss of dignity

Nurses can help make sure patients' distress and wishes are heard. They often share a special bond with patients and are the first to find out about their problems and desires. Nurses should communicate to doctors any knowledge relevant to a patient's request for physician aid-in-dying, especially if it suggests that euthanasia might not be the right choice. Acting as an advocate, nurses can provide the doctor with information on the patient's family and social situation and can let him or her know if the patient wants to try another treatment. Conversely, nurses can help a doctor understand a patient's anguish and can question physicians whose judgment they doubt. Nurses should be included in every stage of the euthanasia process.

If patient and doctor agree that direct euthanasia is the right choice, the doctor will obtain the necessary drugs directly from a pharmacist. He or she should consult with a sympathetic pharmacist on the choice of drug and the dosage level, putting all relevant instructions in writing. The choice of drug depends on the patient's condition and on the desired means of administration; some patients decide against injection and choose to drink their own "hemlock" in their doctor's presence. The doctor and the pharmacist should also take into account any tolerance a patient may have built up to narcotic analgesics, as well as any other medications that may already be in the patient's system (interactions with these drugs can enhance or cancel out the final drug's effect). The ideal drug offers a quick and painless death without unpleasant side effects such as hallucinations, anxiety, convulsions, tightness of the chest, vomiting or motor restlessness. It should induce unconsciousness within minutes (no more than half an hour) and cause death within another half hour.

After the physician administers the drugs, he or she should remain with the patient until death is confirmed. If the doctor cannot stay, a nurse should monitor the patient's condition and keep the doctor informed. It is the doctor, however, who must ascertain death.

Doctors can administer a lethal dose of drugs in one of several ways. The swifter the effect, the more desirable the technique, for the drug will have a stronger effect on the central nervous system. For this reason, experts do not recommend intramuscular (into the muscle) or subcutaneous (under the skin) injection or rectal suppositories. The vagaries of a patient's circulation make it difficult to predict how quickly an intramuscular or subcutaneous injection will take effect. In the case of an intramuscular shot, the effect can be accelerated by locating two places on the body with the best possible circulation and administering an injection at each location. Massaging the sites can further speed distribution of the drug throughout the body. However, neither of these techniques can improve the results of a subcutaneous shot.

Least desirable of all are rectal suppositories, both because of their dubious efficacy and because of the indignities involved in their administration. They must be preceded by an enema, and while they work the patient must remain in an awkward position. In addition, many people have difficulty retaining suppositories (for this reason a barbiturate in the form of sodium salt is best because it relaxes the bowels). A lethal dose is hard to achieve because the drug is absorbed slowly; the doctor may have to administer additional doses after the patient loses consciousness.

Two euthanasia techniques, however, have proven highly effective. Drugs taken orally act relatively swiftly and reliably in hastening death. Because they are easiest to swallow and more quickly absorbed, drugs in liquid form are more desirable than pills or capsules. A recommended oral dose consists of a liquid mixture of pentobarbital sodium or secobarbital sodium dissolved in alcohol, purified water, propylene glycol and orange syrup. Doctors may boost the solution's potency by adding orphenadrine hydrochloride. One of the few drawbacks of such a potion is that it tastes bitter; another is that some patients reject the drug by vomiting. To counter the danger of vomiting, the assisting physician should have an antiemetic on hand, such as metoclopramide (Primperan or Reglan), alizapride (Litican) or phenothiazine derivatives like prochlorperazine (Stemetil or Compazine).

Best of all the physician-assisted suicide techniques is intravenous injection. Drugs administered this way act fastest of all and can be delivered via drip if the patient is already hooked up to an IV device. As a rule of thumb for determining the appropriate intravenous dose, doctors should triple the stated minimum lethal dosage of a drug. For patients who have not built up a tolerance to narcotic analgesics, an injection of morphine hydrochloride should have the desired effect. The choice of drug and dosage level should be determined on a case-by-case basis for drug-tolerant patients. One effective formula is to inject a barbiturate and then follow up a few minutes later with a curare derivative muscle relaxant.

Then, in the words of a dying Hamlet, "The rest is silence."

When Death Arrives

Declaring Death

In the United States, all deaths must be confirmed by a medical doctor or coroner's jury. Either of these parties must ascertain that death has, in fact, occurred and must record a cause of death. If the doctor or coroner does not know the cause of death, he or she may order an autopsy—also referred to as a necropsy or postmortem—to determine the cause.

A death certificate is a legal document; it contains the deceased's name and the cause and date of death and may include personal history information such as birthdate, birth place, social security number, marital status and parents' names. In some states a signed death certificate is required in order to move the body.

Survivors should carefully check all information on the death certificate to make sure it is completed accurately. An incorrect social security number, for example, could cause delays in the payment to survivors of social security or life insurance benefits. Certified copies of the death certificate are necessary for a number of legal and financial transactions, so it is a good idea to request extra copies. Copies can also be obtained later from the registrar of deaths, the state health department or another appropriate official. If you are using the services of a funeral director, often she or he will obtain the death certificate and provide copies.

The Autopsy

Except in cases of murder or suspicious death, permission for the autopsy must be obtained from the next of kin or surviving spouse. Some religions, such as Judaism, prohibit autopsies or other disfigurement of the body for burial, but exceptions may be made for diagnostic or legal reasons. An autopsy to determine the cause of death will delay the completion of a death certificate, so in some cases a temporary death certificate is issued.

Most autopsies take place when there is reason to suspect death by homicide, suicide or other unnatural causes. Cases of suspicious death are overseen by a coroner, who supervises an inquest before a jury.

At the Morgue

When an unidentified person dies in the hospital or an unidentified corpse is discovered by the police, the body is sent to the morgue to await identification. A police investigation may locate next of kin or someone else who can identify the body, in which case it can be released for burial. If no one claims the body within a designated period (ranging from several days to a month or more), the body is sent to the local Potter's Field for interment.

Anyone who claims a body, whether at the morgue, in the hospital or wherever death occurred, must make arrangements for its disposition with a funeral home. By law, only a licensed funeral home can remove the body for burial or cremation.

Making Announcements

Once the death of a person is confirmed, various parties must be informed of the fact. Today, when most deaths in industrialized nations occur in hospitals, doctors are often in the position of announcing the news to the next of kin. Family and friends spread the word of a loved one's death via conversations, telephone calls and letters; they must also inform the deceased's attorneys, business associates, creditors and others with an economic or legal relationship to the deceased.

As in the past, death announcements that must be broadcast quickly (e.g. when rapid burial must take place for religious or public health reasons) can be sent via telegram. Two increasingly popular methods are the broadcast fax, sent simultaneously to several numbers, or E-mail, which likewise can be sent to many addresses at once. Such techniques, of course, are not appropriate when close relatives or friends are being notified. Announcements intended for the entire community or other wide audiences can take the form of newspaper obituaries.

In Western cultures, the announcement of a death is generally a somber process accompanied by sadness. Certain Eastern cultures, however, attach feelings of fear, shame or disgust to any mention of death, which may be considered a taboo, cursed or unclean subject. Throughout the history of both East and West, a variety of rituals have been used to announce deaths to the community. Clergy may deliver formal notice in churches or synagogues, sometimes accompanied by prayers for or expressions of condolence to survivors. In Talmudic times, ancient Hebrews sounded the *shofar*, a ritual ram's horn, to deliver the news of a Jewish death. (See Chapter 10 for more information on announcing a death.)

IX

Making Arrangements

Funerals serve both a ritual and practical purpose. Their ritual purpose is to celebrate and remember the life of the deceased and to help the survivors accept the death. The practical purpose is simple: something must be done with the body. Exactly what that is and how it is accomplished are up to the deceased, if that person expressed any preferences on the subject, and up to the survivors, who must also make certain decisions regarding the fate of the body.

People are increasingly aware that a funeral need not be a complicated, expensive affair to be meaningful. There are more options for the disposition of a body and choices for the manner in which a funeral is conducted than are commonly offered by the conventional funeral industry or acknowledged in our present culture. For that reason, becoming more familiar with the process of arranging a funeral and the choices involved is essential for consumers of funeral goods and services. Then, when the inevitable occurs, they will be more prepared to make practical choices and better able to go about the more important process of grieving.

The emotions that arise when a loved one dies can make dealing with a death extremely difficult. One way to make the practical decisions much simpler is to discuss them in advance. An honest conversation about death and what should be done when it happens need not be morbid; death is, after all, a part of life. A funeral or memorial service consistent with the life of the deceased is a wonderful way to acknowledge that person's place in the lives and memories of the living. Whether these matters have been discussed or not, planning a funeral does not have to be a harrowing experience. One can make considered decisions that result in an appropriate funeral both for the deceased and for her or his survivors.

When Death Comes

The circumstances of a person's death determine what steps are taken immediately afterward. If someone suffers an accident at home or in another nonmedical setting, most likely paramedics or other emergency assistance will have been summoned immediately, because in some cases the person can be revived. If there is no doubt of death, a funeral director or your family physician can be notified to eliminate an expensive and unnecessary visit to a hospital. In questionable circumstances the body will probably be taken to the coroner's office.

If death was expected and has occurred at home as the result of an illness, the attending physician will confirm the death and sign the death certificate. In a hospital or hospice, a physician will determine the cause of death and sign the death certificate.

Survivors should also notify the appropriate clergy member immediately if the deceased was religious. In addition to offering comfort and assistance to the living, she or he can help to make arrangements for the funeral or memorial service.

Removal of the Body

The first consideration after a death is confirmed is the removal of the body. If the death occurred in a hospital, hospice or nursing home, this will most likely be done automatically, and the body will be stored in the institution's facilities, usually for a fee. Some facilities do not have storage capabilities and will want to have the body removed as soon as possible by a funeral director. In the case of an expected death, either at home or in a hospital, often a choice will already have been made about where the body will go: to a funeral home, a crematorium or a medical school.

If the deceased was religious and will have a religious funeral, the body must often be buried within a specified time. Other factors in deciding what will be done with the body include the type of funeral planned and whether the deceased wished to donate organs or donate the body to a medical school. Organ donation can be decided at the time of or immediately after death; under federal law hospital staff at most hospitals in the United States must ask the family of a qualified donor to consider organ donation. Arrangements for donation of the entire body to a medical school typically need to be made well in advance of death. (See Chapter 8 for a complete discussion of donation.)

Deciding the Fate of the Body

If there is no prior plan for disposition of the body, survivors decide what will be done with it. If the body is in a hospital or nursing home storage facility it will probably have to be removed to a funeral home for storage until the survivors decide about the disposition. This decision need not be made immediately; the body can be refrigerated indefinitely, but there will be a charge for its storage. If the body must be removed before survivors have selected which funeral home to use, any funeral home can be hired to remove and store the body while survivors shop around. Survivors are not legally required to use that funeral home, but they will be charged for all the services rendered, so they should be specific about what the home is or is not authorized to do. For example, some funeral homes will begin the work to embalm a body very soon after they receive it.

The main options for the body are cremation or burial. However, there are several alternatives within these two major categories. For example, a body may be embalmed, viewed, then cremated and the ashes buried in a cemetery; or the body may be prepared by a funeral director or other person authorized by the state and buried in a cemetery or on private land. Making funeral arrangements is not very different from planning a wedding or an important birthday party: exactly what form it takes depends on the people involved as well as on how much survivors can afford or want to spend. Of course, state and local laws regulate what may be done with a body. In some states it is not legal to bury someone in any place other than a cemetery, or even to scatter a person's cremated remains. Survivors should check with the local health department on the laws affecting their area.

Earth Burial

Burial in a cemetery is historically the most common choice in the United States. Many people like the idea of having a "final resting place," someplace that loved ones can visit to honor their memory. Some areas of the United States permit burial outside of cemeteries. In either case, the location should be a main consideration in selecting a burial site: loved ones will want to be able to visit it for a long time to come.

Funerals involving an earth burial can range from very simple to lavish. The simplest option is a direct, or immediate, burial, in which the body is transferred from the funeral home to the burial site and interred. Direct burial can include a graveside funeral, or a memorial service may be held at a later date.

The other options to choose from in an earth burial include a funeral service, which can be held either in a house of worship (with or without the body present) or in the funeral home, a visitation (also called a wake) and a graveside interment service. These events may be public or private, held by invitation. A visitation is a designated time when family and friends can view or sit near the body in either an open or closed casket and offer their support and condolence to mourners. It can be held either at the family's home or at a funeral home.

Embalming

Embalming is not necessary in most instances, except in the case of infectious disease, when most states mandate embalming. The family may view the body without it being embalmed, but if an open-casket visitation is held most states require that the body be embalmed. Embalming temporarily delays the breakdown of tissues. It does not prevent decomposition—it only makes the body more presentable for a few days while the funeral process takes place. Embalming is an option and should not be performed by the funeral director unless survivors request it. As with other funeral services survivors must be notified of the price in advance. If survivors do not plan a public viewing of the body and do not wish to have the body embalmed, they should specifically inform the funeral director of the decision.

To embalm a body, the blood is replaced with chemical embalming fluid. The chemicals sanitize and temporarily preserve the tissues. The organs are removed, soaked in embalming fluid and replaced. The body's orifices are closed to prevent leakage. The embalmer also cleans and prepares the body for viewing, arranging the hair, applying makeup and positioning the body. Factors that affect the final result include the condition of the body and the embalmer's skill. If you would like the body to be embalmed, providing a photograph taken during the deceased's lifetime helps to achieve an accurate, natural presentation of the body. (See Chapter 4 for more on embalming.)

People have widely different views on embalming and the purpose it serves. Some grief counselors advise that seeing the deceased helps survivors realize and accept the death, an important step in the grieving process. Some people feel it is gruesome and does not present the deceased as she or he appeared in life. It is wise to discuss in advance whether one believes in embalming or not, so loved ones know which choice to make.

Cremation

People are increasingly choosing cremation as a method of disposition. It can take place after traditional funeral services are held, or the body can be cremated immediately in a direct cremation, with a memorial service held afterward. Cremation can be a less expensive alternative to a traditional burial because some charges associated with a funeral, such as visitation or a cemetery grave site, can be eliminated. However, some people choose to have full funeral services and simply have the body cremated and the ashes buried instead of interring it intact, in which case the costs are similar.

In cremation the body is taken to a crematorium in a casket or other container. While the body must be in a container of some kind, it can be very inexpensive. A very simple container made of corrugated cardboard can be obtained through a funeral director or the crematorium. There is often a delay of 24 to 48 hours before a body can be cremated to make sure there is no question of wrongdoing associated with the death that would be concealed by cremating the body.

Cremated remains can be disposed of in any number of ways. They can be interred in a cemetery or on private property, they can be scattered in a place chosen by the deceased or the family or they can be placed in a mausoleum or columbarium. A columbarium is a designated building or room with small openings along the wall in which cremated remains are placed. Glass is sometimes placed over the opening through which an urn or other container can be viewed, or engraved plaques are placed over these openings. The remains can also be placed in an urn or other decorative container and kept around the house. The choices are many.

Cremated remains are not a health hazard, but in some areas of the country scattering them is forbidden or restricted, and in some places local laws require that an official record of scattering be filed. The local board of health has information on the laws that govern an area.

Two other options that vary according to local law are attendance at the cremation and casket rental. It is possible in some areas of the United States to be present at the facility when the body of a loved one is cremated, although the actual cremation is not viewed. In some areas it is possible to rent a casket for viewing and then to cremate the body in a less expensive container. However, since by law the interior of the casket must be refurbished to be reused, renting a casket is not cheap.

Entombment

The process of entombing a dead person is much the same as for earth burial, except that the remains are held in an above-ground depository, called a mausoleum or tomb. The mausoleum can be large, as for a family tomb, or designed to hold a single body. Depending on geographic location, the price of entombment can be much higher than an earth burial. Those choosing entombment must make the same kinds of choices regarding casket and ceremonies as those choosing earth burial.

The Funeral Director

Most survivors engage the services of a funeral director to carry out their plans for disposition of the body and other services associated with the funeral. Funeral directors are paid for carrying out various activities associated with death, such as transporting the body and preparing it for disposition, that most people are not—and do not want to be—familiar with. In some areas of the United States it is possible to perform some or all of these services independently, a decision that requires both careful planning and family and community support. This option is discussed below. However, most Americans retain the services of a funeral director.

The Role of the Funeral Director

A funeral director is the coordinator of the many elements involved in a death. Sometimes the funeral director is the one who files the death certificate as well as other legal documents, such as papers required by the Veterans and Social Security administrations. If there is to be a religious service the funeral director will contact the clergy to coordinate the timing of the service. The funeral director may also make arrangements for flowers and limousine service, file an obituary with the local paper and act as an agent with the cemetery. If a visitation or a funeral are held at the funeral home, the funeral director and the staff will direct and coordinate the event, both behind the scenes and in public. The level of the funeral director's involvement and what services she or he performs is up to survivors.

Funeral homes are regulated by federal law, the most important being the Federal Trade Commission Funeral Rule. The Rule, discussed later in this chapter, requires that the funeral director supply consumers with price and legal information. Consumers should be aware of their rights, and they always have the right to ask questions.

Selecting a Funeral Director

Families that live in an area for a long time may be familiar with the local funeral directors from previous funerals. In this case they have the benefit of experience to guide them through the whole process. They may have many years of family and religious traditions to follow, in which case the deceased's funeral will probably be much like those of prior decedents, and the same church as well as the same funeral home will be used. However, in this increasingly mobile culture—where most people live far from their place of birth and many people live far from other family members—survivors must often plan funerals from scratch.

When considering potential funeral directors, survivors should look for someone they feel they can trust, who will act with their best interests in mind. Even more important, however, is to know how much a funeral should cost. Consumers can conduct their own price survey by calling several different funeral homes, or they can contact The National Coalition for Fair Funeral Prices or the Funeral and Memorial Societies of America for information on how to conduct a complete survey.

Funeral directors are just like other business people: they provide a service to consumers for a fee. The fact that the consumers of funeral goods and services have just been confronted with a shocking and unfamiliar occurrence gives unscrupulous funeral directors the opportunity to take advantage of the consumers if they wish. This is another reason consumers should be aware of their choices before death forces them to learn all about funerals at a difficult time.

Tips on shopping for a funeral director:

- Try a familiar establishment. Those who have attended other funerals in the area probably noticed if the staff was competent and professional and if the affair was well conducted.

- Ask for recommendations from trusted friends and associates who have used funeral homes in the area. Clergy members can be a resource; they deal with funeral directors often and will probably be familiar with several. However, they are unlikely to be familiar with the price differences among the funeral homes. Survivors should also be aware that clergy sometimes receive payments, gifts or other incentives from funeral homes and may not be objective in their recommendations. Double-check the funeral home suggested by a clergy member.

- Call the local Better Business Bureau, listed in the White Pages. Ask whether there have been any complaints about the funeral homes under consideration.

- Sit down with the telephone book and call several funeral directors. This initial call will give a first indication of how the staff of the funeral home treats customers. Survivors should receive straightforward answers to their questions and concerns. Ask for the total cost of a funeral with a specific casket and services—since the cost of a funeral depends largely on the cost of individual items and services, this will help clarify the funeral home's response. Funeral homes are required to give price information on the phone.

Those who don't have time to shop around but who need the services of a funeral director immediately need not make their decisions at random. Here are some tips for an abbreviated search:

- Ask at least a few questions of the funeral home staff. If not treated with respect, hang up and try another funeral home.

- Remember that there is no obligation to use the funeral home that removes and stores the body for the remaining services. If a storage establishment was called in a hurry and its prices are too high or the facility unsuitable, choose another home. The first home will charge for any services performed.

- If the death occurs at a location away from where the funeral will be held, ask the funeral director who will most likely handle the arrangements for a referral to a reputable funeral director to handle the transportation of the body. Some firms specialize in preparation and shipping; survivors should instruct them to do the minimum to avoid high charges.

Making Plans

The Arrangement Conference: What to Expect

Once the decision on a funeral director has been made, among the first things she or he will ask are:

1. Who has died and where is that person's body?
2. Who declared the death?
3. Who is the next of kin and will that person be the one to make arrangements?
4. Generally, what type of funeral is planned?

The funeral director will also schedule an appointment to make specific arrangements. At this meeting, called an arrangement conference, survivors contract with the funeral director for the goods and services she or he will provide.

To be prepared for this meeting, survivors should gather any papers necessary to supply or confirm information for the death certificate, such as a social security card, birth certificate for place and date of birth and other vital information about the person. Papers confirming cemetery plots that may have been purchased, participation in a memorial society or a prepaid funeral should also be located.

Survivors should bring clothing for the deceased to wear, whether or not they plan to have an open casket. Funeral homes often have burial clothing for purchase, but it is typically expensive and of poor quality. Also, having the deceased wear clothing of his or her own is more appropriate. Survivors should bring dentures, if the deceased wore them, and a photograph so the body can be prepared in a way that is consistent with her or his appearance (whether or not it is embalmed).

Survivors should also be prepared to make definite decisions about the fate of the body and the type of service preferred. The funeral director will need to know at this arrangement conference the specific funeral and visitation plans survivors would like to make so that she or he can designate staff, reserve a visitation room in the funeral home and coordinate the religious ceremony with the clergy member. If survivors are not sure of their plans, the funeral director can help them make these choices, but ultimately it is their own decision and they must be comfortable with the arrangements.

By law, the funeral director must present at this meeting an itemized list of goods and services the funeral home provides and the cost of each item. He or she may not, as was commonly done in the past, offer only "package deals" that do not state the prices for individual items. Indeed, the itemized list of prices, called a General Price List or GPL, must be made available to anyone who walks into a funeral home and requests it. The GPL is discussed in the Consumer Protection section below.

In coordination with the funeral director, survivors develop the plan and the schedule for the funeral. Decisions about disposition of the body, whether to embalm, the visitation (if any) and ceremonies are finalized. There are two types of ritual ceremonies to honor the deceased, funeral and memorial services. A funeral is a service held with the body present, while a memorial service does not involve the body. A memorial service may be held at the time of death or later and can take many forms, from religious to nonreligious.

In deciding on the arrangements for the ceremony itself, survivors should consider several things:

- How far away family members and friends are and whether they will be traveling to attend.

- Whether services will be announced in the newspaper and open to the public or by invitation only.

- How many people are likely to attend if the affair is public.

- Where the ceremony will take place: in a church, in the funeral home, in a private home or outdoors.

These and other factors will partly determine what services will be required of the funeral director. Placing an announcement, room rental, transportation (limousines and drivers in addition to a hearse) are all available from the funeral home. However, survivors may hire the funeral director to simply perform the services involved with the body and may handle funeral or memorial arrangements themselves. The simplest funerals are, of course, the most affordable. See the Funeral/Cremation Price Survey table below for sample prices of "no-frills" funerals around the U.S.

Funeral/Cremation Price Survey

City	Direct Burial($)	Cremation($)
Baltimore	1,035	695
Boston	952	695
Chicago	640	390
Dallas/Houston	875	575
Denver	1,122	586
Los Angeles	610	415
New York/Long Island	545	390
Phoenix	800	375
Pittsburgh	650	390
St. Louis	400	445
Seattle	629	497
Tampa	581	431

Source: "Fraud in the Funeral Industry," *Consumers Digest*, September/October, 1995.

In addition to the basic services, survivors may have the funeral home contract for other items involved in a funeral, such as contacting and paying for the services of a member of the clergy, flowers and the cemetery arrangements. The funeral home provides these additional services for the convenience of the bereaved, and may add a service fee to the cost. However, federal law requires that customers be informed whenever such markups are made (see Consumer Protection on page 248).

The next of kin or another person legally authorized by the will must be the one to sign the contract with the funeral director, and is the person legally responsible for paying for the arrangements. It is important to remember that this is a legally binding contract with the funeral home, so survivors should make sure they understand each element of the agreement and its cost. If they do not understand something, they should ask about it. If the funeral director makes recommendations, for example, about which cemetery or what type of service to choose, survivors should understand why she or he is suggesting that particular choice. This type of guidance from the funeral director can be helpful and save time and effort if the funeral director knows what survivors want and has their best interests in mind. For instance, one cemetery may be less expensive than another, or have more space available. Or the funeral director may have scheduling conflicts and may advise survivors to wait a day for the funeral for that reason.

Ask for Help

There are a number of things that must happen fairly quickly upon someone's death. While the next of kin of the deceased must be the primary performer in most of these actions, asking people to help can be beneficial for all involved. It takes some of the burden off the main decision-maker—who is also the one most affected by the death—and allows others to participate in the activities and decisions.

1.   The bereaved should ask someone they trust—who is not directly affected by the death—to come along to the meeting with the funeral director. This person will be more objective about the decisions to be made and can ask questions loved ones may forget to ask.

2.   After the survivor has made the most important calls to immediate relatives, someone can help make a list of the remaining calls to be made and can ask friends and relatives to assist in informing others about the death. Survivors should remember to inform the decedent's business colleagues and contacts.

3.   A number of people close to the deceased should be involved in planning the funeral. This can make the event more meaningful and facilitate the grieving process.

4.   Someone should answer the telephone and keep a careful record of people who have called and stopped by. Gifts and donations should also be noted so they can be acknowledged later.

5.   Someone should be designated to coordinate meals for the first few days.

6.   People traveling from a distance will need hotel or other accommodations. A friend can help by providing telephone numbers of local hotels or by helping the guests make plans to stay with other relatives or friends.

7.   To lighten everyday burdens, survivors can make special arrangements for pet care or other needs of the household, such as cleaning. If the deceased's house is empty for a time, a neighbor should check on the house to prevent burglary.

Selection of Merchandise

The Casket

After survivors have decided on the disposition and ceremony arrangements with the funeral director, they are shown into a display room for the selection of a casket. (A casket is not the same as a coffin, a six-sided burial container. Coffins are not manufactured in the United States and not widely available here.) At this point survivors should be especially aware of how the funeral director handles the display and sale of caskets. The casket selected has a great impact on the overall cost of the funeral. Caskets can range in price from about $200 for the simplest manufactured casket to many thousands of dollars for a luxury model.

The funeral director makes money on the sale of caskets—he or she is, after all, in business to make a profit. Caskets are marked up from two to seven times the manufacturer's price. For example, the price of a cheap casket from the manufacturer is approximately $150 to $200, and can sell at retail for anywhere from $375 to $1,400, depending on what the traffic will bear. See page 242 for a table of burial container cost comparisons.

Inexpensive caskets should be readily available for examination. Consumers should not feel pressured into buying something they cannot afford. Having a trusted companion to assist in casket selection can be especially helpful. Ideally this person should be not directly affected by the emotional element of the process, and thus be more able to help make a considered choice.

A funeral director is not obligated to offer an economy model casket, but a good business person will have a variety of styles available—at both the high and low end of the price range. If consumers do not see something they can afford, they should ask to see the least expensive casket. If the funeral director is evasive or implies that the deceased deserves better, they are being manipulated and should go elsewhere. They can also ask if the interior of a casket is available in a different color or fabric, as sometimes cheaper caskets are displayed with unattractive color combinations to discourage the customer's interest in them.

If consumers do not see a model they like at a price they are willing to pay, they can call other funeral homes and ask for casket prices for comparison, and purchase the container from a different company than the one providing funeral services. If they shop around this way, they should make sure to get both the manufacturer's name and model number, because funeral homes sometimes assign their own model numbers to caskets to discourage consumers from doing this. Consumers can also provide their own casket (see Alternative Caskets on page 243).

Whatever the budget, the two major considerations in casket selection are appearance and cost. If survivors have chosen cremation for the disposition of the body, they will probably want to select the least expensive option. For a ceremony with the casket on display, its appearance may be a concern. Some denominations drape the casket in a large cloth, or shroud, to eliminate this factor and indicate that people are all equal in death.

Caskets are made of one of four basic materials: wood, metal, sealed metal or fiberglass. Wood and either sealed or unsealed metal are the most frequently used materials. Fiberglass caskets are very expensive and not commonly available.

There are many variations and styles of caskets. The least expensive wooden caskets are typically made of pressed wood covered with fabric on the outside and the inside. Wooden caskets move up in price according to the quality and finish of the wood, exterior decorative elements (a carved religious or other symbol), metal fittings and style of the interior. The interiors of inexpensive wooden caskets are usually finished with fabric tacked flat; more expensive interiors have finer fabric that is gathered or cushioned and may have mattress springs.

Metal caskets also range in price, but the least expensive metal casket typically costs more than an economical wooden casket. The material used to make metal caskets ranges from welded 20-gauge steel to buffed and polished copper, stainless steel or bronze. Metal caskets can be "sealed" or "unsealed." Sealed metal caskets have rubber gaskets and locking devices and while the implication may be that this provides some protection for the body, such caskets do not prevent decay or the eventual intrusion of water and other grave site substances. The style and quality of the interior also affects the price of a metal casket.

Burial Container Cost Comparisons

Type	Retail($)	Wholesale($)	Profit(%)
Cloth-covered	500	167	199
Pine (solid)	1,897	749	153
Oak (solid)	2,600	801	224
Steel (16g)	2,255	1,074	109
Poplar (solid)	3,050	386	690
Cherry (solid)	3,550	1,284	176
Steel (stainless)	4,050	989	309
Mahogany (solid)	8,500	1,810	369
Bronze (48 oz.)	31,000	3,725	732
Copper (solid)	33,000	1,625	1,930

Alternative Caskets

If the cost and design of manufactured caskets does not appeal to the consumer, or if he or she is interested in a simple, inexpensive substitute, it is possible to make a casket or to order one from someone other than a funeral director. Provided that the casket meets certain minimum requirements, the funeral home or crematorium must accept it. Some people order or make the casket in advance. It can be either stored or used as a piece of furniture: a storage chest, legs can be attached to make a table or shelves inserted for use as a closet. Casket plans and the caskets themselves can be purchased via mail order. (See the Resources list beginning on page 304.)

Burial Vaults and Grave Liners

Burial vaults and grave liners are concrete or metal structures that fit into the grave; the casket is placed inside. A grave liner is the cheapest option. Made of concrete, it holds up the ground around the casket to prevent the ground from sinking as the casket breaks down over time. Burial vaults serve the same purpose, but they are more expensive because they are made of costlier materials such as copper or steel. Burial vaults and grave liners are not required by law, but many cemeteries stipulate their use in order to prevent the grave from subsiding, which cuts down on the overall upkeep of the cemetery. When selecting a cemetery, consumers should ask if burial vaults or grave liners are necessary.

Another practical purpose of a burial vault is that it allows the grave to be reopened and another casket interred on the same site. If a cemetery is running out of room, or if a family's plot is filling up, this may be an advantage to the consumer. It is often less expensive to buy a burial vault and use the vertical space than it is to buy additional space for a grave. Burial vaults, like metal caskets, may be sealed or unsealed. Sealed vaults cannot keep out water or dirt in the long term and serve no real purpose except peace of mind to the buyer.

Urns

If survivors elect cremation for disposition of the body, they may want to buy an urn or other container specifically designed to hold the cremated remains. Like caskets, urns come in many styles and prices. Consumers may purchase one from the funeral director at the time of the arrangement conference or have one specially designed and made. The volume an urn will contain is usually part of its description; it should be big enough to hold all of the remains.

Buying an urn is completely a matter of choice, as there are no legal requirements for the storing of cremated remains. They may stay in the container supplied by the crematorium and be buried in the ground or at the back of a closet at home. In fact, some crematoriums report that cremated remains are sometimes never claimed by the family.

If the remains will be placed in a columbarium or another facility such as an urn garden, there may be specific guidelines for the style and appearance of the container. Consumers should check with the facility they are interested in before buying an urn.

Monuments, Markers and Headstones

The site chosen for placement of the remains partly determines what sort of marker is appropriate, as does price. Markers are often not purchased until after the interment, so consumers have some time to select something appropriate. At a minimum, markers include the name of the deceased and her or his birth and death dates. Some people select a meaningful quote or phrase to have engraved.

The simplest markers are bronze or marble plaques set flush with the ground (some cemeteries allow no other kind). More elaborate markers are made of carved marble or cast metal. Monument companies should have a variety of styles available and may offer custom options. As with caskets, consumers should shop around until they find something they like.

In the whole selection process consumers should weigh the relative importance of each item of merchandise. Do they want to pay more for a casket and burial liner that no one will ever see after the funeral than for a marker that will be a visual reminder of a loved one? Each of these choices is very personal, and depends on what survivors value, how much they can spend and how they want to memorialize the deceased. Survivors should not let convention or other people's opinions convince them that one way is superior to another or that the only way to dignify the deceased's memory is to spend a lot of money.

Selecting a Cemetery, Mausoleum or Other Facility

When making a choice regarding the resting place of the remains, location is the most important thing to consider. Do survivors want to visit the site often? Or would they rather remember their loved one's ashes being scattered from a mountain top or over the sea?

Cost, of course, is another factor. Prices depend on what part of the country is involved, but generally, buying space in a mausoleum is the most expensive option, three to ten times the cost of earth burial in some cases. The cost of a spot in an urn garden, a columbarium and a cemetery are probably comparable to each other.

If the family owns a plot in a cemetery, it is important to establish who owns the rights to it and who will be buried in the spaces that are open. At the time of the original purchase a deed was issued; the direct descendants of the owners have the right to continue the use of the plot.

Veterans of any of the military branches who received any discharge except a dishonorable discharge are eligible for free burial in a national cemetery. The veteran's spouse and minor children can also be buried in a national cemetery. Placement in a national cemetery depends on the availability of space, so the location of the cemetery may not be ideal for the survivors. Wherever a qualified veteran is buried, the Veterans Administration will provide a marker free of charge and may pay partial burial costs. These are benefits that must be applied for at the time of death. If the deceased is eligible, survivors should contact the local Veterans Administration office to apply.

Consumers should inquire about the following items when selecting a cemetery or other burial facility:

- A price list of all charges, including the cost of opening (digging) the grave or of opening the mausoleum or columbarium, and the perpetual care fee (usually a one-time fee for maintenance of the site). Cemeteries are not required by law to disclose their fees in advance.

- Whether grave liners are required.

- Restrictions on who may be placed in the facility. Sites associated with a particular religion often require certification (such as a document of last rites) that the deceased was in fact of that religion.

- Any other restrictions imposed. Each facility has different rules.

- Requirements for markers. Some cemeteries allow only flat bronze or marble markers; others may allow or require a larger marker.

Other concerns consumers should think about as they select an interment site include the following:

- Is there room for other family members to be in the same facility?

- Is the facility well kept? In a cemetery, consumers should inspect many graves, not just the ones shown by the director of the cemetery.

- Do buyers have a choice of grave sites? For example, they may want to select a site with a certain view or near a grove of trees.

The Obituary

Obituaries, funeral notices and death notices are the ways people publicly announce a death. These may merely announce the death or may include the date and time of any visitation or funeral and memorial services planned so that the public may attend. If the deceased was prominent in a community other than the one in which she or he died, survivors may ask the newspaper there to announce the death so that all the deceased's friends and associates can know of the death.

Death notices simply state that a person died, and are usually published free of charge. Obituaries are often handled like wedding announcements; there is typically a form to be filled out and the newspaper staff writes it up. Or, if the individual was prominent in the society, the newspaper will write a longer obituary piece. Newspapers have separate space given to funeral notices, which are assembled by the family or the funeral director and paid for by the family. Survivors should check with their funeral director and their local papers about the procedures for placing obituaries.

Alternatives to Traditional Funerals

Do It Yourself

Not too long ago, most activities associated with death were performed by the deceased's family: people washed and prepared the dead for burial, held a visitation at home and buried the deceased in a family plot on private property. Today the funeral requirements and regulations are sufficiently complex that not many people would be inclined—or in some states, be allowed—to perform certain death services. For example, some states require that funeral directors make all of the arrangements, in which case the only opportunity for an individual approach is in the matter of the funeral service or memorial ceremony.

However, in some states it is possible to perform at least some of these services for the dead without relying on a funeral director. Since these activities are governed by law, survivors should thoroughly investigate the regulations that apply in their area if they have an interest in caring for the dead themselves. They can contact the local health department for information on the legal aspects. A death certificate signed by an official is required in all instances of death.

Bear in mind that the process will require substantial family and community support to be carried out effectively. Caring for the dead is a significant emotional endeavor, and while some of the practical activities such as transportation are not burdensome, they should be carefully thought out well in advance. Religious or community groups usually have the most success with alternative funeral arrangements. Two books, Lisa Carlson's *Caring for Your Own Dead* and Earnest Morgan's *Dealing Creatively with Death* (See the Resources list beginning on page 304.) cover this subject at length and are good resources for people interested in researching alternative options.

The following are some of the options survivors have in caring for their own dead, and the legal aspects to consider:

- **PREPARATION:** Loved ones can wash and dress the deceased themselves before the body is removed from the place of death.

- **RETAINING THE BODY UNTIL DISPOSITION:** There is usually an interval of a day or two before cremation or burial takes place. Survivors can hold the body at home rather than at a storage facility until the time for cremation or burial. State and local laws govern the length of time a body may be held before it is buried or cremated.

- **TRANSPORTATION OF THE BODY:** A hearse is not a legal requirement for transporting a body. Survivors can use any vehicle that is large enough to hold the casket to transport the body to the burial site or crematorium. However, permits may be required to transport a body, and some facilities may not accept delivery from anyone other than a licensed funeral director.

- **BURIAL:** In some states survivors may bury a body on private land. Local codes generally dictate that the burial be a certain distance from a water supply.

Funeral and Memorial Societies

In the 1950s and 1960s, in a reaction against the high cost of funerals, many people formed funeral and memorial societies. These nonprofit organizations negotiated with a local funeral director to provide simple, low-cost burial or cremation to its members. Currently, many funeral and memorial societies are still active, and in addition to providing prearrangement forms for funeral planning, they provide information on legal requirements, consumer education, making a complaint, organ donation and living wills and durable powers of attorney. Membership in a society involves a modest entrance fee, and members are encouraged (but not required) to volunteer. Interested parties can contact the Continental Association of Funeral and Memorial Societies (see the Resources list beginning on page 304).

Prearranged Funerals

For those who wish to forestall survivors' anguish or even squabbling over the arrangements of their funeral, it is possible to make these plans oneself, either by writing them down or by making the arrangements with a local funeral director. While these plans are not legally binding, they can provide guidance for survivors at a difficult time. Individuals should make sure, however, to discuss the plans in advance with their family so their decision will not be a surprise. Next of kin is the person legally authorized to make the funeral arrangements, so if that person disagrees with the deceased's last wishes, she or he may decide instead to follow a different scheme. Also, those who make them should be sure their plans can be located before the final arrangements are made and carried out.

Consumer Protection: The Federal Trade Commission Funeral Rule

The first step toward being a good consumer of funeral goods and services is to be educated about the options, one's own personal desires for a funeral and, of course, one's rights. Remember that consumers always have the right to ask questions. The Federal Trade Commission (FTC) Funeral Rule contains basic components that protect consumers' rights. Consumers can obtain a copy of the revised Funeral Rule from the FTC.

The most important government regulations regarding the funeral industry are contained in the FTC Funeral Rule, which went into effect on April 30, 1984 (revised July 19, 1994). The fundamental purpose of the FTC Funeral Rule is to require funeral homes to provide consumers with accurate, itemized information about the goods and services they provide. (The Rule also applies to cemeteries, crematories and other businesses that provide funeral goods and services.)

The Funeral Rule mandates certain legal disclosures and includes penalties of up to $10,000 per violation. The Rule specifically prohibits funeral directors from:

1. misrepresenting legal, crematory and cemetery requirements

2. embalming for a fee without family permission

3. requiring the purchase of a casket for direct cremation

4. requiring consumers to purchase particular goods or services as a condition for purchasing other goods or services

5. engaging in other deceptive or unfair practices

According to the Funeral Rule, consumers are not required to buy the casket from the same funeral home that provides other services. Additionally, the

Rule stipulates that funeral homes cannot add a surcharge or casket-handling fee for using a casket purchased elsewhere. The Rule further requires funeral homes to provide consumers with itemized price lists for specific goods and services as well as a statement listing the goods and services selected. The provisions of the Rule apply both to pre-need and at-need arrangements.

The General Price List

The General Price List (GPL) is the cornerstone of the Funeral Rule. It is an itemized price list of the most basic funeral goods and services. The FTC also requires that the GPL include a number of specific legal disclosures relating to the rights of consumers. GPLs are designed to:

1. help consumers compare prices among funeral homes

2. ensure that consumers purchase, on an itemized basis, only those goods and services that they want

Who Gets a GPL?   The FTC requires that funeral homes provide a copy of their General Price List to anyone who asks, in person, about funeral goods and services or their cost—including journalists, consumer protection groups and individuals. The request need not come from a person wishing to make funeral arrangements at the time or even in the future. Furthermore, consumers must be able to keep the copy they receive. Funeral directors who simply offer a GPL to be read on the spot, show one in their book or read from one are not satisfying the requirements of the Rule. They must physically hand the consumer a copy of the GPL that he or she can take home. No fee may be charged for this list, nor can any other restrictions be placed upon providing this information.

Although the Funeral Rule does not require that funeral homes hand out GPLs to everyone who walks in the door (whether they ask for one or not), GPLs must be offered when the funeral director begins to discuss arrangements, specific goods and services or prices with a customer. Regardless of where this discussion takes place—be it at the family's home, a hospital or at a nursing home—funeral directors must provide GPLs (and carry copies with them for this purpose). The only exception allowed is when a funeral director encounters the bereaved while he or she is simply transferring the body from the place of death to the funeral home. The funeral director need not provide a GPL at this time—and may ask permission to embalm the body—but he or she must also disclose that embalming is required by law only in special cases, and he or she must refrain from further discussion about goods and services.

It may be useful to note that some funeral homes prepare alternative

GPLs for the funerals of children and infants as well as for funerals sold on a volume basis to government agencies, religious groups and memorial societies. However, funeral homes that use alternative price lists must still comply with all the provisions of the Funeral Rule regarding mandatory disclosures and itemized prices. The following sample represents a GPL that meets federal requirements.

Sample 1

ABC FUNERAL HOME
100 Main Street
Yourtown, USA 12345
(123) 456-7890

GENERAL PRICE LIST

These prices are effective as of [date].

The goods and services shown below are those we can provide to our customers. You may choose only the items you desire. However, any funeral arrangements you select will include a charge for our basic services and overhead. If legal or other requirements mean you must buy any items you did not specifically ask for, we will explain the reason in writing on the statement we provide describing the funeral goods and services you selected.

Basic Services of Funeral Director
and Staff and Overhead .... $_____

> Our services include: conducting the arrangements conference; planning the funeral; consulting with family and clergy; shelter of remains; preparing and filing of necessary notices; obtaining necessary authorizations and permits; coordinating with the cemetery, crematory, or other third parties. In addition, this fee includes a proportionate share of our basic overhead costs.

> This fee for our basic services and overhead will be added to the total cost of the funeral arrangements you select. (This fee is already included in our charges for direct cremations, immediate burials, and forwarding or receiving remains.)

Embalming .... $_____

> Except in certain special cases, embalming is not required by law. Embalming may be necessary, however, if you select certain funeral arrangements, such as a funeral with viewing. If you do not want embalming, you usually have the right to choose an arrangement that does not require you to pay for it, such as direct cremation or immediate burial.

Other Preparation of the Body .... $_____
> [list individual services and prices]

Transfer of Remains to the Funeral Home
(within _____ mile radius) .... $_____
> beyond this radius we charge _____ per mile

Use of Facilities and Staff For Viewing
at the Funeral Home .... $_____

Use of Facilities and Staff For Funeral Ceremony
at the Funeral Home .... $_____

Use of Facilities and Staff For Memorial Service
at the Funeral Home .... $_____

Use of Equipment and Staff For Graveside Service .... $_____

Hearse .... $_____
Limousine .... $_____

Caskets .... $_____ to $_____
   A complete price list will be provided at the funeral home.

Outer Burial Containers .... $_____ to $_____
   A complete price list will be provided at the funeral home.

Forwarding of Remains to Another Funeral Home .... $_____
   Our charge includes: basic services of funeral director and staff; a proportionate share of overhead costs; removal of remains; embalming or other preparation of remains, if relevant; and local transportation.

Receiving Remains from Another Funeral Home .... $_____
   Our charge includes: basic services of funeral director and staff; a proportionate share of overhead costs; care of remains; transportation of remains to funeral home and to cemetery or crematory.

Direct Cremation .... $_____
   Our charge for a direct cremation (without ceremony) includes: basic services of funeral director and staff; a proportionate share of overhead costs; removal of remains; transportation to crematory; necessary authorizations; and cremation if relevant.

   If you want to arrange a direct cremation, you can use an alternative container. Alternative containers encase the body and can be made of materials like fiberboard or composition materials (with or without an outside covering). The containers we provide are a fiberboard container or an unfinished wood box.

  A. Direct cremation with container
   provided by the purchaser .... $_____

  B. Direct cremation with
   a fiberboard container .... $_____

  C. Direct cremation with an unfinished wood box .... $_____

Immediate Burial .... $_____
   Our charge for an immediate burial (without ceremony) includes: basic services of funeral director and staff; a proportionate share of overhead costs; removal of remains; and local transportation to cemetery.

  A. Immediate burial with casket provided
   by purchaser .... $_____

B. Immediate burial with alternative
    container [if offered] .... $_____

C. Immediate burial with cloth covered
    wood casket .... $_____

Information Required on the GPL   The FTC mandates that at least 16 separate items be listed on the GPL (more may be) in addition to six specific legal disclosures. The disclosures cover the consumer's right to purchase only those goods and services that they want, the fact that embalming is generally not required by law, the consumer's right to purchase an alternative container for direct cremations, the funeral home's basic services fee, casket prices and outer burial containers.

The Rule prohibits funeral homes from listing any of these 16 items as "free" or "no charge" because the costs are invariably recovered elsewhere in the bill. The purpose of this regulation is to prevent funeral homes from concealing costs in the nondeclinable basic services fee (see item 5 below). Prices for the following items must appear:

1. Forwarding of remains to another funeral home.

2. Receiving of remains from another funeral home.

3. Direct cremation.

4. Immediate burial.

The fees listed for these first four services must include a charge for the funeral home's basic services. Therefore, should a consumer purchase one of these services, he or she should not be charged a separate facilities, staff or equipment fee. The Rule also requires that the GPL describe all the services provided for in the quoted price.

For direct cremations, the GPL must state price options that include the price for a consumer-provided casket as well as the price for at least one type of alternative container. The price of the actual cremation may or may not be included in the funeral home's price (depending on whether the home owns a crematory). If an additional fee must be paid to a third-party crematory, this fee should be treated as a cash advance item (see Cash Advance Items on page 260), and it must be made clear to the consumer that there will be an additional charge.

For immediate burials, the GPL must state price options that include the price for a consumer-provided casket as well as the price for at least one type of casket or alternative container. Some funeral homes list this price as a fee to be added onto their casket prices. Note that the Funeral Rule requires funeral homes to provide alternative containers only for direct cremations and not for immediate burials. Note also that this price generally does not include cemetery costs.

5.   Basic services of funeral director and staff and overhead.

This fee covers the basic services that are part of any funeral, including conducting the arrangements conference, obtaining the necessary permits, preparing the funeral notices, sheltering the remains and coordinating with the cemetery or crematory. It may also include a portion of the funeral home's overhead. It cannot include charges relating to specific services listed separately on the GPL, any of which the consumer may decline to purchase.

The basic services fee (with a description of the services provided) may be listed as a separate fee or it may be included in the casket prices. If it is included in the casket prices, the casket price list must identify the amount that will be added onto the total cost of the funeral arrangements (as a basic services fee) should the consumer provide a casket.

The basic services fee is the only nondeclinable fee allowed by the Funeral Rule, unless state or local law requires otherwise (as in the case of local embalming requirements). Funeral homes may not charge any other nondeclinable fees or any other fees relating at all to services, facilities or overhead—such as a "basic facilities fee," a "casket-handling charge," or a "funeral director's fee"—that should be properly included in the basic services fee.

6.   Embalming.

The price for embalming should include the embalmer's professional services as well as the use of the preparation room, its equipment and all supplies. The embalming listing in the GPL must include the disclosure that embalming is required only in special cases (such as in the case of transport to another country or a formal viewing) and almost never for direct cremations or immediate burials. Note that embalming is not required by federal law under any circumstances.

7.   Other preparation of the body.

This includes such services as cosmetic work for viewing, and washing and disinfecting of unembalmed remains.

8.   Use of facilities and staff for viewing.

9.   Use of facilities and staff for funeral ceremony.

10. Use of facilities and staff for memorial service.

These three services may be charged at a flat or an hourly rate. The fees should include charges for the staff as well as the facilities used in connection with the event. However, if the event is held at a separate location, such as a church or a home, a separate fee for staff services should be provided.

11. Use of equipment and staff for graveside service.

This fee is intended to reflect the cost of a graveside service when the family chooses not to have a funeral ceremony at the funeral home or elsewhere. It should include both staff services and any equipment that the funeral home may provide, such as a tent and chairs. As with the listings above, service and equipment fees should not be itemized separately.

12. Transfer of remains to funeral home.

13. Hearse.

14. Limousine.

These charges may be billed as a flat fee, an hourly rate, according to mileage or as a combination of these methods such as a flat fee plus a mileage charge for distances beyond a certain radius from the funeral home.

15. Casket.

16. Outer burial container.

Prices for caskets and outer burial containers may be listed either on the General Price List or on separate price lists as long as the GPL lists a price range and discloses the availability of separate price lists. Additionally, regarding outer burial containers, either the General Price List or the separate price list must contain the disclosure that most state and local laws do not require the purchase of an outer burial container (although many cemeteries do).

Casket and Outer Burial Container Price Lists

The FTC Funeral Rule also mandates price listings for caskets and outer burial containers provided separately by funeral homes. Each price list must include the retail price of each casket, alternative container or outer burial container that does not require special ordering as well as enough descriptive information so that the consumer can identify and understand what he or she is buying. Providing a model number or a photograph of the casket is not sufficient to comply with the rule; the type of information that must be provided includes the material (gauge of metal or type of wood), the exterior trim and the interior lining—for example, "oak-stained soft-wood with red velvet interior" or "reinforced concrete grave liner."

As with the General Price List, funeral directors must show these casket and outer burial container price lists to anyone who asks, in person, about caskets, alternative containers, burial containers or their prices. Furthermore, funeral directors must show customers these price lists before showing them the actual items. However, unlike the GPL, funeral directors are not obligated to provide consumers with copies of the casket and outer burial container price lists for them to keep and take home. The sample price lists shown below meet federal requirements.

Sample 2

ABC FUNERAL HOME
CASKET PRICE LIST

These prices are effective as of [date].

Alternative Containers:

1. Fiberboard Box .... $_____
2. Plywood Box .... $_____
3. Unfinished Pine Box.. $_____

Caskets:

1. Beige cloth-covered soft-wood
   with beige interior .... $_____

2. Oak stained soft-wood
   with pleated blue crepe interior.. $_____

3. Mahogany finished soft-wood
   with maroon crepe interior .... $_____

4. Solid White Pine
   with eggshell crepe interior .... $_____

5. Solid Mahogany
   with tufted rosetan velvet interior .... $_____

6. Hand finished solid Cherry
   with ivory velvet interior.. $_____

7. 18 gauge rose colored Steel
   with pleated maroon crepe interior
   (available in a variety of interiors) .... $_____
8. 20 gauge bronze colored Steel
   with blue crepe interior.. $_____

9. Solid Bronze (16 gauge) with brushed finish
    white ivory velvet interior .... $_____

10. Solid Copper (32 oz.) with Sealer (Oval Glass)
    and medium bronze finish
    with rosetan velvet interior.. $_____

Sample 3

ABC FUNERAL HOME
OUTER BURIAL CONTAINER PRICE LIST

These prices are effective as of [date].

In most areas of the country, state or local law does not require that you buy a container to surround the casket in the grave. However, many cemeteries require that you have such a container so that the grave will not sink in. Either a grave liner or a burial vault will satisfy these requirements.

1. Concrete Grave Liner .... $_____

2. Acme Reinforced Concrete Vault (lined).. $_____

3. Acme Reinforced Concrete Vault
    (stainless steel lined).. $_____

4. Acme Solid Copper Vault .... $_____

5. Acme Steel Vault (12 gauge) .... $_____

Telephone and Mail Inquiries

The Funeral Rule requires funeral homes to provide all readily available information to consumers over the telephone. Consumers can request general information or, if they wish, specific information from the General Price list or the casket and outer burial container price lists. However, the Rule does not require funeral homes to send out GPLs in response to telephone or mail requests (although some states do require funeral homes to mail price lists upon request).

Callers are explicitly not required to give their names, addresses or phone numbers in order to have their questions answered, nor can they be required to come to the funeral home in person.

The Statement of Funeral Goods and Services Selected

The FTC Funeral Rule requires funeral directors to provide their customers with a Statement of Funeral Goods and Services Selected. This statement lists and totals the prices of the goods and services chosen by that particular consumer. Its purpose is to allow consumers to evaluate their choices and make any desired changes.

The goods and services listed on this statement, which may be presented in contract form, should generally correspond to the way the items are listed on the GPL so that consumers can easily compare the two documents.

The Rule requires that the Statement be prepared and given to the consumer at the end of the arrangements conference. When the arrangements are made in person, the Statement must be provided at this time. Mailing it to the consumer at some later time or presenting it to the consumer at the funeral does not satisfy the requirements of the Rule. If arrangements are made over the telephone, the Statement should be provided at the earliest possible time. Statements that meet federal guidelines resemble the sample statement included here.

Sample 4

ABC FUNERAL HOME
STATEMENT OF FUNERAL GOODS AND SERVICES SELECTED

Charges are only for those items that you selected or that are required. If we are required by law or by a cemetery or crematory to use any items, we will explain the reasons in writing below.

Deceased: _____

Purchaser: _____

Address: _____

Tel. No. _____

_____   _____

Date of Death   Date of Arrangements

Basic Services of Funeral Director and Staff and Overhead .... $_____

Embalming .... $_____

If you selected a funeral that may require embalming, such as a funeral with viewing, you may have to pay for embalming. You do not have to pay for embalming you did not approve if you selected arrangements such as a direct cremation or immediate burial. If we charged for embalming, we will explain why below.

Other Preparation of the Body

    1. Cosmetic Work for Viewing.. $_____
    2. Washing and Disinfecting Unembalmed Remains .... $_____

Transfer of Remains to the Funeral Home.. $_____

Use of Facilities and Staff For Viewing .... $_____

Use of Facilities and Staff For Funeral Ceremony .... $_____

Use of Facilities and Staff For Memorial Service .... $_____

Use of Equipment and Staff For Graveside Service .... $_____

Hearse .... $_____

Limousine .... $_____

Casket .... $_____

Outer Burial Container .... $_____

Forwarding of Remains to Another Funeral Home... $_____

Receiving Remains from Another Funeral Home .... $_____

Direct Cremation .... $_____

Immediate Burial .... $_____

CASH ADVANCE ITEMS

We charge you for our services in obtaining: [specify relevant cash advance items].

    Cemetery charges... $_____
    Crematory charges .... $_____
    Flowers .... $_____
    Obituary notice .... $_____
    Death certificate.. $_____
    Music... $_____

        Total Cash Advance Items... $_____

TOTAL COST OF ARRANGEMENTS (including all services, merchandise,
and cash advance items) .... $_____

If any legal, cemetery, or crematory requirement has required the purchase of any of the items listed above, we will explain the requirement below:

_____

_____

_____

Reason for Embalming:

_____

Information Required on the Statement of Funeral Goods and Services Selected   The Statement should list the individual goods and services selected by the consumer during the arrangements conference, as well as the itemized prices of these goods and services. Fees listed separately on the GPL may not be lumped together on the Statement as, for instance, "Automotive Equipment." (In the case of funeral packages, only the package price need be listed, as long as the individual goods and services are listed on, and the consumer has already been offered, the GPL. In no case may a consumer ever be required to buy a funeral package.)

Additionally, the FTC requires that the Statement include written explanations of the specific reasons for nondeclinable charges that may be required by state or local law or by the cemetery or crematory. Finally, if there is a charge for embalming, the Statement must include the reason why the body was embalmed, either because the bereaved requested embalming or because of a specific legal requirement. The Statement must include a specific disclosure that if the body has been embalmed without the explicit approval of the family or without a legal requirement, consumers are not required to pay any embalming fee. "Explicit approval" means just that: granting permission to "prepare" the body, for example, does not constitute permission to embalm.

Cash Advance Items

Cash advance items are goods and services for which the funeral home must pay a third party on behalf of a consumer, such as death certificates, crematory services, pallbearers, clergy, flowers, musicians and so forth. The Funeral Rule requires that cash advance items be listed separately on the Statement with a price for each item.

Funeral homes are allowed to mark up, charge a fee for or receive a rebate for cash advance items. However, if they do so, they must disclose this fact on the Statement—that is, that the price the consumer is paying is not the same as the price the funeral home is being charged. (Although the Rule does not require disclosure of the amount of the funeral home's markup, nor limit this amount, some states do.)

The Federal Funeral Industry Practices Revised Rule

Originally passed in 1984, the Funeral Rule, as it is commonly called, was revised in 1994 to meet the changing needs of American consumers and the evolving nature of the American funeral business. The text of the law is as follows:

Part 453 - Funeral Industry Practices Revised Rule

Section:
453.1 **Definitions.**
453.2 **Price disclosures.**
453.3 **Misrepresentations.**
453.4 **Required purchase of funeral goods or funeral services.**
453.5 **Services provided without prior approval.**
453.6 **Retention of documents.**
453.7 **Comprehension of disclosures.**
453.8 **Declaration of intent.**
453.9 **State exemptions.**

Authority: 15 U.S.C. 57a(a); 15 U.S.C. 46(g); 5 U.S.C. 552.

§ 453.1 Definitions

(a) <u>Alternative container</u> An "alternative container" is an unfinished wood box or other non-metal receptacle or enclosure, without ornamentation or a fixed interior lining, which is designed for the encasement of human remains and which is made of fiberboard, pressed-wood, composition materials (with or without an outside covering) or like materials.

(b) <u>Cash advance item</u> A "cash advance item" is any item of service or merchandise described to a purchaser as a "cash advance," "accommodation," "cash disbursement," or similar term. A cash advance item is also any item obtained from a third party and paid for by the funeral provider on the purchaser's behalf. Cash advance items may include, but are not limited to: cemetery or crematory services; pallbearers; public transportation; clergy honoraria; flowers; musicians or singers; nurses; obituary notices; gratuities and death certificates.

(c) <u>Casket</u> A "casket" is a rigid container which is designed for the encasement of human remains and which is usually constructed of wood, metal, fiberglass, plastic, or like material, and ornamented and lined with fabric.

(d) <u>Commission</u> "Commission" refers to the Federal Trade Commission.

(e) <u>Cremation</u> "Cremation" is a heating process which incinerates human remains.

(f) <u>Crematory</u> A "crematory" is any person, partnership or corporation that performs cremation and sells funeral goods.

(g) <u>Direct cremation</u> A "direct cremation" is a disposition of human remains by cremation, without formal viewing, visitation, or ceremony with the body present.

(h) <u>Funeral goods</u> "Funeral goods" are the goods which are sold or offered for sale directly to the public for use in connection with funeral services.

(i) <u>Funeral provider</u> A "funeral provider" is any person, partnership or corporation that sells or offers to sell funeral goods and funeral services to the public.

(j) <u>Funeral services</u> "Funeral services" are any services which may be used to: (1) care for and prepare deceased human bodies for burial, cremation or other final disposition; and (2) arrange, supervise or conduct the funeral ceremony or the final disposition of deceased human bodies.

(k) Immediate burial An "immediate burial" is a disposition of human remains by burial, without formal viewing, visitation, or ceremony with the body present, except for a graveside service.

(l) Memorial service A "memorial service" is a ceremony commemorating the deceased without the body present.

(m) Funeral ceremony A "funeral ceremony" is a service commemorating the deceased with the body present.

(n) Outer burial container An "outer burial container" is any container which is designed for placement in the grave around the casket including, but not limited to, containers commonly known as burial vaults, grave boxes, and grave liners.

(o) Person A "person" is any individual, partnership, corporation, association, government or governmental subdivision or agency, or other entity.

(p) Services of funeral director and staff The "services of funeral director and staff" are the basic services, not to be included in prices of other categories in § 453.2(b)(4), that are furnished by a funeral provider in arranging any funeral, such as conducting the arrangements conference, planning the funeral, obtaining necessary permits, and placing obituary notices.

§ 453.2 Price Disclosures

(a) Unfair or Deceptive Acts or Practices

In selling or offering to sell funeral goods or funeral services to the public, it is an unfair or deceptive act or practice for a funeral provider to fail to furnish accurate price information disclosing the cost to the purchaser for each of the specific funeral goods and funeral services used in connection with the disposition of deceased human bodies, including at least the price of embalming, transportation of remains, use of facilities, caskets, outer burial containers, immediate burials, or direct cremations, to persons inquiring about the purchase of funerals. Any funeral provider who complies with the preventive requirements in paragraph (b) of this section is not engaged in the unfair or deceptive acts or practices defined here.

(b) Preventive Requirements

To prevent these unfair or deceptive acts or practices, as well as the unfair or deceptive acts or practices defined in § 453.4(b)(1), funeral providers must:

(1) Telephone Price Disclosure

Tell persons who ask by telephone about the funeral provider's offerings or prices any accurate information from the price lists described in paragraphs (b)(2) through (4) of this section and any other readily available information that reasonably answers the question.

(2) Casket Price List

(i) Give a printed or typewritten price list to people who inquire in person about the offerings or prices of caskets or alternative containers. The funeral provider must offer the list upon beginning discussion of, but in any event before showing caskets. The list must contain at least the retail prices of all caskets and alternative containers offered which do not require special ordering, enough information to identify each, and the effective date for the price list. In lieu of a written list, other formats, such as notebooks, brochures, or charts may be used if they contain the same information as would the printed or typewritten list, and display it in a clear and conspicuous manner. Provided, however, that funeral providers do not have to make a casket price list available if the funeral providers place on the general price list, specified in paragraph (b)(4) of this section, the information required by this paragraph.

(ii) Place on the list, however produced, the name of the funeral provider's place of business and a caption describing the list as a "casket price list."

(3) Outer Burial Container Price List

(i) Give a printed or typewritten price list to persons who inquire in person about outer burial container offerings or prices. The funeral provider must offer the list upon beginning discussion of, but in any event before showing the containers. The list must contain at least the retail prices of all outer burial containers offered which do not require special ordering, enough information to identify each container, and the effective date for the prices listed. In lieu of a written list, the funeral provider may use other formats, such as notebooks, brochures, or charts, if they contain the same information as the printed or typewritten list, and display it in a clear and conspicuous manner. Provided, however, that funeral providers do not have to make an outer burial container price list available if the funeral providers place on the general price list, specified in paragraph (b)(4) of this section, the information required by this paragraph.

(ii) Place on the list, however produced, the name of the funeral provider's place of business and a caption describing the list as an "outer burial container price list."

(4) General Price List

(i)(A) Give a printed or typewritten price list for retention to persons who inquire in person about the funeral goods, funeral services or prices of funeral goods or services offered by the funeral

provider. The funeral provider must give the list upon beginning discussion of any of the following:

(1) the prices of funeral goods or funeral services;

(2) the overall type of funeral service or disposition; or

(3) specific funeral goods or funeral services offered by the funeral provider.

(B) The requirement in paragraph (b)(4)(i)(A) of this section applies whether the discussion takes place in the funeral home or elsewhere. Provided, however, that when the deceased is removed for transportation to the funeral home, an in-person request at that time for authorization to embalm, required by § 453.5(a)(2), does not, by itself, trigger the requirement to offer the general price list if the provider in seeking prior embalming approval discloses that embalming is not required by law except in certain special cases, if any. Any other discussion during that time about prices or the selection of funeral goods or services triggers the requirement under paragraph (b)(4)(i)(A) of this section to give consumers a general price list.

(C) The list required by paragraph (b)(4)(i)(A) of this section must contain at least the following information:

(1) The name, address, and

telephone number of the funeral provider's place of business;

(2) A caption describing the list as a "general price list"; and

(3) The effective date for the price

(ii) Include on the price list, in any order, the retail prices (expressed either as the flat fee, or as the price per hour, mile or other unit of computation) and the other information specified below for at least each of the following items, if offered for sale:

(A) Forwarding of remains to another funeral home, together with a list of the services provided for any quoted price;

(B) Receiving remains from another funeral home, together with a list of the services provided for any quoted price;

(C) The price range for the direct cremations offered by the funeral provider, together with:

(1) a separate price for a direct cremation where the purchaser provides the container;

(2) separate prices for each direct cremation offered including an alternative container; and

(3) a description of the ser-

vices and container (where applicable), included in each price;

(D) The price range for the immediate burials offered by the funeral provider, together with:

(1) a separate price for an immediate burial where the purchaser provides the casket;

(2) separate prices for each immediate burial offered including a casket or alternative container; and

(3) a description of the services and container (where applicable) included in that price;

(E) Transfer of remains to funeral home;

(F) Embalming;

(G) Other preparation of the body;

(H) Use of facilities and staff for viewing;

(I) Use of facilities and staff for funeral ceremony;

(J) Use of facilities and staff for memorial service;

(K) Use of equipment and staff for graveside service;

(L) Hearse; and

(M) Limousine.

(iii) Include on the price list, in any order, the following information:

(A) Either of the following:

(1) The price range for the caskets offered by the funeral provider, together with the statement: "A complete price list will be provided at the funeral home."; or

(2) The prices of individual caskets, disclosed in the manner specified by paragraph (b)(2)(i) of this section; and

(B) Either of the following:

(1) The price range for the outer burial containers offered by the funeral provider, together with the statement: "A complete price list will be provided at the funeral home."; or

(2) The prices of individual outer burial containers, disclosed in the manner specified by paragraph (b)(3)(i) of this section; and

(C) Either of the following:

(1) The price for the basic services of funeral director and staff, together with a list of the principal basic services provided for any

quoted price and, if the charge cannot be declined by the purchaser, the statement "This fee for our basic services will be added to the total cost of the funeral arrangements you select. (This fee is already included in our charges for direct cremations, immediate burials, and forwarding or receiving remains.)" If the charge cannot be declined by the purchaser, the quoted price shall include all charges for the recovery of unallocated funeral provider overhead, and funeral providers may include in the required disclosure the phrase "and overhead" after the word "services"; or

(2) The following statement: "Please note that a fee of (specify dollar amount) for the use of our basic services is included in the price of our caskets. This same fee shall be added to the total cost of your funeral arrangements if you provide the casket. Our services include (specify)." The fee shall include all charges for the recovery of unallocated funeral provider overhead, and funeral providers may include in the required disclosure the phrase "and overhead" after the word "services." The statement must be placed on the gen-

eral price list together with the casket price range, required by paragraph (b)(4)(iii)(A)(1) of this section, or together with the prices of individual caskets, required by (b)(4)(iii)(A)(2) of this section.

(iv) The services fee permitted by § 453.2(b)(4)(iii)(C)(1) or (C)(2) is the only funeral provider fee for services, facilities or unallocated overhead permitted by this part to be nondeclinable, unless otherwise required by law.

(5) Statement of Funeral Goods and Services Selected

(i) Give an itemized written statement for retention to each person who arranges a funeral or other disposition of human remains, at the conclusion of the discussion of arrangements. The statement must list at least the following information:

(A) The funeral goods and funeral services selected by that person and the prices to be paid for each of them;

(B) Specifically itemized cash advance items. (These prices must be given to the extent then known or reasonably ascertainable. If the prices are not known or reasonably ascertainable, a good faith estimate shall be given and a written statement of the actual charges shall be provided before the final bill is paid.); and

(C) The total cost of the goods and services selected.

(ii) The information required by this paragraph (b)(5) may be included on any contract, statement, or other document which the funeral provider would otherwise provide at the conclusion of discussion of arrangements.

(6) Other Pricing Methods

Funeral providers may give persons any other price information, in any other format, in addition to that required by § 453.2(b)(2), (3), and (4) so long as the statement required by 453.2(b)(5) is given when required by the rule.

§ 453.3 Misrepresentations

(a) Embalming Provisions

(1) Deceptive Acts or Practices

In selling or offering to sell funeral goods or funeral services to the public, it is a deceptive act or practice for a funeral provider to:

(i) Represent that state or local law requires that a deceased person be embalmed when such is not the case;

(ii) Fail to disclose that embalming is not required by law except in certain special cases, if any.

(2) Preventive requirements

To prevent these deceptive acts or practices, as well as the unfair or deceptive acts or practices defined in §§ 453.4(b)(1) and 453.5(2), funeral providers must:

(i) Not represent that a deceased person is required to be embalmed for:

(A) direct cremation;

(B) immediate burial; or

(C) a closed casket funeral without viewing or visitation when refrigeration is available and when state or local law does not require embalming; and

(ii) Place the following disclosure on the general price list, required by § 453.2(b)(4), in immediate conjunction with the price shown for embalming: "Except in certain special cases, embalming is not required by law. Embalming may be necessary, however, if you select certain funeral arrangements, such as a funeral with viewing. If you do not want embalming, you usually have the right to choose an arrangement that does not require you to pay for it, such as direct cremation or immediate burial." The phrase "except in certain special cases" need not be included in this disclosure if state or local law in the area(s) where the provider does business does not require embalming under any circumstances.

(b) Casket for Cremation Provisions

(1) Deceptive Acts or Practices

In selling or offering to sell funeral goods or funeral services to the public, it is a deceptive act or practice for a funeral provider to:

(i) Represent that state or local law requires a casket for direct cremations;

(ii) Represent that a casket is required for direct cremations.

(2) Preventive Requirements

To prevent these deceptive acts or practices, as well as the unfair or deceptive acts or practices defined in § 453.4(a)(1), funeral providers must place the following disclosure in immediate conjunction with the price range shown for direct cremations: "If you want to arrange a direct cremation, you can use an alternative container. Alternative containers encase the body and can be made of materials like fiberboard or composition materials (with or without an outside covering). The containers we provide are (specify containers)." This disclosure only has to be placed on the general price list if the funeral provider arranges direct cremations.

(c) Outer Burial Container Provisions

(1) Deceptive Acts or Practices
In selling or offering to sell

funeral goods and funeral services to the public, it is a deceptive act or practice for a funeral provider to:

(i) Represent that state or local laws or regulations, or particular cemeteries, require outer burial containers when such is not the case;

(ii) Fail to disclose to persons arranging funerals that state law does not require the purchase of an outer burial container.

(2) Preventive Requirement

To prevent these deceptive acts or practices, funeral providers must place the following disclosure on the outer burial container price list, required by § 453.2(b)(3)(i), or, if the prices of outer burial containers are listed on the general price list, required by § 453.2(b)(4), in immediate conjunction with those prices: "In most areas of the country, state or local law does not require that you buy a container to surround the casket in the grave. However, many cemeteries require that you have such a container so that the grave will not sink in. Either a grave liner or a burial vault will satisfy these requirements."
    The phrase "in most areas of the country" need not be included in this disclosure if state or local law in the area(s) where the provider does business does not require a container to surround the casket in the grave.

(d) General Provisions in Legal and Cemetery Requirements

(1) Deceptive Acts or Practices

In selling or offering to sell funeral goods or funeral services to the public, it is a deceptive act or practice for funeral providers to represent that federal, state, or local laws, or particular cemeteries or crematories, require the purchase of any funeral goods or funeral services when such is not the case.

(2) Preventive Requirements

To prevent these deceptive acts or practices, as well as the deceptive acts or practices identified in §§ 453.3(a)(1), 453.3(b)(1), and 453.3(c)(1), funeral providers must identify and briefly describe in writing on the statement of funeral goods and services selected (required by § 453.2(b)(5)) any legal, cemetery, or crematory requirement which the funeral provider represents to persons as compelling the purchase of funeral goods or funeral services for the funeral which that person is arranging.

(e) Provisions on Preservative and Protective Value Claims

In selling or offering to sell funeral goods or funeral services to the public, it is a deceptive act or practice for a funeral provider to:

(1) Represent that funeral goods or funeral services will

delay the natural decomposition of human remains for a long-term or indefinite time;

(2) Represent that funeral goods have protective features or will protect the body from gravesite substances, when such is not the case.

(f) Cash Advance Provisions

(1) Deceptive Acts or Practices

In selling or offering to sell funeral goods or funeral services to the public, it is a deceptive act or practice for a funeral provider to:

(i) Represent that the price charged for a cash advance item is the same as the cost to the funeral provider for the item when such is not the case;

(ii) Fail to disclose to persons arranging funerals that the price being charged for a cash advance item is not the same as the cost to the funeral provider for the item when such is the case.

(2) Preventive Requirements

To prevent these deceptive acts or practices, funeral providers must place the following sentence in the itemized statement of funeral goods and services selected, in immediate conjunction with the list of itemized cash advance items required by § 453.2(b)(5)(i)(B): "We charge you for our services in obtaining:

(specify cash advance items)," if the funeral provider makes a charge upon, or receives and retains a rebate, commission or trade or volume discount upon a cash advance item.

§ 453.4 **Required Purchase of Funeral Goods or Funeral Services.**

(a) Casket for Cremation Provisions

(1) Unfair or Deceptive Acts or Practices

In selling or offering to sell funeral goods or funeral services to the public, it is an unfair or deceptive act or practice for a funeral provider, or a crematory, to require that a casket be purchased for direct cremation.

(2) Preventive Requirement

To prevent this unfair or deceptive act or practice, funeral providers must make an alternative container available for direct cremations, if they arrange direct cremations.

(b) Other Required Purchases of Funeral Goods or Funeral Services

(1) Unfair or Deceptive Acts or Practices

In selling or offering to sell funeral goods or funeral services, it is an unfair or deceptive act or practice for a funeral provider to:

(i) Condition the furnishing of any funeral good or funeral service to a person arranging a funeral upon the purchase of any other funeral good or funeral service, except as required by law or as otherwise permitted by this plan;

(ii) Charge any fee as a condition to furnishing any funeral goods or funeral services to a person arranging a funeral, other than the fees for: (1) services of funeral director and staff, permitted by § 453.2(b)(4)(iii)(C); (2) other funeral services and funeral goods selected by the purchaser; and (3) other funeral goods or services required to be purchased, as explained on the itemized statement in accordance with § 453-3(d)(2).

(2) Preventive Requirements

(i) To prevent these unfair or deceptive acts or practices, funeral providers must:

(A) Place the following disclosure in the general price list, immediately above the prices required by § 453.2(b)(4)(ii) and (iii): "The goods and services shown below are those we can provide to our customers. You may choose only the items you desire. If legal or other requirements mean you must buy any items you did not specifically ask for, we will explain the reason in writing on the statement we provide describing the funeral goods and services you selected." Provided, however, that if the charge for "services of funeral director and staff" cannot be declined by the purchaser, the statement shall include the sentence: "However, any funeral arrangements you select will include a charge for our basic services" between the second and third sentences of the statement specified above herein. The statement may include the phrase "and overhead" after the word "services" if the fee includes a charge for the recovery of unallocated funeral provider overhead;

(B) Place the following disclosure in the statement of funeral goods and services selected, required by § 453.2(b)(5)(i): "Charges are only for those items that you selected or that are required. If we are required by law or by a cemetery or crematory to use any items, we will explain the reasons in writing below."

(ii) A funeral provider shall not violate this section by failing to comply with a request for a combination of goods or services which would be impossible, impractical, or excessively burdensome to provide.

§ 453.5 Services Provided Without Prior Approval

(a) Unfair or Deceptive Acts or Practices

In selling or offering to sell funeral goods or funeral services to the public, it is an unfair or deceptive act or practice for any provider to embalm a deceased human body for a fee unless:

(1) State or local law or regulation requires embalming in the particular circumstances regardless of any funeral choice which the family might make; or

(2) Prior approval for embalming (expressly so described) has been obtained from a family member or other authorized person; or

(3) The funeral provider is unable to contact a family member or other authorized person after exercising due diligence, has no reason to believe the family does not want embalming performed, and obtains subsequent approval for embalming already performed (expressly so described). In seeking approval, the funeral provider must disclose that a fee will be charged if the family selects a funeral which requires embalming, such as a funeral with viewing, and that no fee will be charged if the family selects a service which does not require embalming, such as direct cremation or immediate burial.

(b) Preventive Requirement

To prevent these unfair or deceptive acts or practices, funeral providers must include on the itemized statement of funeral goods and services selected, required by § 453.2(b)(5), the statement: "If you selected a funeral that may require embalming, such as a funeral with viewing, you may have to pay for embalming. You do not have to pay for embalming you did not approve if you selected arrangements such as a direct cremation or immediate burial. If we charged for embalming, we will explain why below."

§ 453.6 Retention of Documents

To prevent the unfair or deceptive acts or practices specified in § 453.2 and § 453.3 of this rule, funeral providers must retain and make available for inspection by Commission officials true and accurate copies of the price lists specified in §§ 453.2(b)(2) through (4), as applicable, for at least one year after the date of their last distribution to customers, and a copy of each statement of funeral goods and services selected, as required by § 453.2(b)(5), for at least one year from the date of the arrangements conference.

§ 453.7 Comprehension of Disclosures

To prevent the unfair or deceptive acts or practices specified in § 453.2 through § 453.5, funeral providers must make all disclosures required by those sections in a clear and conspicuous manner. Providers shall not include in the casket, outer burial container, and general price lists, required by §§ 453.2(b)(2)-(4), any statement or information that alters or contradicts the information required by this Part to be included in those lists.

§ 453.8 Declaration of Intent

(a) Except as otherwise provided in § 453.2(a), it is a violation of this rule to engage in any unfair or deceptive acts or practices specified in this rule, or to fail to comply with any of the preventive requirements specified in this rule;

(b) The provisions of this rule are separate and severable from one another. If any provision is determined to be invalid, it is the Commission's intention that the remaining provisions shall continue in effect.

(c) This rule shall not apply to the business of insurance or to acts in the conduct thereof.

§ 453.9 State Exemptions

If, upon application to the Commission by an appropriate state agency, the Commission determines that:

(a) There is a state requirement in effect which applies to any transaction to which this rule applies; and

(b) That state requirement affords an overall level of protection to consumers which is as great as, or greater than, the protection afforded by this rule;

then the Commission's rule will not be in effect in that state to the extent specified by the Commission in its determination, for as long as the State administers and enforces effectively the state requirement.

By direction of the Commission.

Donald S. Clark
Secretary

Fraud in the Funeral Industry

Despite the enactment of the FTC Funeral Rule, surveys have shown that there is still extensive noncompliance with its provisions. Consumers commonly complain of funeral directors:

- persuading them to purchase elaborate funerals at a time when they are least able to resist

- promoting expensive caskets when the deceased is to be cremated (a casket is not required for cremation)

- wildly overcharging for cash advance items such as flowers

- refusing to provide General Price Lists or to cite prices over the telephone (actions required under the FTC Rule)

- showing only the most expensive caskets

- delivering goods and services other than, or in addition to, those selected

Furthermore, there still exists a confusing network of state and local laws that can baffle even some funeral directors who mean well.

In any case, the best strategy in avoiding fraud is consumer education about the Funeral Rule and the specific laws that apply in their city and state. But unless consumers are aware of these requirements, unprincipled funeral directors may ignore the law as best they can.

Unfortunately, state funeral licensing boards are often of little help. A majority of the seats on these boards are usually filled by funeral professionals more concerned with their industry than with the rights of consumers. Some boards, especially those controlled by large funeral home chains, have been known to make regulations that force smaller, inexpensive operations to raise their prices or go out of business. For example, a state licensing board may pass a regulation requiring funeral homes in that state to have a full-time embalmer (only a part-time embalmer is necessary in most cases), the extra cost of which drives up prices. Similarly, state legislatures under the influence of wealthy funeral industry lobbyists may pass laws requiring the embalming of a body with contagious diseases, although the prevailing opinion among public health specialists is that this serves no public health purpose.

A basic principle to remember is that funeral homes make their living selling goods and services that address the needs of survivors. Be wary when funeral directors make guilt-producing remarks about "honoring" the deceased, such as "You only have one chance to do this right." The dead have no specific needs. It is the survivors' needs that must be met.

Common Funeral Home Fraud and What to Do About It

1. Embalming requirements.

Even though embalming is required only in special cases, many funeral directors still tell consumers that it is necessary "for practical purposes." Consumers should be suspicious of these claims. Unless they are planning a formal viewing and there will be a delay before the ceremony, there is probably no need to embalm the body, especially for closed-casket funerals when refrigeration is available. Consumers should also be aware that a private final viewing of the body by the immediate family does not constitute a formal viewing in this sense and does not necessitate embalming.

2. Cemetery or crematory requirements.

Some unscrupulous funeral directors may try to sell goods or services based on their representation of cemetery or crematory requirements. For instance, they may claim that a particular cemetery requires a reinforced concrete grave liner. Any requirements cited by the funeral director should be stated in writing on the Statement of Funeral Goods and Services Selected. Consumers can then contact the cemetery or crematory directly to verify that such requirements in fact exist.

3. Hidden overhead charges.

There are only three acceptable ways for funeral homes to recover overhead expenses. They can include overhead as part of their basic services fee; by spreading the cost among several goods and services; or by using a combination of these methods. Except for the basic services fee, there can be no additional nondeclinable charges for overhead such as a "facilities fee" or a "staff fee."

4. Claim regarding preservation.

The FTC Funeral Rule specifically prohibits funeral homes from making claims that a particular treatment, casket or outer burial container will preserve the body indefinitely or even for a long time. This prohibition includes claims that caskets or outer burial containers will keep out dirt, water or other grave site substances. The purpose of embalming is merely to preserve the body the few days necessary to arrange a formal viewing, if one is desired.

5. Bait and switch.

One of the easiest ways for shady funeral homes to rip survivors off is by selling them one casket but providing another, especially for cremations. To protect themselves, and to make sure that the casket chosen in the showroom is the casket delivered, consumers should make notes at the time of purchase so they will recognize the casket later. (The same is true of outer burial containers.) In particular, they should note the name of the manufacturer and the model number, and ask the funeral director to provide a copy of the brochure or the descriptive invoice provided by the manufacturer. In this way, they have the paperwork necessary to prosecute a claim should the funeral home switch caskets.

6. Flowers.

Flowers are another commodity that are often baited and switched—that is, the arrangement received has fewer, older and cheaper flowers than the one pictured in the florist's arrangement book. To avoid this problem, consumers should have the florist's order specify the number and variety of the flowers. It is also wise to order arrangements that can be taken home, such as everlastings or other dried flowers.

7. Recommendations from clergy.

Although members of the clergy have been at the forefront of the battle against funeral abuses, there are some members of the clergy whose ethics in this regard are not so scrupulous. Some clerics have been known to accept donations, personal gifts and even kickbacks from funeral directors in exchange for recommendations to parishioners. For this reason, many clerics are reluctant to call attention to funeral homes that exploit or defraud consumers. Therefore, it's always better to research the situation than to rely solely on the advice of a priest, minister or rabbi.

8. Vultures.

There exists an entire class of con artists who support themselves by swindling the bereaved, especially widows. They appear shortly after a funeral notice has been printed in the local newspaper, often claiming that they are owed a nonexistent debt or that the deceased had recently ordered an expensive item from them (commonly a Bible) but had not yet paid the balance due. Another favorite scam is claiming that the deceased had a life insurance policy on which one payment remains before the survivor can collect. In these cases, survivors should always satisfy themselves that representations are legitimate. Before any money changes hands, survivors should consult the attorney who is handling the probate of the will. A less brazen version of fraud is perpetrated by investment counselors who, in order to receive the commissions involved, suggest a survivor rearrange the deceased's investment portfolio.

9. "Special" discounts.

Occasionally, funeral homes will list artificially high prices on their GPLs and then offer many of their customers "special" discounts. This practice is specifically prohibited by the Funeral Rule.

10. Pre-need contracts.

When entering into a pre-need contract, consumers should be careful about terms such as "nontransferable," "noncancellable" and "nonrefundable." They may in the future need to leave the area, in which case they should be able to reclaim money already paid, transfer the contract by gift or sale or at least stop making payments. Because pre-need contracts are, by definition, entered into when time is not pressing, it may be wise to consult an attorney before signing one.

Complaints

Consumers who experience a problem with any aspect of the services performed by a funeral home should first speak to the funeral director. They should state their problem and their concerns—most often, once they voice their dissatisfaction the funeral home will make an effort to resolve the issue. As business people they are most likely concerned about their reputation and their standing in the community.

Consumers Beware

Consumer complaints are on the rise in the area of prepaid funeral arrangements. In prepaying a funeral, the consumer contracts with a funeral provider for specific funeral services. There are some significant drawbacks to prepaying a funeral. For example, if the company goes out of business customers may not be able to recover their money, or if they move or for another reason must use the services of another funeral provider, their money may not be refunded. There are several important precautions consumers should take when entering into a prepaid contract.

1. A lawyer should be consulted before any agreement is signed.

2. The contract should be made with an established, reputable company. Consumers can call the Better Business Bureau to check whether there have been complaints about the firm under consideration.

3. Consumers should make sure the price plan is guaranteed. The company may try to add charges or increase the cost of certain items.

4. The funds should be held in a guaranteed trust.

5. The contract should allow the right of cancellation.

For those concerned about paying for funeral arrangements, in most cases the same financial advantages of buying a prepaid funeral contract can be gained from putting the money in a savings account, trust fund or credit union.

If speaking to the funeral director does not resolve the problem, other options include contacting the state and national funeral directors association, state licensing boards and the local and state consumer protection agencies. If consumers suspect fraud, they should contact the district attorney, state attorney general or the Federal Trade Commission. The FTC cannot resolve individual problems or disputes, but it does monitor trends in industry and will investigate some complaints and inform funeral directors of the Funeral Rule in case of noncompliance.

X
Saying Good-bye

Saying a final farewell to a loved one is one of the most painful situations we face in life. Getting a divorce, moving, changing jobs, suffering an illness or undergoing other changes mean loss, but no loss is as all-encompassing as death. In fact, the death of a loved one tops the list of stressful events. Making one's way through the emotional trauma, financial decisions and etiquette dilemmas can be exhausting. Unfortunately, coping with loss is inescapable. However, there are some ways to make it more bearable.

Informing Friends and Family

One of the hardest parts of dealing with death is telling the bad news to others. Telling relatives, friends, business associates and neighbors usually will be very difficult. Survivors should take care of themselves when delivering bad news. They might ask another person to go with them or sit with them while they make calls. They should allow themselves to have whatever emotions they are experiencing. They must be tactful, but it will not do any good to hide one's feelings.

Some survivors may find it too difficult to contact people; they can ask other relatives or friends to help. It may be a good idea to develop a list of people who need to be notified, to make sure no one is forgotten, and then divide up the list. As people are contacted, they should be asked if they know others who should be added to the list.

As difficult as it is to deliver such news, receiving the news is also traumatic. Depending on the nature of the death, people's relationship to the deceased and their location, it may be better to tell people face to face, rather than over the phone.

If possible, survivors should have friends and relatives contact people they know so they can be of comfort when the news is delivered. Survivors may also want to contact another relative, friend or a minister or rabbi to be with people when they receive the news.

Unless the deceased had been ill for a long time, the death will be shocking. Most people will not be able to digest everything at once. Those who deliver the news should not go into a lot of detail. They should give general information about how and when the person died, family plans and funeral arrangements. The wake, memorial service or funeral can serve as times to talk more in-depth. However, the bearers of the bad news should be prepared to give more specific information if someone requests it.

Messengers should be gentle, but direct. It will only make things worse if they prolong delivering sad news. They must be prepared for a wide range of reactions from people, who may burst into tears, get silent or act oddly detached. Those just receiving word should be allowed the time they need for the news to sink in. Whether on the phone or in person, the contact person should try to stay with the recipient long enough to ensure that he or she is okay. If necessary, they might be helped to find someone else who can assist in consoling them.

Also, survivors delivering the news of a death should be aware of the effects caused by the reactions of others. For example, someone who is very emotional about the loss may be angered that another relative isn't as demonstrative. Conversely, those who haven't dealt with their emotions may find that when someone else begins to weep, their own tears may be triggered.

Police officers, social workers, firefighters, chaplains, nurses and doctors are often put in the difficult spot of having to deliver death news to strangers. These are high-stress jobs where it's easy—and many even feel wiser—to become immune to heartache. However, it's better to deal compassionately with survivors. Though it is frightening and painful to feel the sorrow of death time and time again, it may be healthier than the alternative.

In his book *Love, Medicine and Miracles*, Dr. Bernie Siegel talks about how doctors and nurses benefit when they embrace their emotions when working with dying patients. Others who see death on a regular basis might also gain from allowing themselves to feel the variety of emotions associated with death and grief. The families and friends who have to hear that their loved ones have died will grieve easier if they are dealt with honestly and compassionately from the very beginning.

See the section on Controversial Deaths (page 287) for information on how to handle informing people about deaths due to AIDS, suicide or violence.

Writing the Obituary

If possible, it is a good idea to prepare obituaries before death and dying are on the family's minds. It might be helpful to select a family secretary who chronicles important facts about family members that can be given to the press and the mortuary when the time comes. Key information to relay includes: when and where the person lived, their survivors, organizations they belonged to and important accomplishments. Also, add the family's plans for a memorial. Let people know if there are charities that they would like to have receive memorial gifts.

If the obituary will be used for a program at the memorial service, survivors may also want to include any religious writings, quotes or poetry that will help mourners. If they have a mind to, it is also meaningful to share a favorite poem, Bible passage or saying the person had. One can include special stories about the person to make their memories more alive.

What Should I Say?: Offering Condolences

If you wish me to weep, you yourself
must first feel grief.

—HORACE

It's hard to know what to say upon hearing that a friend, relative or colleague has lost someone they love. As much as one loves one's friends, the hard reality is that one cannot and should not try to take their pain away. A friend cannot feel their grief for them and cannot change the truth. The best a friend can do is bear witness to their pain.

The urge to comfort and condole during a loss is natural. However, it's the rare person who is so empathetic and such a good communicator that he or she knows exactly what to say. Most people struggle awkwardly through clichés and silence. Modern society does not teach people how to handle their feelings and help others emotionally. It's easy to feel awkward and uncomfortable.

Supporters should not pull away from a grieving person for fear of making mistakes. They should stand by their friends and do the best they can. If they don't know what to say, they might try telling their friend just that. They can express how inadequate and helpless they feel. A supporter may truly empathize, but he or she cannot assume they know how the bereaved person feels. The bereaved should be given the room to tell supporters how they feel. Their friends should listen and validate the mourner's feelings. It also may be helpful to share how they felt in a similar situation.

Friends can provide better support if they avoid certain phrases. It isn't helpful for the bereaved to hear comments like: "It was God's will." "You'll have other children." "You should be happy she's out of her misery." "I know exactly how you feel." "He wouldn't want you to be upset." People say these things to help, but instead they can leave the bereaved feeling angry, guilty, frustrated or alone.

When writing a sympathy note, the same rules apply. The response should be personal and warm, perhaps remembering the deceased's characteristics. It may recall a funny anecdote or conversation. If the writer does not know much about the deceased or doesn't know the grieving person well, he or she can simply say "Our prayers are with you" or "I'm keeping a good thought for you." If it feels comfortable, they might share a favorite piece of religious or inspirational writing. Whether in person or in writing, words of condolence are best kept simple and heartfelt.

Some other tips on the art of condolence:

- Friends should contact the bereaved as soon as they hear the news. They should not wait until they know the "right thing" to say or write.

- It may feel right to ask a friend how he or she is feeling and what he or she needs. (Keep in mind, however, that a grief-stricken person may not be able to answer. Helpers should be prepared to offer a specific service—run errands, watch the kids, help write thank-you notes, etc.)

- Listen. Grieving people often feel compelled to tell the "death story" over and over again. Listening will help friends process their grief.

- No one should assume they know how the grieving person is feeling. In a situation where one person would feel sad, another might feel relieved and vice versa.

- Experts on etiquette say handwritten notes are warmer. But for those who truly don't know what to say, a nice sympathy card with a brief inspirational quote or a short note attached will do.

Ways to Be of Continued Support

People tend to bring food to families in mourning. It's a traditional way of showing sympathy and pitching in to help. However, there may be ways to be more helpful. All one needs to do is ask.

If a loved one is in mourning, friends should not abandon them after the funeral. Often, planning for the funeral keeps people busy so they don't have to face their loss. In addition, during the time prior to and immediately after the funeral, people are around to help them. It is after some time has passed that people are sometimes left alone with their grief. This is the time a friend or relative needs support most.

Friends might call or send notes to the grieving person often. People may say, with the best intentions, "Let me know if there's anything I can do," and expect the grieving person to call them. But the mourner cannot be expected to ask. They may be embarrassed to ask for help. They may feel like they don't want to be a burden. Or, quite commonly, they may need help, but not be sure what they need. Grief can be confusing; the object of support is to try to make it simpler.

On the other hand, people sometimes know exactly how much contact they need. Depending on the person's personality, friends might feel free to ask them how frequently they want to be called, written to or visited.

Friends should be willing to listen to the grieving person. One of the biggest problems grieving people have is that loved ones want to rush them through their grief. People don't want them to feel bad. Plus, sadness and anger are difficult emotions for people to face. If a friend brings up painful feelings, it is best not to change the subject. Friends should not feel obligated to offer advice on how they can feel better. They should just listen.

Planning the Service

Unfortunately, people usually have to plan a funeral or memorial during a time of intense emotional pain and shock. If the deceased has left instructions or made arrangements, most of the decisions already will be made. If not, it will be up to survivors to choose what the deceased will wear, the casket and how the service should be conducted.

If a loved one is dying and the family is unaware of his or her wishes, one might want to bring up the subject. Or perhaps some relatives or friends are having difficulty talking about the funeral. Another relative, trusted friend, clergyman or grief counselor can help survivors through the process of making these tough decisions.

The wishes of the deceased, family traditions and religious customs will help decide the type of service that is appropriate. A memorial service is usually held in cases where the body hasn't been recovered or isn't suitable for viewing, or when mourners can't be present at the funeral. Sometimes, family members will hold a private funeral and have a public memorial service. Wakes were traditionally held at the home of the deceased, but today wakes usually take place at the funeral home. If it is appropriate, the casket is open for mourners to say farewell to the deceased.

The purpose of a funeral is to help mourners express their feelings, pay tribute to the departed and begin the healing process. Different cultures handle funerals in different ways. African-Americans in New Orleans might dance in the streets on the way back from the cemetery, choosing to celebrate life and putting an end to mourning. Quakers, Native Americans and the Amish sometimes participate personally in preparing the body for the funeral. Survivors of those who have died of AIDS often turn the service into a celebration of the deceased's life, or into a political demonstration, because of the nature of the AIDS crisis, which claims so many young people.

Jews often have *chevra kaddishes* (sacred burial societies) that protect the body from desecration and cleanse and dress it for burial. In many states, families legally can handle all burial arrangements without working with a funeral director. Those who are interested in personally preparing a loved one's body should check with the local health department for the state statutes that apply (see Chapter 9).

Planning the funeral or memorial is an individual decision. Some families conduct services that are full of personal meaning and participation. Favorite music and poems are read. Relatives and friends are invited to share a special story about the departed. Other families prefer a more traditional service, led by a rabbi or pastor; preferring to share their memories and stories during a meal after the funeral. There is no right or wrong way to hold a funeral. However, survivors will want to honor the personality of the person who has passed on and keep in mind the wishes of the family. The funeral may not please everyone, but an effort should be made not to insult anybody.

Following are some of the decisions survivors will need to make:

- Will the casket be open? This decision depends on the family's feelings and religious convictions and the condition the body is in.

- Will children attend? Grief experts suggest children be allowed to participate in grief rituals. (See the section Helping Children Cope with Grief on page 300.)

- Who will deliver the eulogy? Will family and friends be allowed to speak?

- Where will the service take place? At a church, synagogue or temple, the funeral home, a relative's home, the cemetery?

If the Person Will Be Cremated

The choice between cremation or burial is usually made by the person who has passed away, either in their will or by what they expressed to their next of kin. If, however, the person never said what they preferred, the decision will be up to survivors. Again, cultural and religious background may preclude cremation. Some factors to consider: the personality of the deceased, the survivors' beliefs about death, the reaction of other relatives and cost.

Once the decision has been made for cremation, the next step will be to plan a memorial service. The memorial is subject to the same guidelines as a funeral. Survivors may want to hold the service at a church or synagogue, funeral parlor, at home or in a park.

Survivors also need to decide whether to keep the ashes in an urn or dispose of them. Many people sprinkle their loved one's remains in a natural setting: the backyard, a favorite hiking trail, a lake or on the ocean. However, others have dropped ashes from a plane or off the top of a building. Whatever is legal and will be of meaning to the survivors and to the departed is acceptable.

Etiquette for Mourners

Guests at a funeral should bear in mind that etiquette will vary by culture and religion. The best way to make sure one's actions are appropriate is to ask. One might try to contact someone in the family who is less emotionally affected by the loss or ask the funeral home director, priest or rabbi for more information. Guests probably don't want to bother immediate family members with questions about what to wear and how to act.

Some families relish floral displays and sympathy cards. However, some prefer that people make a charitable donation in honor of the deceased. Sending money to organizations that fund research in heart disease, cancer, AIDS and other diseases or to a local hospice is a lovely way to remember the deceased and help others. It's also proper to send money to an organization that the person supported, such as giving money to the humane society in honor of an animal lover.

As with birthdays, weddings, bar mitzvahs and other occasions, it is considered proper etiquette to thank the people who showed their support during a death in the family. However, unlike those happy occasions, mourners may have a difficult time showing their appreciation.

It is appropriate to send a simple thank-you card with a brief, handwritten note. Survivors can ask other family members to share this responsibility or take it over entirely. When they feel ready, they can write or call people to thank them for their support.

Sitting Shiva

Many Jews observe *Shiva,* a seven-day mourning period during which friends and relatives console the bereaved and share in their pain. In addition, it can be a time of laughter, story-telling and remembering. The closest relatives of the deceased—spouse, parents, children and siblings—are obliged to participate in the period of Shiva. Custom and law demands that mirrors are covered with white cloth and a memorial candle is lit to burn for the Shiva period.

Close relatives do not leave the place of Shiva, unless necessary. Nor do they typically have haircuts, shaves or wear makeup. They are allowed only quick showers.

It is unsuitable to call mourners during the Shiva period. Visitors customarily wait until spoken to by one of the mourners before they speak. They do not address mourners when entering or leaving. It is also inappropriate to take flowers or gifts to a Jewish mourner; better to make a donation in honor of their departed loved one. Visitors are asked to listen to the mourners share their experiences or, on occasion, to distract them from their pain.

Delivering a Eulogy

It is quite an honor to speak at a service for a departed relative or friend. Giving the eulogy offers a chance to pay tribute, comfort survivors, say things one wished to say to the deceased and bring a sense of closure so that healing can begin.

It also can be frightening. Even under the best of circumstances, public speaking is one of the biggest fears people have. To speak in front of a group of people when feeling emotionally vulnerable can be especially scary.

Those asked to give a eulogy may not want to; they should politely decline. It's better to say no now than to feel like a hypocrite at the service.

Those who decide to speak should keep seven tips in mind:

- Plan beforehand. Speakers cannot expect to remember everything they want to say. They should write down a few points or type up their entire speech; if they are overcome with emotion, someone else can read their thoughts.

- Except for practiced speakers, eulogists should make it short. If they are not given a specific amount of time to speak, 15 or 20 minutes should be enough to express any praise and feelings of loss. They may need to speak even more briefly if they are one of several speakers.

- Speakers should strive to be themselves. If it comes naturally to tell a funny story about a loved one, do so. Those who can never remember the punch line to a joke, should not make this the time to be humorous. They should say whatever they feel comfortable sharing.

- Eulogies should be personal. Those who didn't know the person well should focus on what they do know. They might talk about shared interests, hobbies or occasions. It is best to avoid flowery, greeting-card language. A eulogy should be real and specific.

- Eulogies should be discreet. Now is not the time to confess or apologize for wrongdoings.

- Speakers should not be afraid of showing emotion. If they are angry about the way the person died, they should say so. If they feel like crying, they should cry.

- Speakers should keep their audience in mind. Elderly people, children and others who don't appreciate bawdy language may be present. It is best to avoid profanity and slang that may be offensive.

Paying Tribute

Even those who don't participate in the funeral have other ways to pay tribute to a loved one. One time-honored tradition is to wear black to symbolize grief. In other cultures, different colors symbolize the color of death. In the Far East, white is the color of death.

Another way to pay tribute is to write an elegy. Elegy means "song of mourning" and is derived from the Greek word *elegeia.* An elegy can be a poem that can be shared with family members and friends of the deceased, published in a newspaper or magazine or something to save to look back on.

Other ways to pay tribute include:

- Placing meaningful objects in the casket, such as a lock of hair, photograph or other inexpensive personal mementos.

- After the service, one might ask mourners to drink a toast in honor of the deceased. They should be sure nonalcoholic drinks are available for those who want them.

- Guests might be asked to wear the deceased's favorite color.

- Mourners can make a list of all the people they love who are still alive and tell them how much they mean.

The Grief Process

When Elizabeth Kübler-Ross wrote *On Death and Dying* in 1969, she outlined five common stages that dying people go through. The five stages—

denial, anger, bargaining, depression and acceptance—were later applied to people grieving the death of someone else.

Other interpretations of the grief process incorporate phases of disorganization, fear and protest. Using these descriptions helps people make sense of grief. It is sometimes helpful to know that there are common feelings and symptoms that grieving people experience. However, anyone who has grieved will tell you that grief is not an orderly and predictable process. The combination of emotions that are possible to feel while grieving is infinite; everyone's grief process will be different.

Clearly, sadness is a primary part of grief, but other emotions factor in as well. Following are some of the common emotions grieving people feel.

Denial

The denial phase is characterized by feelings of shock, disbelief and numbness. When the news of a death first hits it can be hard to believe. Even when the person was old or ill, it can be difficult to comprehend the finality of death. Denial temporarily protects the grieving person until they are prepared to handle the loss. At one level they know the person has died, but on another level they aren't ready yet to accept that reality.

People in denial may say things like: "I can't believe this is happening." "This can't be true." "This isn't real." "There must be some mistake." They may act like everything is fine or say they don't feel anything. Other indications of denial include:

• a refusal to plan or attend the funeral

• insisting the person is not dead

• keeping overly busy

Even after the funeral, a measure of denial may be evident. A widow may expect her dead husband to walk in from work in the evening for dinner. A child may hear his or her departed mother's voice or see her on the street.

One should not try to rush through this phase. Denial is a natural, normal phenomenon. Grievers will let go of denial when they are ready. However, if a few weeks after the funeral someone still has not begun acknowledging reality, a counselor should be consulted.

Disorganization

When people are ready to deal with the blow they've been dealt, their hearts thaw enough to start feeling the flood of emotions. Fear, resentment, doubt, relief, anger and sadness swirl around in such a massive wave of emotions that it may feel impossible to separate one from another. The effort to unravel and feel each one clearly will feel overwhelming during the disorganization phase.

The disorganization phase is marked by feeling dazed or confused. A simple trip to the grocery store becomes a great chore. Decisions that were made effortlessly before a loss now feel monumental.

Conversely, grieving people may feel compelled to make big changes. Their inner life has changed so much that they want to change external things. They may decide to move, quit jobs, divorce or marry. Grief experts recommend that, when possible, the bereaved delay making such life-changing decisions for at least a year. They should be careful, too, about making decisions about what to do with a loved one's belongings during this phase.

Anger

The anger stage is also referred to as the protest stage. When terminally ill patients acknowledge that they are, indeed, dying, they move into the anger phase. They question, "Why me?" For grieving people the question "Why me?" becomes "Why my loved one?" It's common for grieving people to feel mad at medical professionals who didn't "save" their loved ones. They may also feel angry with God and begin to question their faith. How could God allow plane crashes, bombings, gang fights, disease and destruction? Why would God take my mother, my son, my lover?

Even agnostics and atheists may ponder the nature of good and evil and the mysteries of the universe.

Anger can be a frightening emotion, especially for women. Women often are taught that to be angry is to be bad. People may be afraid their rage will overwhelm them and drive them to violence or madness. Unless one is planning to act on anger by hurting someone, anger is nothing to fear. However, those who are being destructive or self-destructive, or who are afraid they will be, should consult a therapist.

Anger can be helpful. Mothers Against Drunk Drivers is an example of how one group puts its anger to good use: changing laws and educating people about the dangers of driving while intoxicated.

Feeling angry can help survivors recover. Indeed, holding in anger can lead to depression and hostility. Survivors should try to express their anger in healthy ways. They might punch a pillow, write in a journal, talk it out, get in a car and scream or go for a walk.

Guilt

In the struggle to make sense of a death, people may even feel angry at themselves. They may torture themselves with questions like: "Why didn't

I . . . ?" and "If only . . ." Sometimes it's easier to blame themselves than to accept the reality that death is part of life.

Part of the nonacceptance of death is the desire to have one more chance with their loved ones. They might feel they could have made their loved ones more comfortable in their last days. They could have been better children, partners, parents, friends. The "could haves" and "should haves" eat people up with remorse. No matter what they did for their loved ones, they believe they could have done more.

Chances are they did the best they could. Feeling guilty for not protecting or saving a deceased loved one or for not being a better person is natural. However, blaming oneself will not bring a dead loved one back.

Occasionally, there are real instances when a survivor is guilty of causing a death. Perhaps the person accidentally shot someone or crashed into them while driving. Even then, the process of personal forgiveness must take place. Those who are feeling guilty because of a death should try to sort out real guilt from false guilt. They should know that it will take a long time to make peace with themselves, but it can be done. They might seek a trusted friend who will allow them to express their remorse repeatedly. Professional help probably will be required to help people recover from actual guilt.

Bargaining

Bargaining is the stage in which terminally ill patients begin to negotiate with God. When they were angry, they may have demanded that they be healed. Now, they are willing to bargain. They may pray "I'll never swear, cheat, lie, steal again if I'm allowed to live."

But how does bargaining affect people who have already lost a loved one? What could grieving people hope to achieve by negotiating with God? They want their loved ones back. Denial and sadness are a part of bargaining. It's common for grievers to pray that the deceased didn't die. To yearn for their loved ones so much that they beg them to return to them.

While it seems irrational, trying to negotiate the resurrection of the deceased can be a normal part of the healing process. Eventually, grievers will accept that no matter what they do, their loved ones are never coming back.

Depression

Bargaining does not work. The deceased loved one is still dead. There is no way to escape the truth. Grieving people have no hope but to surrender to reality. This is when depression can set in. Depression manifests itself in hopelessness, sluggishness, apathy, isolation and sadness.

Grieving people might lose their interest in activities that used to bring them pleasure. Food, music, sex, hobbies and friends often don't bring joy as they used to do. They are too weighted down by pain to feel happy. The sadness and loneliness can be unbearable. Grieving people yearn for their loved ones with such intensity that they may even ache.

While it may not feel like it, grief depression is temporary and rarely requires medication. How long feelings of depression will last vary from person to person. However, it's common for people to feel depressed for months. And some people may suffer from grief depression off and on for years.

Fear

Fear is an ordinary part of the grief process. The awareness of death is so heightened that all the dangers of the world seem imminent. Grievers may become obsessed with all the ways it is possible to die. People may have a free-floating sense of anxiety; not having anything specific which scares them, they may simply feel suspicious of goodness and happiness.

People who are grieving may temporarily be unable to distinguish between realistic fears and unrealistic fears. They may become hypochondriacs, fearing they will contract the disease that killed their loved ones. Or they may be afraid to ride in planes or cars if their loved ones were killed in transportation accidents.

There are realistic fears, of course. Someone who had unprotected sex with a person who died from AIDS-related causes, or someone with a family history of disease should see a doctor. They will feel much better knowing the truth about their health. And, if disease is present, they might catch it before it becomes deadly, or change their lifestyle and add years to their life.

It may be helpful for people feeling overwhelmed by fear to talk to other mourners, grief counselors or religious advisers.

Acceptance

Finally, after much despair and struggle, people accept the reality of their loved one's death and begin to heal. The acceptance phase is also referred to as reorganization or reconciliation, and possibilities arise. Life doesn't look as dim. Hope is regained.

Survivors begin to become interested in life again. Food tastes good again. They are able to laugh and enjoy friends and family more often. They think of their loved ones without feeling overwhelming sadness. They even feel like they learned something from their loss.

Recovering grievers might say they feel like different people. They may not go back to their old hobbies and activities, instead choosing to participate in new interests. In the acceptance phase, however, they are unafraid of their new identity. They become even more grateful for their lives and the lives of their loved ones. And, in their gratitude, they are able to move on. As the saying goes, "what doesn't kill you, makes you stronger."

Physical Symptoms

Grieving people undergo changes in appetite and sleep patterns. Survivors might not be able to sleep at all or they may find themselves wanting to sleep all the time. They may avoid food or eat more than usual.

Grief hurts. Not just emotionally but physically. Survivors might have headaches, chest pains, stomach aches or feel nauseous. They might feel dizzy, dazed or weak. Or be susceptible to colds and flu.

It's common to "be sick with grief." However, exercise, relaxation techniques and proper nutrition may help alleviate some physical discomfort. One should see a doctor if symptoms persist or get worse.

Spiritual Aspects of Grief

Bereaved people often experience a variety of metaphysical or spiritual occurrences. For example, most grieving people report dreaming of their deceased loved ones. Often, the dead will "speak" to their survivors and ask questions or assure them that they are okay. More disturbing, grievers sometimes have nightmares in which they aren't able to save their loved ones and they are forced to reexperience their deaths. Working out psychic trauma through dreams is normal and healthy.

It is also common for bereaved people to have hallucinations where they see or hear their departed loved ones. Or they may "feel the presence" of the deceased. Depending on the personality and beliefs of the survivor, these experiences can be either soothing or scary. They are quite normal. However, those who are unnerved by the experience should talk to a grief counselor.

Controversial Deaths and Complicated Grief

Unexpected deaths are always shocking and difficult to deal with. But grieving someone who was murdered, killed in a tornado or run over by a drunk driver is especially tough. Grieving someone who committed suicide, died from AIDS-related causes or in some other "socially unacceptable" way, too, can be complicated.

If a survivor or someone he or she cares about seems to be having an especially difficult time dealing with death, there may be complications preventing the resolution of issues and the move to the next stage.

There is a long list of situations that could make the grief process even harder than usual. A common situation that causes complicated grief is if the death comes when the survivor is already going through a tough time—a divorce, job change or move. Having more than one stressor to deal with can make one feel like he or she is going over the edge. Also, having to get through the logistics of one situation sometimes can make it easier to avoid the others, thereby delaying grief.

Other events that may complicate grief include:

- If the body of the deceased has not been recovered or is disfigured.

- If there are multiple deaths. Sometimes fate is cruel and people lose several family members or friends at once or back to back. The pain of such losses can be overwhelming. The financial and emotional burden of planning and paying for more than one funeral at a time can be astounding.

Violent Death

If all death is a shock to the sensibilities, then death by violence is a complete outrage. There is no way to comprehend the senselessness of murder. Mourning someone who was killed is sure to bring on horror, shock, rage, fear and helplessness in measures the average person is not equipped to handle.

Surviving the purposeful or accidental killing of a loved one violates everything one may know to be good and true. It can rob one of faith and trust in mankind and God. The pain is indescribable.

It may be impossible to feel safe knowing that a loved one was killed by a drunk driver, in a robbery or raped and murdered. In such cases, the anger that many grieving people feel can become rage. Survivors want justice and also may want revenge: "an eye for an eye."

In addition to planning a funeral, informing friends and family and bearing such immense pain, there may be additional challenges. Family members may be asked to identify the body, to identify the murderer or to testify in court. They also may be expected to work with police officers, prosecutors and coroners. If the bereaved don't suffer through a lengthy trial, they may have to endure the pain of never knowing who killed their loved one and why.

A growing consideration for friends and relatives of victims of violence is the necessity of dealing with the media. Television and newspaper reporters often confront mourners while they are confused, angry, shocked or distressed. Mourners find they are living their nightmares under a spotlight.

Survivors also may have to endure the social stigma attached to homicide. If they are lucky enough to enjoy a certain socioeconomic status, they may have to grapple with their illusions that murder only happens to minorities, gang members, people who live in the "wrong" part of town or "bad" people.

Those who are mourning someone who was killed should seek out others who understand the trauma they have experienced. Support groups such as Parents of Murdered Children and Other Survivors of Homicide Victims (POMC) can help families deal with the public ordeal of mourning a violent death. Survivors can also look for other support groups, social workers, ministers, counselors and therapists who can help them work out the stress and pain unique to those who must live with the knowledge that violence doesn't happen only to "other people."

AIDS

As with other terminal illnesses, grief connected with AIDS often begins when HIV is first diagnosed. As new treatments are developed, HIV-positive people are living longer and with better quality of life. And as society becomes more educated about HIV and AIDS, the stigma is beginning to lessen. However, for many people AIDS is still a disease marked with shame, fear and embarrassment. Often families are unwilling to acknowledge that a loved one died from AIDS-related causes for fear of being ostracized or looked down on.

Homosexual men also may not feel safe expressing their grief at the death of their lovers. Gays may experience prejudice because of their sexual orientation and their relationship with someone who died from AIDS. Their partners' families may not recognize or validate their relationships. On top of the anguish of missing their dead partners, they may have to battle for the right to show their love. Unlike heterosexual mates, gays may lose the right to select the casket, the cemetery, keep the deceased's ashes or arrange the funeral. Ancient, basic ways of dealing with grief are denied them.

For the partners of someone who has died due to AIDS, grief can be especially complex. If a surviving partner is infected, he or she will have to face his or her own illness and mortality, in addition to grieving. Partners may also feel angry at the deceased, thus causing feelings of guilt. If the partner is not infected, he or she could feel guilty for surviving.

Those recovering from the loss of someone with AIDS need to grieve fully. Keeping a secret about the cause of death or lying about the cause of death will add to their stress. If they cannot tell coworkers, neighbors or other associates, they should find a support group that can help.

It may be helpful to give people correct information about HIV and AIDS when telling others about an AIDS-related death. Their discomfort may be alleviated when they know the facts about how the virus is spread. Local hospice and AIDS organizations can provide pamphlets, brochures and information on support groups.

Suicide

Denial, sadness, anger, fear, guilt, longing and other emotions associated with grief also apply in the case of suicide deaths. However, grieving for people who killed themselves can be especially difficult because of the disgrace attached to suicide. Some religions believe that committing suicide is a sin and, therefore, the deceased won't go to heaven. Grievers may blame themselves for the person's death or worry that others blame them. Or they may fully understand that they were not responsible for another person taking his life, but feel socially pressured to feel guilty.

Because of the taboo attached to suicide, family members may feel ashamed to tell people how the person died. Relatives might want to cover up the true cause of death to avoid embarrassment or causing pain to other loved ones. Financial concerns are another reason a family might consider lying about the cause of death. Insurance policies for hospitalization and death sometimes have clauses that deny coverage in the case of suicide.

Recovering from the suicide of a loved one can be even more painful for those who discover the body. They are left having to deal with the image of the often gruesome death scene in their minds or living in the place where a loved one took their own life.

Those mourning someone who committed suicide probably will spend a lot of time wondering why. They might ask "Why didn't I see this coming?" "What could I have done to stop it?" "Why did the person commit suicide now?" Survivors might start to remember "clues" the person gave by what they said or did.

The reality is that survivors may never understand why loved ones killed themselves. Unless the person was terminally ill or incapacitated, psychologists say suicide is most often linked to depression. Untreated depression causes an imbalance of chemicals in the brain that can make it virtually impossible to be happy. People who kill themselves due to depression want to escape deep emotional pain. Mourning a suicide death will be easier for those who understand depression. They can get help from a school counselor, grief counselor, therapist or grief support group.

Another component of suicide that will determine how people grieve is the method of death. It is almost impossible to understand someone jumping from a building, lighting themselves on fire or shooting themselves. The more violent or grotesque the method, the more difficult it will be to mourn.

As with other types of death, part of the suicide grief process might be a sense of relief. Sometimes, grievers were aware of the deceased's pain. The deceased might have tried unsuccessfully before to kill themselves or exhibited other unbalanced behavior. They might have been threatening to kill themselves, holding their friends or family emotional hostage. Even with extreme sadness, anger and guilt, you may naturally feel relieved that the waiting is over.

Survivors also may worry about being mentally ill themselves. Depression and other mental illnesses do sometimes run in families. However, there is a difference between the "crazies" that grieving people feel and chemical depression. Depression can be successfully treated with therapy and medication. Those who are confused about the appropriateness of their feelings should talk to a pastor, rabbi, grief counselor or psychologist. Survivors who are thinking of taking their own life should see a counselor immediately.

To successfully mourn a suicide death, one needs to resolve one's sense of guilt. The person who killed him- or herself made the decision to do so. It probably wasn't rational or logical, but it was his or her decision.

Survivors also need to be honest about how the person died. Keeping track of lies will only add to their stress and validate the idea that they have something to be ashamed about.

Those mourning the death of a suicide should learn as much as they can about suicide. Reading books on suicide and going to suicide-survivor support groups will help them understand that they are not alone.

Euthanasia and Self-Deliverance

Euthanasia, or mercy killing, occurs when a terminally ill or brain-dead person is killed or allowed to die. Self-deliverance allows the hopelessly ill to take their own lives. Some people believe that euthanasia and self-deliverance are compassionate, dignified choices, but others believe these acts are a form of murder, of "playing God." If a loved one asks to be relieved of his or her pain or decides to end his or her own agony, or if the family must make the tough choice of "pulling the plug," consciously helping someone die is a difficult decision.

How people cope with grief after euthanasia depends on the deceased's medical status and their religious and cultural beliefs. Survivors who disapprove of assisted suicide or who weren't involved in the decision might experience feelings similar to suffering a more typical suicide loss. Even if they agree with a person's right to die, they might feel pangs of guilt. And though they may be greatly relieved that the person was spared from suffering and indignity, they probably still will feel deep sadness and loss.

Hospice organizations, grief counselors and groups like the National Hemlock Society can offer information and support.

When a Child Dies

For many people, the most heartbreaking death is when a child dies. For the parents, the shock and pain may seem overwhelming. The first few weeks may be filled with numbness and denial. No matter what their child's age, parents expect to die before their children; it's the natural order of things. Therefore, it can be incomprehensible that their child is gone. Bereaved people often question "why?" but the death of a child seems to beg the question even more.

Even after a prolonged illness, parents may be shocked that their child actually died. As long as the child was alive, even the slimmest chance for recovery offered a ray of hope. It may take weeks or months for the full impact of their child's death to sink in. Denial is a natural reaction. It's necessary to cushion the blow from the despair and guilt parents inevitably will feel.

While trauma can bring couples and families closer together, the death of a child often places extra strain on a marriage and on the family. The emotional wreckage may cause additional problems or bring to light problems that already existed. But even the healthiest of relationships will feel the stress.

Husbands and wives, pressed to their emotional limits by grief, may crack under the pressure. Spouses travel through their own grief journeys at their own rates. He may be unable to even admit that he is hurting, while she is demanding communication. She may feel nothing but emptiness, while he rages. The pressure on couples after losing a child is enormous. Such mourners should pay special attention to their marriage. If problems are arising that aren't being resolved, they should seek the help of a rabbi, pastor or marriage counselor.

The surviving siblings also will be deeply affected by the death. Parents can help their children by knowing how children grieve and allowing them to have their feelings. Parents need to be aware that remaining children may feel guilty, confused or unable to cope. Parents should try to help children understand that they are not the cause of their parents' sorrow, nor or they responsible for "fixing" things in the family. (See the section on Helping Children Cope with Grief on page 300 for more information on how children handle death and grief.)

Parents may hold back from recovering from the loss of their child out of guilt. How can they possibly be happy and enjoy life again knowing that their child is gone? Some couples are blessed with wise friends and family members who help them through this most difficult of times. Some are blessed with strong marriages that allow each spouse to lean on the other. Single parents, divorced or separated parents or parents who are unable to depend on their spouses have to go it alone. They seek support in God, therapists, grief counselors and such organizations as Compassionate Friends and Mothers Against Drunk Drivers. Whatever works for the family is the right answer.

After the death of a child, things will never be the same again. But one can go on. Recovery doesn't mean forgetting. As with any other death it is possible to move on and heal.

Some tips on coping with the death of a child:

- Survivors should include friends and family in mourning rituals. Grandparents, siblings, aunts, uncles, cousins, godparents, baby-sitters, schoolmates and neighbors need to express their grief, too.

- Grieving families can get involved. Helping to lobby lawmakers, educate the public and console other grieving families can relieve the sense of helplessness many feel at the death of a child.

- Parents should pay attention to their surviving children. They can help children remember that they are loved, and that their parents don't blame them for the family's sadness.

- Survivors should accept their emotions. Grieving parents recover like alcoholics, "one day at a time."

- Parents should acknowledge and accept feelings of guilt. No parent is perfect and almost all grieving parents feel like they failed their child. Unresolved guilt and blame can destroy individuals, marriages and families.

When a Spouse Dies

The death of a husband or wife will have a profound impact on the surviving partner, especially if they had been married for a long time. The loss of a life mate is the loss of many people: confidante, best friend, lover, companion and coparent.

It's not only the loss of the person that is so painful, but the loss of the familiar, the routine. The loss of kisses good-bye in the morning and recounting the day at dinner. Partners may have to adjust to living alone and sleeping alone for the first time in many years. They have to learn to make parenting and financial decisions on their own. They may have to adjust to celibacy until their grief is healed, then face an unfamiliar world of dating and sex.

Most widows and widowers report intense feelings of loneliness. After all, they had purposefully joined their lives with another, "making two into one." Why shouldn't they feel traumatized at changing from a "we" to an "I"?

Unfortunately, to add to their loneliness and isolation, widows and widowers sometimes are deserted by their friends. Married couples may feel threatened by the awareness that death could shatter their lives too. They also may feel uncomfortable about having newly single people around.

In addition, widowed people may feel pressured to grieve "correctly." Family members and friends may expect them to never stop grieving and be horrified when they start to recover. Other relatives or friends might try to rush a widow or widower through the grief process. As with all deaths, there is no right way to mourn.

In addition to the deep emotional loss, there will be legal and financial decisions. It may be hard to concentrate on wills and property when all one can think about is how much one misses one's spouse. If there is someone whose advice the survivor trusts, he or she should ask them for help through the maze of decisions left to be made. If possible, they should wait until they are more clearheaded before selling a home, moving to a different city or changing jobs.

When people lose lovers, they may find their pain being discounted by others. The death of a boyfriend or girlfriend sometimes isn't considered as important as the death of a husband or wife. However, the loss of a beloved partner is always distressing. Some general suggestions for mourning a spouse or lover:

- Survivors should grieve at their own pace.

- It helps to create new routines and traditions with children, family and friends or just by oneself.

- Those who live alone might consider adopting a pet for companionship.

- Joining a support group is especially helpful for widowed people.

When a Parent Dies

The death of a parent is a loss that almost everyone will suffer. As no one expects to die before their parents, it's the only loss they are supposed to suffer. It is life's pattern: one generation falls back to clear a path for the next. However, that doesn't mean it doesn't hurt.

And it doesn't mean people will be prepared. Because of modern medical advances, most adults expect their parents to live well into their 70s and 80s. And even when parents die at an advanced age, their adult children often are ill equipped to handle the sorrow, guilt and longing they feel.

American society makes it even harder to mourn the loss of a parent because it discourages adults from grieving a dead parent "too much." Experiencing grief over a parent, particularly an older parent, isn't considered as "legitimate" as mourning a spouse or child. Grieving offspring often are expected to "get over it."

Contrary to that thinking, denial, depression and disorganization are typical reactions to a parent's death—no matter what the griever's age. Offspring in their 60s may feel shocked and saddened about the death of their 80-year-old parents. And years after the loss of a parent, many adults occasionally cry or feel upset when they remember their parent.

The parent-child relationship is unique; we only get one mother and one father. This relationship forms the crux of our identity long into adulthood. It makes sense, then, that the loss of this relationship will affect survivors. Indeed, because of the powerful bond between parents and children, the loss can leave deep psychological scars.

When a parent dies, adult children grieve what their mother or father symbolized to them. While parents are alive, there is always the chance that they'll give the unconditional love, attention or approval children always wanted. When they die, so do those hopes and dreams.

In addition to the trauma of the loss, adults usually become more conscious of their own mortality after their parents die. They no longer have a psychological buffer between themselves and death; they are now on the front lines.

But a parent's death also can mark an important turning point in an adult's life. Grieving a parent can be a developmental push into maturity. When a person heals, the end of their mourning can open an exciting new range of possibilities.

Ways to mourn a parent's death:

- Survivors should remember they are entitled to grieve no matter how old they are or how old their parent was.

- A letter to the parent describing all the ways they disappointed or hurt the survivor may help him or her forgive the dead parent. One might place the letter in the casket or store it in a private place. Those who are not ready to forgive their parent can write out their feelings and then burn the letter.

- Survivors should talk to people about their parent. They can find others who have lost a parent and encourage them to share their grief experiences as well.

Grief is Crazy-Making

A grieving person is not losing his or her mind, but grief can make it feel that way. Survivors go back and forth with their emotions, one minute feeling fine and then seemingly from out of nowhere feeling upset. They may be forgetful and distracted and misplace things. They may go over and over the person's death so many times that they are sick of hearing themselves. They may lose track of the time or day. They may even see or hear the person who has passed on.

These are natural reactions to a death. The bereaved should be assured that grief doesn't last forever and they will survive it. It may be helpful for them to read books about loss and grief, or to join a support group.

How Long Does Grief Take?

There is no right answer to how long a person should or will grieve. Everybody's grief process is different. It will depend on the survivor's personality, the nature of their relationship to the person who died, how old they are, how old their loved one was and how they died.

Even gender affects how people grieve. Typically, men are expected to be stoic and in control and, therefore, can have a difficult time expressing hurt and confusion. Women, on the other hand, are "allowed" to feel sad, but not angry. It may be especially hard for women to accept that anger is often a healthy part of grief.

Generally, grief experts have found that people typically grieve for about a year. However, many years after a death a survivor may feel sad, lonely, angry or guilty about it. It's not the amount of time that passes after a death that's important, but how survivors use that time to do their grief work. If they avoid doing the work of grief, the healing process will take longer.

Following are some general suggestions on how survivors can take care of themselves after suffering a loss:

- They should try to get some exercise. Even walking 10 or 20 minutes a day will release natural chemicals in the brain called endorphins that will fight depression and help a person feel better.

- They should watch what they eat. Grieving people may undereat or overeat. Neither is good for one's health.

- They should honor their emotions. They don't have to be strong or in control. Crying really does help. Researchers even suspect that tears cried in sorrow are chemically different from tears cried in joy.

- They should avoid numbing themselves with alcohol or drugs. A glass of wine or beer from time to time is one thing. Using booze to "try to forget" is another. Abusing alcohol and drugs won't erase sorrow and it may cause more problems.

- They should get enough rest. As with appetite, they may feel like sleeping all the time or not be able to sleep at all. Survivors should listen to their body.

- They should get some support. If family and friends are supportive, survivors can lean on them and allow them to give. Those who don't have people who can share their grief can join a support group. Many hospices, hospitals, churches and counselors offer grief support groups.

- They should talk about it. Telling the "grief story" is an important part of healing. Reviewing the circumstances of the person's death over and over again is natural. Survivors may find themselves repeating the same stories about the person and how they died. They may even have a recurring dream or nightmare about the person as a way to help them work through their grief. Again, if friends and family aren't willing to listen, survivors should find other means of support. They might even want to consider talking to a professional counselor.

- They should be gentle with themselves. It may take a long while before they feel like their old self. Survivors deserve all the time they need to heal.

- They should pamper themselves. Taking long baths, lighting candles, watching favorite videos, getting a massage can relieve stress.

- They can call on their faith. Sometimes when we lose someone, it's hard to believe in good. We may question the existence of a higher power. However, a survivor's questioning can lead to a more profound understanding of spirituality and faith.

Mourning

Grief is the complex web of emotions people feel after a death. Mourning is how they express those emotions. When they are sad, people may cry or show the world their pain in another way. They have many ways of communicating to dead loved ones that they miss them. Mourning is important to heal from a loss. William Worden, author of *Grief Counseling and Grief Therapy*, discussed the "four tasks of mourning":

1. to accept the reality of the loss
2. to work through to the pain of grief

3. to adjust to an environment in which the deceased is missing

4. to emotionally relocate the deceased and move on with life

Not everyone will feel grief. Individuals' spiritual, cultural or psychological beliefs may lead them to believe the death of a person isn't something to feel sad about. Some people accept death as part of the natural cycle of life, without going through a process of grief. If the person who died was aged, on life-support systems, in pain or had a diminished quality of life, the death might bring more relief than sorrow.

Each person's and culture's response to death is unique. Lakotas and many other Native Americans believe that death is a natural part of life. It is sacred and isn't questioned. Denial and anger, therefore, are not typical grief reactions in the Lakota culture.

However, no matter how survivors feel or think after a person dies, it's important to commemorate the loved one's life. It seems to be a universal human need to honor the dead and celebrate their lives.

Rituals

The funeral or memorial is typically the ritual that allows people to express their feelings of loss. However, there is no need for rituals to end there. Rituals are important because they give a formal outlet for emotion. Many people who are in mourning feel comforted by having rituals that they can count on to pay tribute to their loved ones. Rituals also help mark the time since their loved one has passed on.

Rituals don't have to be elaborate ceremonies. Other people don't have to be involved. Something as simple as leaving a favorite flower at the person's grave once a month can be a healthy ritual. Other rituals that might be helpful include:

- Lighting a candle on special days. Jews participate in this ritual on the anniversary of a death by lighting a *yahrzeit* candle for the day.

- Creating an altar with photos and mementos of the deceased.

- Burning herbs, incense or essential oils. Scents can help soothe as well as create a sacred atmosphere.

- Creating a memorial box or scrapbook and collecting writings, photos and mementos that recall the loved one and help heal grief.

- Participating in holidays, like the Mexican Day of the Dead (El Dia de Muertos), the Day of Atonement, Passover and Memorial Day, that honor the dead.

- Writing a letter to the loved one to say good-bye. It can be buried with them, planted with their ashes or burned if it holds unpleasant memories.

- Planting a tree or flowering bush in honor of the loved one. Each year when it leafs or blossoms, it recalls the departed.

Rituals are not an excuse to stay stuck in grief. They are intended to help people get on with their lives when they are ready.

Visiting the Grave

Do not stand by my grave and weep.
I am not there. I do not sleep.
I am a thousand winds that blow.
I am a diamond glint of snow.
I am the sunlight on ripened grain.
I am the gentle autumn rain.
When you awake in the morning hush,
I am the swift, uplifting rush
of quiet birds in circling flight.
I am the soft starshine at night.
Do not stand by my grave and cry.
I am not there. . . I did not die.

—NATIVE AMERICAN, AUTHOR UNKNOWN

Many people believe the grave site is the place where they can make contact with their departed loved ones. They feel comfortable talking to the deceased at the grave. They leave flowers or letters or even photos as a way of paying tribute and "communicating" with their loved ones. Others believe—as illustrated in the above Native American poem—that though the body is present, the spirit is gone.

No matter what one's belief about an afterlife, visiting the grave for the first time can be a shock. It can help to take a friend along to provide company if needed. Those who want to be left alone at the grave can ask their friend to stay in the car for a bit.

Anniversaries, Holidays and Other Special Occasions

After a death, holidays, birthdays and anniversaries may feel like occasions to be endured rather than celebrated. Holidays call special attention to a loss. It seems the whole world is happy and together while the bereaved is missing a piece of him- or herself.

Survivors should take some time to think about when their holidays are, remembering not just religious and public holidays like Thanksgiving,

Hanukkah and Christmas, but also personal occasions. They can be marked on the calendar and a coping strategy can be planned.

Survivors may choose not to celebrate a holiday or they may choose to celebrate in a different way. Changing traditions can make it easier to cope with a holiday. For example, one might decide to take the family to a restaurant for Thanksgiving dinner instead of gathering at home. Even small changes, opening gifts at a different time of day, can make holidays less painful.

Those in mourning can delegate tasks to others. Holidays already can be stressful and depressing. The survivor who feels overwhelmed should ask for help. They can let the children decorate and bake desserts, ask a relative to do the shopping.

The deceased can be incorporated into celebrations. Survivors might reserve a ceremonial place at the table or light a long-burning candle (don't leave it unattended) in a place of honor. They can donate money or give a gift in honor of the loved one.

Some survivors find it comforting to forget their own pain for a while to help others in need. They may invite someone who would be alone to spend the day with the family. They can volunteer to serve meals at a homeless shelter or deliver meals to shut-ins.

The anniversary of a loved one's death can be especially painful. Ironically, many grieving people say that it is often the days or weeks prior to or after the actual death date that are the most difficult. The anniversary can be almost anticlimactic. Other difficult anniversaries to be prepared for are: the day one found out the person was sick, the day one found out he or she was dead and the day of the funeral.

Helping Children Cope with Grief

Our society has difficulty dealing with loss, making it easy to avoid dealing with children's grief, but helping children cope with grief is important to their development.

How a child reacts to death will depend on a number of factors, including: how close they were to the person who died, the child's age, other stresses in the child's life, the nature of the death and the amount of support given the child.

The primary factor affecting how a child recovers from a loss is how the parents respond to death. Children's response to death will be as healthy and straightforward as the adults in their lives allow. If children have been taught to accept and express their emotions, they will have an easier time working through their feelings of loss. If they live in a family that encourages open communication, they will feel comfortable asking questions, which will help alleviate confusion.

Even very young children need information to make sense of death. Unless they hear honest information, children's imaginations can make terrifying assumptions. Telling a child "Grandpa died in his sleep," can make him or her afraid to go to sleep at night; he or she could be afraid of dying also.

The finality of death is difficult for adults to accept. For young children, it might be impossible. They might understand that "Grandma is in heaven," but ask why can't they call her on the phone. Of course, parents should use the simplest language possible. Children don't need a medical account. But they do need information.

As with adults, children's grief process isn't a tidy series of emotions and symptoms. The process typically includes shock, denial, fear, disorganization, anger, guilt, sadness and acceptance. In addition to those feelings, children may go through periods of regression. They might start talking in baby talk again, ask for bottles, refuse to walk on their own, want to be held or want to sleep with their parent(s). Regression is usually temporary and should be accepted. Parents should be cautioned against avoiding their own feelings of loneliness and fear by encouraging their children's overdependence.

Children's denial may take on the form of acting "older" than they are. They might pick up the messages from relatives and friends of the family like: "Big boys don't cry." "Be strong for daddy." "Don't think about it." This only delays the grief process.

Adults often try to shield children from their own pain. They may try not to cry or argue in front of the children. They may even lie about their emotions and say "I'm not crying" when it's clear that they are. This sends a very confusing message to children. The healthiest thing kids can learn is that they are entitled to their emotions. It's okay for them to feel mad at daddy for dying and never coming back. It's okay for them to feel sad that grandma will never read them another story.

Some kids may not want to talk about their feelings. They may feel embarrassed or ashamed. They may feel responsible for being strong for their parents or siblings. Adults should not pressure children to open up if they don't want to. They should be assured that a parent will be there whenever they want to talk, but also be allowed time to deal with their feelings. Adults also might offer them the opportunity to express their feelings through writing or art.

Probably one of the most important grief issues for a child to deal with is guilt. Young children have magical thinking. They believe in fairies, dragons and monsters. They also believe that the power of their thoughts can make things happen. For example, a boy might believe mommy died because he was bad or he was mad at her and wished she would go away.

Answering questions about life and death can be one of the toughest things about helping a child cope with grief. Honesty is the best policy. Parents should share their spiritual beliefs with a child. For adults who are uncertain, it's appropriate to admit that they aren't sure about heaven and hell. Letting a child know that an adult is not sure about what happens after death can help him or her accept his or her own confusion. It's also a good lesson about the mysteries of life.

Children tend to repeat the same questions over and over. That's how they learn. Each time they are allowed to speak about the death, it becomes a little more understandable and the pain lessens.

Parents can encourage children to ritualize their losses and allow them to participate in mourning. Parents often think it will be better for children not to attend the funeral. Quite the contrary: it can put to rest the child's anxieties and confusion and help them reach closure, just as for adults. Letting children place pictures, letters or photos in the casket, choose a special song to play at the funeral or other activities can be an important part of their grief recovery process. Of course, it's best for the parents to use their judgment. If they feel the child will be traumatized or frightened, they can create other methods for the child to say good-bye. Even if children don't attend the funeral, they should be allowed rituals to help them come to terms with the death.

The best way to help a child mourn is for their parents to openly and honestly mourn themselves. If parents allow themselves to experience the wide range of grief emotions, the child will follow suit. Parents who work to heal themselves are better able to help their children.

Adolescents

Teenagers are primarily concerned with discovering who they are and how they fit with their peers, family and society. To suffer a death loss during the teen years can make the self-defining process even more difficult; especially if the deceased is one of the parents the teen is trying to separate from.

The work of adolescence is about separating from parents to form a unique identity, rebelling and experimenting to discover oneself. Being forcibly separated from a mother or father when a teen is trying to psychologically separate may cause the teen to feel guilty. Like the child who thinks "Daddy died because I was mad at him" a teenager might feel somehow responsible for causing a parent's death.

A teenager's grief may be expressed as "acting out": smoking, drinking or taking drugs, being promiscuous, skipping school or fighting. Or becoming hyperresponsible and trying to ease the family's burden by taking the place of their missing parent or sibling. Or trying to remain normal, so as not to be different from friends. In the case of grieving teens, being "normal" might call for boys not to cry and girls to be "nice"—no matter how they feel.

If teens are allowed to express their emotions and face their pain, they will heal. Parents should allow adolescents to explore their feelings without smothering them. They will be much more likely to seek out support if they don't feel they will risk losing any hard-won independence. However, while teens might pretend that everything is okay, the death of a parent, sibling or other close relative will affect them. They may need permission to grieve.

Saying good-bye, a good good-bye, is one of the harder tasks we face in life. But as we grow and learn, we discover that life is full of good-byes, full of mourning. But there is an end to mourning.

One way to tell that mourning is complete is when thoughts of the deceased bring more pleasure than pain. Survivors are able to speak about the loved one's death and life with equal ease. The sadness never completely disappears, but it changes. Over time, with attention, people are able to put their grief behind them and move on with their lives. As one woman who lost her best friend, father and sister within a three-year span said, "It never goes away, but—day by day—it gets a little easier."

Resources

Organizations

American Association of Retired Persons
601 E Street NW
Washington, DC 20049

The American Cemetery Association
1895 Preston White Drive, Suite 220
Reston, VA 22091
(703) 391-8400
A sponsor of the CCSC, this organization will
answer consumer questions and publishes a
pamphlet called "Cemeteries and Memorial Parks:
Questions and Answers."

American Cryonics Society
165 Gibraltar Court
Sunnyvale, CA 94089
or:
P.O. Box 1509
Cupertino, CA 95015
Cemetery Consumer Service Council
P.O. Box 2028
Reston, VA 22090
(703) 391-8407
Contact this organization or the CCSC committee
in your state for information and to make
complaints regarding cemeteries. This organization is
run by the cemetery and cremation industries.

**Continental Association of Funeral and Memorial
Societies**
6900 Lost Lake Road
Egg Harbor, WI 54209
(800) 458-5563

Cremation Association of North America
401 North Michigan Avenue
Chicago, IL 60611
(312) 664-6610
This industry organization offers several pamphlets
and will answer questions about cremation. The
pamphlets are free, but the organization requests a
self-addressed, stamped envelope (79 cents postage)
with your request.

Funeral and Memorial Societies of America, Inc.
6900 Lost Lake Road
Egg Harbor, WI 54209-9231
(414) 868-3136
This association, formerly called the Continental
Association of Funeral and Memorial Societies, will
provide an up-to-date list of memorial societies in the
U.S. and Canada (send a self-addressed, stamped
envelope with your request). They also offer advice
and information on funeral prices and practices, legal
developments pertaining to funerals, anatomical gift-
giving and living wills and durable powers of attorney.
They also monitor state and federal funeral legislation.

Funeral Service Consumer Assistance Program
1614 Central Street
Evanston, Illinois 60201
(800) 662-7666
The FSCAP, a division of the National Research and
Information Center, will act as liaison between the
consumer and funeral director in complaints.
Complaints not resolved are referred to the
American Arbitration Association.

Hemlock Society
P.O. Box 11830
Eugene, OR 97440-4030
(503) 342-5748

International Order of the Golden Rule (funeral homes)
P.O. Box 3586
Springfield, IL 62708
(217) 793-3322

Jewish Funeral Directors of America
399 East 72nd Street
New York, NY 10021
(212) 628-3465

The Living Bank (organ donation)
(800) 528-2971
In Texas: (713) 961-9431

Memorial Society of British Columbia
624 Sixth Street, Room 212
New Westminster, British Columbia B3L 3C4
Canada

Monument Builders of North America
3158 Des Plaines Avenue, Suite 224
Des Plaines, Illinois 60018
(708) 869-2031
Contact with complaints regarding monuments (an industry organization).

National Coalition for Fair Funeral Prices
P.O. Box 9097
Chandler Heights, Arizona 85227
(602) 253-6814
The Coalition, a volunteer organization, will furnish wholesale price lists for caskets made by major manufacturers so you can gauge markup, and provides information on how to conduct a detailed, complete price survey in your area, as well as advice on how to arrange a funeral. The number above is a 24-hour phone line with a recorded message about funeral costs, reasonable price ranges, names and phone numbers of the local funeral homes whose prices are in that range.

National Funeral Directors Association
11121 West Oklahoma Avenue
Milwaukee, WI 53227-4096
(414) 541-2500
The NFDA is the major funeral industry organization. They have a pamphlet called "Making Funeral Arrangements" available to the public and will respond to requests for information and questions regarding funerals and dealing with funeral homes.

National Funeral Directors and Morticians Association
1800 East Linwood Boulevard
Kansas City, MO 64109
(816) 921-1800

National Hospice Organization
1901 North Moore Street, Suite 901
Arlington, VA 22209
(703) 243-5900

National Selected Morticians
5 Revere Drive, Suite 340
Northbrook, IL 60062-8009
(708) 559-9569

Network for Organ Sharing
Richmond, VA
(800) 756-3483

Government Agencies

Conference of Funeral Service Examining Boards
2404 Washington Boulevard, Suite 1000
Ogden, UT 84401
(801) 392-7771

Federal Trade Commission—National Division of Marketing Practices
6th Street and Pennsylvania Avenue NW
Washington, DC 20580
(202) 326-2000

Federal Trade Commission—Southeast
1718 Peachtree Street, N.W., Suite 1000
Atlanta, GA 30367
(404) 347-4836

Federal Trade Commission—New England
101 Merrimac Street, Suite 810
Boston, MA 02114-4719
(617) 424-5960

Federal Trade Commission—Midwest
55 East Monroe Street, Suite 1437
Chicago, IL 60603
(312) 353-4423

Federal Trade Commission—Midwest
668 Euclid Avenue, Suite 520-A
Cleveland, OH 44114
(216) 522-4207

Federal Trade Commission—Southwest
100 N. Central Expressway, Suite 500
Dallas, TX 75201
(214) 767-5501

Federal Trade Commission—Mountain
1405 Curtis Street, Suite 2900
Denver, CO 80202-2393
(303) 844-2271

Federal Trade Commission—West
11000 Wilshire Boulevard, Suite 13209
Los Angeles, CA 90024
(310) 575-7575

Federal Trade Commission—Mid-Atlantic
150 William Street, Suite 1300
New York, NY 10038
(212) 264-1207

Federal Trade Commission—West
901 Market Street, Suite 570
San Francisco, CA 94103
(415) 744-7920

Federal Trade Commission—Northwest
2806 Federal Building, 915 Second Avenue
Seattle, WA 98174
(206) 220-6363

Mail-Order Caskets and Plans

Alameda Cremations
1516 Oak Street, Suite 208
Alameda, CA 94501
(510) 865-3435
Plans to make your own casket are available for
$9.95.

Out of the Woodworks
5583 Bancroft S.E.
Alto, MI 49302
(616) 868-6925

Plain Pine
Harmon Road
Monterey, MA 01245
(413) 528-9937
A brochure from this furniture maker is available;
caskets are made of pine and currently priced at
$500, $750, and $900.

St. Francis Center
5135 MacArthur Boulevard NW
Washington, DC 20016
(202) 363-8500
The St. Francis Center is now a regional nonprofit,
nondenominational organization providing
counseling, education and training for people with
life-threatening illnesses and the bereaved. However,
they have a pamphlet called "How to Build Your
Own Coffin."

Bibliography

Achebe, Chinua. *Things Fall Apart*. New York: Fawcett, 1959.

Adler, Mortimer J. *Angels and Us*. New York: Collier Books, Macmillan Publishing Co., 1982.

Albury, W.R. "Ideas of Life and Death," in *Companion Encyclopedia of the History of Medicine*. W.F. Bynum and Roy Porter, eds. New York: Routledge, 1993.

Alighieri, Dante. *The Inferno, The Purgatorio* and *The Paradiso*. Translated by John Ciardi. New York: New American Library, 1961.

Alvarez, A. *The Savage God: A Study of Suicide*. New York: W.W. Norton & Company, 1990.

Arbeiter, Jean and Lind D. Cirino. *Permanent Addresses: A Guide to the Resting Places of Famous Americans*. New York: M. Evans & Co., 1983.

Ariés, Philippe. *The Hour of Our Death*. New York: Alfred A. Knopf, 1981.

Askenasy, Hans. *Cannibalism: From Sacrifice to Survival*. Amherst, NY: Prometheus Books, 1994.

Attwater, Donald. *Penguin Dictionary of Saints*. Revised and updated by Catherine Rachel John. New York: Penguin Books, 1983.

Austin, John. *Hollywood's Unsolved Mysteries*. New York: S.P.I. Books, 1992.

Baden, Michael M. and Judith A. Hennessee. *Unnatural Death: Confessions of a Medical Examiner*. New York: Random House, 1989.

Battin, Margaret Pabst. *Ethical Issues in Suicide*. Englewood Cliffs, NJ: Prentice Hall, 1995.

Bedau, Hugo Adam. *Death is Different: Studies in the Morality, Law and Politics of Capital Punishment*. Boston: Northeastern University Press, 1987.

Bentley, Peter. *The Dictionary of World Myth*. New York: Facts on File. 1995.

Biedermann, Hans. *Dictionary of Symbolism*. New York: Penguin Books, 1994.

Blackmore, Susan. *Dying to Live: Near-Death Experiences*. New York: Prometheus Books, 1993.

Bowker, John. *The Meanings of Death*. Cambridge: Cambridge University Press, 1991.

Boyle, James J. *Killer Cults*. New York: St. Martin's Paperbacks, 1995.

Bozarth-Campbell, Alla. *Life is Goodbye Life is Hello: Grieving Well Through All Kinds of Loss*. Minneapolis, MN: CompCare Publishers, 1982.

Brandreth, Gyles. *Famous Last Words & Tombstone Humor*. New York: Sterling Publishing Co., 1989.

Brenner, Paul R.F. "The Need for Hospice." Jacob Perlow Hospice, Inc. of Beth Israel Medical Center (unpublished article).

Bresler, Fenton. *An Almanac of Murder*. London: Severn House Publishers, 1987.

Briggs, Julia. *Night Visitors: The Rise and Fall of the English Ghost Story*. New York: Faber, 1977.

Carlson, Lisa. *Caring for Your Own Dead*. Hinesburg, VT: Upper Access Publishers, 1987.

Childs-Gowell, Elaine. *Good Grief Rituals*. Station Hill Press, 1992.

Christoph, James B. *Capital Punishment and British Politics: The British Movement to Abolish the Death Penalty 1945–57*. Chicago: The University of Chicago Press, 1962.

Clift, Eleanor. "Fatal Distraction." *Longevity*, December 1995.

Coffin, Margaret. *Death in Early America*. Nashville and New York: Thomas Nelson, Inc., 1976.

Colgrove, M., H.H. Bloomfield and P. McWilliams. *How to Survive the Loss of a Love*. Los Angeles, CA: Prelude Press, 1991.

Colum, Padraic. *Myths of the World*. New York: Macmillan, 1930.

Comfort, Alex. *The Biology of Senescence*. 3rd ed. New York: Elsevier, 1979.

Congregation Anshei Israel. *Jewish Customs of Mourning*. Tucson, AZ: Congregation Anshei Israel, no date.

Conrad, Bonnie Hunt. *When a Child Has Died: Ways You Can Help a Bereaved Parent.* Santa Barbara, CA: Fithian Press, 1995.

Conrad, Joseph. *Heart of Darkness.* New York: New American Library, 1910.

Corr, C.A., and J.N McNeil. *Adolescence and Death.* New York: Springer Publishing Company, 1986.

Crim, Kenneth, ed. *Perennial Dictionary of World Religions.* San Francisco: HarperCollins Publishing, 1989.

Culbertson, Judi and Tom Randall. *Permanent Londoners.* Post Mills, VT: Chelsea Green Publishing, 1991.

———. *Permanent Parisians.* Post Mills, VT: Chelsea Green Publishing, 1986.

Dacy, Norman F. *How to Avoid Probate.* New York: HarperPerennial, 1993.

Dalby, Richard. *The Virago Book of Ghost Stories.* London: Virago, 1987.

Denisoff, R. Serge, and George Plasketes. *True Disbelievers: The Elvis Contagion.* New York: Transaction Publishers, 1995.

Department of Veterans Affairs. *Federal Benefits for Veterans and Dependents.* Washington, DC: United States Government Printing Office, 1995.

Derry, Charles. *The Suspense Thriller: Films in the Shadow of Alfred Hitchcock.* Jefferson, NC: McFarland, 1988.

DeSpelder, Lynn and Albert Strickland. *The Last Dance: Encountering Death and Dying.* Mountain View, CA: Mayfield Publishing Company, 1992.

Dickstein, Leslie, et al. "No Seconds." *Time,* May 23, 1994.

Diocese of Tucson. *Guidelines for the Rite of Christian Burial.* Tucson, AZ: Diocese of Tucson, 1991.

"Doctors Offer Some Support for Kevorkian: Urge 10 Guidelines in Assisting Suicides." *The New York Times,* December 4, 1995.

Donaldson, Norman and Betty Donaldson. *How Did They Die?* New York: St. Martin's Paperbacks, 1989.

Donnelly, Katherine Fair. *Recovering From the Loss of a Child.* New York: The Berkley Publishing Group, 1982.

———. *Recovering From the Loss of a Loved One to AIDS,* New York: Fawcett Columbine, 1994.

Douglas, Jack D. *The Social Meanings of Suicide.* Princeton, NJ: Princeton University Press, 1967.

Drimmer, Frederick. *Until You Are Dead: The Book of Executions in America.* New York: Carol Publishing Group, 1990.

Dukeminier, Jesse and James E. Krier. *Property.* Boston: Little, Brown, 1981.

Dunand, François and Roger Lichtenberg. *Mummies: A Voyage Through Eternity.* Translated by Ruth Sharman. New York: Harry N. Abrams, Inc., 1994.

Edelman, Hope. *Motherless Daughters.* New York: Bantam Doubleday Dell, 1994.

Enright, D.J. *The Oxford Book of Death.* Oxford: Oxford University Press, 1983.

Ericcson, Stephanie. "The Agony of Grief." *Utne Reader,* September/October, 1991.

Faulkner, R.O. *The Ancient Egyptian Book of the Dead.* Austin, TX: University of Texas Press, 1985.

Federal Trade Commission. *Complying with the Funeral Rule.* June 1994.

Feinberg, Linda. *I'm Grieving As Fast As I Can.* Far Hills, NJ: New Horizon Press, 1994.

Finch, Caleb E. and Leonard Hayflick, eds. *Handbook of the Biology of Aging.* New York: Van Nostrand, 1977.

Finnegan, Robert W. "Using First-to-Die Life Insurance in Estate Planning." *Estate Planning,* September/October 1994.

Fitzgerald, Helen. *The Mourning Handbook.* New York: Fireside/ Simon & Schuster, 1994.

Florescu, Radu R. and Raymond T. McNally. *Dracula: Prince of Many Faces.* Boston: Back Bay Books, 1989.

French, Roger. "The Anatomical Tradition," in *Companion Encyclopedia of the History of Medicine.* W.F. Bynum and Roy Porter, eds. New York: Routledge, 1993.

Gargan, Edward A. "For Many Brides in India, a Dowry Buys Death," *The New York Times*, December 30, 1993.

Garrison, Webb. *Strange Facts About Death.* Nashville: Abingdon, 1978.

George, Leona. *Crimes of Perception.* New York: Paragon House, 1995.

Ginsburg, Genevieve Davis. *Widow: Rebuilding Your Life.* Tucson, AZ: Fisher Books, 1987.

Goldman, Linda. *Life & Loss: A Guide to Help Grieving Children.* Bristol, PA: Accelerated Development, Inc., 1994.

Gonzalez-Crussi, F. *The Day of the Dead.* New York: Harcourt Brace, 1993.

Gordon, Albert. *In Times of Sorrow: A Manual for Mourners.* New York: The United Synagogue of America, 1949. Rev. ed. 1959, 1965.

Green, Jonathon. *Famous Last Words.* New York: Quick Fox, 1979.

Greenberg, Blu. *How to Run a Traditional Jewish Household.* New York: Fireside/Simon & Schuster, 1983.

Gruman, Gerald J. *A History of Ideas About the Prolongation of Life.* New York: Arno Press, 1977. Reprinted from the Transactions of the American Philosophical Society, Philadelphia, 1966.

Hacker, Marilyn. *Love, Death and the Changing of the Seasons.* New York: W.W. Norton. 1986.

Haggerty, George. *Gothic Fiction/Gothic Form.* University Park, PA: The Pennsylvania State University Press, 1989.

Hampton, Craig Douglas. *Survivorship Life Insurance.* Chicago: American Bar Association, 1994.

Hayflick, Leonard. *How and Why We Age.* New York: Ballantine Books, 1994.

The Heard Museum. *El Dia de los Muertos.* Phoenix, AZ: The Heard Museum, no date.

Helpern, Milton. *Autopsy.* New York: St. Martin's Press, 1977.

Henry-Jenkins, Wanda. *Just Us: Overcoming and Understanding Homicidal Loss and Grief.*

Omaha, NE: Centering Corporation, 1993.

Hill, T. Patrick and David Shirley. *A Good Death: Taking More Control at the End of Your Life.* National Council for the Right to Die. New York: Addison Wesley, 1992.

Hillman, James. *Suicide and the Soul.* Dallas: Spring Publications, Inc., 1965

Humphry, Derek. *Dying with Dignity: What You Need to Know About Euthanasia.* New York: St. Martin's Press, 1992.

———. *Final Exit: The Practicalities of Self-Deliverance and Assisted Suicide for the Dying.* New York: Dell, 1991.

Internal Revenue Service. *Publication 559: Survivors, Executors, and Administrators.* United States Department of the Treasury, Internal Revenue Service, 1995.

Institute of Occupational Health. *Occupational Epidemics of the 1990s.* Cincinnati, Ohio: National Institute for Occupational Safety and Health, June 9–12, 1992 symposium.

Iserson, Kenneth V., M.D. *Death to Dust.* Tucson, AZ: Galen Press, Ltd., 1994.

Jacobs, Louis. *The Jewish Religion: A Companion.* New York: Oxford University Press, 1995.

Johnson, Robert. *Death Work: A Study of the Modern Execution Process.* Pacific Grove, CA: Brooks/Cole Publishing Co., 1990.

Jones, Barbara. *Design for Death.* Indianapolis: The Bobbs-Merrill Company, 1967.

Kahn, Carol. *Beyond the Helix.* New York: Times Books, 1985.

Kastenbaum, Robert, and Beatrice Kastenbaum, eds. *Encyclopedia of Death.* Phoenix: The Oryx Press, 1989.

Kennedy, Alexandra. *Losing a Parent: Passage to a New Way of Living.* New York: HarperCollins, 1991.

Kersh, Maxine D. "The Empowerment of the Crime Victim: A Comparative Study of Victim Compensation Schemes in the United States and Australia." *California Western International Law Journal,* Spring 1994.

Kevorkian, Jack. "A Modern Inquisition." *The Humanist*, November/December, 1994.

Kilduff, Marshall, and Ron Javers. *The Suicide Cult: The Inside Story of the Peoples Temple Sect and the Massacre in Guyana*. New York: Bantam Books, 1978.

Klawans, Harold L. *Life, Death, and In Between: Tales of Clinical Neurology*. New York: Paragon House, 1992.

Knox, Lucinda Page, and Michael D. Knox, Ph.D. *Last Wishes: A Handbook to Guide Your Survivors*. Berkeley, CA: Ulysses Press, 1995.

Kohn, George C. *Dictionary of Culprits and Criminals*. Metuchen, NJ: The Scarecrow Press, 1986.

Kramer, Kenneth. *The Sacred Art of Dying: How World Religions Understand Death*. Mahwah, NJ: Paulist Press, 1988.

Kronenberger, Louis, ed. *Brief Lives: A Biographical Companion to the Arts*. Boston: Little, Brown and Company, 1971.

Kübler-Ross, Elizabeth. *On Death and Dying*. New York: Collier Books, Macmillan Publishing, 1969.

———. *On Life After Death*. Berkeley, CA: Celestial Arts, 1991.

Kushner, Harold S. *When Bad Things Happen to Good People*. New York: Avon, 1981.

Lamm, Maurice. *The Jewish Way in Death and Mourning*. New York: Jonathan David Publishers, 1969.

Larsen, David. "The Sorrow of a Grown-Up Goodby." *Los Angeles Times*, July 30, 1989.

Lasky, Kathryn. *Days of the Dead*. New York: Hyperion Books, 1994.

Lawrence, Susan. "Medical Education," in *Companion Encyclopedia of the History of Medicine*, W.F Bynum and Roy Porter, eds. New York: Routledge, 1993.

Lentz, Harris M. III. *Assassinations and Executions: An Encyclopedia of Political Violence, 1865–1986*. Jefferson, NC: McFarland & Company, 1988.

Lewis, James R. *Encyclopedia of Afterlife Beliefs and Phenomena*. Detroit: Visible Ink Press, 1995.

Lewis, C.S. *A Grief Observed*. New York: Bantam Doubleday Dell, 1961.

Lippett, Peter E. *Estate Planning: What Anyone Who Owns Anything Must Know*. Reston, VA: Reston Publishing Company, 1979.

Luker, Kristin. *Abortion and the Politics of Motherhood*. Berkeley: University of California Press, 1984.

Lundquist, K.F., D.P. Irish and V.J. Nelsen. *Ethnic Variations in Dying, Death, and Grief*. Washington, DC: Taylor and Francis, 1993.

MacKinnon, Catharine A. *Only Words*. Cambridge, MA: Harvard University Press, 1993.

Maples, William R. and Michael Browning. *Dead Men Do Tell Tales*. New York: Doubleday, 1994.

Marion, John Francis. *Famous and Curious Cemeteries*. New York: Crown Publishers, 1977.

Marongiu, Pietro, and Graeme Newman. *Vengeance: The Fight Against Injustice*. Lanham, MD: Rowman & Littlefield, 1987.

Martingale, Moira. *Cannibal Killers*. New York: Carroll & Graf Publishers, 1993.

Mathews, Tom. "He Wanted to Listen to My Heart." *Newsweek*, February 10, 1992.

McBrien, Richard P., ed. *HarperCollins Encyclopedia of Catholicism*. San Francisco: HarperCollins Publishers, 1995.

McGrath, Alister, ed. *The Blackwell Encyclopedia of Modern Christian Thought*. Cambridge, MA: Basil Blackwell, Ltd., 1993.

McNeil, W.K. *Ghost Stories from the American South*. Little Rock, AR: August House, 1985.

McNeill, William H. *Plagues and Peoples*. New York: Anchor/Doubleday, 1977.

McPherson, T. *American Funeral Cars and Ambulances Since 1900*. Glen Ellyn, IL: Crestline Publishing, 1973.

Menten, Ted. *Gentle Closings: How to Say Goodbye to Someone You Love*. Philadelphia, PA: Running Press, 1991.

Miller, Clarence W. *The Funeral Book*. San Francisco: Robert D. Reed, Publishers, 1994.

Mitford, Jessica. *The American Way of Death*. New York: Simon and Schuster, 1963.

Moody, Raymond. *Life After Life*. Harrisburg: Stackpole Books, 1976.

———. *Reflections on Life After Life*. New York: Bantam Books, 1978.

Morbidity and Mortality Weekly Report, Dec. 16, 1994. InfoTrac Health Reference.

Morgan, Earnest. *Dealing Creatively with Death: A Manual of Death Education and Simple Burial*. Bayside, NY: Zinn Communications, 1994.

Morse, Melvin, and Paul Perry. *Closer to the Light: Learning from the Near-Death Experiences of Children*. New York: Ivy Books, 1990.

Mossman, B.S., and M.W. Stark. *The Last Salute: Civil & Military Funerals, 1921–1969*. Washington, DC: Department of the Army, 1971.

Myers, Edward. *When Parents Die: A Guide for Adults*. New York: Penguin Books, 1986.

Nagy, Kate. "Viaticals for Cancer Patients Gain Popularity in U.S." *Journal of the National Cancer Institute*, 87(4), 1995.

Nash, Jay Robert. *Almanac of World Crime*. New York: Bonanza Books, 1986.

———. *Bloodletters and Badmen*. New York: M. Evans and Company, 1995.

———. *Open Files*. New York: McGraw-Hill Book Company, 1983.

Newman, Lawrence, and Albert Kalter. *Postmortem Estate Planning: Strategies for Executors and Beneficiaries*. New York: Practicing Law Institute, 1993.

"NLM Unveils 'The Visible Man,'" *NLM Technical Bulletin*. Washington, DC: National Library of Medicine, July-August, 1995.

Nolfi, Edward A. *Basic Wills, Trusts and Estates*. Akron, OH: Glencoe/McGraw-Hill, 1995.

Norris, Dr. Joel. *Henry Lee Lucas: The Shocking True Story of America's Most Notorious Serial Killer*. New York: Zebra Books, 1991.

Nuland, Sherwin B. *Doctors: The Biography of Medicine*. New York: Alfred A. Knopf, 1988.

———. *How We Die: Reflections on Life's Final Chapter*. New York: Random House, 1993.

Ott, David E. "Survivor Income Benefits Provided by Employers." *Monthly Labor Review*, 114(6), 1991.

Palmer, Greg. *Death: The Trip of a Lifetime*. San Francisco: Harper San Francisco, 1993.

Panati, Charles. *Panati's Extraordinary Endings of Practically Everything and Everybody*. New York: Harper & Row, 1989.

Pelling, Margaret. "Contagion/Germ Theory/Specificity," in *Companion Encyclopedia to the History of Medicine*. W.F. Bynum and Roy Porter, eds. New York: Routledge, 1993.

Pokorski, Doug. *Death Rehearsal: A Practical Guide for Preparing for the Inevitable*. Springfield, IL: Octavo Press, 1995.

Proposed National Strategies for the Prevention of Leading Work-Related Diseases and Injuries. Washington, DC: NIOSH, 1975.

Puckle, Bertram. *Funeral Customs: Their Origins and Development*. London: T. Werner Laurie Ltd., 1926.

Putnam, James. *Mummy*. New York: Alfred A. Knopf, 1992.

Quigley, Christine. *Death Dictionary*. Jefferson, NC: McFarland, 1994.

Rinpoche, Sogyal. *Tibetan Book of Living and Dying*. San Francisco: HarperCollins Publishers, 1993.

Rosenfeld, Albert. *Prolongevity II*. New York: Alfred A. Knopf, 1985.

Ross, Anne, and Dan Robins. *The Life and Death of A Druid Prince: The Story of Lindow Man, An Archaeological Sensation*. New York: Summit, 1989.

Rothstein, Mark A., Andria S. Knapp and Lance Liebman. *Employment Law*. Westbury, NY: Foundation Press, 1987.

Rushton, Lucy. *Death Customs*. New York: Thomson Learning, 1993.

Saks, Howard J. "Comparing Universal Life and Whole Life Policies for Both Individual and Survivorship Insurance Needs." *Estate Planning,* September/October 1994.

Santino, Jack, ed. *Halloween and Other Festivals of Death and Life.* Knoxville: The University of Tennessee Press, 1994.

Scholl, Sharon. *Death and the Humanities.* Lewisburg, PA: Bucknell University Press, 1984.

Schutze, Jim. *Cauldron of Blood: The Matamoros Cult Killings.* New York: Avon Books, 1989.

Schwartz, Richard A. and Catherine R. Turner. *The Life Insurance Counselor: Life Insurance Products, Illustrations and Due Diligence.* Chicago: American Bar Association, 1989.

————. *Life Insurance Due Care: Carrier, Products and Illustrations.* Chicago: American Bar Association, 1994.

Sellin, Thorsten. *The Penalty of Death.* Sage Library of Social Research, 1980.

Shaw, Eva. *What To Do When a Loved One Dies.* Irvine, CA: Dickens Press, 1994.

Shepherd, Chuck. *News of the Weird,* Internet, http//www.upi.com. July 7, 1995.

Sherr, Lorraine. *Grief and AIDS.* New York: John Wiley & Sons, 1995.

Sifakis, Carl. *Encyclopedia of Assassinations.* New York: Facts on File, 1991.

Signorelli, Nancy. *Mass Media Images and Impact on Health: A Sourcebook.* Westport, CT: Greenwood Press, 1993.

Skala, Ken. *American Guidance for Seniors. . . and their Caregivers.* Falls Church, VA: American Guidance, 1993.

Slater, Scott and Alec Solomita. *Exits: Stories of Dying Moments & Parting Words.* New York: E.P. Dutton, 1980.

Social Security Administration. *1995 Social Security Handbook.* Washington, DC: United States Government Printing Office, 1995.

Spencer, John, and Anne Spencer. *Encyclopedia of Ghosts and Spirits.* London: Headline Book Publishing plc, 1992.

Spencer, Linda. *Knock on Wood.* Nashville: Rutledge Hill Press, 1995.

Stearns, Ann Kaiser. *Living Through Personal Crisis.* New York: Ballantine, 1984.

Sublette, Kathleen, and Martin Flagg. *Final Celebrations: A Guide for Personal and Family Planning.* Ventura, CA: Pathfinder Publishing, 1992.

Sullivan, Lawrence E., ed. *Death, Afterlife, and the Soul. Selections from The Encyclopedia of Religion.* New York: Macmillan Publishing Co., 1987.

Sullivan, Terry and Peter T. Maiken. *Killer Clown: The John Wayne Gacy Murders.* New York: Pinnacle Books, 1983.

Sungolf Plus Leisure Co. *Executions 1601–1926.* London: Sungolf Plus Leisure Co., 1979.

Susman, Ed. "Spare Body Parts," *Longevity,* December 1995.

Tannahill, Reay. *Flesh and Blood.* New York: Stein and Day Publishing Company, 1975.

Thane, Pat. "Geriatrics," in *Companion Encyclopedia of the History of Medicine.* W.F. Bynum and Roy Porter, eds. New York: Routledge, 1993.

"Body Language: The Lure of the Dead." *The New York Times,* October 29, 1995.

The Economist: Book of Vital World Statistics. New York: Times Books, 1990.

Thompson, Henry O. *World Religions in War and Peace.* Jefferson, NC: McFarland, 1988.

Tierney, Patrick. *The Highest Altar: The Story of Human Sacrifice.* New York: Viking, 1989.

Turner, Ann. *Houses for the Dead.* New York: D. McKay, 1976.

Unger, Frederic W. *Epitaphs.* Philadelphia: The Penn Publishing Co., 1904.

United States Railroad Retirement Board. *Railroad Retirement and Survivor Benefits.* Chicago: United States Railroad Retirement Board, 1991.

Van Hoof, Anton J.L. *From Autothanasia to Suicide: Self-Killing in Classical Antiquity.* New York: Routledge, 1990.

Viorst, Judith. *Necessary Losses.* New York: Fawcett Gold Medal, 1986.

Walker, Barbara G. *The Crone.* New York: HarperCollins Publishing, 1985.

Ward, Howard N., M.D., J.D. "Euthanasia: A Medical and Legal Overview". *Journal of the Kansas Bar Association*, vol. 49, Winter, 1980.

Whitaker, Terence. *Haunted England.* New York: Contemporary Books, 1987.

Wigoder, Geoffrey, ed. *The New Standard Jewish Encyclopedia.* 7th ed. New York: Facts on File, 1992.

Wilson, Colin, and Donald Seaman. *The Encyclopedia of Modern Murder.* New York: Arlington House, 1988.

Wilson, Colin, et al., eds. *Colin Wilson's World Famous Crimes.* New York: Carroll & Graf Publishers, 1995.

Wolf, Marvin J. and Katherine Mader. *Rotten Apples: True Stories of New York Crime and Mystery.* New York: Ballantine Books, 1991.

Wolfelt, Alan. *Helping Children Cope With Grief.* Bristol, PA: Accelerated Development, Inc., 1983.

———. *Understanding Grief: Helping Yourself Heal.* Bristol, PA: Accelerated Development, Inc., 1992.

Worden, J. William. *Grief Counseling & Grief Therapy.* 2nd ed. New York: Springer Publishing Company, 1991.

Worker Exposure to AIDS & Hepatitis B. Washington, DC: U.S. Department of Labor, Occupational Safety and Health Administration, 1987.

Wrobleski, Adina. *Suicide Survivors.* Minneapolis, MN: Afterwards Publishing, 1994.

Yarrow, H.C. *North American Indian Burial Customs.* Ogden, VT: Eagle's View Publishing Co., 1988.

Young, Gregory W. *The High Cost of Dying: A Guide to Funeral Planning.* Buffalo, NY: Prometheus Books, 1994.

Zunin, L.M. and H.S. Zunin. *The Art of Condolence.* New York: HarperPerennial, 1991.

Index